Descartes' Dualism

'Unique, remarkable ... the book is simply filled with gems of information and interpretation. It's *essential* reading.'
Journal for the History of Philosophy

'A fascinatingly radical interpretation of Descartes's conception of the mind ... it is also a very compelling one'
Philosophical Books

'Scholarly, reasonable, detailed and ultimately convincing .... Anyone who is interested in Descartes will enjoy it.'
Heythrop Journal

'Ambitious and closely argued .... There is much here with which to agree.'
Teorema

Was Descartes a Cartesian Dualist? In this controversial study, Gordon Baker and Katherine J. Morris argue that, despite the general consensus within philosophy, Descartes was neither a proponent of dualism nor guilty of the many crimes of which he has been accused by twentieth-century philosophers.

In lively and engaging prose, Baker and Morris present a radical revision of the ways in which Descartes' work has been interpreted. Descartes emerges with both his historical importance assured and his philosophical importance redeemed.

Gordon Baker is Fellow and Lecturer in Philosophy at St John's College, Oxford. He has written various books including *Frege: Logical Excavations* (1984), *Wittgenstein: Rules, Grammar and Necessity* (1985), and *Language, Sense and Nonsense* (1984), all co-authored with P.M.S. Hacker, and also *Wittgenstein, Frege and the Vienna Circle* (1988). **Katherine J. Morris** is Supernumerary Fellow of Philosophy at Mansfield College, Oxford. She lectures on Sartre and Merleau-Ponty, and has written on Descartes, Sartre and Wittgenstein.

DESCARTES' DUALISM

Gordon Baker
Katherine J. Morris

London and New York

First published 1996
by Routledge
11 New Fetter Lane, London EC4P 4EE

Simultaneously published in the USA and Canada
by Routledge
29 West 35th Street, New York, NY 10001

First published in paperback 2002

Routledge is an imprint of the Taylor & Francis Group

Typeset in Times
Printed and bound in Great Britain by
St Edmundsbury Press, Bury St Edmunds, Suffolk

British Library Cataloguing in Publication Data
A catalogue record for this book is available from the British Library

Library of Congress Cataloging in Publication Data
A catalog record for this book has been requested

ISBN 0-415-10121-2 (Hbk)
ISBN 0-415-30104-1 (Pbk)

What makes a subject hard to understand – if it's something significant and important – is not that before you can understand it you need to be specially trained in abstruse matters, but the contrast between understanding the subject and what most people *want* to see. Because of this the very things which are most obvious may become the hardest of all to understand. What has to be overcome is a difficulty having to do with the will, rather than with the intellect.

(Wittgenstein, *Culture and Value*, 17)

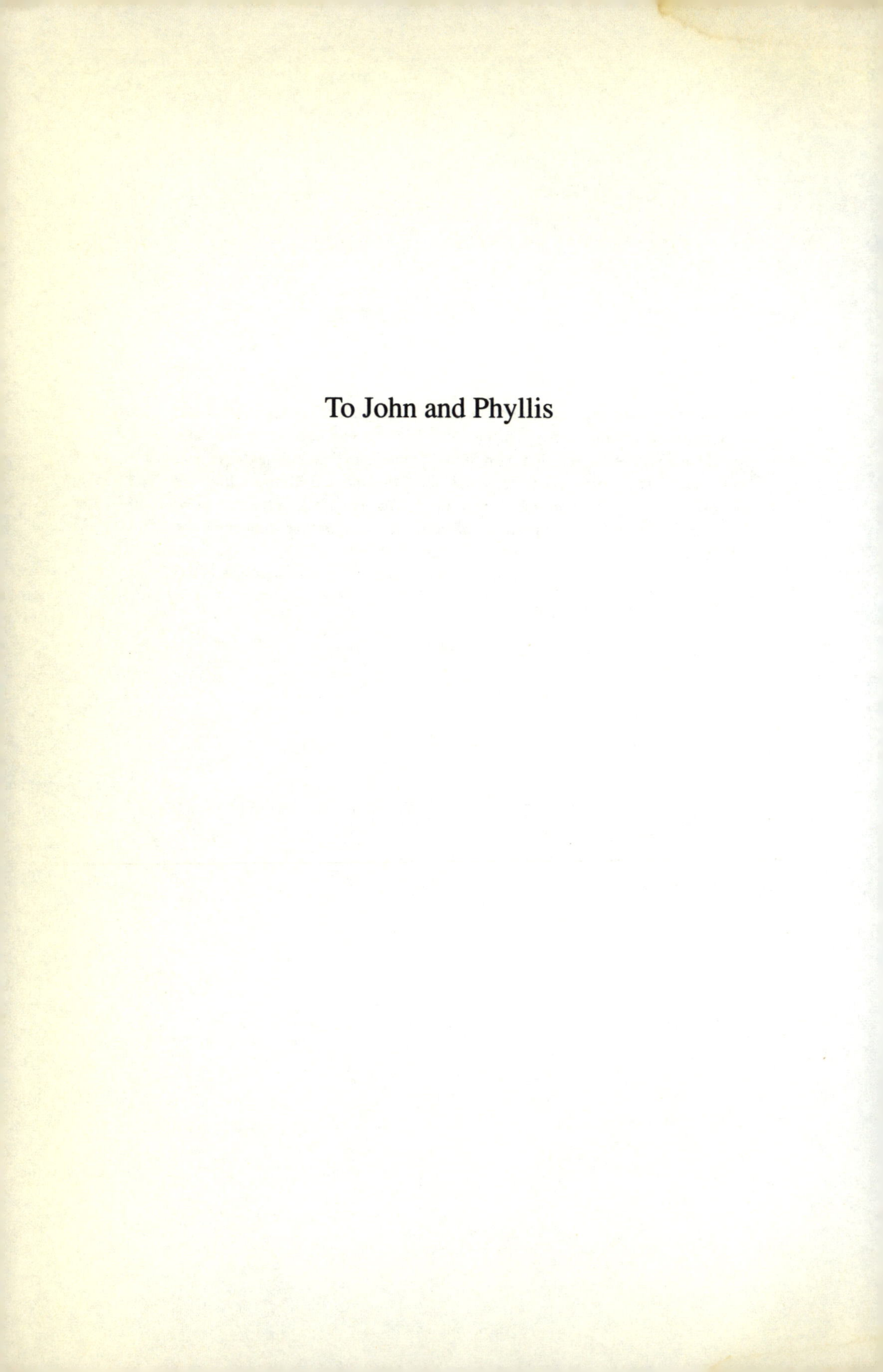

To John and Phyllis

CONTENTS

PREFACE

E. H. Gombrich tells a story to show 'the fate of exotic creatures in the illustrated books of the last few centuries before the advent of photography'. Dürer's famous woodcut of a rhinoceros depicted a bizarre creature apparently covered in armoured plating, complete with spikes and rivets (a veritable *bête-machine*). In 1790, over 250 years after the publication of that woodcut, James Bruce described it as 'wonderfully ill-executed in all its parts', and he held it to be 'the origin of all the monstrous forms under which that animal has been painted ever since'. His preferred engraving, 'designed from the life', is also covered in armour plates, though the rivets and spikes are somewhat reduced in number and size.[1] Whether due to a philosophical Dürer (perhaps more than one) or to the 'preconceived prejudices and inattention' to which Bruce ascribed the faults of later depictions of the rhinoceros, twentieth-century 'engravings' of Descartes' conception of the human being, even those 'designed from the life', have much the same character as Bruce's engraving.

Our principal target in this book is the 'preconceived prejudices' of twentieth-century Anglo-American philosophers. (We frequently use the word 'modern' as shorthand for 'twentieth-century Anglo-American'. We hope this term is neither confusing nor offensive in these 'post-modern' times; but abbreviations are ugly and 'twentieth-century Anglo-American' is, as Austin would have said, rather a mouthful.) This is what underlies our policy of extracting apposite quotations about 'Cartesian' ideas not only from major studies of Descartes, but also from a wide range of authors who do not purport to be writing exegeses of Descartes (e.g. William James, Daniel Dennett, Paul Churchland, Richard Rorty, Peter Strawson, and Peter Hacker). It equally informs our policy of excluding from consideration non-anglophone scholarly commentaries on Descartes. Though French and German scholars offer contrasting views which could serve to highlight some anglophone 'prejudices', their works are not suitable for our purposes in virtue of their being unfamiliar to most anglophone philosophers, and, in addition, they introduce other 'prejudices' which it would be a distraction to address here.

1 E. H. Gombrich, *Art and Illusion* (5th edn), London: Phaidon, 1977, 70–1.

One main modern prejudice relates to ways of seeing the mind and the body; another to ways of seeing different ways of seeing things. There is, for example, widespread agreement today that 'the mental' includes sensations and emotions while excluding virtues and vices. Correlatively, 'the bodily' excludes sensations and emotions (a pain in the foot isn't literally *in the foot*); indeed the body is little more than an ambulatory vat of chemicals that serves to keep the brain alive. But there is also widespread agreement that the modern way of seeing the scope of the terms 'mental' and 'bodily' is, for the most part, the *right way*. If other ways of seeing things are acknowledged to have existed in the past, we thank God (and Descartes) that we have progressed since then.

We think that the first of these prejudices influences not just the authors of monographs on philosophy of mind but, rather more worryingly, the authors of modern scholarly commentaries on Descartes.[2] This tends to blind them to the very different conception of the scope of 'mental' and 'bodily' that, we argue, informs his work. But our greatest fear is that the second of these prejudices will lead readers of our book to conclude that, if our interpretation is correct, there is *less* to be learned from Descartes than even his severest critics had previously supposed. We think that there is *more* to be learned from him than is dreamt of in modern philosophy.

2 Obviously not all modern commentators share the first prejudice; it is to be found principally (although neither only nor universally) in those who are also by way of being philosophers of mind. Nor do all modern commentators share the second, although it is perhaps more widespread. We simply aim to pick out a type.

ABBREVIATIONS AND SHORTENED TITLES

Descartes' works

For the sake of economy, all references are by volume and page to the following two editions. (The only exceptions are references to the *Principles of Philosophy* and the *Passions of the Soul*, which are by book and section number.)

Charles Adam and Paul Tannery, *Oeuvres de Descartes*, 12 vols, Paris: Léopold Cerf, 1897–1910 (AT).

The Philosophical Writings of Descartes, trs John Cottingham, Robert Stoothoff, and Dugald Murdoch, 2 vols, Cambridge: Cambridge University Press, 1985 (CSM). Third vol. with Anthony Kenny, Cambridge: Cambridge University Press, 1991 (CSMK).

Works by other authors

If no particular edition is mentioned, all references are by book and section number.

Aquinas, Thomas, *Summa Theologica* (*ST*).

Arnauld, Antoine, *On True and False Ideas* (1683), trs and ed. Stephen Gaukroger, Manchester: Manchester University Press, 1990 (*Ideas*).

—— *L'Art de Penser* (1662), translated as the *Port-Royal Logic* (*PRL*).

Frege, Gottlob, *Foundations of Arithmetic*, trs J. L. Austin, Oxford: Blackwell, 1959 (*FA*).

Hume, David, *Enquiry Concerning Human Understanding* (*Enquiry*).

—— *Treatise on Human Understanding* (*Treatise*).

Leibniz, G. F., *Letters* (*Lettres*).

—— *New Essays on Human Understanding* (*Essais*).

Locke, John, *An Essay Concerning Human Understanding* (*Essay*).

Malebranche, N., *Recherche de la Verité et Eclaircissements* (*Recherche* and *Eclaircissements* respectively).

Mill, John Stuart, *A System of Logic*, 8th edn, 1872 (*Logic*).

Reid, Thomas, *Essays on the Intellectual Powers of Man* (*Essays*).

Ritter, J. (ed.), *Historisches Wörterbuch der Philosophie*, Basel: Schwabe & Co., 1971 (*Wörterbuch*).

Watts, Isaac, *Logick: or the Right Use of Reason* (1725), London: Garland Publishing, 1984 (*Logick*).

Wittgenstein, Ludwig, 'Cause and Effect: Intuitive Understanding', in his *Philosophical Occasions 1912–1951*, James Klagge and Alfred Nordman (eds), Indianapolis: Hackett, 1993 ('Cause').

—— *Culture and Value*, Oxford: Blackwell, 1980 (*CV*).

—— *Philosophical Investigations*, trs G. E. M. Anscombe, Oxford: Blackwell, 1953 (*PI*).

—— *Tractatus Logico-Philosophicus* (1921), trs D. F. Pears and B. F. McGuinness, London: Routledge, 1961 (*TLP*).

1

VISIONS

THE PROGRAMME

It is common knowledge that Descartes was a Cartesian Dualist. (Perhaps it's nothing more than common sense!) As everyone knows, he held that there are two worlds, one of mental objects and one of material things, including animals and human bodies. The mental objects are 'states of consciousness' (e.g., pains, visual experiences, beliefs and desires, fear and joy), the material objects are more or less complex bits of 'clockwork'. The items in the 'inner world' are apprehended through the exercise of a special infallible faculty called 'introspection', objects in the 'outer world' are perceived by the five senses. Mental states and states of the body are logically independent but causally interrelated: causal interaction is, as it were, the glue bonding mind to body in each individual person.

This conception of a human being is variously developed with much sophisticated refinement in monographs on Descartes. Although the great body of Anglo-American philosophers who subscribe to this general framework of interpretation have severally noted important local misfits and developed some telling objections to this way of interpreting Descartes,[1] like many a *Gestalt*, this one exhibits remarkable powers of recuperating from severe injury: indeed, it seems able to regenerate amputated limbs. Most of its core elements are frequently repeated in encyclopedias or handbooks, and with even more striking unanimity as a preamble to the ritual refutations of Cartesian Dualism with which many monographs on philosophy of mind or cognitive science begin.

Like most items of 'common knowledge', this one is questionable. What we will call 'the Cartesian Legend' is, to a first approximation, the view that Descartes held and expounded this conception of a person. The Cartesian Legend should not, of course, be confused with what Ryle referred to as 'Descartes' Myth' ('the myth of the ghost in the machine'), one version of the position more neutrally called 'Cartesian Dualism'. Rather, the Cartesian Legend is a second-order myth, a myth about a myth. Our choice of the label 'the Cartesian Legend' has multiple motivations.

1 Many of the individual elements of this picture have been cogently criticized in the literature; some of these criticisms will be referred to in the main body of this book.

First, we want to invoke a particular connotation of one meaning of the term 'legend', namely the notion of heroic stature. Many commentators who subscribe to the Cartesian Legend, whether or not they count themselves as admirers of 'Cartesian Dualism', assign to Descartes a status within the history of philosophy which might aptly be called 'superhuman' or 'legendary'. Whether as a hero or a villain, he looms larger than life: Descartes expressed one main aspect of Cartesian Dualism 'with mesmerizing brilliance' (Hacker 1986: 279); one cannot but be 'awed at the breathtaking power of an intellect which could propagate, almost unaided, a myth which to this day has such a comprehensive grasp on the imagination of a large part of the human race' (Kenny 1985: 77).[2] He is the paradigm of a *great* dead philosopher – even if usually the paradigm of a philosophical *malin génie*.[3]

Second, we mean to trade on another prominent connotation of the term 'legend' by using it to distance ourselves from the position under critical investigation. We hope to persuade our readers that the Cartesian Legend is a *fiction*, if more of a superstition than a mistake. It is not that exponents of the Legend have acted in bad faith. On the contrary, they have proceeded, by their own lights, in a careful and scholarly manner, and they have argued with skill and sophistication. None the less, close textual analysis does not directly support, still less decisively prove, the conclusion that Descartes held the main tenets of so-called 'Cartesian Dualism'. More importantly, we will suggest that there are forceful reasons for concluding that he *couldn't* have held this position. Many of its ingredients (both concepts and presuppositions) are absent from or inconsistent with major elements in the framework of his thinking. The Cartesian Legend has much of the character of a projection of distinctively more modern ideas on to an early seventeenth-century thinker.

Third, we mean both to allude to the well-known label 'Descartes' myth' and to distinguish our target from this myth. Our concern is a view *about* that myth. Thus 'advocates (proponents, etc.) of the Cartesian Legend' are not philosophers who hold Cartesian Dualism to be *true* (since most, although not all, of them believe it to be seriously flawed, inconsistent or nonsensical), but rather those who hold that it is true that Descartes was a Cartesian Dualist. The Legend offers a beguiling way of ordering or systematizing the various doctrines and chains of reasoning that he presented in his major works. In this book, we focus on the question of how well or badly this pattern fits his texts, and propose a different pattern for making better sense of his thinking, what we call 'Descartes' Dualism'. We don't intend to debate the philosophical merits of either of these conceptions, not at least along the lines of arguments characteristic of contemporary philosophy

2 In this case, Descartes is being set up as a Goliath whom Wittgenstein is about to slay with the projectile known as the 'private language argument'. To each Hero his Anti-Hero.

3 Descartes is today commonly seen as the *malin génie* in almost every conceivable field: not just philosophy of mind but animal rights, feminism, medicine, and environmental ethics. Our analysis of his ideas may have very wide implications.

of mind. Our primary goal is to arrive at a clearer and deeper understanding of what was Descartes' conception of a person.

In this sense, we finally exploit yet another connotation of 'legend', namely the idea that legends provide fictitious *historical* narratives. Perhaps the Cartesian Legend's continuing to flourish attests less to its intrinsic merits than to the intellectual needs of modern philosophers. Cartesian Dualism is commonly used to set the agenda of philosophy of mind. It is taken to make clear what 'the mind–body problem' is by offering a naive but intuitively appealing solution. The thought is that every philosopher begins naturally as a Cartesian Dualist and then, having worked through its defects, arrives at a more sophisticated position. There is a certain intellectual satisfaction to be gained in supposing that ontogeny, individual philosophical progress, recapitulates phylogeny, a kind of collective historical philosophical progress. Into this feeds the picture according to which Descartes effected a revolution in philosophy by putting scepticism at stage-centre and by locating the foundations of knowledge in immediate subjective experience. It is his invention of Cartesian Dualism which is taken to have decisively altered the course of modern philosophy. He made the opening move in a chess-game; Locke, Berkeley, and Hume carried on and played out the middle game; finally, Kant and Wittgenstein (with an assist from computer science) played the Cartesian conception of the mind into checkmate. This whole story depicts in the mainstream of modern European philosophy just the sort of steady progress that philosophy is often accused of being unable to make. Because Cartesian Dualism holds the pivotal position in this narrative, any serious grounds for calling into question the Cartesian Legend would equally raise doubts about the interpretation of every one of the texts that are integral to this tradition. Everything, including the status of modern philosophy of mind, would be thrown into the melting-pot. Thus in various ways modern Anglo-American philosophers have a large investment in the *truth* of the Cartesian Legend (even if they are equally committed to the falsity of Cartesian Dualism).

Many readers brought up in this tradition may themselves have felt qualms about certain details of the ascription – qualms which they have had to learn to repress. Here, perhaps, is one. It is a staple of the Cartesian Legend, practically the first thing you learn in 'Descartes for Beginners', that according to Descartes 'man is the *only* conscious animal; all other animals . . . are merely complicated, but unconscious, machines'.[4] You may well have found this deeply shocking on first hearing, and might have wondered what on earth could have led a manifestly intelligent philosopher to hold such a manifestly wrong-headed view. (Surely your cat feels pain when you pull its tail; surely it sees the bird in the ivy; surely it remembers where it caught the mouse last spring; surely it is afraid of the neighbour's dog; and surely these are all ways of being conscious.) The Cartesian Legend has an ingenious answer to this. Descartes ('notoriously') confused

4 Anthony Kenny, 'Descartes for Beginners', in his *The Heritage of Wisdom*, Oxford: Blackwell, 1987, p. 119.

consciousness with self-consciousness; having correctly noted that animals are not self-conscious, he was moved to deny that they were conscious (Kenny 1989: 9; Williams 1978: 286). This explains how Descartes could have held the position all right, but only at the expense of seeing this 'great philosopher' as seriously confused.

If you are at all familiar with Descartes' texts, you might have further qualms. On the one hand, he never referred to animals as 'unconscious' or 'insentient'; his usual phrase is 'animals without *reason*' (cf. AT VI: 46; CSM I: 134), and most of the discussions of animals in the correspondence concern the questions of whether animals *think* – 'I cannot share the opinion of Montaigne and others who attribute understanding or thought to animals' (AT IV: 573; CSMK III: 302) – or even whether they have *immortal souls* – 'if they thought as we do, they would have an immortal soul like us . . . and many of them such as oysters and sponges are too imperfect for this to be credible' (AT IV: 576; CSMK III: 304). On the other hand, he frequently referred to animals as feeling passions and what we would call bodily sensations: 'all animals easily communicate to us, by voice or bodily movement, their natural impulses of anger, fear, hunger, and so on' (AT V: 278; CSMK III: 366). Indeed he stated explicitly that in 'denying thought to animals' 'I am speaking of thought, and not of life or sensation' (AT V: 278; CSMK III: 366). The Cartesian Legend has taught us all how to explain such passages away.[5] By 'thought' Descartes meant 'consciousness', and that of course includes pain, fear, anger, hunger, and so on. But there again, Descartes' references to animals 'expressing passions' or 'communicating fear or hunger' are to be taken with a pinch of salt; he meant these terms in an impoverished sense: 'These "passions" of animals are to be regarded as purely physical disturbances in the nervous system, which can generate behaviour, but are not associated with experiences' (Williams 1978: 283).

You might well feel that these 'explanations' generate more questions than they answer. Isn't the word 'thought' an odd word for Descartes to use to encompass fear and hunger? (Aren't 'reason' and 'understanding' even stranger?) And what bearing does the question of whether animals feel hunger or fear have on the question of whether they have immortal Christian souls? (Surely free will and moral responsibility are the more obviously relevant attributes here?)

There are many other worries that you may have felt about this framework for interpreting Descartes. They should, we think, be taken seriously. We have both a 'first-order' aim, to argue for the possibility of a radically different interpretation of Descartes' Dualism, and a 'second-order' aim, to sketch a case for the current *philosophical* interest of this conception which is independent of whether it is a 'live option' for twentieth-century philosophers.

5 Other, perhaps more honest, critics such as Cottingham (1978a: 558) conclude that there is an internal tension in Descartes' thinking here: 'this strange fuzziness is not simply the result of a blind spot which Descartes had when dealing with animals, but connects with a fundamental and unresolved difficulty in Cartesian metaphysics'. See pp. 87–100.

The general first-order aim is to get our readers to see a large-scale pattern which unifies Descartes' detailed and complicated investigation of issues in physics, physiology, epistemology, ethics, theology, and philosophy of mind.[6] Although the ideal would be to effect an all-embracing reorientation of reflections on the whole of Descartes' philosophy, we can't reasonably undertake to carry out this entire campaign in one book. So we will focus attention on one basic element in his system, namely his conception of the nature of a person. Thus the more specific first-order goal is to make a persuasive case for a particular way of seeing his (metaphysical) dualism, to clarify Descartes' own distinctive conception of every human being as being a 'substantial union' of two distinct substances, a perishable, mechanical body and an immortal, rational soul.

Any interpretation of a set of texts is a matter of finding a certain pattern in them, a pattern that is brought out by highlighting certain passages, sidelining others, comparing or seeing connections between passages from different places, etc. Patterns have a tendency to interfere with one another: once you have seen the duck-aspect of Jastrow's diagram, you may find it hard to see the rabbit-aspect (cf. Wittgenstein, *PI* p. 194). Modern Anglo-American philosophy presents Descartes' conception, with a striking degree of unanimity despite many differences of detail, under the label 'Cartesian Dualism'. This well-entrenched picture creates an interference; as long as it persists, it eliminates both the desire for seeking and the possibility of seeing any other pattern in Descartes' work. Hence, by force of circumstance, success at our positive task presupposes achieving a negative aim: breaking the grip of the different pattern now widely superimposed on his texts. So the first part of our project must be critical, in both senses of the word. We will confront this interfering picture with a detailed exposition and analysis of some of Descartes' texts, and will argue that this schema of interpretation is not forced on anybody by the texts that are regularly held to support it.

This much is, of course, characteristic of patterns. We are not forced by the duck–rabbit drawing to read it one way as opposed to the other. Indeed we are not forced to read it either way: it could also perhaps be seen as a pair of scissors or a nutcracker; it could even be seen as a seriously defective drawing of an oval, with a few extraneous dots and wriggly bits. Cartesian Dualism, as an interpretation of Descartes' texts, is not definitively provable as the only way of reading them. Nor (by the same token) is it refutable. But interpretations, like ways of seeing line drawings, can also be more or less natural (as opposed to 'strained'); they can, to a greater or lesser degree, require us to ignore or exaggerate certain lines, or regard them as slips of the pen, or as extraneous or arbitrary. The duck and the rabbit are relatively natural readings of the famous drawing; the defective oval, although possible, is considerably less natural. Cartesian Dualism is, we will argue, a

6 A number of recent commentators have shared our general positive aim of showing the interconnections between Descartes' scientific, metaphysical, logical, and/or theological frameworks; for example, many articles in A. Rorty 1986; Gaukroger, Introduction to Arnauld, *Ideas*; Garber 1992; many articles in Voss 1993.

reading of Descartes' texts roughly on a par with this last example. It doesn't offer enough friction to allow of any definitive *refutation* as a way of organizing Descartes' ideas about persons. With sufficient ingenuity and enough supplementary hypotheses, it can be squared with almost any awkward text. To show (to the extent that such a thing can be shown) that it is a very unnatural reading is not to disprove it, but it ought to make it less attractive, especially if there is an available alternative. This is what we will try to provide.

By the same token, of course, we cannot *demonstrate* that our interpretation of Descartes' Dualism is correct. There is no possibility of imposing this way of seeing Descartes' philosophy on an unwilling reader by sheer force of argument. Our positive first-order aim is simply to make a persuasive case in favour of a different way of developing and organizing the leading ideas of his philosophy. We put a new face on some familiar doctrines (e.g., that animals are automata); spotlight some concepts that have disappeared from view (e.g., the internal senses, Nature); and relate things that are commonly thought to be unconnected (e.g., rationality and moral agency, or metaphysics and logic). The hope is to make perspicuous some neglected aspects of Descartes' thinking: to make everything look different while adhering as faithfully as possible to his texts. In principle this result might be achieved even if authors who offer divergent interpretations of Descartes, or who ascribe to him some form of Cartesian Dualism, would judge that we have scored no decisive points against them. We are, minimally, trying to break a monopoly in the Republic of Letters by setting up a viable competitor in business. Our case should be judged by the usual (flexible and controversial) criteria for preferring one interpretation of a text to another one. We think that it stands up reasonably well to such critical scrutiny.

A vision *of* a complex set of texts aims to uncover a vision *in* those texts: a pattern in the central concepts or the uses of the centrally important words. The vision which the Cartesian Legend finds in Descartes' philosophical writings, i.e. Cartesian Dualism, is utterly familiar. It, for example, links 'thought', 'consciousness', 'sentience', 'privacy', and 'subjectivity'. We try to lay open to view a quite different, even alien, vision, which we call 'Descartes' Dualism'. Its conceptual links are quite different: for example, 'thought' is linked with 'rationality', 'communicability', 'freedom', and 'moral agency', and *contrasted* with 'sentience', 'sensitivity', and 'responsiveness'. Descartes offered a powerful new synthesis of human knowledge; he combined a venerable tradition of Aristotelian logic and metaphysics with the findings of the New Science and with a distinctive theologico-moral crusade in defence of freedom and responsibility in intellectual enquiry. We hope to recapture some of the intellectual excitement that his contemporaries and immediate successors so obviously found in his work. There is much of importance to learn from the exploration of alien visions. Our second-order aim is to try to make out a case for this. The value of such explorations comes not so much from recovering truths – although, importantly, we can learn to see aspects of things which we have collectively lost sight of – as from cultivating the imagination and sympathy required to arrive at a sound understanding of a different point of view, a different vision of things.[7]

Our task makes heavy demands on our readers. Like all authors, we depend on readers' concentration and thoughtfulness, but because of the special nature of pattern-recognition, we need their good will as well.

THE STRATEGY

The structure of this book flows straightforwardly from our description of the enterprise. Following this first chapter, the text splits into four further chapters.

The second chapter presents a thumb-nail sketch of the conception of a human being which contemporary Anglo-American philosophers label 'Cartesian Dualism'. We pick out four doctrines:

1 Thoughts constitute an inner or private world of mental objects which is broadly parallel to the external world of material things; the objects of each world have distinctive properties and stand in various relations to each other.
2 The mind is equated with consciousness; or, equivalently, Descartes extended the term 'thought' to embrace everything that is now called a 'state of consciousness'. (This has the important implication that what he called 'thoughts' need not have propositional content; for instance, a thought may be a headache or the visual experience of a flash of lightning.) The body is a mere unconscious or insentient machine, effectively a complicated bit of clockwork. (Notoriously, so are animals.)
3 Inner objects are apprehended by the subject alone through the exercise of a quasi-perceptual faculty called 'introspection', and the deliverances of introspection are indubitable. External objects, including the subject's own body, are perceived by the five senses.
4 Thoughts and states of the body are logically independent but causally interrelated: in sense-perception, physical causes (e.g., retinal irradiation or vibrations of the ear-drum) produce mental effects (sense-experiences or sense-impressions), and in voluntary action, mental causes (volitions) bring about physical effects (bodily movements). (It is notorious that Descartes could give no defensible account of *how* these causal interactions take place.)

7 A few modern works have shared something of the second-order iconoclastic ambitions of this book, for example, R. Rorty 1980; Myles Burnyeat, 'Idealism and Greek Philosophy: What Descartes Saw and Berkeley Missed', *The Philosophical Review*, vol. 41, no. 1, 1982; Charles Taylor, *Sources of the Self*, Cambridge: Cambridge University Press, 1989. Our first-order purpose distinguishes this book from these paradigms of the 'new historicism'. The 'new historicism' is inclined, as Susan James has put it, to 'write the end [of the historical story] before the beginning' ('Internal and External in the Work of Descartes', in James Tully (ed.), *Philosophy in an Age of Pluralism*, Cambridge: Cambridge University Press, 1994, p. 8), and a result is a tendency to proceed with too little scholarly investigation of texts; all the shibboleths of the Cartesian Legend reappear here (inwardness, subjectivity, states of consciousness, ideas as mental particulars). Why, asks James, 'does the opposition between inner and outer play such a prominent part in contemporary philosophy's telling of its own history?' (p. 9).

The third chapter consists of a close critical examination of the textual support typically given by believers in the Cartesian Legend for each of the four strands of Cartesian Dualism. We try to show that the very texts that are used to prove that Cartesian Dualism is the correct interpretation of Descartes' thinking are open to very different readings. We also argue that the four strands of Cartesian Dualism have clear implications that come into conflict with what is apparently expressed in other parts of his major texts, and we call attention to the kinds of unnatural readings of these texts or the kinds of supplementary hypotheses which are invoked by interpreters to remove these tensions. (In a loose sense, we aim to produce a *reductio ad absurdum*.) We try to identify some of the dubious presuppositions that are required for extracting Cartesian Dualism from Descartes' writings. The upshot, we hope, is that our readers will return the verdict 'Not proven' when presented with expositions of the Cartesian Legend. This third chapter concludes the negative part of our programme.

The fourth chapter is the centre of gravity of the positive first-order aim of the book. Here we develop in some detail the guidelines for constructing a different picture of Descartes' dualism.[8]

1 There are two and only two kinds of (finite) substance, *minds* and corporeal things. We argue that the view that thoughts constitute a world of inner *objects* is inconsistent with his metaphysics, and make out a case for so linking his metaphysics with his logic that the standard 'refutations' of Cartesian Dualism cannot even be formulated within his framework of thought.
2 We argue for the view that his fundamental project was to extend the range of phenomena which can be explained by the principles of mechanics to include the vegetative, sentient, and locomotive functions of living organisms. Hence on the one hand, he *narrowed* the term 'soul' to what had traditionally been called the rational soul (intellect and volition), which was the seat of freedom and moral responsibility. On the other hand, the body itself was a *sentient* machine; so too were animals. They felt pain and saw light, but did not have free will and hence were not moral agents.
3 We argue that he employed the scholastic terms '*conscius*' and '*conscientia*' (usually translated as 'conscious' and 'consciousness' respectively) in the traditional manner, namely to denote knowledge of the operations of the *rational* soul. Modern interpretations have missed the conceptual links between *conscientia* and conscience, hence moral responsibility. They have also failed to distinguish his two terms '*conscientia*' and 'internal sense': the (two) internal senses were for him means for perceiving certain properties of the body, which include pain, bodily appetites, and emotions; these senses were as fallible as the five external senses and were shared with animals.
4 Finally, we argue that he explicitly rejected the idea that there could be any *intelligible* (hence any efficient causal) connection between states of the soul

8 Some individual elements of our own positive interpretation have been put forward by other authors; some cases will be noted in the body of the book.

> and states of the body; the regular correlations between thoughts and bodily states can be explained only by the doctrine that they are instituted or ordained by God. What he called 'the power of the body to act on the soul' (exemplified in human sense-perception) is a power that only a body substantially united to a soul could exhibit; and 'the power of the soul to move the body' (exemplified in human voluntary action) is a power that only a soul substantially united to a body could exhibit.

The crucial concept in making sense of these claims is that of 'our Nature', which was ordained by God for our welfare (including our moral welfare) and which, having been ordained by God, has a certain kind of necessity. Thus the mind and the body of a human being are in a certain sense internally related. Implicit in this picture is support for our general positive first-order claim that Descartes' Dualism cannot be understood in isolation from principles that belong to metaphysics, logic, ethics, and theology.

The final chapter connects this with our second-order aim: we try to clarify the philosophical interest of tracing a different pattern in Descartes' philosophy. The entrenchedness of the Cartesian Legend in Anglo-American philosophy is arguably a by-product of a set of unnoticed and unexamined assumptions that shape modern philosophy of mind and cognitive science. Exposing the nature and sources of the Cartesian Legend is a way of bringing to light many semi-conscious or unconscious prejudices, both about minds and bodies, and about the importance of history of philosophy to philosophy. (What you fail to notice is very likely to be something that is always in your field of vision.) Developing some sensitivity to other frameworks of thinking that are visible, though unremarked, in the work of some of the Great Dead Philosophers might prove a way to arrive at an improved self-understanding. Modern philosophers might conceivably cultivate more humility, refraining from condemning Descartes' thinking as primitive and acknowledging the possibility that conceptual blinkers are as prominent in twentieth-century Anglo-American philosophy as they were among seventeenth-century French rationalists.

Although this book focuses on Descartes' Dualism, the considerations brought to bear on this issue range over the whole body of his philosophy. It is essential to understanding his philosophy to proceed in this way. If we are right about the high degree of integration of his ideas, then there is no quick way to achieve a clear view of his conception of a person as the substantial union of a body with a rational soul. We will see this in good light only once dawn has broken over the whole landscape of his thinking.

Five preliminary notes

1 References to Descartes' works in translation are principally to the Cottingham, Stoothoff, Murdoch, and Kenny translation (CSM). There are some places where this generally excellent translation seems to us to be defective, however; in such

cases, rather than detailing and justifying our modifications, we simply mark our modified version with an asterisk (*) after the page reference. Interested readers can check both our and their versions against the original texts in Adam and Tannery (AT).

2 We call attention to certain words by capitalizing them. All occurrences of the term 'Nature' (and the cognate terms 'Natural' and 'Naturally'), except when it is used as a synonym for 'essence', are capitalized in order to emphasize the (now unfamiliar) connotation of being 'ordained by God'. (See below pp. 168–72.) We capitalize 'Imagination' to call attention to the (now neglected) fact that its scope is far more extensive than the modern English word, regularly covering in Descartes' usage memory, anticipation, and desire or goal-seeking as well as imaging or visualizing things, i.e. a 'faculty of the soul' whose scope is comparable in width to the correlative faculties of sense-perception and intellect.

3 Most of our attention is devoted to sense-perception (*sentire*) and locomotion or movement (*agere*). Moreover, in treating sense-perception, we focus on the external senses and the first internal sense (by which pain, hunger, and thirst are perceived). In following this policy, we say virtually nothing about Imagination or about the emotions (the latter being linked with the second internal sense). This means, of course, that our discussion is not comprehensive: but we are trying to effect a reorientation. Our picture is already complex, and including further detail at this stage might obscure the overall pattern we hope to make visible.

4 Chapters 2–4 have parallel structures. They treat the same four themes in the same order, and also to some degree the main subdivisions of these themes. This policy is designed to help readers with particular interests to take short-cuts or to go cross-country in following our arguments. The parallel sections of these chapters are not meant to be self-contained; on the contrary, they have important implications for each other. But they do target general topics where our interpretation of Descartes' texts diverges sharply from the Legendary one.

5 The two authors (both he and she, individually and jointly) use 'he', 'him', 'his', 'himself' as gender-neutral pronouns.

2

CARTESIAN DUALISM

Cartesian Dualism is the conception of the person which the Cartesian Legend attributes to Descartes. The aim of this chapter is to sketch out this conception more fully. At its heart is a compelling vision, so simple that it could 'be written on the back of a postcard' (Kenny 1989: 1). Kenny epitomizes this vision in two sentences: 'Man is a thinking mind; matter is extension in motion'. We expand Cartesian Dualism to four theses:

1 There are two worlds, the one populated by physical objects, the other by mental objects.
2 Physical objects are essentially (bits of) clockwork; mental objects are essentially (states of) consciousness.
3 Physical objects are public and observable, though fallibly, via the senses; mental objects are private and (quasi-) observable via the infallible faculty of introspection.
4 Physical objects and mental objects interact causally within a human being; hence mind and body are externally or contingently related.

THE 'TWO-WORLDS VIEW'

Descartes held that there were two (and only two) kinds of (created) substance, namely minds or thinking substances and bodies or corporeal substances.[1] This dualistic metaphysics is presented by the Cartesian Legend in the form of the claim that there are 'two parallel but independent *worlds*, that of mind and that of matter, each of which can be studied without reference to the other' (Russell 1946: 590, italics added). This formulation of his Dualism we call 'the Two-Worlds View'; it is widespread and noteworthy:

1 Here is the clearest statement of this doctrine: 'I recognize only two ultimate classes of things: first, intellectual or thinking things, i.e. those which pertain to mind or thinking substance; and secondly, material things, i.e. those which pertain to extended substance or body' (*Principles* I.48; CSM I: 208). But even this passage is not entirely straightforward. First, '*things* which pertain to' mind or body include the essential *attributes* of each. (On his use of the word 'thing', see p. 133 n.206. Second, the term 'substance' is normally used as a count-noun, but here as a mass-noun.

> Dualism is the idea that there are two worlds. There is the physical world which contains matter, and energy, and all the tangible contents of the universe including human bodies. Then there is another psychical world: mental events and states belong to a private world which is inaccessible to public observation.
>
> (Kenny 1989: 1; cf. Ryle 1949: 63)[2]

It is even claimed that the Two-Worlds View was a specifically Cartesian *revolution*: Descartes' '*new* mind–body distinction . . . was not a distinction between human faculties but a distinction between two series of events . . . . It was more like a distinction between two worlds than like a distinction between two sides, or even parts, of a human being' (R. Rorty 1980: 51–2).

The metaphor is striking, but what exactly is the content of the Two-Worlds View? Apparently this: just as the physical world is 'populated' by physical objects (tables, chairs, human bodies), the mental world is 'populated' by mental objects (mental events and states). Space is occupied by corporeal things, the mind by incorporeal things. Each kind of thing has its own distinctive kinds of properties.[3] Constitutive of what we call the Two-Worlds View is the joint supposition that there are mental *particulars* in addition to physical particulars like tables, chairs, and human bodies, and that the category of mental particulars includes mental *events and states*.

The term 'particular' is not used by philosophers uniformly or in any precise way, but it is meant to introduce a *logical* concept in contrast to a metaphysical one (like *Descartes*' notion of 'substance'!). Roughly, a particular is something to which we can make 'identifying reference' using 'singular terms',[4] something which can figure as the 'logical subject' of a (singular) judgement (thus supporting existential generalization, substitution of identicals for identicals, etc.), and something to which the distinction between 'numerical' and 'qualitative' identity applies.[5] Consequently, we cannot treat explicit talk of 'two *worlds*' as the sole criterion for holding the Two-Worlds View. Commentators may commit themselves to it in various ways. Here is a selection of clear instances.

2 Quinton talks about one *world*, but one which contains two fundamentally different kinds of thing: 'For the dualist, then, the contents of the world . . . can be divided into physical things, states and events which are in space and fallibly known and mental things, states and events which are not in space and are either infallibly known or are only identifiable by their analogy to things that are' (A. Quinton, *The Nature of Things*, London: Routledge, 1973, pp. 314–17). For our purposes this also counts as an expression of the Two-Worlds View.

3 Already there is a problem: the properties of corporeal things are 'modes of extension'; but the properties of mental things are not Descartes' correlative 'modes of thinking', but are said to be privacy, indubitability, etc.

4 This terminology comes from Strawson 1959.

5 This concept of a particular was explained and exploited in Russell's doctrine of logical atomism: 'Particulars = terms of relations in atomic facts. Df. That is the definition of particulars, and I want to emphasize it because the definition of a particular is something purely logical. The question whether this or that is a particular, is a question to be decided in terms of that logical definition . . . . The whole question of what particulars you actually find in the real world is a purely empirical one which does not interest the logician as such' (Russell 1956: 199).

1 According to Descartes, 'Whenever anyone actually sees, tastes, hears, smells, etc. something there is a perception before the mind'.[6]
2 'Some knowledge, such as knowledge of the existence of our sense-data, appears quite indubitable, however calmly and thoroughly we reflect upon it' (Russell 1912: 151).
3 'How can Descartes explain the fact that we ascribe our states of consciousness to the very same thing as corporeal characteristics?' (cf. Strawson 1959: 94ff.).
4 'How does Descartes get from the existence of his own thought to the existence of "an I"?' (cf. Williams 1978: 101).
5 'Is a pain a mental or a physical event for Descartes?'[7]

Without acknowledging mental particulars, it is difficult to make sense of these theses, objections, or questions.

'CONSCIOUSNESS AND CLOCKWORK'

Descartes held that the essence of mind is thought, the essence of body extension. The Legend interprets these terms in a characteristic way, aptly expressed as the contrast between 'consciousness and clockwork' (Kenny 1966: 353).

Consciousness and the 'Expansion Thesis'

The essence of mind is thought; but what is thinking, or thought? When Descartes asked himself, 'What is a thing which thinks?', he replied: 'a thing which doubts, understands, affirms, denies, is willing, is unwilling, and also imagines and has sensory perceptions' (*Meditation* II (AT VII: 28; CSM II: 19)).

The Legend offers this distinctive interpretation: '*cogitatio* [thought] includes not only intellectual meditation but also volition, emotion, pain, pleasure, mental images, and sensations' (Kenny 1966: 352). The term '*cogitatio*' covers 'more than the modern English term "thought" naturally covers, including not merely ratiocination but also any form of conscious state or process or activity whatsoever'.[8] Sometimes this extremely wide scope of the term '*cogitatio*' is presented as standard seventeenth-century usage: 'The term 'thought' – *pensée*, *cogitatio* – had, in Descartes' time, a much wider meaning than it has now. It embraced not only "thought" as it is now understood, but all mental acts and data'.[9] Indeed, on this basis, '*cogitatio*' is sometimes *translated* as 'experience' or 'consciousness' (Anscombe and Geach 1954: xlvii–xlviii). More usually, commentators see his use of the term as innovative, though they say nothing about his motivation for

6 Barry Stroud, *Hume*, London: Routledge, 1977, p. 26.
7 Cf. John Cottingham, 'Descartes' "Sixth Meditation": The External World, "Nature" and Human Experience', *Philosophy* 20 (Supp.) 1986, pp. 73–89.
8 Williams 1967: 347; cf. Russell 1946: 587.
9 A. Koyré, Introduction to Anscombe and Geach 1954: xxxvii.

the change.[10] The idea that Descartes *expanded* the term '*cogitatio*' to cover all (and only) 'states of consciousness' we will call 'the Expansion Thesis'.[11]

Explaining more precisely the content of the Expansion Thesis requires elucidating the Legendary understanding of the expression 'state of consciousness', although it is doubtful that anything very precise can be said.[12] States of consciousness are not distinguished from mental states; the same things are generally treated as paradigms of both.[13] States of consciousness are associated with a characteristic 'logic' and epistemology ('first-/third-person asymmetry', often construed in terms of 'privacy', 'indubitability', 'subjectivity', and so on; see pp. 18–20). They include manifestations of 'sentience' as well as of 'sapience', so that pain, hunger, fear, joy, and so on are thought of as 'states of consciousness'.[14] Many of these are commonly associated with a characteristic 'phenomenology' ('qualia', 'raw feels', the 'What's it like?'). They are usually conceived of as 'non-propositional', 'non-cognitive', or 'lacking intentionality'.[15] Empiricists have commonly treated certain states of consciousness, especially sense-experiences, as the pre-cognitive, non-linguistic basis for making empirical judgements. (And Descartes is commonly taken to hold this conception in his (allegedly) aiming to locate the foundations of knowledge in immediate subjective experience.) When we use the terms 'consciousness', 'conscious', and 'states of consciousness', it is this sort of conception we will be invoking.[16]

The Expansion Thesis could be expressed by saying that Descartes counted sensations and the like as thoughts;[17] but thus put, it needs to be distinguished from two others.[18] The Expansion Thesis sees 'thought' as having been expanded so as to include anger, pain, mental images, hunger, etc. Such an expansion involves, in effect, removing the *cognitive* connotations of the word 'thought',

10 A few attempt to explain his motivation (Cottingham 1978b, Malcolm 1977), but they are not proponents of the Expansion Thesis.

11 This is roughly the view that Rée (1974: 94ff.) designated as 'pluralism', by contrast with what he described as Descartes' 'reductionism'. His terminology presupposes a view about Descartes' motivations which we do not share.

12 Note that we are concerned here only with twentieth-century Anglo-American philosophers. The use of the term 'consciousness' and its cognates varies enormously between different traditions and different periods. See pp. 100–24.

13 Mill distinguished the two, for instance, in treating generosity as an attribute or state of mind but not a state of consciousness (*Logic* I.iii.14).

14 This is obviously a powerful source of the idea that Descartes made a blunder in denying minds to animals, since they are manifestly sentient.

15 Hence many Anglo-American philosophers have accused Brentano, and by implication the French phenomenologists, of making a mistake in taking intentionality to be the defining feature of mental states. (Of course, terms like 'intentionality' are as variable and contestable as 'consciousness'.)

16 To avoid the danger of anachronism, we will not make use of these terms in expounding our own conception of Descartes' Dualism; hence we leave untranslated the two Latin terms '*conscientia*' and '*conscius*' (see pp. 101–2).

17 Cf. Rée 1974: 94 n. 11: 'Such accounts as these have the implausible implication that Descartes was not particularly keen on "separating the mind from the senses"'.

18 Elsewhere (Baker and Morris 1993) we did not make this distinction; and K. Morris (1995) treated all of these theses as variants of the Expansion Thesis. We here focus our discussion more sharply by concentrating solely on the Expansion Thesis 'properly so-called'.

thus redefining 'thought'.[19] This thesis is to be distinguished from what we could call the 'Annexation Thesis', according to which Descartes in effect annexed pain, mental images, and anger into the mind by removing the *non-cognitive* connotations of the words 'pain', 'anger', 'mental image', etc. (Pain and anger are, contrary to popular belief, in fact *cognitive* phenomena, namely thoughts.)[20] Both of these theses are to be distinguished from a third, to be called the 'Courtesy Thesis'. On this view, Descartes did not consider pain, sense-perception, images, etc. to be '*cogitationes simpliciter*', but referred to them as 'thoughts' as it were by courtesy, because they are objects of 'reflective awareness' (which *is* a *cogitatio simpliciter*).[21]

We focus here on the Expansion Thesis, although what we say has bearings on its cousins. It is this thesis which has captured the imagination of philosophers (and cognitive psychologists, literary critics, environmentalists, et al.) outside the circle of Descartes scholarship. More precisely, what grips them is its consequence that he expanded the boundaries of the *mind*. According to this reading, he broke with the medieval tradition, which located 'the boundary between spirit and nature' 'not between consciousness and clockwork', but 'between intellect and sense. It was understanding and judging and willing, not feeling aches or seeing colours or having mental images, which . . . set mind apart from matter' (Kenny 1966: 360; cf. Geach 1957: 116–17). By extending the term 'thought' (the essence of the mind) so as to cover all states of consciousness, Descartes is said to have been the first to locate the boundary between mind and body in its modern (proper?) site. By this innovation, he is credited with having 'created a new philosophy of mind' and having altered 'the whole perspective in which [philosophy] viewed the relationship between the mental and the physical' (Kenny 1966: 352).

By shunting the interest of the Expansion Thesis away from the concept of thought and on to the concept of mind, its proponents sidestep the question of the *motivation* for the expansion of '*cogitatio*' as opposed to the motivation for the expansion of '*mens*'. (Here the Annexation and Courtesy Theses have a distinct advantage.) They see nothing remarkable in the idea that Descartes used the word 'thought' to collect together pains, mental images, sense-perceptions, emotions, *and thoughts* in virtue of what they have in common (cf. R. Rorty 1980: 54ff.),

19 See, for example, Kenny 1966, 1968, 1989; Williams 1978; Wilson 1978 (although with refinements); R. Rorty 1980; and Strawson 1959. This is the 'classical', most commonly held version of the Expansion Thesis.

20 See Malcolm 1977 and perhaps Curley 1979; Williams (1978: 286) hints at the possibility of interpreting Descartes' alleged thesis in this way, but his own account is the Expansion Thesis.

Anscombe and Geach consider a version of the 'Annexation Thesis', namely the idea that Descartes was 'maintaining that all mental acts, in spite of their apparent differences, are "really" thoughts (in the way that McTaggart maintains . . . that all mental states are "really" perceptions) and are only "misperceived" as being anything else'. They object to this interpretation on the grounds that 'Descartes expressly denies that the "evil genius" could make me "misperceive" the contents of my own mind' (Anscombe and Geach 1954: xlvii–xlviii).

21 Cottingham 1978b, 1986, and 1993: 156.

and nothing paradoxical in the suggestion that his 'introduction of *cogitatio* [a word apparently evoking rationality] as the defining characteristic of mind is tantamount to the substitution of privacy for rationality as the mark of the mental' (Kenny 1966: 360). (Otherwise one might be tempted to suppose that a word so redolent of *sapience* was a poor choice for somebody who allegedly wished to give pride of place to *sentience*.)[22]

Further puzzlement might arise from the Legend's claim that, when Descartes expanded the term 'thought' to cover sense-perception, he redefined the term 'sense-perception' to mean 'what is common to the genuine case [e.g., of seeing] and the doubtful case [i.e. hallucinating]' (Kenny 1968: 73). He is thereby credited with having invented a new, and dubious, category of mental entities, namely 'sense-impressions' or '*sense-data*'.[23] This innovation is central to 'the most far-reaching aspect of Descartes's revolution in philosophy', viz. seeing epistemology as the starting-point of philosophy.[24] It permitted the seventeenth century 'to pose the problem of the veil of ideas, the problem which made epistemology central to philosophy' (R. Rorty 1980: 50–1). This achievement is what warrants the common description of Descartes as 'the founder of modern philosophy' (Russell 1912: 18; Russell 1946: 580).[25] Is there nothing strange in the idea that Descartes (the paradigm anti-empiricist) invented the idea of 'pure data in experience to serve as logically certain foundations for knowledge'?[26]

22 Rée (1974: 94) suggests that 'Descartes' belief that all non-physical aspects of human beings could be reduced to thought is often concealed from modern readers because . . . words like "mind" and "mental" have lost their austerely intellectualistic connotations'. This is undoubtedly right and important; but it is equally striking that the word 'thought' has by no means lost these connotations, yet his recurrent thesis that the essence of the mind is thought is still read 'non-intellectualistically'.

The Legend might try to motivate Descartes' choice of terminology. For example, might he have been selling his readers a decisive change without calling attention to it?

23 Also Williams 1978: 79. (The view is very common.)

24 M. A. E. Dummett, *Truth and Other Enigmas*, London: Duckworth, 1978, pp. 88–9. Cf. Williams 1967: 346. (This view too is very common.)

25 Others describe him as 'the father of modern philosophy' (e.g., Tom Sorrell, 'Descartes' Modernity', in Cottingham 1994: 29); yet others, just for variety, as 'the founding father of modern philosophy' (Roger Scruton, *A Short History of Modern Philosophy*, London: Ark/Routledge, 1984, p. 29).

Here, for once, we find ourselves in profound agreement with Bernard Williams: 'the effect of taking the tradition of modernity as given, with Descartes as its founder, can only be deeply settling and undisturbing, since it confronts us exactly with what we thought we had already. Our sense of the situation will be unsettled only when we come to see Descartes and the other supposed contributors as stranger than they seem while they are still regarded as the constituents of the tradition' ('Descartes and the Historiography of Philosophy', in Cottingham 1994: 26).

26 Michael Pendlebury, 'Experience, Theories of', in Dancy and Sosa 1992: 126. A number of commentators (notably Wilson) have of course rejected the Legendary view that 'Descartes introduces "sensory ideas" as the indubitable residue that remains when judgements about external objects are called into question' (Wilson 1994: 210). This goes some distance towards undermining the Legendary view of Descartes as a kind of honorary British empiricist, even though it does not entail rejection of the idea that he held there to *be* such a 'residue'.

Clockwork and the 'Contraction Thesis'

The Legend says little explicitly on the topic of the body, yet what it describes as the Cartesian conception of the mind has clear implications for the Cartesian conception of the body.

First, the Legend sets out from the principle that the essence of mind is thought, and the essence of body is extension. Interpreting 'thought' as 'consciousness', it must interpret 'extension' so that it excludes any form of consciousness. The body cannot be conscious. Moreover, the behaviour of everything extended can be explained by mechanical principles. Consequently, the human body must be a *machine* whose movements are to be explained 'along purely mechanical lines: the nerves are little pipes through which the fast-moving vapour called the "animal spirits" flows, so as to inflate the muscles and cause movement' (Cottingham 1986: 107). The Legend takes it to be pleonastic to add the adjective '*unconscious*' to the noun 'machine'. This is the burden of describing Descartes' boundary between mind and body as that between 'consciousness and clockwork' (Kenny 1966: 353).

Second, there is a clear implication of the Legend's claim that Descartes expanded the scope of the terms 'thought' and 'mind' relative to his predecessors. In so far as the terms 'mind' and 'body' are logically *correlative* (each, as it were, taking in the other's washing), the allegedly pre-Cartesian view must have been that non-cognitive 'states of consciousness' (pains, joy, images) are not mental, but bodily. For Descartes' predecessors, 'the boundary between spirit and nature was . . . between intellect and sense. It was understanding and judging and willing, not feeling aches or seeing colours or having mental images, which . . . set mind apart from matter' (Kenny 1966: 353).[27] We wish to highlight this implication by introducing the label 'the Contraction Thesis': the correlate of Descartes' expansion of the mental *must* be a corresponding contraction of the bodily. The Legend is committed not only to maintaining that he held the body to be essentially non-conscious ('mere clockwork'), but also to seeing this doctrine as innovative *vis-à-vis* his predecessors. What could have been his motivation for this change? Like the parallel question about the motivation for the Expansion Thesis, this receives no answer from the Legend.

'CARTESIAN INTROSPECTION' AND 'CARTESIAN OBSERVATION'

G. F. Stout discussed a picture, 'historically traceable to Descartes', according to which 'the body, like other material objects, is known only through external perception, whereas self-consciousness reveals only mind' (Stout 1964: 259). This is precisely the Legend's conception of our knowledge of our own minds and

27 Compare: 'For Descartes' predecessors the imagination was not part of the mind, but was thoroughly bodily' (Kenny 1989: 10). Cf. W. Matson, quoted in R. Rorty 1980: 47.

bodies. The Legendary Descartes expressly held that we know the contents of our own minds through 'self-consciousness' or (what is often said to be the same thing) 'introspection' – the contents of other minds being known only via a problematic inference from their behaviour. By implication the Legendary Descartes adhered to the principle that states of one's own body can be known only through the five (external) senses. (The Legend certainly never challenges this, and it wholly neglects the two internal senses.)

The mind: Cartesian Introspection

Cartesian Dualism equates the mind with consciousness. According to the Legend, 'Many people go along with Descartes [*sic*] in identifying the mental realm as the realm of consciousness. They think of consciousness as an object of introspection' (Kenny 1989: 2).[28]

The Legend's notion of 'states of consciousness' includes certain logical or epistemological properties that are gestured at by the phrase 'first-/third-person asymmetry'.[29] It is often held that concepts designating 'states of consciousness' (e.g., the concept of pain) 'work' differently in the first- and third-person cases. For instance (it is said), nothing would count as my being mistaken in saying 'I have a pain', by contrast with 'He has a pain'; nothing would count as my being in pain but not knowing it, whereas it makes perfect sense to speak of *his* being in pain but *my* not knowing this; it makes sense to say 'I feel my pain', but not 'I feel his pain'; the question 'How do you know he's in pain?' is a sensible one, but not the question 'How do you know *you're* in pain?', since I do not ascribe pain to myself on evidence or grounds. It is claimed to be a crucial feature of the concept of pain that first-person present-tense avowals of pain by the sufferer have an authoritative status. And a parallel point is supposed to hold quite generally for 'states of consciousness' (or 'psychological concepts').[30]

According to the Legend, Descartes offered a (mistaken) general explanation of these grammatical data. He held that the contents of the mind are known through 'introspection, a looking into oneself, a form of perception or "inner sense"',[31] allegedly in an attempt to capture the 'important grammatical connections and

28 Ryle's use of the term 'introspection' diverges from this. He sees Cartesian Dualism as invoking a 'twofold Privileged Access' to one's own mental states: 'a mind cannot help being constantly aware of all the supposed occupants of its private stage' and 'it can also deliberately scrutinise by a species of non-sensuous perception at least some of its own states and operations'. The first route he calls 'consciousness', the second 'introspection' (1949: 154). Thus, for Ryle, both 'consciousness' and 'introspection' designate ways of acquiring knowledge about one's own mental states. On this point Curley remarks that 'if consciousness is as good a way of knowing one's own mind as it is supposed to be, it is difficult to see what contribution introspection could make' (1979: 172)!

29 This phrase is explained in Hacker 1990: 187–8.

30 'If I want to know what sensations somebody is having, what he seems to see or hear, what he is imagining or saying to himself, then I have to give his utterances on the topic a special status.' In all such cases, 'the subject is in a position of special authority' (Kenny 1966: 360).

31 David Pears ('Avowals', in Dancy and Sosa 1992: 37) talks of 'the Cartesian idea that a person discloses the contents of his mind by identifying inner objects and describing them'.

features of first- and third-person psychological utterances' (Hacker 1986: 279). The results are the notorious doctrines of 'the epistemological transparency of thought' (Wilson 1978: 151;[32] cf. Cottingham 1986: 39) and of 'Cartesian Privacy' (Kenny 1966: title; cf. Williams 1978: 84–6).

The doctrine of the Epistemological Transparency of Thought states that introspection is essentially and universally infallible. Its deliverances are 'immune from illusion, confusion or doubt' (Ryle 1949: 14).[33] States of consciousness 'intimate themselves' to introspection: 'If I think, hope, remember, will, regret, hear a noise, or feel a pain, I must, *ipso facto*, know that I do so' (Ryle 1949: 158). Alternatively, 'mental processes are phosphorescent, like tropical sea-water' (Ryle 1949: 158–9).[34] There are variations around this central core: 'self-intimation', for instance, is sometimes taken, not to be an 'actuality' concept as in Ryle's famous characterization, but a 'potentiality' concept: 'Everything in a mind at a time is available to consciousness, introspectively available, at that time' (Armstrong 1984: 121–2). The first conception is supposed to generate an infinite regress and to lead to the notorious problems of divided attention; the second is taken to be refuted by findings in psychoanalysis.[35]

The doctrine of Cartesian Privacy turns on the idea that introspection gives 'asymmetrical' access to our own mental states (i.e. a route unavailable to others, cf. Hacker 1986: 279; Ryle 1949: 154), a route that is epistemically superior to any access that others may have: it is the only 'direct', non-inferential route ('while I can have direct knowledge of my own states and operations, I cannot have it of yours . . . I can satisfy myself that you have a mind at all only by complex and frail inferences from what your body does' (Ryle 1949: 155, cf. 14)).[36] 'The workings of one mind are not witnessable by other observers; its career is private. Only I can take direct cognisance of the states and processes of my own mind' (Ryle 1949: 11; cf. Williams 1978: 85).[37] Thus, ironic though it might seem for

32 Note that Wilson is highly critical of the ascription of many aspects of this doctrine to Descartes.

33 Cf. Armstrong (1984: 122); Sydney Shoemaker, 'Self-Knowledge and Self-Identity' (in Dancy and Sosa 1992: 467).

34 This characterizes Rylean 'consciousness' as opposed to 'introspection'. On his view, introspection does not involve what he calls self-intimation (although it does involve what others would call 'self-intimation'): it is supposed to be 'an attentive operation and one which is only occasionally performed, whereas consciousness is supposed to be a constant element of all mental processes' (Ryle 1949: 164).

35 Sometimes, of course, the focus of the 'Freudian' attack is the alleged incorrigibility of introspective reports rather than their self-intimation (construed as 'availability to consciousness'). The precise boundaries between these various notions are variable and open to dispute; it is no part of our task to try to make them precise.

36 Ryle (1949: 154–5) and others use the term 'privileged access' for the combination of asymmetry and superiority. The term is sometimes used (e.g., by Dalmiya 1992: 219) to denote the idea that the subject has an *infallible* route to his own mental states.

37 Kenny, rather strangely, interprets privacy in such a way that it follows from the alleged infallibility of introspection: 'Experiences [e.g., sense-impressions] . . . seem to be exempt from doubt by the person whose experiences they are. Descartes took this kind of indubitability as the characteristic property of thought. Such experiences are private to their owner in the sense that while others can doubt them, he cannot' (Kenny 1989: 9–10); and Dalmiya (1992: 219) interprets it in terms of asymmetrical access alone.

the paradigm rationalist, 'The introduction of *cogitatio* as the defining characteristic of mind is tantamount to the substitution of privacy for rationality as the mark of the mental' (Kenny 1966: 360).[38]

Cartesian Introspection is explicitly modelled on *sense-perception*. 'The world of Matter is known through external/outer sense-perception. So cognitive access to Mind must be based on a *parallel* process of introspection' (Dalmiya 1992: 219). Introspection is thus a kind of quasi-perception, 'the *faculty* or information-processing mechanism whereby I come to acquire' 'knowledge' of my own psychological states, with 'peculiarities' which are meant to explain the 'peculiarities of first-person psychological awareness and reports' (Dalmiya 1992: 222).

The body: Cartesian Observation

Unlike mental processes and states, 'bodily processes and states can be inspected by external observers. So a man's bodily life is . . . a public affair' (Ryle 1949: 11). The Legend supplies no parallel account of Descartes' view about our knowledge of states of our *own* bodies. But what we call the thesis of Cartesian Observation seems to be the only option: according to the Legendary Descartes, 'the body, like other material objects, is known *only* through external perception' (Stout 1964: 259, italics added).

First, what apart from 'sense-perception' *could* be the source of our knowledge of the (physical) states of our own bodies? The Legend sees one's own body as part of the external world, and it seems tautological to say that the five (external) senses are, immediately or proximately, the source of all knowledge about the external world.

Second, 'external' sense-perception has properties that seem tailor-made for the Legendary body. The body is mere clockwork; it is definitive of 'clockwork' concepts that they do not exhibit first-/third-person asymmetry. The same point holds of the concept of the objects of sense-perception. What is perceived is not 'epistemologically transparent'. ('It only makes sense to talk of perceiving x if it makes sense for x to occur unperceived, or of misperceiving x' (Hacker 1987: 70), and it always makes sense to say that something was in the visual (or auditory, etc.) field of someone, only he did not notice it.) The objects of sense-perception

38 Cf. Andrew Woodfield (ed.), *Thought and Object*, Oxford: Clarendon, 1982, p. vii: 'Descartes, Locke, Hume, and indeed the majority of great philosophers, appear to have held that the specific nature of a thought or belief is fixed by its subjective content . . . . According to the conception of mind which prevails in our culture (a conception often called "Cartesian" although it is actually far older than Descartes), thoughts are by nature private to the person experiencing them; so there must be a way of individuating them which respects that privacy'.

Cartesian Privacy is said to include not only the kind of 'epistemological privacy' described here, but also so-called 'privacy of ownership' (sometimes expressed as 'Another's thought is another thought'), in so far as the two are seen as distinct. 'Privacy of ownership' is principally a consequence of the Two-Worlds View. Here our concern is Introspection and hence we confine ourselves to 'epistemological privacy'.

are necessarily public. (Access to the objects of sense-perception is held to be at best contingently asymmetrical, and at best contingently superior: 'Things looked at, or listened to, are public objects, in principle observable by any suitably placed observer' (Ryle 1949: 163).) Thus conceived, external sense-perception seems to be logically and epistemologically well-suited to the Legend's clockwork-body.

'CARTESIAN INTERACTION'

Causal interaction is a central element of the Cartesian Legend. 'What exactly is the special relationship between the mind and the (part of) the body to which it is "joined"? On this question, at least, Descartes had a definite, unambiguous answer . . . that mind and body are *causally* related' (Dicker 1993: 218). This causal relation is two-way. On the one hand, 'a physical change in the optic nerve [has] among its effects a mind's perception of a flash of light' (Ryle 1949: 19). On the other, 'a mental process, such as willing, cause[s] spatial movements like the movement of the tongue' (Ryle 1949: 19).[39]

> On [his][40] view the will is a phenomenon, an episode in one's mental history, an item of introspective consciousness. Volition is a mental event whose occurrence makes the difference between voluntary and involuntary actions. For an overt action to be voluntary is for it to be preceded and caused by a characteristic internal impression or conscious thought.
>
> (Kenny 1989: 32; 1975: 13)

It is often said to be characteristic of Descartes' version of dualism, as over against other versions (Occasionalism, Pre-Established Harmony, etc.), that he held that mind and body causally interact: his view is sometimes labelled 'interactionism' in honour of this fact (and interactionism is called 'Cartesian Interactionism' in honour of him).[41]

This doctrine raises some difficulty about how to understand Descartes' famous claim that 'I am not merely present in my body as a sailor is present in a ship, but am very closely joined and, as it were, intermingled with it' (AT VII: 81; CSM II: 56). Some take it simply as a rather misleading restatement of causal interactionism itself: 'Though Descartes conceded that "I am not merely present in my body as a sailor is present in a ship", but am rather ". . . intermingled with

39 The doctrine of 'volitions', those 'acts, or operations, "in the mind", by means of which a mind gets its ideas translated into facts', 'is just an inevitable extension of the myth of the ghost in the machine': 'to say that a person pulled the trigger intentionally . . . [according to most versions of the myth] is to express a causal proposition, asserting that the bodily act of pulling the trigger was the effect of the mental act of willing to pull the trigger' (Ryle 1949: 63).

40 Kenny calls this the 'introvert' view, which he says 'can be illustrated by Descartes, Hume and William James' (1975: 12).

41 Many philosophy of mind books present dualism in this way. A particularly splendid example of this genre occurs in Haugeland (1985: 38–9): his 'Box 4' (labelled 'Dualist Desperados') contains Interactionism, Parallelism, Occasionalism, and Epiphenomenalism, with Descartes himself placed firmly in the first box.

it . . .", the intermingling is causal, and the unity contingent' (Hacker 1990: 244–5). Others suppose that if you take it seriously, it is actually *incompatible* with Cartesian Interaction: 'Descartes' talk of "intermingling" can at best be taken as a way of describing how we *seem* to ourselves to be joined to our bodies, rather than as a literal, true account of the connection' (Dicker 1993: 218). Yet others claim that although 'Descartes may have a more purely metaphysical level of explanation in mind. . . the entire content of Descartes's denial that he is a pilot in a ship is phenomenological – it is exclusively about what the experience of being embodied is like' (Williams 1978: 280).

This picture of two worlds, one of physical objects known through sense-perception and one of mental objects known through infallible introspection, which (mysteriously!) causally interact with each other, is a familiar one. It undoubtedly has a powerful appeal to many twentieth-century Anglo-American philosophers. Most commentators suppose that it is deeply flawed. Many of them find the idea of pinning this picture on to Descartes highly attractive, with the consequence that they judge *his* thinking to be highly problematic or downright incoherent. Our next task is to examine their case for convicting him of the sins of Cartesian Dualism.

3

A SHADOW OF A DOUBT

Cartesian Dualism, as we have just depicted the doctrine, has a twofold importance. First, it presents an attractive, even if naive or simplistic, picture of the nature of a person. It seems a very natural starting-point for philosophical reflection on the concepts of the mind and the body, and it is a landmark for plotting progress (collective or individual) in philosophy of mind. The doctrine seems all at once captivating, pernicious, and demonstrably confused. Second, it is thought to give a correct interpretation, at least in broad outline, of Descartes' reflections on the nature of a person. It is claimed to reveal the pattern that alone makes sense of his thinking. His alleged invention of Cartesian Dualism is central to his reputation as the Founder of Modern Philosophy, and it makes him the Anti-Hero of twentieth-century philosophy of mind.

In this chapter, we focus on the second of these two claims. We refrain from playing the popular party-game of constructing refutations of Cartesian Dualism, though we make some allusions to these manoeuvres in working out interpretations that make better sense of his writings.

Having ready to hand a clear sketch of Cartesian Dualism (in Chapter 2) makes it possible for us to search Descartes' texts carefully for clear support for its component theses. Attributing to Descartes the specific ideas characteristic of Cartesian Dualism must surely be grounded in unambiguous textual evidence. We show that the Legend conspicuously fails to meet this requirement. Indeed, we argue that there is no solid *textual* foundation whatever for ascribing *any* single element of Cartesian Dualism to Descartes. On the contrary, many of the Legend's exhibits provide at least *prima facie counter*-evidence. The Legend is not struck by things that, once called to our attention, may be the most striking features of its citations.

Our immediate programme is to exploit Descartes' texts to discredit Cartesian Dualism as the correct interpretation of his philosophical system. (We are following his exhortation to challenge arguments from authority.) At the same time, we indicate features of his arguments that may point towards a better account. Our more remote purpose is to create the possibility of making visible a radically different pattern in his thinking.

THE TWO-WORLDS VIEW

The Legendary Descartes is committed to what we have called the Two-Worlds View, the thesis according to which there are mental particulars other than minds which have some substantial resemblances to physical particulars.

There is some unclarity about the precise content of this thesis. Exploiting Strawson's distinction between particulars which are 'identifiability-dependent' on other particulars and those which are not (1959: 40ff.), we might distinguish two versions of the view: (a) that these further mental particulars are 'identifiability-dependent' on minds; and (b) that they are not.[1] It is unclear to which of these the Legend supposes Descartes to be committed. It is quite clear, however, that (b) is incompatible with his ontology.[2] Given Descartes' own conception of substance as 'a thing which exists in such a way as to depend on no other thing for its existence' (*Principles* I.51; CSM I: 210), (b) would seem to imply that there were mental *substances* other than minds, which is inconsistent with his clearly stated dualistic view according to which the only types of substance (apart from God) were minds and corporeal things.[3] Version (a) seems more plausible and less clearly in conflict with his ideas, but even it is arguably incompatible with his logical and metaphysical framework (see pp. 60–9).

What textual evidence supports taking the Two-Worlds View as Descartes' 'unofficial metaphysics'? *Principles* I.9 (CSM I: 195) elucidates how the verb '*cogito*' is to be understood in the argument '*Cogito, ergo sum*'. 'By the term "thinking" [*cogitatio*] I understand . . .' The question here is what counts as the *activity* of thinking; or what the term 'cogitation' means here. What is at issue is the nature of intelligent substance: here 'thinking' stands to incorporeal substance as 'extension' stands to corporeal substance (cf. *Principles* I.63–4; CSM I: 215–16). The same point holds in respect of *Meditation* II (AT VII: 28; CSM II: 19): having proved that he is a thinking thing (*res cogitans*), Descartes raised the question 'What is a *thinking* thing?' and proceeded to elucidate what counts as

1 The latter view is constitutive of Russell's conception of particulars: 'Particulars have this peculiarity, among the sort of objects that you have to take account of in an inventory of the world, that each of them stands entirely alone and is completely self-subsistent. It has that sort of self-subsistence that used to belong to substance' (Russell 1956: 202).

2 Hume's famous claim, that his 'impressions' or 'perceptions' might just as well be called *substances*, 'since all our perceptions are different from each other, and from every thing else in the universe, they are also distinct and separable, and may be consider'd as separately existent, and may exist separately, and have no need of any thing else to support their existence' (*Treatise* I.iv.5), is a version of (b). It was quite self-consciously anti-Cartesian.

3 There is a locution, namely 'mind-stuff', current in some quarters (R. Rorty 1980: e.g., p. 17; Dennett 1993: e.g., p. 33; Churchland 1984: e.g., p. 8) which seems to embody a misconception of Descartes' concept of substance. When Dennett raises the question of whether 'mind-stuff' might turn out to be, not immaterial, but 'a scientifically investigatable kind of matter', rather like ectoplasm (p. 36), he evidently understands 'mental substance' as a kind of 'immaterial plasticine' *out of which* minds and mental states are 'made' (cf. also Hacker 1990: 520). But minds are not *made* of 'mental substance' according to Descartes, they *are* mental substances (and indeed the only mental substances apart from God). He normally used 'substance' as a count-noun, not a mass-noun.

forms of thinking: doubting, understanding, affirming, etc.[4] The present participle '*cogitans*' is cashed out into the string of participles '*dubitans, intelligens, affirmans, negans, volens, nolens, imaginans & sentiens*'.

Of course we can see these passages as clarifications of what counts as 'thought'. But this term can be interpreted in two ways: either as an abstract noun like 'thinking' or 'cogitation' or as a count-noun like 'idea' or 'proposition'. Used in the first sense, 'thought' does pick out the subject-matter of these two passages. But used in the second sense, 'thought' (i.e. 'a thought') introduces altogether different considerations, especially the criteria for individuating thoughts. The Legend regularly paraphrases these two passages by making use of the *count-noun* 'thought'. 'Descartes . . . uses the verbs [*cogitare* and *penser*] to record many experiences which we would not naturally describe as thoughts' (Kenny 1966: 353–4). This is what opens the way to picturing instances of thinking on the model of the soul's standing in certain relations to *entities* (thoughts) that make up an 'inner realm', but this Legendary gloss has no warrant in the commonly cited passages.[5] Arguably, just here is where a decisive move in the conjuring trick is made.

The Two-Worlds View, in one or another version, is, in effect, the centre of gravity of the whole system of thought called Cartesian Dualism. Without it, the other main elements lose much of their motivation, plausibility, and charm. Moreover, most of the standard 'refutations' of Cartesian Dualism depend directly upon it; without it they are plainly question-begging. Consequently, to the extent that it is inconsistent with Descartes' ontology, metaphysics, and logic, there will be a strong suspicion that the other components of Cartesian Dualism are too. But even if it were consistent with his texts, it would be a gratuitous interpretation of his thought unless it were either required or directly supported by his writings. The Legend is wholly committed to pinning on to Descartes a logico-metaphysical doctrine which is arguably both anachronistic and unwarranted.

The centrality of the Two-Worlds View

The Expansion Thesis

The idea that Descartes extended the boundary of the mental to include all states of consciousness or subjective experiences is typically so formulated that it embodies the Two-Worlds View. The underlying picture is that there are

4 The relation of 'thinking' to particular 'modes of thinking' is discussed at AT V: 221 (CSMK III: 357). This passage, in comparing this relation to the relation of extension to particular shapes, *may* suggest that the various modes of thinking are determinates which fall under the determinable 'thinking'.

5 The plural 'thoughts' ('*pensées*') occurs in AT II: 36 (CSMK III: 97), but here the topic is the differentiation of different species of 'operations of the soul' (e.g., meditating and willing, seeing, hearing, and deciding on one movement rather than another), each of which is called 'a thought' ('*une pensée*'). The phrase 'a thought' occurs in a different context where it clearly is equivalent with the expression 'a soul' (AT III: 694; CSMK III: 228).

indubitably such *things* or *particulars* as toothaches, hunger-pangs, itches, feelings of fear and joy, visual sense-impressions, mental images, etc. Hence, given a commitment to dualism, you are inevitably faced with the task of how to allocate these various entities to the two realms: the mental and the physical. The Legendary Descartes followed our natural intuitions [*sic*] by assigning them all to the category of *mental* particulars. They are conceived to be entities (though perhaps not full-blown substances) which can be the logical subjects of singular judgements.[6] On this view, in telling a doctor 'The pain in my knee is throbbing', I make a (logically) subject-predicate judgement ascribing a 'phenomenological property' to a mental particular. The Expansion Thesis is thus glossed as Descartes' having enlarged the range of *things* to be included under the generic count-noun 'a thought'.[7] It is never formulated as the claim that Descartes extended the range of *properties* predicated of the rational soul ('modes of thinking'). In that form, it would lose much of its charm.

Cartesian Introspection

This Legendary faculty is taken to be modelled on *sense-perception*. 'A natural counterpart to the theory that minds constitute a world other than "the physical world" is the theory that there exist ways of discovering the contents of this other world which are counterparts to our ways of discovering the contents of the physical world' (Ryle 1949: 154; cf. Dalmiya 1992: 219). Just as objects in the physical world (including one's own body) are perceived through the five senses, objects in the inner world are perceived through the 'inner sense'. The very idea of an infallible quasi-perceptual and logically private access to one's own states of mind draws on the Two-Worlds View.[8] Post-Cartesians held that

> . . . only the owner of an inner world can *apprehend its occupants* by means of introspection. 'Internal sense' or 'inner sense' is the source of our knowledge of the *subjective objects* in our private inner world, and it gives us an *immediate, non-inferential acquaintance* with them . . .
>
> (Hacker 1990: 46–7, some italics added)

The 'objects of introspection' are conceived as the counterparts of the 'objects of (external) sense-perception'; they are mental *entities* that are 'perceived' to have certain ('mentalistic') properties just as planets and billiard balls are perceived to have certain physical properties like shape, size, and colour. The deliverances of

6 'Feelings, or states of consciousness, are assuredly to be accounted among realities [objects, or nameable things], but they cannot be reckoned either among [Aristotelian] substances or attributes' (Mill, *Logic* I.iii.1).

7 Mill used the expression 'a feeling' (or 'a state of consciousness') for the same purpose (*Logic* I.iii.3).

8 The link between the two must be what explains the widespread idea that Wittgenstein's private language argument contains decisive criticisms of the concept of introspection. (He did not there mention the topic.)

introspection are viewed by the Legend as singular judgements whose logical subjects are particular 'thoughts' or states of consciousness: they all have the form '*cogitatur*' (or 'this particular thought is occurring'). In this respect they parallel singular perceptual judgements. If Cartesian Introspection were depicted as '*self*-consciousness', i.e. as issuing uniformly in singular judgements whose logical subject is the *Thinker*, this attractive parallelism would be lost.

Cartesian Interactionism

According to the Legend, the mind and body of an individual person are 'glued' together by various kinds of causal interaction: in sense-perception, changes in the body bring about changes in perceptual experiences, while in voluntary action, mental entities (volitions) bring about bodily movements. There is a tendency to conceive of efficient causation as a relation between *things* or *particulars* ('objects', on Hume's account, or 'events' as Davidson (1980) prefers). This tendency creates a powerful gravitational field: making causation plausible involves discovering or inventing appropriate things. Consequently, the possibility (or intelligibility) of any causal interaction between mind and body seems to require just the mental particulars that the Two-Worlds View providentially supplies:[9] the idea that states of consciousness are *things* (mental entities or particulars) makes them at least *prima facie* eligible as candidates for being causes or effects. (The only remaining question is whether the relevant causal hypotheses are true.) In this way, the Two-Worlds View has a pivotal role in making logical room for Cartesian Interaction.

A cynic might suggest that the Two-Worlds View is a doctrine whose sole recommendation is that it *apparently* makes sense of something which is *really* unintelligible. Descartes himself noted and criticized a parallel movement of thought in the case of 'real attributes' or 'substantial forms'. In his view, the scholastic doctrine that 'heaviness' or 'gravity' can cause the movement of matter (independently of the impact of other moving matter) rests on mistaking modes of material things for things or substances in their own right. (It exhibits one form of the basic confusion of modes and substances.) If this mistake is corrected, then the very idea that some thing called 'heaviness' or 'gravity' can be an efficient cause will seem evidently absurd. (As it were, no*thing* can't move something.) How would the Legend exclude the hypothesis that Descartes would have launched the very same attack on the doctrine that thoughts are *things* or *particulars*?[10]

9 Ryle notes this point in respect of the 'Myth of Volitions': an advocate of 'the paramechanical theory of the mind' will 'speak glibly of "experiences", a plural noun commonly used to denote the postulated non-physical episodes which constitute the shadow-drama on the ghostly boards of the mental stage' (1949: 64).

10 This is a conspicuous component in Arnauld's attack on Malebranche's doctrine of ideas. He rejected the contention that ideas are 'real spiritual beings', holding that they must be considered not as '"beings" properly speaking' (i.e. substances), but as *modes* of (thinking) substances (Arnauld, *Ideas*: ch. 27).

It is equally noteworthy that Cartesian Interactionism depends for much of its persuasiveness on the prior acceptance of the Expansion Thesis. What the Legend casts in the role of the mental effects of bodily conditions are not perceptual *judgements* but rather perceptual *experiences* (sense-impressions or sense-data) that provide the 'basis' for making judgements. The idea that acts of judgement could themselves be caused by physical states of the sense-organs doesn't seem plausible in itself, and it hardly squares with Descartes' stress on our complete freedom to make (and to suspend) judgement about any thought.[11] In the same way, what the Legend envisages as the mental causes of voluntary movements are not prudential or moral *judgements* (e.g., 'It would promote my welfare to eat'), but rather certain mental acts ('acts of the will', 'ghostly pushes and pulls') that somehow initiate bodily movement. In so far as judgements provide *reasons* for action, they might naturally be regarded as implausible candidates for being *causes* of movements.

Standard 'refutations' and the Two-Worlds View

Cartesian Dualism is commonly held to be fraught with difficulties. In some cases, the difficulty is thought to lie close to the surface, while in others it has taken the genius of other great philosophers to bring it to light. Most of the standard 'refutations', we argue, depend directly on the Two-Worlds View. If this case can be made out, then the claim that it depicts Descartes' 'unofficial metaphysics' must demand very secure textual support.

For present purposes, we can distinguish two kinds of objection to Cartesian Dualism. The first concerns knowledge of others' thoughts and of other minds. The second focuses on each person's knowledge of his own mind and his states of consciousness.

The first line of criticism stresses the 'subjectivity' of the so-called 'Cartesian foundations of knowledge'. The argument starts from the premise that the *Cogito* is grounded in indubitable reports of the occurrence or existence of various states of consciousness. Various conclusions are drawn about the impossibility of objective human knowledge: I can't be certain that there are any thoughts other than my own, and even if I could ascertain that there are other thoughts, I can't be certain that there are any minds other than my own to whom these thoughts 'belong'. More generally, knowledge of my own thoughts can't provide any basis for demonstrating even the *possibility* of shared, intersubjective knowledge; there is no conceivable way to ground public knowledge in essentially first-person thoughts. Thus many critics have accused Descartes of being committed to scepticism about other minds as well as embarking on an epistemological project that is self-evidently hopeless.

All of these criticisms originate in the Two-Worlds View, for their germ is the

11 This freedom explicitly embraces all of the 'operations of the soul', including the 'functions of seeing and hearing' (AT II: 36; CSMK III: 97).

notion of the impossibility of ascertaining the numerical identity of my thoughts with the thoughts of others. The notion of a particular is bound up with the possibility of distinguishing qualitative from numerical identity. So, for instance, we distinguish Smith's car from Jones' car, even though both are the same make, model, colour, and year of manufacture: they are numerically distinct though qualitatively identical. This general point applies in principle to mental particulars. Hence, as a corollary of the Two-Worlds View, the question is opened up whether one person can ever have the very same (numerically the same) thought on two occasions, or whether two persons can ever have numerically the same thought. Indeed, it is commonly claimed that Descartes gave a definitively negative answer to this question: for him, 'Another's thought is another thought'. (This aspect of 'Cartesian Privacy' is often called 'privacy of ownership'.)[12] This idea *couldn't* be developed independently of saddling him with the Two-Worlds View. Questions about numerical identity make sense only in respect of *particulars*.

The other line of criticism questions the very possibility of self-knowledge given a 'Cartesian framework'. The most long-standing of these objections is the impossibility of solving the problem of the 'unity of consciousness'. On the one hand, it is taken to be incontrovertible that introspection gives no acquaintance with the Thinker, but only with individual thoughts. (Hume is commonly claimed to have established this fact.) Hence the most primitive subjective judgements are reports of ownerless states of consciousness or passing thoughts. On the other hand, Descartes provided no materials for answering the question: 'How do two thoughts need to be related to each other in order to be the thoughts of a single Thinker?' As a consequence, he is accused of having no cogent reason to affirm 'I am a thinking substance (*res cogitans*)'. For all he said, experiences might have no 'owners' at all, or what he called 'my' thoughts might have belonged to a myriad of distinct thinking things.

A second objection of this genre is that the very possibility of certain knowledge about my own states of mind presupposes the possibility of certainty about *others*' states of mind. (Kant is usually claimed to have established this important principle by a 'transcendental deduction'.) Since Descartes is accused of leaving room for scepticism about other minds, he is thereby convicted of a second offence, i.e. not satisfying the conditions for achieving genuine *self*-knowledge.

A third objection is that his conception of grounding all knowledge in immediate experience presupposes the intelligibility of a (logically) 'private language'. On this view, my understanding of the terms that I use to designate the entities of my own 'inner world' *must* be based on a kind of private ostensive definition, i.e. on my baptizing things (feelings, sensations, images) with which I am directly acquainted; this conception depicts these words as not being subject

12 So-called 'Cartesian Privacy' is sometimes held to have two distinct components, one being 'privacy of ownership', the other being 'epistemic privacy' of the sort discussed under the heading 'Cartesian Introspection': Anthony Kenny, *Wittgenstein*, London: Penguin, 1973, p. 185; Hacker 1990: 46–64; Malcolm argues against the distinction (1977: 104ff.).

to public (behavioural) criteria of correctness. Yet this account demonstrably does not satisfy the objective conditions for a word to have a meaning. (Wittgenstein is credited with this discovery in his 'private language argument'.) As a consequence, all of the 'reports of immediate experience' which are envisaged in Cartesian Dualism as constituting the foundations of knowledge turn out to have no significance at all when considered within that framework. No set of descriptions of an essentially private inner world of feelings, emotions, sensations, etc. which is logically independent of outward behaviour could be intelligible, hence it couldn't provide the foundations of knowledge.

The possibility of raising all of the questions which are judged to leave Cartesian Dualism in the lurch depends on ascribing to him the Two-Worlds View. The whole framework of discussion is one admitting the possibility of singular judgements whose *logical subjects* are mental particulars other than minds. Moreover, most of the questions to which Descartes was unable to provide answers are ones the answers to which would have to take the form of genuine relational judgements, at least one term of which must be a mental particular other than a mind. In particular, the question of the criteria for assigning states of consciousness to minds must be answered by specifying a condition to be satisfied by a particular state of consciousness for it to stand in the relation of 'belonging to' to a particular soul; and the question of the 'unity of consciousness' must be answered by specifying a relation between two particular thoughts that suffices for them both to belong to the same mind. If Descartes' logico-metaphysical system excluded (as it were, 'geometrically') the possibility of raising all of these questions (see Chapter 4, pp. 60–9), it can't be a fault of his dualism that he failed to provide answers to them – you might as well fault a bridge player for taking a trick with the ace of trumps on the grounds that the ace is the lowest card of the suit in cribbage. On *these* grounds, God Himself couldn't indict Descartes at the Last Judgement for failure to make fully responsible use of his faculty of reason.

We have sketched a defence of Descartes' Dualism by calling attention to an unsupported presupposition in the prosecution's refutation, namely the presumption that he subscribed to the metaphysics of the Two-Worlds View. But this defence leaves open a more indirect attack on his position. If the Two-Worlds View is indeed required for making sense of Cartesian Dualism, then clear direct evidence for his advancing other strands of Cartesian Dualism would count as strong indirect evidence for his holding the Two-Worlds View. This gives us indirect as well as direct interests in evaluating the textual evidence for the other components of Cartesian Dualism.

CONSCIOUSNESS AND CLOCKWORK

Consciousness and the Expansion Thesis

We turn first to consider what textual support there is for the Expansion Thesis, i.e. for the claim that Descartes radically widened the term '*cogitatio*' to encompass emotions, sensations, imagination, sense-perception, bodily appetites, and the like. Two texts, in which Descartes explained his usage of the term 'thought', are repeatedly cited and treated as constituting the nucleus of an indisputable positive case:[13]

> (1) By the term 'thought', I understand everything which we are aware of as happening within us, in so far as we have awareness of it. Hence, *thinking* is to be identified here not merely with understanding, willing, imagining, but also with sensory awareness [*sentire*]. For if I say 'I am seeing, or I am walking, therefore I exist,' and take this as applying to vision or walking as bodily activities [*& hoc intelligam de visione, aut ambulatione, quae corpore peragitur*], then the conclusion is not absolutely certain. This is because, as often happens during sleep, it is possible for me to think I am seeing or walking, though my eyes are closed and I am not moving about; such thoughts might even be possible if I had no body at all. But if I take 'seeing' or 'walking' to apply to the actual sense or awareness of seeing or walking [*Sed si intelligam de ipso sensu sive conscientia videndi aut ambulandi*], then the conclusion is quite certain, since it relates to the mind, which alone has the sensation or thought that it is seeing or walking [. . . *ad mentem, quae sola sentit sive cogitat se videre aut ambulare*].
>
> (*Principles* I.9 (AT VIIIA: 7–8, CSM I: 195))

> (2) But what then am I? A thing that thinks. What is that? A thing that doubts, understands, affirms, denies, is willing, is unwilling, and also imagines [*imaginari*] and has sensory perceptions [*sentire*].
>
> (*Meditation* II (AT VII: 28; CSM II: 19))

On this basis alone, many commentators urge us to stamp the Expansion Thesis with 'QED'. Although tempting, this would be irresponsible.

First, a very general point. According to Descartes, 'all the modes of thinking . . . can be brought under two general headings: perception, or the operation of the intellect, and volition, or the operation of the will' (*Principles* I.32, CSM I: 204). Descartes conceived of *judgement* (and also suspension of judgement) as the operation *of* the will *on* a 'perception' of the intellect. 'Making a judgement requires not only the intellect but also the will' (*Principles* I.34, CSM I: 204). 'All that the intellect does is to enable me to perceive the ideas which are subjects for possible judgements' (AT VII: 56; CSM II: 39). It is only with the affirmation or denial of such a 'perception' (i.e. only with judgement) that truth or falsity comes in (cf. AT VII: 37, CSM II: 25–6; AT VII: 56, CSM II: 39). But it only makes *sense* to speak of affirming, denying, or suspending judgement on 'cognitive' or 'propositional' items. The essential connection of these items with the possibility of articulate expression seems to be in part what motivates the choice

13 Other passages sometimes cited as evidence for the Expansion Thesis are mentioned *en passant* below.

of the phrase 'perception *of the intellect*'. Consequently, in so far as pain or joy are thought of as non-cognitive or non-propositional, it makes no more sense to talk of them as 'perceptions of the intellect' than it does to speak of affirming pains or suspending judgement on feelings of joy. Where in this classificatory scheme, then, are these non-cognitive items meant to fit? (Would there be any plausibility in holding that Descartes meant us to classify pain and joy as 'operations of the will'?)

But second, it is explicit in passage (1) that Descartes was *disambiguating* the expression '*sentire*' (usually translated as 'sense-perception', 'sensation', or 'feeling'). He asserted that 'seeing' (or 'I am seeing') can be taken in two ways: as referring either to a 'bodily activity' or to 'the actual sense of seeing'. The argumentative strategy of passage (1) is that expressions such as 'I am seeing', taken in one sense, do not render the conclusion '*sum*' certain, whereas taken in another sense, they do. He engaged in a parallel disambiguation in the paragraph immediately following (2):

> (3) I am now seeing light, hearing a noise, feeling heat. But I am asleep, so all this is false. Yet I certainly *seem* to see, to hear, and to be warmed. This cannot be false; what is called 'having a sensory perception' [*sentire*] is strictly [*proprie*] just this, and in this restricted sense of the term [*& hoc praecise sic sumptum*] it is simply thinking.
>
> (AT VII: 29; CSM II: 19)

Here he distinguished between two senses of the expression 'having a sensory perception' ('*sentire*'), in one of which (a 'restricted sense') *sentire* counted as thinking, in the other of which (by implication) it did not.[14] Moreover, he was perfectly explicit about seeing the term '*imaginari*' too as ambiguous in a parallel way: 'The sense in which I include imaginations in the definition of *cogitatio* or thought is different from the sense in which I exclude them' (AT III: 361; CSMK III: 180).

This point ought to be uncontroversial. The Legend, however, does not see

14 Cottingham rightly raises the question of why *sentire* and *imaginari* are given a special status in this list of 'modes of thinking' in passage (2), though he may be wrong to pose it in the form of why they are 'tacked on to the rest of the list almost as an afterthought' (1986: 123). The obvious answer (but not Cottingham's) is that the reader is meant to understand that in only *one* sense do these *ambiguous* expressions signify modes of *thinking*.

Indeed another recurrent form of words ought to be seen in the same light, namely 'in so far as it depends on the soul' vs. 'in so far as it depends on the body'; passages containing variants on the first of these locutions are sometimes cited as supplementary evidence for the Expansion Thesis, but with no attention directed to the highlighted phrases. Thus he spoke of 'the modes of thinking which I refer to as cases of sensory perception and imagination, *in so far as they are simply modes of thinking*' (AT VII: 34–5; CSM II: 24); again, he asserted that he used the word 'thought' to cover 'the activities of seeing and hearing and deciding on one movement rather than another, *so far as they depend on the soul*' (AT II: 36; CSMK III: 97). It seems amply evident that these highlighted phrases subserve the function of indicating one sense of an ambiguous expression; the other sense is indicated by variants on the second form of words, as when he asserted that he did not 'deny sensation [to animals], *in so far as it depends on a bodily organ*' (AT V: 278; CSMK III: 366). (All italics added.)

Descartes as here being engaged in simple or straightforward disambiguation, but rather in discovering – or legislating – the true sense of 'sense-perception'. Its exponents interpret the phrase 'seeming to see' in (3) – or 'the sense of seeing' in (1) – as referring to visual impressions or 'sense-data', i.e. 'what is common to the genuine and the doubtful case' of having perceptual experiences (Kenny 1968: 73). In (3), so we are told, Descartes was asserting that 'sensation [*sentire*] *strictly so called*' 'consists' in such 'impressions' or 'sense-data' (Kenny 1968: 71, italics added).[15]

What we want to highlight is the subtle shift from the phrase 'in the restricted sense' to the phrase 'strictly so called'. Talk of a 'restricted' sense of 'having a sensory perception' is a natural follow-on to drawing attention to an ambiguity; talk of a 'strict' sense is much more a natural follow-on to a bit of conceptual legislation. It is very much in the latter light that advocates of the Cartesian Legend see (3). The view is that he 'sheared off' (Williams 1978: 79) or 'extracted' a sense-datum from what we ordinarily call 'sense-perception' and dubbed that '"*sentire*" in the *strict* (proper, genuine) sense'. To use the term 'sense-perception' to apply to an activity of the sense-organs in response to light (hence, e.g., to say that animals 'see light') is on this view improper, loose usage: in Descartes' view, according to the Legend, animals only 'see' in a poor, etiolated sense: they do not have 'genuine sensations' (Kenny 1989: 8) or 'real passions' (Malcolm 1977: 42).[16]

Now, it might well be thought that this is a superficial problem. The exponents of the Legend could simply modify their position to one according to which '*sentire*' was ambiguous between designating purely bodily states and designating states of consciousness.[17] But it is not as easy as that. First, '*sentire*' covers 'feeling pain' and 'feeling hunger' as well as 'seeing light' and 'hearing noise'. Most

15 A supplementary indirect argument for the idea that Descartes subscribed to 'visual impressions' is grounded in his description of 'some of his thoughts' as 'as it were the images of things' and his subsequent questions about whether any of these 'ideas' 'resembled' things existing outside him (AT VII: 37–8; CSM II: 25–6). It is sometimes suggested that only if such ideas were 'sense-data' or 'visual impressions' could they intelligibly be said to 'resemble' things. It is perspicuous, however, that the entire line of reasoning underlying this interpretation of the expression 'resemblance' presupposes the Two-Worlds View. Otherwise it would be impossible to raise the question whether the same property is predicated of the *idea* of, say, a tomato as is predicated of a tomato in judging 'This tomato is red'. We argue for a less naive interpretation of the notion of resemblance on pp. 130–2.

16 Malcolm (as well as Grene (1985: 37–8)) here quotes a letter in which Descartes allegedly asserted that animals do not have 'real feeling' or 'real passion' (*vray sentiment*, *vray passion*) (AT II: 41; CSMK III: 100). In fact, the claim is hypothetical: someone brought up exclusively among automata *would*, upon encountering an animal for the first time, have no reason to ascribe 'real sensations or real passions' to the animal. And what is at issue is whether the observable similarity between our actions and the actions of animals gives us good reason to conclude (as we habitually do, since we rely too much on our senses) that they 'act by an interior principle like the one within ourselves, that is to say, *by means of a soul* which has feelings and passions *like ours*' (AT II: 39; CSMK III: 99, italics added).

17 Some of the more simple-minded criticisms of Cartesian Dualism could then no longer be raised, e.g., that he actually contradicted himself in asserting (1) that animals did not think, (2) that sense-perception and sensation were modes of thinking, and (3) that animals could see and feel pain; such criticisms would be seen to rest on equivocation.

proponents of the Legend are extremely reluctant to say that there is *any genuine* sense in which 'feeling pain' or 'feeling hunger' refers to something non-mental, since for them that would mean something *non-conscious*. (But they are also reluctant to recognize that for Descartes 'feeling pain' and 'feeling hunger' are instances of *sentire* in the first place: they do not suggest that passage (3) entails 'shearing off a *painful* sense-datum'.) Second, to accept that Descartes was actually asserting that the expression '*sentire*' is ambiguous is completely to undermine the simple *textual* case for the Expansion Thesis. Advocates of the Legend *could not* then, without further ado, simply point to passages where Descartes classified sensations, sense-perception, etc. as thoughts (*cogitationes*) in order to demonstrate that the Expansion Thesis is correct. On the contrary, one must consider how, if at all, so-called 'perceptual experiences' fit into the framework of Descartes' analysis of 'sense-perception' ('*sentire*') lest one commit the fallacy of equivocation. Moreover, the case for saying that in passages (1) and (3) Descartes was picking out *a* sense of the expression 'having a sensory perception', in which it designates a 'sensation' or 'sense-datum' or 'conscious experience', would be no more solid than a *conjectural* interpretation of judgements of the form 'It seems to me that I see light'. Shoring up this conjecture would require a demonstration that there is either no alternative or at least no more plausible alternative interpretation of judgements of this form; but, as we will show later, the first disjunct is certainly false, and the second is open to dispute.

Indeed we will go further. We will argue that the Legendary interpretation is one which Descartes *could not* have held, given his logico-metaphysical framework.[18] And we will argue that his 'disambiguations' play an absolutely central role in his global strategy for getting his readers to break their bad intellectual habits of youth. They expose forms of the fallacy of equivocation that are in Descartes' view both widespread and pernicious (as much for virtuous conduct as for rational scientific enquiry). These disambiguations aren't simply tacked on as an afterthought, nor can acknowledgement of them be so. They are an essential, though generally unremarked, component of Descartes' Dualism (see pp. 70–87).

We have argued that the Legend misrepresents the role or purpose of both the passages most commonly cited to demonstrate Descartes' adherence to the Expansion Thesis. In addition, however, it makes nonsense of the content of passage (1), and this casts serious doubt on the acceptability of its interpreting passage (3) as introducing the notion of sense-impressions, perceptual experiences, or sense-data.

Passage (1) is intended to clarify the question of exactly what 'I-thoughts' are admissible premises in the argument schema of the *Cogito*. In particular, would either 'I see' [*Video*] or 'I am walking' [*Ambulo*] fit the bill? Both of these judgements are reports of paradigms of what the Aristotelian tradition called 'operations of the sensitive soul'. The first reports an exercise of the power of

18 Here we go further than Curley, who (rightly!) sees in Descartes 'no commitment to sense data, or any other contentious entities' (1979: 53).

perception (*aisthesis*), the second an exercise of the power of locomotion (*kinēsis kata topon*).[19] Passage (1) manifestly treats these two representative I-thoughts *symmetrically*. How is this to be made intelligible? If Descartes' purpose in distinguishing two senses of the term 'see' is to 'shear off' a visual sense-datum and to argue that having this experience is what is strictly or properly called 'seeing', did he have the parallel intention of isolating a sense-datum of *walking* and arguing that this immediate experience is what is strictly or properly called 'walking'? This seems implausible: his account of perception (even by the 'internal senses') leaves no room for any 'kinaesthetic sensations' of bodily movement, and even if it did, the idea that in its proper or primary sense the verb 'walk' signifies having such a sensation seems an unmotivated blunder. Does the Legend seriously want to take passage (1) to argue that '*walking* (in the strict sense)', just like 'seeing (properly so called)', is a form of *thinking*?[20] (Should we conclude that unthinking animals only 'walk' in a loose, etiolated sense? Do they only go through the motions of walking?) The Legend's interpretation threatens to yield a *reductio ad absurdum* when rigorously applied to (1).[21] Thus it undermines the credibility of its own principal witness for the Expansion Thesis. Any adequate interpretation of Descartes' Dualism must make good sense of the symmetry between seeing and walking in passage (1). We think that the Legend's evident failure in this task is symptomatic of very deep and far-reaching misunderstandings.

Clockwork and the Contraction Thesis

We stressed in Chapter 2 that the Legend gives little attention to the topic of the Cartesian body. Its commitment to 'the Contraction Thesis' – the claim that the essence of the body was 'clockwork' (pleonastically unconscious) – was inferred from its advocacy of the Expansion Thesis. Hence absence of direct textual evidence for the Expansion Thesis seems to put both in jeopardy. Conversely, both might be resuscitated provided that there *is* direct evidence for the Contraction Thesis.

There is no doubt whatsoever that Descartes held that the human body could be regarded as a *machine*, although this thesis (the *Corps-Machine* Doctrine) is far less widely disseminated than the parallel thesis that non-human animals could

19 Aristotle, *De Anima*, 432^{a}15–18.

20 Proponents of the Legend are unlikely to accept this view. In fact we will argue (pp. 75–7) that Descartes held that the ambiguous expression 'is walking' refers in one sense to a mode of thinking. But since we see the expression as ambiguous (hence as having *two* strict and proper senses, not as having only one which does not apply to animals) we are not drawn into the conclusion that animals don't really walk!

21 To mitigate this difficulty, one translation (Anscombe and Geach 1954: 183) inserts unauthorized parentheses around each occurrence of the phrase 'or walking'! As F. R. Leavis once said, 'It would be foolish to make a fuss whenever the academic mind behaves characteristically, but there is a classical quality about this instance' (*The Common Pursuit*, Harmondsworth: Penguin, 1962, p. 60).

be seen as machines (the *Bête-Machine* Doctrine).[22] The *Treatise on Man* describes the body of a hypothetical man, a body not united with a soul:[23]

> I suppose the body to be nothing but a statue or machine made of earth, which God forms with the explicit intention of making it as much as possible like us. Thus God not only gives it externally the colours and shapes of all the parts of our bodies, but also places inside it all the parts required to make it walk, eat, breathe, and indeed to imitate all those of our functions which can be imagined to proceed from matter and to depend solely on the disposition of our organs.
>
> (AT XI: 120; CSM I: 99)

This may strike a modern reader as wholly anodyne. It seems to ascribe to the body powers of metabolism and movement, and it suggests that these have mechanical explanations. What is so revolutionary about *this* conception of the body?

Matters begin to look different once we take note of the symmetry in Descartes' treatment of the body and his account of non-human animals (or brutes). Whatever conclusions hold of one must also apply to the other. It may well seem *obviously* pleonastic to add 'unconscious' to 'machine' (cf. Kenny 1989: 1). This implies not only that the human body is unconscious, but also that brutes are. This seems at best counter-intuitive and unmotivated, at worst perverse and morally offensive. The *Bête-Machine* Doctrine *is* clearly an established element of Descartes' philosophy, and it *seems* to put the Contraction Thesis beyond doubt.

This case needs more critical examination. To begin with, proponents of the Legend load the dice in their favour by describing the opposition between mind and body as one between consciousness and *clockwork*. It *may* well be pleonastic to talk about 'unconscious clockwork'.[24] Moreover, Descartes did sometimes draw analogies between the human body and clockwork.[25] But he did not equate

22 The explanation of this asymmetry is perhaps that many twentieth-century Anglo-American philosophers suppose that it doesn't make sense to say that a human body sees a tree, feels hungry or angry, desires exercise, etc.; these properties must be attributed to a person, not to a person's body. By contrast, the *Bête-Machine* Doctrine is seen as outrageous. Consequently, the second doctrine has a notoriety not shared with the first. This asymmetry constantly crops up: e.g., although Cottingham (1986: 129) sees Descartes as having 'dumped' *animals* 'into the non-conscious inanimate world of mere extension', he does not similarly spring to the defence of the human body.

23 It is perhaps worth noting that, for Descartes, a human body without a soul is not a corpse; 'what differentiates a corpse from a living human being' was *not* 'the fact that the living human being is animated by a mind' (*pace* Hacker 1990: 244), but is compared by Descartes to the difference between 'a watch or other automaton . . . when it is wound up . . . [and] the same watch or other machine when it is broken' (*Passions* I.6; CSM I: 329–30).

24 Those who believe that a machine might think tend to focus attention on electronic computers, not on mechanical calculators. The difference may not be purely rhetorical.

25 In the *Description of the Human Body*, for instance, his aim was 'to give such a full account of the entire bodily machine that we will have no more reason to think that it is our soul which produces in it the movements which we know by experience are not controlled by our will than we have reason to think that there is a soul in a clock which makes it tell the time' (AT XI: 226; CSM I: 315).

'machine' with 'clockwork'. 'Clockwork' seems to be limited to mechanisms that are within the power of human beings to fabricate (although, as we stress on pp. 92–3, seventeenth-century clocks were none the less objects of admiration), whereas 'machine' definitely did not carry this connotation in his usage. We might see certain texts as emphasizing just this important *contrast* between the human body-machine and clockwork:

> We see clocks, artificial fountains, mills, and other such machines which, although only man-made, have the power to move of their own accord in many different ways. But I am supposing this machine *to be made by the hands of God*, and so I think you may reasonably think it capable of a greater variety of movements than I could possibly imagine in it, and of exhibiting more artistry than I could possibly ascribe to it.
>
> (AT XI: 120; CSM I: 99, italics added: cf. AT VI: 56; CSM I: 139)

What Descartes took to be the conceptual limitations on the abilities of these 'machines' needs to be established by careful investigation of his texts, not by off-hand remarks about 'clockwork'. If the Legend is to base its proof of the Contraction Thesis on Descartes' adherence to the *Corps-Machine* Doctrine, then it needs to *show* that there is a contradiction in talking about a 'conscious machine' given *Descartes'* conception of a machine and *our* (twentieth-century) conception of 'conscious'. Without a careful exploration of both of these conceptions, the textual case for the Contraction Thesis is definitely inconclusive.[26]

Any cogent advocacy of this Thesis must consider Descartes' *list* of those of 'our functions which can be imagined to proceed from matter and to depend solely on the disposition of our organs':

> the digestion of food, the beating of the heart and arteries, the nourishment and growth of the limbs, respiration, waking and sleeping, the reception by the external sense organs of light, sounds, smells, tastes, heat and other such qualities, the imprinting of the ideas of these qualities in the organ of the 'common' sense and the imagination, the retention or stamping of these ideas in the memory, the internal movements of the appetites and passions, and finally the external movements of all the limbs.
>
> (AT XI: 202; CSM I: 108)

It may be unclear exactly what to make of the various items on this list; *prima facie*, they are the features of animal and human behaviour that Aristotelian psychology ascribed to the vegetative and sensitive souls. Some of them are apparently forms of sentience, and for this reason advocates of the Legend cannot afford to ignore them. We have argued already that Descartes held the expression

26 Loeb (1981: 113): 'Here we are confronted with a philosopher of obvious intelligence, appealing to an exceedingly weak argument in support of a grossly implausible conclusion'. He infers the necessity of distinguishing 'between the articulated grounds for the conclusion, and the motive which led the philosopher to accept it'. We infer the necessity of questioning whether either his doctrine or his grounds has been understood aright.

sentire and its particularizations ('seeing light', 'feeling hunger', etc.), as well as predicates of action or locomotion like 'is walking', to be ambiguous: each of them refers in one sense to something purely bodily ('vision or walking as bodily activities'), in another sense to something purely mental (whatever 'the sensation or *conscientia* of seeing or walking' may be). On the face of it at least, what is here being ascribed to the bodily machine in this passage are just these predicates in their 'bodily' sense ('the reception by the external sense organs of light', 'the internal movements of the appetites and passions', 'the external movements of all the limbs', etc.). Since the bodily machine is supposed not to have been attached to a soul, it cannot think and hence cannot be ascribed these predicates in their 'mental' sense. But does it follow that the body-machine is not *conscious*? (i.e. does it follow that 'seeing light' or 'feeling hunger' in the bodily sense of these expressions designate non-conscious activities?) Only if it has *already* been shown that 'thought' is to be equated with 'consciousness'. This passage counts as evidence for the Contraction Thesis only if the Expansion Thesis has already been demonstrated. Otherwise it is to be read as affirming that animal *sentience* is a function of the body, not an operation of the soul.[27]

The same point holds for Descartes' conception of brutes. On his view, they too can be viewed as machines without minds or rational souls and their behaviour is fully explicable on mechanical principles. If machines or automata could be constructed which 'had the organs and outward shape of a monkey or of some other animal that lacks reason, we should have no means of knowing that they did not possess entirely the same nature as these animals' (*Discourse V* (AT VI: 56; CSM I: 139)). The list of 'functions' of the body applies equally to *animals* (AT VI: 46, CSM I: 134; AT VI: 55–6, CSM I: 139); there is a sense (the 'purely bodily' sense) in which brutes see light, feel hunger, etc. (AT V: 278, CSMK III: 366; AT IV: 574–5, CSMK III: 303, etc.). But these same predicates in their 'purely mental' sense do not apply to them. It is commonly inferred that Descartes held that brutes are non-conscious (e.g., that 'the "passions" of animals are to be regarded as purely physical disturbances in the nervous system, which . . . are not associated with experiences' (Williams 1978: 283)). Commentators spin stories to explain why Descartes fell into this egregious and scandalous error, for instance, that he confused 'consciousness' with 'self-consciousness' and thus wrongly thought that consciousness, like self-consciousness, required language (Kenny 1989: 9). But the original inference from 'non-thinking' to 'non-conscious' manifestly presupposes the truth of the Expansion Thesis.

27 The '*Corps-Machine*' Doctrine has been subject to criticism by phenomenologists and feminists; Descartes is standardly seen as the *malin génie* behind this view. We think that given *his* conception of a machine, *his* '*Corps-Machine*' doctrine is far less objectionable than that which is ascribed to him, without criticism, by the Legend. If his analogy between animals and the human body were taken seriously, the whole Legendary line of argument could be stood on its head: since animals and human bodies have analogous functions and since animals are manifestly sentient, so too is the human body. We pursue this suggestion on pp. 91–100.

CARTESIAN INTROSPECTION AND CARTESIAN OBSERVATION

The mind: Cartesian Introspection

The notion of Cartesian Introspection, although it 'neither originates with Descartes nor is it adopted only by those who embrace the doctrines propounded by him', was none the less articulated by Descartes 'with mesmerizing brilliance' (Hacker 1986: 278–9; cf. Kenny 1989: 2). It is a major component in the myth of the ghost in the machine which is claimed to 'hail chiefly from Descartes' (Ryle 1949: 11). It is surely fair to ask *where* he articulated this picture so brilliantly. Advocates of the Legend rarely offer much direct textual evidence.[28]

An immediate obstacle to answering this question is a terminological uncertainty. There are at least *two* terms which look like serious candidates for expressions signifying the notion of 'introspection', namely '*conscientia*' (usually translated as 'consciousness' or 'awareness', sometimes as 'inner awareness')[29] and '*sensus internus*' (literally, 'the internal sense'). Are these terms synonymous in his usage? If not, how are they individually to be explained, and what is the relation between these concepts? *Prima facie*, either 'internal sense' or 'inner awareness' might be construed as Descartes' expression for the Legendary faculty of 'inner sense' or 'introspection'.

In fact, the 'internal sense' (or rather, the two internal senses) can be ruled out straight away as a plausible candidate for this role. Descartes' view is that there are not five senses, but seven (*Principles* IV.190; CSM I: 280–1). Five of these are external (touch, taste, smell, hearing, and sight) and two are internal (the means for apprehending 'natural appetites' and 'emotions' respectively). The two internal senses are depicted as straightforward sense-modalities: they have bodily sense-organs, they are as fallible as the external senses (AT VII: 76–7; CSM II: 53), and they are possessed by animals as well as human beings.[30] They are apparently seen as the means whereby we perceive certain properties of our own *bodies*. (This idea collides with the Legendary notion that pain, hunger, and emotions are all essentially mental states.) Descartes' internal senses bear no resemblance whatsoever to the organ-less, infallible, quasi-perceptual means for perceiving the contents of our own minds which Cartesian Introspection is held to be. Consequently, in default of a demonstration that he used the phrase 'internal sense' equivocally, we can safely put aside as irrelevant to our present enquiry those few passages that discuss the internal senses.

There is, nevertheless, a further positive point in mentioning the internal senses

28 In one extreme case, the *only* such evidence offered for ascribing this view to him consists in quotations from Locke and Hume (Armstrong 1984: 122, 123)!

29 In CSM's version, 'inner awareness' translates *intime conscii*, for example, in *Principles* I.66 (CSM I: 216); but sometimes it is not *conscientia* at all, but *cognitio*, which appears in the English guise of 'awareness' (e.g., AT VII: 422; CSM II: 285).

30 Animal sense-perception of pain is discussed in some detail in the *Treatise on Man* (AT XI: 141–2; CSM I: 101–2).

here. We think the inclination to pin so-called Cartesian Introspection on to Descartes arises, in large part, from a failure to distinguish the objects of the internal senses from the objects of *conscientia*. (We return to this suggestion on pp. 50 and 136.)

Having eliminated the internal senses as suspects in the Case of Cartesian Introspection, we can examine the textual evidence for identifying *conscientia* as this notorious malefactor.

Analogies with sense-perception

Cartesian Introspection is commonly supposed to be a *quasi*-perceptual faculty. It is far from obvious whether there is a conception of sense-perception shared by Descartes and the Legend to serve as a basis for this analogy (see pp. 120–3). In addition, it is problematic how exactly the proponents of the Legend are to explicate the analogy. After all, by their own admission, introspection *lacks* most of the properties that they agree with Descartes in deeming to be essential to genuine sense-perception! For example, 'introspection [unlike sense-perception] involves the functioning of no bodily organ' (Ryle 1949: 163), and (by contrast with introspection) 'things looked at, or listened to, are public objects' and 'sense perception is never exempt from the possibility of dullness or even of illusion' (Ryle 1949: 163–4).

In fact, both the attraction of the analogy and the explanation of its content lie in the Legendary parallelism between the Two Worlds. Introspection is held to play the same role in cognition of 'inner objects' as sense-perception does in cognition of 'outer objects'.

Of course the precise content of this analogy depends crucially on how one analyses sense-perception. One popular way of spelling out the parallelism suggests that sense-perception is a matter of acquaintance with physical states, events, and objects; and in like manner, introspection may be seen as a matter of 'acquaintance' with mental states, events, and objects. It is a form of direct, immediate, or non-inferential awareness of states of consciousness, or a species of what Russell calls 'knowledge by acquaintance'.

> We are not only aware of things, but we are often aware of being aware of them. When I see the sun, I am often aware of my seeing the sun; thus 'my seeing the sun' is an object with which I have acquaintance.
>
> (Russell 1912: 49–50)

On this model, the logical form of judgements manifesting *conscientia* is a relation between the Thinker (or a mind) and a mental particular. In Russell's view, this cognitive relation *must* be immune to the possibility of error.

It needs to be asked whether this model of *sense-perception* is one that Descartes could have exploited. It presupposes that he took the normal form of a sensory (or sense-based) judgement to be the assertion of a relation between the percipient and what he perceives. So, for instance, I might say 'I see the sun', and this statement is held to be logically of relational form. We will argue that this is an analysis that he *could not* have offered of this form of judgement (see p. 62ff.). Moreover, of course, when this analogy is carried over to introspection (conceiving this as acquaintance with 'inner objects'), it clearly presupposes the Two-Worlds View.

But then this is clearly not the only possibility for describing the normal form of sense-based judgements. Another makes use of indirect statements: 'I see *that* the sun is shining', 'I feel *that* the fire is getting hotter', 'I hear *that* the sheep are demanding some hay'. Treating these as primitive reports of sense-experiences yields a notion of sense-perception that is essentially propositional. On this view, sense-perception, in Russell's jargon, is not mere 'knowledge by acquaintance', but 'knowledge of truths'.[31]

One possible way of exploiting this more sophisticated analysis of sense-perception for an analogy with introspection would surely be this: that just as sense-perception gives us knowledge of truths about external objects, introspection gives us knowledge of truths about *the mind*; the parallel would be between 'I see that *the sun* is shining' and 'I introspect that *I* think that . . .'

This, however, is *not* the use which is made of it. Rather, it is routinely combined with the Two-Worlds View, together with a vague analogy between the Eye and the Mind. The upshot is that, just as the eye isn't part of the visual field,[32] the mind can't be an object of introspection, i.e. the Thinker *cannot* be the logical subject of judgements manifesting *conscientia*; only the existence of particular states of consciousness can be the subject-matter of indubitable reports of introspection. (In a certain sense, the term '*self*-knowledge' is a misnomer, since it cannot be knowledge *of* oneself.) But is there *any* textual justification for preferring the Legendary version (e.g., 'that a particular thought is occurring') as the canonical specification of the content of *conscientia*, as opposed to 'that *I* have a particular thought' (i.e. 'that *I* think that . . .', 'that *I* have a particular mental property')?

The upshot of this investigation is surely the verdict 'Not proven' in so far as the Legendary conception of introspection rests primarily on an analogy with sense-perception.

The properties of Cartesian Introspection

Cartesian Introspection is credited with a number of marvellous properties: all of its objects are infallibly known and 'self-intimating' (hence the contents of the mind are 'epistemologically transparent' to introspection); and it is supposed to give us 'privileged access' to the contents of our own minds (so that states of mind are characterized by 'Cartesian Privacy'). What is the textual evidence for ascribing these properties to *conscientia*?

31 Kenny, for example, seems to embroider on this 'propositional' analysis of sense-perception in treating *conscientia* not as awareness of a thought, but as awareness of the *occurrence* of a particular thought, i.e. awareness *that* a particular thought is occurring (1968: 72–3).

32 Wittgenstein, *TLP* 5.663: 'really you do *not* see the eye'.

'Epistemological Transparency'

Self-intimation Let's review the first sentence of passage (1). This is sometimes taken to demonstrate that the contents of the Cartesian mind 'intimate themselves' to *conscientia*:[33]

> (1′) By the term 'thought' [*cogitatio*], I understand everything which we are aware [*nobis consciis*] of as happening within us, in so far as we have awareness [*conscientia*] of it.[34]

This passage is sometimes glossed as implying that Descartes 'makes it true by definition that if I think, I know that I think' (Kenny 1968: 49; cf. Ryle 1949: 158).[35] Somewhat less soberly, Descartes allegedly held that 'mental processes are phosphorescent, like tropical sea-water' (Ryle 1949: 159).

But the sheer difficulty of interpreting (1′) should throw doubt on taking it as unequivocal evidence for the 'self-intimation' doctrine. What does 'happening within us' ('*in nobis fiunt*') mean? Does it mean 'within our bodies', 'within our minds', or is it non-committal about this question? What are the consequences of answering this question in one or other of these ways? We might, for example, treat 'things that happen within us' as the equivalent of Aristotle's phrase 'what we do' (*ho prattomen*) which includes everything from dying, sleeping, growing grey-haired with age, and breathing to walking, standing one's ground in battle, speaking in the assembly, and making a judgement. Some of these 'things we do' may be purely bodily movements or changes; others may be purely mental acts or events. Yet others may need to be further analysed or refined. 'In so far as we have *conscientia* of them' might be a suitable criterion for carrying out this analysis; hence an appropriate introduction to the subsequent disambiguation of the terms 'walk' and 'see'.

Again, why is '*cogitatio*' tied *twice over* to *conscientia*? Is the phrase '*nobis consciis*' ('we being *conscius*') redundant? If not, what exactly is its function?

33 Wilson (1978: 98, 152) also cites 'there can be nothing within me of which I am not in some way aware' (AT VII: 107; CSM II: 77), and a passage which explicitly refers back to this: 'nothing can be in me, that is to say, in my mind, of which I am not aware' (AT III: 273; CSMK III: 165).

34 *Cogitationis nomine, intelligo illa omnia, quae nobis consciis in nobis fiunt, quatenus eorum in nobis conscientia est* (AT VIIIA: 7). A non-committal translation of the whole sentence would be: 'By the word "thought" I understand all things which take place within us, we being *conscius* [*nobis consciis*], in so far as there is *conscientia* of them in us'. The Latin is ambiguous as to whether the second occurrence of '*in nobis*' ('in us') refers to the awareness or the things of which we are aware. Since 'the things' at issue have already been stated to be 'within us', CSM's translation of this last clause as 'in so far as *we have* awareness of [them]' seems justified.

See p. 105 for further clarification of the phrase '*nobis consciis*'. It is noteworthy that the French text eliminates any counterpart of the phrase '*nobis consciis*': '*Par le mot de penser, j'entends tout ce qui se fait en nous de telle sorte que nous l'appercevons immediatement par nous-mesmes*' (AT IXB: 28).

35 He adds, 'It is here that the indubitability of the premise of "*cogito ergo sum*" is to be found' (cf. also Kenny 1968: 70–1). But this is surely a mistake: 'if I think, I know that I think' is an expression of what we on p. 19 called 'self-intimation', not 'incorrigibility' (a point also made by Curley (1979: 87)). Curley also (pp. 185f.) argues against the claim that the *Cogito* requires a premise which is either 'self-intimating' ('conscious' in his terms) or incorrigible.

What of the qualification '*in so far as* [*quatenus*] we have *conscientia* of them'? Are there different degrees of *conscientia* of some things that occur within us? Or are there complex things occurring within us of some of whose *parts* we are fully *conscius*, though we are wholly ignorant of others of their parts? Or is it that we confuse together under the heading 'things that occur within us' distinct things – for example, two forms of 'walking' or of 'seeing' – and that we can use presence or absence of *conscientia* as the principle for differentiating between them?

Even if we could settle these perplexing questions, we might be no closer to justifying the claim that Cartesian thoughts 'intimate themselves' to *conscientia*. According to the usual version of this picture, minds (through introspection) have *actual* thoughts, as opposed to potential knowledge, about their own states. This is built into the perceptual model of introspection: though one might otherwise think of *conscientia* as something like the *potential* or *capacity* for me to say how things are with me, the Legend's analogy between introspection and sense-perception invokes an actual achievement (an experience of 'as-it-were seeing' or an impression of 'inner sense'). (This is what generates the standard objections, namely splitting my attention among several things, disturbance of observations by emotions, and infinite regress.)[36] The idiom of 'self-intimation' manifestly demands more than the *possibility* of knowledge about one's own 'thoughts'. But where in passage (1′) is it implied that *conscientia* of having a thought needs to be *actually* thinking *another* thought?

Might some other texts provide less equivocal testimony? Undoubtedly the most promising candidates are passages elaborating the principle (or 'axiom') that the soul must be *conscius* of having a thought at the time of having this thought. On one understanding of the phrase 'operations of the soul', this is equivalent to the scholastic principle that the soul must have *conscientia* of its own (present) operations. There is good textual evidence that Descartes did indeed adhere to this doctrine in both forms (see pp. 114–5.). But none of these passages provides any good reason for claiming that *conscientia* of having a thought, or being *conscius* of an operation of the soul, need consist in having a thought or making a judgement about a mode of thinking. What Descartes called 'reflection' (AT V: 149; CSMK III: 335) or 'reflective knowledge' (AT VII: 422; CSM II: 285) *may* consist of thinking such second-order thoughts, but it seems that '*conscientia*' designates the power or potentiality which is exercised *in* reflective thinking. He apparently distinguished 'reflective knowledge' from 'internal knowledge' (*cognitio interna*) to head off the argument that *conscientia* generates an infinite regress:

> no one can be certain that he is thinking or that he exists unless he knows what thought is and what existence is. But this does not require reflective knowledge . . . still less does it require knowledge of reflective knowledge, i.e. knowing that we know, and knowing that we know that we know, and so on *ad infinitum*. This kind of knowledge cannot possibly be obtained

36 Ryle 1949; also Hobbes (AT VII: 173; CSM II: 122–3).

about anything. It is quite sufficient that we should know it by that internal knowledge which always precedes reflective knowledge.

(AT VII: 422; CSM II: 285*)

Although all of these texts require further elucidation, no text that asserts that the soul must be *conscius* of its own present thinking requires, or even suggests, that *conscientia* must consist in making a true judgement rather than in having a cognitive *capacity.* (Moreover, Descartes' defence of the principle that the soul must be *conscius* of having a thought *at the very moment of having it* (e.g., AT VII: 246; CSM II: 171) suggests that *conscientia* is not by definition restricted to knowledge of present operations of the soul, unlike introspection (otherwise the words 'at the very moment of having it' would be superfluous). But then the idea that *all* of its objects *must* be self-intimating loses every shred of plausibility.)

Of course, even if *conscientia* is interpreted as a 'potentiality' rather than an 'actuality' concept – for example, 'Everything in a mind at a time is available to consciousness, introspectively available, at that time' (Armstrong 1984: 121–2) – it may still be thought open to objections from the 'discoveries' of psychoanalysis. How one responds to such objections depends on having answers to two quite different kinds of questions. First, what did *Descartes* build into the notion of 'potential' knowledge or 'capacity' for reflection? Is it, for instance, a capacity that improves with practice? Or can it be interfered with? (What is the textual evidence for Descartes' holding the crude doctrine which *would* be open to 'refutation' by the 'discoveries' of psychoanalysis?)[37] Second, what exactly is the status of psychoanalytic theory? Is it better to see the Unconscious as a discovery, like the planet Pluto, or as a motivated change in concepts, perhaps like complex numbers?[38] Unless it is unequivocally the former, it can hardly be said to *refute* even the crudest version of the 'self-intimation' doctrine (even if Descartes had demonstrably held it).

The minimal conclusion is that there is no *straightforward* textual case for the claim that the contents of the mind 'intimate themselves' to *conscientia*. 'Self-intimation' is a very simple (even crude) picture with very crude defects, whereas Descartes' conception of *conscientia* is clearly not a *crude* picture (cf. pp. 112–18).[39]

Infallibility The other aspect of 'the epistemological transparency of the mind' is the essential infallibility of Cartesian Introspection.[40] This faculty results in incorrigible reports or judgements about the states of one's own mind; and

37 Curley (1979: 177ff.) makes some relevant observations.

38 Wittgenstein suggests that the psychoanalytic doctrine of the Unconscious is a complex amalgam of hitherto unnoted psychological reactions and a new form of description (or 'notation'). As a consequence, both its exponents and its opponents are apt to misconceive the nature of the debate (*The Blue and Brown Books*, Blackwell: Oxford, 1964, pp. 57–8).

39 See also Wilson 1978: ch. IV.2.

40 Introspection is, by definition, 'an immediate and infallible spiritual awareness'. Reports of Cartesian thoughts are 'exempt from doubt by the person whose experiences they are' (Kenny 1989: 9, 51).

(according to the Legend), 'it is not just the occurrence of *thought* that cannot be doubted, but the occurrence of the particular thought in question' (Kenny 1968: 72–3).[41] This formulation clearly presupposes the Two-Worlds View. (No reason is given for admitting, let alone for preferring, the formulation 'having *conscientia* that such-and-such a thought has occurred' instead of the formulation 'having *conscientia* that *I* have such-and-such a thought'.) So we might put on the table an alternative formulation of the infallibility claim as well, namely if I think (judge) that *I* have a 'thought', then I must really have that 'thought'.[42] The doctrine of infallibility is also so understood that it presupposes the Expansion Thesis. The 'thoughts' of which the occurrences cannot be doubted are taken to include all manner of 'states of consciousness'. It is argued, for example, that an experience of toothache is an appropriate premise for the *Cogito* because anybody's sincere claim to have a toothache is indubitable. More generally, it is said, Descartes took reports of immediate subjective experiences to be the foundation of knowledge precisely because they are infallibly known through *conscientia*.

It is common to cite part of passage (3) as evidence for the doctrine of infallibility (e.g. Kenny 1968: 73; Wilson 1978: 151):

> (3′) I am now seeing light, hearing a noise, feeling heat. But I am asleep, so all this is false. Yet I certainly *seem* to see, to hear, and to be warmed. This cannot be false . . .

Does this show that Descartes took judgements about the contents of my own immediate experiences to be infallible? Did he argue that sincerity excludes the possibility of making mistaken judgements about one's own 'states of consciousness'? Does (3′) even prove the narrower principle that, if I think (judge) that I think that *p*, then I think that *p*?

Even when isolated from the Two-Worlds View and the Expansion Thesis, (3′) is anything but straightforward to interpret. What is it that 'cannot be false'? And what does 'cannot be false' *mean*? On one reading, the final sentence states that the *judgement* that I have the property 'seeming to see light' must be true. (What the content of this judgement is would still be open to debate. It might be, say, that I have the property 'having the thought that I see light'; or that I have the property of 'having just now judged that I see light'.)[43] On another reading, the

41 Cottingham (1986: 39ff.) distinguishes between a narrower and a wider reading of the *Cogito* on the basis of this distinction.

42 Descartes 'makes it clear that the certainty of the *cogito* applies to any mode of *cogitatio*; what can be indubitable is not merely the bare proposition "I am thinking" but also more determinate statements about my states of consciousness – that I am doubting this or that, that I am imagining certain things, that it seems to me (at least) that I am seeing certain physical objects, and so on. All such statements of "immediate experience" are recognized as being, if true, indubitably so' (Williams 1967: 347).

43 The very same grammatical construction (in indirect speech) is used to report the (mistaken) *judgement* that an amputee makes about a 'phantom pain': '*se* sibi videri *adhuc interdum* dolorem sentire *in ea parte corporis qua carebant*' (AT VII: 77, italics added).

utterance 'I seem to see light' amounts to a refusal to make a judgement; the final sentence then states that the (unasserted and undenied) thought or idea that I see light (the thought on which I am now suspending judgement) cannot, 'strictly speaking', be false (or true!) since truth and falsity only come in with judgement (AT VII: 37; CSM II: 25–6).[44] On the latter reading, of course, passage (3′) would be *irrelevant* to the issue of the infallibility of *conscientia*. The former reading leaves a host of problems about the content of the judgement that must be true (see pp. 115–18). In any case, there is no way of expounding this passage so that it provides cogent justification for the *general* claim that for any *p* whatsoever, if I judge that I think that *p*, then I think that *p*;[45] it is expressly limited to thoughts that count as instances of sense-perception (*sentire*).

The bridge from passage (3′) to the doctrine of the Epistemological Transparency of Mind is unsupported speculation. The Legend's reasoning makes no attempt at all to clarify what Descartes understood by 'operations of the soul' or 'modes of thinking', to explore the range of things of which he claimed that we have *conscientia*, or to connect *conscientia* with the concepts of conscience and moral agency (see pp. 108–11). Attention to these matters shows that the speculation is definitely indefensible.

Cartesian Privacy

According to the Legend, Cartesian Introspection conforms to the Principles of Asymmetry and of Superiority. It thus gives each person 'privileged access' to his own states of mind – a 'conception [that] could hardly help sowing the seeds of scepticism about other minds'.[46] This whole package of ideas is labelled 'Cartesian Privacy'. This is the aspect of Cartesian Dualism which Wittgenstein-inspired critics most love to hate; but *nothing* whatever is offered in the way of textual evidence for ascribing it to Descartes.[47] This notion is supposed to be the hallmark of Descartes' revolutionary conception of the mental (Kenny 1989: 9–10). But it hangs in an argumentative vacuum. This makes it rather difficult to criticize the Legend's *case* for highlighting Cartesian Privacy in the account of Cartesian Dualism! But we can clarify some peripheral features of this puzzling situation.

First, although it might be a 'grammatical' truth about *conscientia* that I can have *conscientia* only of my own thoughts, not of those of another (so there is a first-/third-person asymmetry built into the concept), does it follow that *conscientia* gives me 'asymmetrical *access*' to my own thoughts? The term

44 Kenny excludes such an interpretation on the grounds that Descartes held that one cannot have a thought *about* a thought (1968: 76) (see pp. 64–5); this rests on a misreading of AT VII: 175.

45 Nor, by the way, is this strong claim required for the *Cogito*. (Curley (1979: 185ff.) notes this point.)

46 Hacker 1990: 245. This is often supported by the passage about my seeing hats and cloaks, not men, when I look out of the window on a square (AT VII: 32; CSM II: 21).

47 Curley rightly points this out (1979: 193).

'access' carries certain implications. It suggests a contrast between a route and a destination. But did Descartes himself depict *conscientia* as a form of awareness that provides the source or basis of self-knowledge, or rather as a kind of articulate, propositional knowledge about one's own mode of thinking? In the latter case, the phrase 'asymmetrical access' would risk conflating the route with the destination. Moreover, 'access' suggests an external relation between the 'accessing' and what is 'accessed'. Just as the sun's shining is one thing, my seeing the sun another, so too my having a thought should be one thing, my being *conscius* of having it another. But it is far from obvious that Descartes saw the relation between my having a given thought and my *conscientia* of my having that thought as conforming to this model of an external relation. Indeed, the definition of '*cogitatio*' ('thought') in passage (1′) suggests just the opposite: something that happens within me is a thought only *in so far as* I have *conscientia* of it.[48]

Second, there is room to question whether *conscientia* gives us '*Superior* Access'. We noted before that the Legend prefers to think of *conscientia*, not as articulate knowledge, but as inarticulate immediate awareness on the model of a sense-impression.[49] Furthermore, the content of the awareness is not that *I* think that such-and-such (i.e. that *I* have a particular 'mode of thinking'), but rather that such-and-such a thought is occurring (i.e. that a mental particular is present to consciousness); hence the normal form of the associated knowledge-claim is taken to be not '*cogito*', but rather '*cogitatur*'. The term 'awareness' and the phrase 'a thought is occurring'[50] are both calculated to divorce the concept of *conscientia* from articulate judgements about having thoughts which are themselves essentially articulate or propositional. The schema '*cogitatur*' is taken to report, e.g., having the experience of a pain in the foot. Though unsupported by textual evidence, this whole conception is essential to making sense of treating privacy as the mark of the mental. Otherwise why should we attribute to Descartes the view that it is 'an inessential, contingent matter that consciousness has a connection with expression in speech and behaviour'? Or the linked idea that others 'can only infer to our conscious states by accepting our testimony or making

48 There are other parallel affirmations of an internal connection between thinking and *conscientia*: 'The fact that there can be nothing in the mind, in so far as it is a thinking thing, of which it is not aware [*conscius*], seems to me to be self-evident' (AT VII: 246; CSM II: 171: cf. AT V: 149; CSMK III: 335).

49 This conception is apparent from criticisms of introspection. For instance, Malcolm offers a *reductio* of Brentano's conception of 'inner perception' that turns on raising questions that make sense only about *experiences*: 'According to Brentano every "mental phenomenon" (joy, doubt, fear, sorrow, intention, etc.) is directed upon an object; and further, this mental direction upon an object is itself the object of an inner consciousness or inner perception. If a person is joyous . . . the person has an inner consciousness of his joy . . . . *When* . . . – and for *how long*?' (Malcolm and Armstrong 1984: 27).

50 The same point holds of other descriptions of the alleged objects of introspection: these are called 'states and operations of [one's] mind' or 'episodes in the stream of consciousness' (Ryle 1949: 12, 14), 'events which happen in our minds' (Russell 1912: 49–50), 'mental events, states, and processes' (Kenny 1989: 4–5) or 'all the operations of the mind' (Kenny 1966: 355).

causal inferences from our physical behaviour' (Kenny 1989: 2)?[51] Unless Descartes is thought to have held the picture of 'looking' within oneself, as into a kaleidoscope, in order to 'discern' the states and events to be found there and thereby to acquire an experiential basis for grounding reports of them, would there be any reason to attribute to him the idea that *conscientia* and its linguistic expression are externally related? But if *conscientia* were articulate knowledge of articulate thoughts, then the notion of 'Superior Access' would be wholly inappropriate. There is nothing essentially private about articulate thinking and reasoning.[52]

In fine, the Legend's ascribing to Descartes the doctrine of 'Cartesian Privacy' seems to rest on *less* than nothing. The case for it is entirely indirect, and it makes several presuppositions that are inconsistent with his leading ideas.

The body: Cartesian Observation

As we saw earlier (p. 17), Stout described a picture ('historically traceable to Descartes') according to which 'the body, like other material objects, is known only through external perception, whereas self-consciousness reveals only mind'. Although the Legend has little to say on this topic, there seemed to be every reason to suppose that it would agree with Stout's view that the Cartesian body is known only via the external senses (the thesis of Cartesian Observation).

The ascription of this doctrine rests squarely on *overlooking* Descartes' 'internal senses':[53] sense-modalities in addition to the 'external senses' or 'external perception', which were presented as means for perceiving certain states of one's own body.[54] Just as, with the external senses, we perceive how things are outside our bodies, with the internal senses we perceive how things are inside our bodies. Therefore, the general thesis of Cartesian Observation definitely misrepresents Descartes' own position.

This is not the worst of it. The 'things inside the body' perceived by the internal senses apparently included many things that might now be called 'states of consciousness': pain, hunger, and thirst (with the first internal sense), fear, anger, and joy (with the second). (This point has clear implications for the Expansion Thesis, and hence for the Contraction Thesis.) And since the internal senses are instances of *sentire*, the doctrine of the systematic ambiguity of *sentire*-predicates is applicable to these forms of *sentire*. Expressions such as 'feeling pain' and

51 We will argue (pp. 86–7) that running together 'speech' and 'physical behaviour' as Kenny does here would from Descartes' point of view manifest a serious confusion.

52 As Kenny rightly insists (1966: 360).

53 The irony here is that the quotation from Stout subserves his attempt to argue for the existence of internal senses in many ways analogous to those which Descartes believed us to possess.

54 But not for perceiving everything that either we or Descartes would call 'states of one's body'. In particular, not states of the sense-organs (the eyes, the ears, etc.), the functioning of the body-machine (the movement of the animal spirits, the transmission of nerve impulses, the motions of the pineal gland, the circulation of the blood, etc.), or animal movement (locomotion and goal-directed behaviour).

'feeling thirst' have both a purely bodily and a purely mental sense, and Descartes normally used the idiom 'the sensation of pain (or thirst)' to refer to the purely mental sense of these expressions. Consequently, what he called 'the sensation of pain' must be sharply distinguished from pain, a point which makes a large difference for the interpretation of many passages.

The very fact that the Legend so persistently neglects the internal senses is of interest in its own right. 'Internal sense' never occurs in indices of books analysing Descartes' thought. Even explicit references to the internal senses are regularly ignored, misread, or misreported.[55] Here is an exemplary case:

> Sometimes towers which had looked round from a distance appeared square from close up . . . In these and countless other such cases, I found that the judgements of the external senses were mistaken. And this applied not just to the external senses but to the internal senses as well. For what can be more internal than pain? And yet I had heard that those who had had a leg or an arm amputated sometimes still seemed to feel pain intermittently in the missing part of the body.
>
> (AT VII: 76–7; CSM II: 53)

This passage from *Meditation* VI clearly asserts that the case of amputees who seem to feel pain in a missing limb exemplifies an error in an (*internal-*)sense-based judgement which is exactly parallel to the error in the (external-)sense-based judgement made by someone who takes a square tower in the distance to be round. The amputees erroneously judge that they have pains in their missing limbs.[56] In this way, they are deceived by their first internal sense.[57] The same conclusion holds of somebody who, suffering from dropsy, makes the (mistaken) judgement, 'I am thirsty'. Descartes' explicit purpose here is to prove that the internal senses are no less fallible than the external senses.

Exponents of the Legend draw very different and mutually inconsistent

55 One of the few sustained discussions of the phantom limb case in Descartes is Lott (1986); he, however, misidentifies the *objects* of the relevant internal sense, and supposes that what is in question is proprioception. Hence he, rather like Williams (*infra*), reads the sentence which immediately follows this passage ('So even in my own case it was apparently not quite certain that a particular limb was hurting, even if I felt pain in it') as meaning that Descartes 'is not quite certain that he has, say, an arm or a leg in which to feel pain' (p. 243).

56 On the face of it, this could be understood in more than one way. One possibility might be that the erroneous judgement on the part of the amputee is *that the pain he perceives is in the missing limb*, i.e. that he 'mislocates' his pain (cf. Rée (1974: 96), one of the few who notices that Descartes held that judgements about pain can be mistaken). Another might be that the erroneous judgement is *that his limb hurts*. The first, in effect, treats pain as a corporeal substance, the second treats pain (or painfulness) as a mode or property of a physical object (viz. a limb; see pp. 128–34 for reasons for preferring the second reading).

57 Descartes also held that one can make erroneous judgements about what one *Imagines*, although Imagination is not an internal sense (*pace* Kenny 1989: 10): for example, one may be mistaken in supposing oneself to be imagining a chiliagon, for 'if I want to think of a chiliagon . . . I may construct in my mind a confused representation of some figure; but it is clear that this is not a chiliagon. For it differs in no way from the representation I should form if I were thinking of a myriagon, or any figure with very many sides' (AT VII: 72; CSM II: 50).

conclusions from this passage. Their reports of it virtually never *mention* the internal senses, hence provide no explanation of why this should be a case of erroneous *sense-based* judgement and no explanation of what Descartes took the parallel to be between feeling a phantom pain and mistaking the shape of a tower. Many accounts pay little heed to his notion that cases of 'deception by the senses' must always be cases of making false *judgements* – suggesting, for instance, that the 'phantom limb patients . . . suffer . . . misleading sensory data' (Cottingham 1993: 144). Some accounts leave the content of the erroneous judgement unspecified: 'even "internal" senses like that of pain may mislead ([e.g.] . . . the patient who on waking from an operation feels pain "in the arm" even though the limb has in fact been amputated') (Cottingham 1993: 80). And others elaborate some content which is both implausible and alien to Descartes' argument, claiming, for example, that the amputee 'falsely thinks *that his foot has not been amputated*, because he feels a pain "in" it' (Williams 1978: 249, italics added). All manner of means are adopted by various exponents of the Legend to make sense of a point that Descartes evidently took to be quite straightforward.

This treatment of this famous passage is puzzling enough to call for some explanation. By viewing pains, appetites, and emotions as *mental entities*, the Legend removes the logical space that is occupied in Descartes' system by the two internal senses. He took pain, hunger, and fear to be objects of *sense*-perception. Hence they must in some sense be modes of extension (sc. properties of the body) that have the power to modify local motions within the appropriate sense-organs (see pp. 129–34). Moreover, the internal senses are shared by humans and mindless animals. The Legend categorizes pain, hunger, and fear as *mental* entities: all of them are paradigms of 'thoughts' under the Expansion Thesis. Consequently, they are no more possible objects of sense-perception than are volitions or geometrical theorems. They are, as it were, too close to the mind to be *perceived* (even by an 'internal' *sense*). The conflict between these two lines of thought seems intolerable. The Legend seems to deal with it by repressing the doctrine of the internal senses, in particular by taking references to the internal senses as references to the *quasi*-perceptual faculty of *conscientia* (or 'inner awareness'). Because the Legend takes *conscientia* to be essentially infallible, this mistaken identification requires the further repression of the explicit thesis that the internal senses are fallible. A tempting conclusion to draw is that Cartesian Introspection is nothing more than the muddled artefact of this conflation.

CARTESIAN INTERACTION

According to the Legend, Descartes held that mind and body causally interact; this is said to be distinctive of his version of dualism, as over against other versions (occasionalism, pre-established harmony, etc.). Causation is taken to be the 'glue' that unites the Cartesian mind with the Cartesian body, or the 'ghost' with the 'machine'.

The causal interaction between mind and body is supposed to be two-way.

Descartes certainly held that the soul has the 'power' to move the body, especially in (human) voluntary action, and that the body has the 'power' to act on the soul, especially in sense-perception (AT III: 665; CSMK III: 218). In both cases, this 'power' is taken by the Legend to be a causal power, comparable to the power of moving matter to set other matter into motion by impact.

We will consider separately the textual evidence for each half of the two-way causal interaction embodied in Cartesian Dualism. Then we consider some more general doubts and difficulties.

Two-way causal interaction

Sense-perception

There are numerous passages cited as textual evidence for taking Descartes' conception of sense-perception to involve the doctrine that sensory 'thoughts' are the mental effects of corporeal causes. The favourite texts come from the *Treatise on Man* and the *Passions*.[58] This one is typical:

> (4) [If] the tiny fibres which make up the marrow of the nerves are pulled with such force that they are broken . . . the movement which they cause in the brain will give occasion for the soul . . . to have the sensation of *pain* [*le mouvement . . . donnera occasion à l'ame . . . d'avoir le sentiment de la* douleur] . . . . [A]ccording to the various other ways in which they are stimulated, the fibres will cause the soul to perceive all other qualities [*ils luy feront sentir toutes les autres qualitez*].
>
> (AT XI: 143–4; CSM I: 102–3*)

This textual evidence is demonstrably inconclusive for at least two reasons. First, no passage states explicitly that any movement in the body (whether in a sense-organ or in the brain) is the (efficient) cause of a thought or idea. Instead, some passages make use of familiar idioms which in many everyday contexts are used to express causal notions; especially frequent is the form 'to make something do something' ('*faire faire quelque chose à quelque chose*'). Does it follow from Descartes' employment of this idiom in passage (4) that he is committed to a particular causal analysis of mind–body interaction? No more than it would follow from his using the same idiom in describing a transaction with a craftsman (e.g., '*faire faire des andouillettes au boucher*') that he held ordering sausages from a butcher to be a case of efficient causation. Even Malebranche made use of everyday causal locutions, especially transitive verbs of action. Would it be reasonable to conclude that he thereby contradicted his ('official'?) occasionalism?

58 *Passions* I.31 (CSM I: 340) is cited in Cottingham (1986: 121) and Williams (1978: 289); Kenny (1968: 225) quotes from *Passions* I.35 (CSM I: 341–2). Cottingham (1986: 119) also cites AT III: 424 (CSMK III: 189–90): 'we know by experience that our minds are so closely joined to our bodies as to be almost always acted upon by them', and AT III: 664 (CSMK III: 217–18): the soul, 'being united to the body . . . can act and be acted upon along with it'.

Second, the burden of proof is on the Legend to vindicate the thesis that Descartes was an interactionist *as opposed to* an occasionalist. This conclusion does not follow from passage (4). The first idiom employed there is striking, and it seems straightforward evidence for an occasionalist interpretation: a movement in the brain is described as '*giving occasion to the soul* to have the sensation of pain'. The same phraseology then recurs in the discussion of 'titillation' (*chatouillement*) (AT XI: 144; CSM I: 103). Consequently, we might well take this conception to be built into Descartes' own understanding of the final sentence of (4). On this interpretation, the phrase '*ils luy feront sentir*' could actually be *paraphrased* as '*ils donnent occasion à l'ame de sentir*', and then passage (4) could be cited as confirming Descartes' Occasionalism and disconfirming the doctrine of Causal Interaction.

In fact, the idiom 'to give occasion to the soul to form the idea of . . .' is a prominent and recurrent feature in the *Treatise on Man* and in the *Optics*. It appears in dozens of passages that offer analyses of various forms of sense-perception. No doubt this helps to explain the consensus among late nineteenth-century Anglo-American philosophers that Cartesian Dualism embodied an occasionalist account of sense-perception (see pp. 139–40). It equally indicates deficiencies in the Legend's case for his advocating a *causal* theory of perception.

Of course, a more sophisticated version of the Cartesian Legend might perceive an ambivalence in Descartes' position and conclude that he never resolved the tension between the two positions.[59] This suggestion might help to reconcile apparently divergent judgements about his role in the history of modern philosophy. On the one hand, according to Russell (1921: 35) and Hume, occasionalism was a direct descendant of Descartes' own theories. On the other hand, according to the standard Legendary view, 'the scandal of Cartesian interactionism helped to encourage both Malebranche's "occasionalism" . . . and also the theory of the "pre-established harmony"' (Williams 1978: 287–8).[60] Perhaps Descartes' successors were more acutely aware of the problems with interactionism, and so they chose to develop the occasionalist rather than the interactionist strand of his writings, even though both were present there. But this more sophisticated line still presupposes, without argument, that there is a *tension* between using causal idioms and expressing occasionalism (see *infra*).

There are some hidden commitments of the interactionist account. The most obvious one is to the Two-Worlds View. It is difficult to make much sense of the idea of any sensation's being the effect of a condition of the body unless this sensation itself is considered to be some kind of mental 'object'. Descartes' 'Unofficial Metaphysics' once again has a pivotal role in the Legend's thinking.

Somewhat less obviously, the Expansion Thesis is presupposed in taking a

59 Cf. Gaukroger, Introduction to Arnauld, *Ideas*.

60 'The problem [of Cartesian Interaction] seemed so intractable that even theories that made God the intermediary between the mind and body of a person were seen by leading thinkers of the day as genuine improvements' (Dicker 1993: 222).

causal theory of perception to be even a *possible* interpretation of Descartes' position. Sense-impressions or perceptual experiences seem to be things of which it makes sense to say that they might be caused by states of the body. This is less clearly intelligible in the case of propositional thoughts. In the case of sense-based *judgements*, it would seem to be excluded by Descartes' explicit commitment to the moral position that every person is completely free in making judgements and hence fully responsible for all of his judgements. What is 'the sensation of *pain*' ('*le sentiment de la* douleur') mentioned in passage (4)? If it is (as we argue later (pp. 72–4)) not the experience of pain (something given), but rather the sense-based *judgement* 'I have a pain' (something active),[61] then the very idea that *this* could have a bodily movement as its efficient cause would be absurd.

Voluntary action

A causal analysis of voluntary action is a very prominent feature of Cartesian Dualism. It is a popular target of attack when depicted as a 'paramechanical hypothesis' according to which the machine' is driven by the 'ghostly pushes and pulls' of its attendant genie. One might reasonably expect the Legend to provide some direct textual evidence to support the attribution of this doctrine to Descartes.

Ryle lays out 'The Myth of Volitions' with great authority and without a single scrap of textual evidence.[62] It is 'just an inevitable extension of the myth of the ghost in the machine' (Ryle 1949: 63). On this view, 'the workings of the body are motions of matter in space' (Ryle 1949: 63), and the question, 'What makes a bodily movement voluntary?', is wrongly supposed to be a causal question (Ryle 1949: 67). The core of the Cartesian myth of volitions is the thesis that 'in some way which must forever remain a mystery, mental thrusts, which are not movements of matter in space, can cause muscles to contract' (Ryle 1949: 63–4).

Kenny gives the appearance of going further. He cites a passage from *Passions* I.19 (CSM I: 335–6): 'It is certain that we cannot will anything without thereby perceiving that we are willing it . . . . [But] this perception is really one and the same thing as the volition'. Having paraphrased this (with no analysis of Descartes' conception of a perception, sc. a 'perception of the intellect'!) as the thesis that 'the way to understand the will is to regard it as a perception of a certain kind', he immediately draws the conclusion that 'his [doctrine] is the same as one more clearly put by Hume, when he defined the will as "the internal impression we feel and are conscious of when we knowingly give rise to any new motion of the body or new perception of the mind"' (1975: 12). This seems closer to a flight of fancy than an argument.[63]

61 Compare the notion that sense-perception involves conceptual or intellectual activity. 'Minimally, it must be possible to decide whether or not to judge that things are as one's experience represents them to be. How one's experience represents things to be is not under one's control, but it is up to one whether one accepts the appearance or rejects it' (McDowell 1994: 11).

62 As Curley drily notes, 'A priori historians are not required to footnote their claims' (1979: 175).

63 The passage surely concerns the idea that we have *conscientia* of all our thoughts, including our volitions. See p. 113.

Could one do better? Descartes' reference to 'the soul's power to move the body' (AT III: 665; CSMK III: 218) might be held to entail this half of the interactionist doctrine. But any discussion of this power needs careful handling: in this very passage Descartes cautioned us against conceiving 'the way in which the soul moves the body by conceiving the way in which one body is moved by another' (AT III: 666; CSMK III: 218). We should be very sure that we understand what confusion he is trying to avert before ascribing to him the Legendary view of volition. Again, Descartes referred to 'deciding on one movement rather than another, so far as they depend on the soul' (AT II: 36; CSMK III: 97), as well as to patterns of human activity that are to be explained in terms of how 'our reason makes us act' (AT V: 57; CSM I: 140) and to a 'principle of motion' which 'consists in mind or thought' (AT VII: 231; CSM II: 162). But these remarks give no grounds whatever for ascribing to him the doctrine that voluntary action is to be analysed in terms of volitions that are efficient causes of bodily movements. Do we not need at least to consider the possibility that thoughts are *final* causes of movements?

This serious lacuna in the Legend might seem less scandalous if we bear in mind that Descartes' texts contain very little discussion of voluntary action apart from the special case of making judgements (where mind–body interaction seems to be out of the question). But then half of the Legend's account of causal interaction is, at best, purely speculative.

Attention ought also to be given to an important indirect argument which many earlier philosophers have taken to be conclusive support for the thesis that Descartes should be ascribed an *occasionalist* account of voluntary action. Russell, for example, held Cartesians to be committed to the view that the mind cannot in principle bring about the movement of matter (1946: 584). This has two main sources in Descartes' texts. First, it is an axiom (known by the Natural light) that matter can be moved only by the impact of other moving matter. Second, it is a fundamental principle of Cartesian physics, something known by pure reason, that the total quantity of motion is constant. Together these principles exclude the very possibility that a thought (or even a soul's having a thought) could make a difference to, or interfere with, the motion of a body. The realization of mind–body interaction in this form would require a source of motion other than impact as well as the generation of motion *ex nihilo*. As a consequence, the strength of the evidence *against* Descartes' having given such a 'paramechanical' analysis of voluntary action is apparently directly proportional to the strength of the documentation *for* his adherence to these two (metaphysical) principles; and the latter appears to be very strong indeed. The alternative is to accept that the fundamental principles of his physics are logically incompatible with one of the leading ideas of his dualism. But why should we prefer drawing the conclusion that his thinking was internally inconsistent to drawing the conclusion that he must have been an occasionalist?[64]

64 Philosophers of mind having a 'scientific' bent criticize dualistic interactionism on the ground that interaction between something physical and something non-physical is incompatible with well-established physical laws, say (for simplicity) the law of the conservation of momentum.

General difficulties

Apart from the deficiencies in the textual evidence for Descartes' having subscribed to the doctrine of causal interaction between mind and body, there are several more general problems about this component of the Legend.

First, the whole discussion of causal interaction tends to be conducted in a curious conceptual vacuum. The notion of 'cause–effect' is multi-facetted, and there is considerable variation among the conceptions held by different philosophers. Presumably it must be *Descartes*' own conception that is relevant to the question whether his analysis of sense-perception or his analysis of voluntary action contains elements of mind–body causal interaction. But little effort goes into clarifying his concept of (efficient) causation. This must be reckoned a serious strategic weakness in the Legend.

Remedying this defect might have dramatic consequences. Suppose for the moment that he took it to be an *essential* feature of causal interaction that the cause make the effect fully *intelligible*. (We shall argue for this view on pp. 145–52.) Now reconsider the common objection that his doctrine of causal interaction of mind and body is indefensible because of his total inability to explain *how* the mind can act on the body or *how* the body can act on the mind. Critics regularly ask, with heavy rhetorical emphasis and much irony, '*How* can the mind causally affect the body, and vice versa?' (Dicker 1993: 219; cf. Williams 1978: 288; Kenny 1968: 222–3; Cottingham 1986: 119, etc.). This rhetorical request for a 'how' looks like a demand for an intelligible connection between cause and effect, and the critics who pose the question think thereby to checkmate Descartes because they take it to be clear *a priori* that there can *be* no 'how', nothing comparable to a mechanism. Some add the accusation that Descartes tried to disguise this 'intractable problem' from himself by locating the site of mind–body interaction in the pineal gland, evidently in the forlorn belief that by making the site *small* enough, he could make the logical problem disappear! (Cf. Kenny 1968: 225; Cottingham 1986: 121–2.) Others see the 'animal spirits' as playing this role: 'Descartes tried to make things easier for the soul by having it influence motions of very fine and light "animal spirits" rather than have it directly move heavy lumps of matter.'[65] Many critics note Descartes' own acknowledgement that there were 'insuperable difficulties' with Cartesian Interaction. In reply to Burman's

They argue that momentum would be gained in the physical world every time the mind interfered with the body, and that momentum would be lost every time the body interfered with the mind. (There are less crude versions of the objection which take into account quantum physics.) Thus, 'for a dualist, the price of admitting mind–body interactions would be forfeiture of modern physics' (Haugeland 1985: 37). One conclusion might be that Descartes must have been an occasionalist; these philosophers evidently prefer to see Cartesian Dualism as 'fundamentally antiscientific' (Dennett 1993: 37), this despite Descartes' passionate advocacy of the programme of constructing a comprehensive and fully rational science of corporeal substances.

65 Jaegwon Kim, 'Causality, Identity, and Supervenience in the Mind–Body Problem', in Peter A. French, Theodore Uehling, and Howard K. Wettstein (eds), *Studies in Metaphysics*, Minnesota Studies in Philosophy, vol. IV, University of Minnesota Press: Minneapolis, 1979, p. 31. Cf. Keeling 1968: 165; Churchland 1984: 9, etc.

question 'how can the soul be affected by the body and vice versa when their natures are completely different?', he 'lamely admitted' (Cottingham 1986: 119): 'This is very difficult to explain, but here our experience is sufficient, since it is so clear on this point that it cannot be gainsaid' (AT V: 163, CSMK III: 346).

But far from reluctantly *conceding* this point, Descartes seemed prepared to assert as an explicit, positive part of his doctrine that there *could be* no intelligible connection between soul and body, and evidently held that anyone who supposed that there could be thereby showed that he misunderstood the nature of the soul and the body: 'in the case of body and soul, you cannot see any . . . connection, *provided that you conceive them as they should be conceived*, the one as that which fills space, the other as that which thinks' (AT III: 421; CSMK III: 188, italics added). This suggests that the very same argument that is taken by critics of Cartesian Dualism to prove the incoherence of causal interaction could be seen, from his own perspective, as a conclusive reason for denying that there is any such thing as (efficient) causal interaction between body and soul (in either direction). The Legend arguably commits the fallacy of *ignoratio elenchi*.

Second, failure to explore Descartes' own conception of causation underwrites the whole course of twentieth-century debate about whether he advocated causal interactionism or some form of occasionalism. Critics assume, without any argument whatever, that in *his* usage the idioms of 'causing' and 'occasioning' are *incompatible*. This is far from obvious. We already noted the fact that he made use of both idioms in the course of expounding a single uniform argument (as in passage (4) above). Various of his successors, both immediate (e.g., Arnauld) and more remote (e.g., Reid), saw no logical conflict between these ways of speaking, and they even made use of the concept of 'occasional causes' to develop one doctrine of the relation of mind and body. The very idea that there are two distinct strands in Descartes' conception of sense-perception or of voluntary action, or the claim that he vacillated between two accounts, is seriously question-begging.

What is required is a scholarly examination of his texts. Many issues need clarification. His usage of the term 'cause' needs to be placed against the background of the Aristotelian doctrine of the different forms of causation: efficient, final, formal, and material. Moreover, his conception of efficient causation among corporeal things must be related to his conception of the nature of mechanisms and mechanical interaction. Furthermore, there is good reason to believe that he took the word 'cause' to be *systematically ambiguous*, meaning different things in reference to causal interaction between corporeal substances and in reference to interaction between incorporeal and corporeal substances; it is surely for this reason that he warned against the danger of confusing 'the notion of the soul's power to act on the body with the power one body has to act on another' (AT III: 667; CSMK III: 219). Finally, we need a well-documented, comprehensive account of how causal idioms interlock with 'occasionalist' ones in Descartes' writings. (This might benefit from some comparison with earlier uses, if any, of such phrases as 'gives occasion to (something) to (do something)'.)[66]

The logical grammar of certain terms that he uses in connection with his discussions of mind–body interaction also requires clarification. He described a person as the union of body and soul '*so united by Nature* that the soul can move the body and feel the things which happen to it' (AT III: 694; CSMK III: 228*, italics added), and he added the explanation that 'our body is so constructed that certain movements in it *follow by Nature* upon certain thoughts' (AT V: 65; CSMK III: 237*). What does 'by Nature' mean? Moreover, this phraseology is linked to a denial of 'resemblance' between a movement and a thought to which it gives rise: 'certain motions of the heart [are] *connected by Nature* with certain thoughts, which they *in no way resemble*' (AT IV: 603–4; CSMK III: 307*, italics added). Given Descartes' alleged adherence to the scholastic principle that an effect must resemble its cause (AT V: 156; CSMK III: 339–40; cf. Cottingham 1986: 25–6), clarifying his conception of 'resemblance' seems crucial for arriving at *his* conception of *causal* interaction (see pp. 149–52).

Third, the doctrine of Cartesian Interactionism makes a mystery of Descartes' celebrated formulation of the doctrine of the substantial union: 'I am not merely present in my body as a sailor is present in a ship, but am very closely joined and, as it were, intermingled with it' (AT VII: 81; CSM II: 56). Commentators feel threatened by a dilemma. On the one hand, if mind and body are glued together by two-way causal interaction, what is the *contrast* drawn here between my relation to my body and the sailor's relation to his ship? Aren't both of them essentially forms of efficient causation? On the other hand, if my relation to my body is to be *contrasted* with the (presumably) causal interactions of the sailor to his ship (e.g., when he is informed that it has suffered damage and is leaking), what is the nature of the soul's power to move the body and to be affected by what happens to the body? Wouldn't this become completely mysterious (like Williams' 'psychokinesis' (1978: 288ff.))?

The Legend makes some attempts to deal with this antinomy. One is the suggestion that the description of the soul's being 'intermingled' with the body cannot be taken 'literally'. In one sense this is true enough: mind and body are not intermingled in just the way that salt and water are intermingled in a salt solution. Descartes himself clearly saw it as metaphorical – hence the prefix 'as it were' ('*quasi*') – and he explicitly rejected Gassendi's analogy with the intermingling of two bodies (AT VII: 390; CSM II: 266). But this doesn't mean that the doctrine is not to be taken seriously. The fact that I am intermingled with my body is something which is taught to me by '*Nature*', and 'everything that I am taught by Nature contains some truth' since it is bestowed on me by God (AT

66 Note that occasionalism was *not* originally tied to *dualism*: it was a quite general doctrine concerned with allegedly 'causal' relations. This point is acknowledged in Hume's accusation that Descartes 'insinuated that doctrine of the universal and sole efficacy of the Deity' (*Enquiry* VII.i, n. 1), the doctrine that blossomed into full-fledged occasionalism in Malebranche.

VII: 80–1; CSM II: 56). If Nature teaches me that I am not present in my body as a sailor is present in a ship when in fact I *am*, when I would surely have to conclude that God is a deceiver.

Another strategy is to suggest that the intended contrast with the sailor in his ship is to be drawn in some dimension other than causal interaction. Though in both instances the two entities are connected by two-way relations of efficient causation, there is something more involved in the substantial union of mind and body. What could this be but the 'phenomenology of being embodied', the what-it-is-like-to-be-a-human-being? 'What Descartes is drawing attention to here is the peculiar phenomenology of sensation – its special subjective character as present to our consciousness' (Cottingham 1986: 126).[67] This interpretation looks anachronistic, and by Cottingham's own admission is hard to square with Descartes' 'Official Dualism'. The fact that the Legend is driven to adopt this desperate remedy mightr seem a powerful argument against ascribing to Descartes the Doctrine of Cartesian Interaction which generates the problem.

The Legend 'sees' the main elements of Cartesian Dualism in Descartes' texts in the same way that Dürer's successors 'saw' armour plating when they draw the rhinoceros 'from the life'. Achieving a more faithful representation is less a matter of discovering something hitherto unknown than one of learning to see what is right in front of your own eyes and of having the courage to draw what you see.

Our hope is to catalyse a similar transformation of the impression made by Descartes' thinking on modern readers. This is less a matter of adducing novel textual evidence than of probing more critically the exhibits already on display, of taking a wider look around at elements of his thinking already familiar to you, and of resisting the temptation to repress your doubts about the Legend as infantile. In this setting the Cartesian Legend's 'decisive evidence' loses much of its probative force.

67 'The entire content of Descartes's denial that he is a pilot in a ship is phenomenological' (Williams 1978: 280); yet it is evident that the phrase 'very closely joined and, as it were, intermingled' is *equivalent* to the manifestly 'metaphysical' phrase 'substantially united' (AT VII: 228; CSM II: 160), and how are we to understand that?

4

DESCARTES' DUALISM

Cartesian Dualism is, for Anglo-American thinkers in the late twentieth century, a highly compelling vision: it is seen as a tempting, if deeply flawed, conception of the relation of the mind and the body. As we saw in Chapter 3, the direct textual evidence that Descartes propounded it is not compelling. In this chapter we take the argument two stages further. We show that Descartes' own vision, although equally elegant and immensely exciting to his contemporaries, was entirely different. It was grounded in the most basic elements of the Aristotelian tradition of logic, metaphysics and psychology (even though it cut out many of the intricacies of medieval scholasticism). As a consequence, we argue, the leading ideas of Cartesian Dualism are entirely *at odds* with the very framework of Descartes' thinking. In many cases, he would have condemned much now taken for granted (including a great deal which is ascribed to him by the Cartesian Legend) as 'confused ideas': ideas manifesting the very misconceptions at which he directed his philosophical therapy!

The heart of Cartesian Dualism was a simple and compelling vision. The same is true of Descartes' Dualism, the (different) vision which we will elicit from his texts. We can summarize it in the following four maxims:

1 There are two and only two kinds of (finite) substances: corporeal things and thinking things (minds or rational souls).
2 The essence of the mind is thought, the essence of the body is extension.
3 Human bodies and their properties are objects of sense-perception. Minds and their properties cannot be objects of sense-perception.
4 Interaction between mind and body is 'rationally unintelligible'; in a human being, a mind and a body are 'substantially united'.

These four maxims are (or should be) uncontroversially part of Descartes' doctrine. (That is no doubt all to the good, in a minimalist summary of his dualism!) But each of them has implications and refinements that are alien to modern thinkers and hence seldom noted now. The task of this chapter is to put flesh on the skeleton: to elucidate Descartes' conception of the nature of the embodied soul and the ensouled body.

THE TWO-SUBSTANCES VIEW

Descartes characterized an individual person as a composite thing, a combination of a body (a corporeal substance) and a rational soul (an incorporeal substance). This is the indisputable core of his dualism. He added some glosses to this central idea: a person is 'a substantial union' of mind and body; this union is an *ens per se*, not an *ens per accidens*; in a person the soul and the body are 'intimately conjoined and, as it were, intermingled', etc. (We discuss these glosses on pp. 163–91).

Let's start with a thumb-nail sketch of Descartes' logico-metaphysical system. The only mental *substances* are individual rational souls (or minds). He imposed a strong 'metaphysical' requirement on what counts as a substance: any (finite) substance must be capable of existing independently of any other (finite) substance, requiring 'only the ordinary concurrence of God in order to exist' (*Principles* I.51; CSM I: 210).[1] The notion of substances plays a crucial role in his analysis of the logical forms of judgements: every singular judgement must predicate a *property* of *a substance*.[2] Hence, in his view, it must predicate of *a mind* a mode of thinking or of *a corporeal substance* a mode of extension. These two schemata exhaust the logical structures of singular judgements.

We make a case for a tight and thorough-going integration of metaphysics and logic as one of the keys to understanding his dualism. In our view, Descartes' metaphysics and his logic are intermingled and closely conjoined. In this respect, his thinking has close parallels with the metaphysical underpinnings of Frege's function/argument analysis of judgements or with the metaphysics underlying Wittgenstein's contrasting account of the nature of the propositions of logic in the *Tractatus*. In all these instances, the anatomy of forms of judgement is held to have foundations 'deep in the nature of things'. Bringing to light this aspect of Descartes' thinking will make clear that the Two-Worlds View is *inconsistent* with his dualism.

For this purpose, we must call to mind three of the well-entrenched doctrines of traditional Aristotelian logic:

1 Every judgement must be subject-predicate in form.[3]

1 The qualification 'finite' is to be understood for the remainder of this section.

2 'A substance, as understood in the Aristotelian-scholastic tradition in which Descartes grew up, is, in the first place, simply a subject of predication, a bearer of attributes' (Cottingham 1986: 84). This remark is broadly correct, and it needs to be respected scrupulously in expounding Descartes.
Mill treated this position as one familiar from traditional logic; hence he felt the need to contradict it explicitly. He claimed that the Aristotelian dichotomy of substance and attribute cannot account for the fact that we can frame judgements in which something is affirmed or denied of 'feeling', 'sensations', or 'states of mind'. Though not substances, these are 'assuredly to be accounted among realities'; indeed, they are 'the simplest class of nameable things' (Mill, *Logic* I.iii.1–2).

3 This doctrine applies to particular and universal judgements, as well as singular judgements. (Both Frege and Russell, who were educated in the 'Old Logic', were familiar with this doctrine and took it to be a fundamental error in the syllogistic conception of logical form.) As a consequence, the *concepts* of subject and predicate differ between syllogistic logic and the predicate calculus: for example, the first system affirms, the second denies, that the judgement expressed by 'All men are mortal' is subject-predicate in logical form.

2 Singular judgements are distinct from particular and from universal judgements.[4] (These three kinds of judgements differ from each other in 'quantity'.)
3 Every judgement must have a unique logical analysis into subject and predicate. Consequently, a single judgement can't have different logical analyses revealing it to have different logical subjects.[5] ('Different subject, *ergo* different judgement'.)

All of these doctrines were staple parts of standard instruction in logic in Descartes' day. None of them was subjected to sustained criticism in expositions of syllogistic logic. On the contrary, students were taught manoeuvres to defend them against apparent counter-examples.[6] They learned to supply logical subjects where these appeared to be lacking, especially in so-called 'impersonalia' such as 'It is raining', which might be paraphrased as 'Water droplets are falling'[7] (cf. *PRL* II.i). They also learned to deal with judgements apparently having more than one logical subject (by treating judgements framed with transitive verbs as conjunctions of two subject-predicate judgements[8] or as two distinct judgements each involving 'substantial attributes').[9] Descartes was evidently instructed in this tradition. He explicitly alluded to the doctrine of substantial attributes in making repeated use of a hackneyed example: 'clothing, regarded in itself, is a substance, even though when referred to the man who wears it, it is a quality' (AT VII: 441; CSM II: 297).[10] There is no reason for supposing that he didn't sincerely accept

4 This is not contradicted by the observation that singular judgements behave like universal judgements in respect of syllogistic inferences. On the contrary, noting this symmetry presupposes that the forms are distinct (cf. *PRL* II.iii).

5 There is nothing comparable to the different partial analyses of relational judgements in the predicate calculus; i.e. to seeing one and the same judgement 'aRb' now as predicating a property of a, now as predicating a (different) property of b. The closest analogue in syllogistic logic is 'substantial predication', but in this case a single (or atomic) sentence is held to express a conjunction of two distinct judgements.

6 The possibility of these manoeuvres is of crucial importance for defusing the worry that the logical strait-jacket of syllogistic logic is so constrictive that it would leave no room for many of the judgements commonly made in everyday life. It is only the *logical analysis* of the judgement 'Socrates taught Plato' which is constrained.

7 'Those who would support the claim that many judgements are one-termed by pointing to the so-called *impersonalia* (propositions such as "It is snowing", "It is raining", and the like), make the mistake of confusing linguistic relationships with logical ones. For despite their simple form, it is obvious that these short sentences invariably designate a state of affairs with several elements (e.g., "It is snowing" means "Flakes are falling")' (Schlick 1974: 44).

8 All propositions compounded out of active verbs and their objects are *complex*, and must really contain, in some sense, *two* propositions. For example, 'Brutus killed a tyrant' means that Brutus killed someone and he whom Brutus killed was a tyrant; this explains why it can be contradicted in two distinct ways (*PRL* II.vi).

9 For example, '*He* was wearing this jacket' and '*This jacket* was worn by him' express two distinct judgements each of which predicates a 'substantial mode' of a true substance. The adjectives 'clothed' and 'armed' are instances of such modes (*PRL* I.ii). More generally, 'when we consider two substances together, we may regard one as a mode of the other. Thus . . . to be dressed is, in relation to the [dressed] man, only a mode or phase of existence under which we regard him, although the parts of the dress may be themselves substances' (*PRL* I.vii).

10 Cf. 'some accidents, considered in themselves, may be substances, as clothing is an accident with respect to a human being' (AT III: 460; CSMK III: 200).

the basic syllogistic doctrine that every judgement must be of subject-predicate form.[11] In his day, it would have had a status comparable to the entrenchment in twentieth-century thought of the principle 'Existence is not a predicate', i.e. the first thing you would learn in Baby Logic.

To these three logical doctrines there correspond three logico-metaphysical principles:

4 The *only* components of singular judgements are things (or substances) and affections of things (modes or attributes of things).[12] He formulated this point in the idiom that nothing else has any 'existence outside our thought' (*Principles* I.48; CSM I: 208). (We clarify this much-misunderstood idiom on pp. 133–4.)
5 (As an immediate consequence of his metaphysical dualism) every singular judgement must *either* predicate a mode of thinking[13] of an incorporeal substance (a rational soul or mind) *or* predicate a mode of extension of a corporeal substance.[14] (A singular judgement can have no other logical form, however different its grammatical form may be.)
6 There are no (genuine) relations:[15] no singular judgement can have more than one substance among its (logical) components.[16] Every singular judgement has

11 It is alleged that 'Descartes sustained a life-long contempt' for the 'run-down traditional logic which was then current' (Williams 1978: 27). This is an over-simplification of his position. His contempt focused on using syllogistic reasoning as a method of discovery: see Stephen Gaukroger, *Cartesian Logic*, Oxford: Clarendon Press, 1989.

12 Descartes followed scholastic practice in distinguishing between attributes of a substance ('without which the substance is unintelligible' (*Principles* I.62 (CSM I: 214)) and modes of those attributes (the various 'forms' which the essential attribute of a substance can take), which can by extension be regarded as modes of the substances themselves (cf. *Principles* I.64, 65 (CSM I: 215–16)). Hence, in his usage, 'mode of extension' is interchangeable with 'mode of a corporeal substance'. We generally use the term 'mode' without distinguishing modes from attributes.

13 It is important to note that the expression 'mode of thinking' must be understood to embrace *all* real affections of rational souls. In particular, it must include intellectual powers as well as performances: for instance, what is predicated in the judgements 'I am able to multiply any pair of two-digit numbers in my head' and 'He is fluent in Mandarin'. And it must include moral attributes: for instance, the states of character predicated in the judgements 'He is generous' and 'She is indignant about that slight'. For Descartes, all modes of thinking belong to a single logico-metaphysical category. (This raises obvious issues about the scope and infallibility of 'Cartesian Introspection'.)

14 In this way, the syllogistic forms of judgement become infused with metaphysical content. 'I would like to say: the old logic [Russell's term for syllogistic logic] contains more convention and physics than has been realized. If a noun is the name of a *body*, a verb is to denote a movement, and an adjective to denote a property of a body, it is easy to see how much that logic presupposes' (Ludwig Wittgenstein, *Philosophical Grammar*, Oxford: Blackwell, 1974, p. 204).

15 Note Locke's qualms about relations. Though he described the relation of cause and effect as 'the most comprehensive relation, wherein all things that do, or can exist, are concerned', he also observed that no relation is 'contained in the real existence of things, but [is] something extraneous and superinduced', and that relations 'have no other *reality*, but what they have in the Minds of Men' (*Essay* II.xxv.8,11; II.xxx.4).

16 J. Morris (1980: 368) notes this commitment in Descartes, although he is inclined to think of it as a 'failing'. (It is a common criticism of syllogistic logic that it cannot formalize the logic of relations.)

exactly two components: one substance,[17] one mode. No more, and no less. (Therefore it must have a unique logical analysis into subject and predicate.)

These principles may sound bizarre to twentieth-century ears, but apart from one refinement (the rigorous imposition of the corporeal/incorporeal dichotomy), there is nothing that would sound unorthodox to someone educated in the Aristotelian tradition and nothing that didn't persist for another two hundred years as generally received wisdom. Descartes' texts give evidence that he attached great importance to each of these principles and that he employed them in elaborating some major arguments. We see no evidence that he jettisoned this 'scholastic baggage' or even for the weaker claim that he exploited these principles merely rhetorically, i.e. to present his ideas in the style favoured by the Academic Establishment of his day.[18]

Before trying to demonstrate textual evidence for Descartes' adherence to these principles and exploring some of the consequences of that adherence, we must forestall a tempting form of misunderstanding. The ideas we are ascribing to him are doctrines about the correct *logical analysis* of judgements. They cannot be properly paraphrased as doctrines about what an everyday speaker (or even a philosopher) might say that judgements are *about*; *a fortiori*, they do not impose any limitations on what judgements may be about (or be said to be about). In particular, Descartes didn't deny that it was possible to make judgements that twentieth-century logicians would call judgements about things that aren't substances: for example, you can perfectly well state '11 is a prime number', 'The pain in my foot is agonizing', or 'The doctrine of transubstantiation is difficult to understand'. Rather, he denied that any of these judgements has a logical form that matches its apparent grammatical form. He held that all of them must be radically reformulated (in different ways) to exhibit their true logical forms. Similarly, he didn't deny that it was possible to make judgements that twentieth-century logicians commonly say express relations: for instance, 'Brutus killed Caesar', '4 is greater than 2', or 'The earthquake caused the house to collapse'. Nor did he refrain from making judgements apparently of these kinds or from incorporating them in geometrical demonstrations or mechanical explanations. What he did deny is that any of these judgements really has the logical form of a binary relation, i.e. that it exemplifies the logical form exemplified in the predicate calculus by the formula 'aRb'. (According to syllogistic logic, there is no such form of judgement.)[19] Consequently, he followed the tradition of syllogistic logic

17 This is part of the very concept of a substance in the Aristotelian tradition, i.e. part of what is to be understood by characterizing substances as the subjects of predication or the bearers of attributes (cf. Cottingham 1986: 84). It is *not* part of the modern concept of the logical subject of a singular statement (e.g., Strawson's category of particulars). In this respect, there is an important change in the *concept* of a logical subject (see pp. 211–12).

18 This interpretation is a major theme in Gaukroger 1995.

19 This point is frequently misunderstood. An exemplary instance is found in Russell: he described the logical doctrine that every judgement *must* be subject-predicate in form as an 'untenable metaphysical hypothesis' (1956: 109). He took it to be a consequence of the 'Old Logic' that 'either there can be only one thing in the universe [*monism*], or, if there are many things, they cannot possibly interact in any way [*monadism*], since any interaction would be a relation, and

in proposing different (and non-uniform) ways of analysing what is said by each of these so-called 'relational judgements'. This doctrine is comparable to Davidson's celebrated analysis of adverbs: the true logical form of adverbial modification of verbs of action is claimed to be predicating properties of special entities (events).[20] Any genuine singular judgement whose grammatical form doesn't exhibit attaching an appropriate predicate-expression to the name of a substance must be capable of being reformulated in a sentence that perspicuously exhibits its true logical form. Although a judgement may *appear* to have another logical form, its *real* form must be predicating of a substance an appropriate mode. Whatever *cannot* be reformulated in this perspicuous form cannot be a *genuine* singular judgement at all.

It is a defining feature of Descartes' Dualism that the logical subject of any singular judgement whose content is mental or incorporeal *must* be a mind or rational soul. (This is the antithesis of the Two-Worlds View.) This principle is certainly unnoticed, but it isn't in the least speculative, and it has profound importance for grasping much of his thinking. It is made explicit in his reply to Hobbes' objection that Descartes committed a fallacy in reasoning 'I am thinking, therefore I am a mind, or intelligence, or intellect or reason'; it is not valid to argue 'I am thinking, therefore I am thought' ('*ego sum cogitans, ergo sum cogitatio*'). Hobbes accused Descartes of conflating a subject (*subjectum*) with its acts or faculties; it is one thing to be a being (*ens*), another to be a property or essence of a thing (AT VII: 172–3; CSM II: 122). Descartes began his rebuttal by stating that it is irrelevant for Hobbes to point out that 'one thought cannot be the *subject* of another thought' ('*unam cogitationem non posse esse* subjectum *alterius cogitationis*') (AT VII: 175; CSM II: 124, italics added). He then went on to argue that 'it is certain that a thought cannot exist without a thing that is thinking; and in general no act or accident can exist without a *substance* for it to belong to'. Since there are 'acts of thought', there must be a substance in which they inhere, and 'we call the *substance* in which they inhere a "thinking thing" or a "mind"' (AT VII: 176; CSM II: 124, italics added). The topic of debate is clearly the logical analysis of judgements which concern particular acts of thinking, and the terms 'subject' and 'substance' are used interchangeably.[21]

relations are impossible' (1912: 95). Finally, he argued in support of the metaphysical thesis that there *must be* relations (1912: 95–7), and he concluded from the existence of asymmetrical relations that not all judgements can be of subject-predicate form (*Principles of Mathematics*, London: George Allen & Unwin, 1903, pp. 226, 446–8). This reasoning turns on Russell's conviction that rigorous adherence to Aristotelian logic is straightforwardly incompatible with acknowledging the intelligibility of the declarative sentences 'The moon is the cause of the tides in the English Channel' and 'Plato was older than Aristotle'. This is a blatant *non sequitur*: it presupposes that the logical forms of the predicate calculus are essential to describing the *syntax* of grammatical sentences in English.

20 And refuting either doctrine by citing alleged counter-examples is equally futile. As if Davidson's analysis were incompatible with the grammaticality of the sentence 'She ran across the quad *quickly*'!

21 'It has been *usual* also in the Description of *Substance* to add, it is that which is the *Subject* of Modes or Accidents . . .' (Watts, *Logick*, I.ii.2; cf. I.ii.3, some italics added).

Wouldn't a different interpretation of this passage be preferable? It is argued that Descartes here started out by denying that there is any such thing as a thought *about* a thought (Kenny 1968: 61, 76);[22] or that he held the view that any genuine judgement must be *about* something extra-mental (Kenny 1968: 123). But he clearly held no such view. On the contrary, he thought that each person can reflect on his own thinking and achieve certain knowledge about his modes of thinking (e.g., AT V: 149; CSMK III: 335). (This form of self-knowledge falls under the label '*conscientia*'.) There is nothing absurd about the supposition that one thought may be about another thought; for instance, I can make the judgement 'I [subject] have the property that [predicate] I think or judge that I see light'. What Descartes held to be absurd was something different, namely that any thought could be the *logical subject* of a singular judgement. A thought is not a *substance*, hence *not* something in which any property can inhere. He took for granted here that thinking (or having a thought) is not a substance, but a *mode* of a substance. Hence he argued that he was fully justified (by a general metaphysical principle) in inferring that any mode (or act) of thinking must inhere in a substance. Thus, *pace* Hobbes, '*Cogito, ergo sum res cogitans*' is a valid inference.

This principle must be applied to any judgement that a twentieth-century logician would analyse as a singular statement about a mental particular (a state of consciousness, an individual experience). In Descartes' view, the possibility of someone's stating 'The thought that I just had was brilliant' doesn't prove that his universe of discourse must include *things* called 'thoughts'; the speaker isn't 'ontologically committed' to the existence of 'inner objects'.[23] Instead, Descartes required that the logical analysis of what is said take the form of predicating an incorporeal property of the speaker's soul. What is constrained is not the thoughts that someone may have, but the logical analysis of thoughts.

This point about the analysis of 'psychological judgements' has many important consequences. First, it affects how the *Cogito* is to be understood. It invalidates the common criticism that Descartes begged the crucial question in formulating the premise as '*I* think' ('*cogito*') rather than as 'Thinking occurs' ('*cogitatur*'). In his view, there *can* be *no* judgement about thinking (or the occurrence of a thought) whose logical subject is not a substance. To predicate a mode of thinking *of a thinking thing* is the *minimal* move in the language-game. A thought (or an act of thinking) isn't a substance, and there is no such thing as a mode which doesn't inhere in a substance. Consequently, there is no (genuine) judgement about

22 This would apparently make nonsense of the rider 'For who, apart from him [i.e. Hobbes], ever supposed that [there] could be?', as well as failing to connect with the remainder of the paragraph.

23 Further issues are raised about thoughts like 'The pain in my foot is agonizing'; it is only the Expansion Thesis that would license seeing this thought as (unambiguously) about something mental in the first place. As we will see below (pp. 133–4), 'pain' does not name a mental object, nor does it name a physical object. Rather, 'being painful' is a *mode* of a part of the body. Descartes would not have been checkmated by the rhetorical question 'If it isn't the pain in my foot that is so unbearable, *what* is?' For he could obviously have explained the difference between my having a mild pain and my having an unbearable one without having to represent this conceptual difference as one of predicating contrasting properties of a mental (or bodily!) particular.

the occurrence of a thought which is any weaker (or more non-committal) than the judgement '*I* think'. Descartes' conception leaves no logical room for contrasting '*cogito*' with '*cogitatur*' (as Lichtenberg did in accusing Descartes of committing a fallacy in drawing the conclusion '*sum*'). To admit that contrast is definitively to jettison his logico-metaphysical framework.

This observation about the *Cogito* affects one's understanding of what Descartes referred to as the 'restricted' sense of *sentire* (sense-perception) which is expressed by the formula 'It seems to me that (I see light, I feel warmth, etc.)' (AT VII: 29; CSM II: 19). Since this form of judgement is explicitly said to report a mode of thinking, it must be understood as predicating something of a thinking thing. In other words, its logical subject must be *the thinker* himself, and the logical predicate must be the property of having a particular thought (e.g., having the thought or making the judgement that I see light). So a perspicuous paraphrase would be, '*I* think or judge that (I see light, I feel warmth, etc.)' (cf. *Principles* I.11–12; CSM I: 196–7). We might call it a *personal* judgement, not an *impersonal* one (like 'It's raining'); Descartes expressed it quite perspicuously by putting its main verb in the *first-person* singular (using the deponent personal form '*videor*' rather than the impersonal form '*mihi videtur*' to formulate the prefix 'It seems to me that . . .'). The notion that the restricted sense of *sentire* characterizes reports of the occurrence of perceptual experiences or sense-data is altogether inadmissible if it is taken to eliminate commitment to the existence of a thinker (or 'subject of experience'); the logical subject of such a judgement cannot be a perceptual experience or a sense-datum. (It is equally inadmissible to suppose that 'It seems to me that I see light' is to be characterized as expressing a genuine *relation* between a thinker and a mental *entity*.) (See pp. 72–5.)

A further consequence is that *conscientia*, as knowledge of one's own states of mind, must have the form of I-thoughts. The characteristic expression of *conscientia* is 'I (substance) have the thought that . . . (predicate)'. This is an essential (conceptual) difference between *conscientia* and Humean introspection, whose characteristic expression is 'The thought that . . . is occurring' (see pp. 118–24).

Finally, upholding the principle that the logical subject of a singular judgement must be a substance allows us to make sense of a movement of his thought that might otherwise seem simply unmotivated. Descartes held that the properties commonly predicated of persons in everyday speech *must* be subdivided into two jointly exhaustive and mutually exclusive sub-sets: some are really properties of minds, others really properties of bodies. An obvious explanation would be that he subscribed to the principle that every singular judgement must have a (genuine) *substance* as its logical subject. Taking for granted the premise that a person is not a single substance but a combination of two distinct substances, you could motivate the bifurcation of properties characteristic of Cartesian Dualism. A person *can't* be the logical subject of any judgement. Hence every judgement framed with personal pronouns or phrases apparently making singular reference to persons has a grammatical form that conceals its true logical form; it *must* be analysed into a judgement about a soul or a body (or some combination of such judgements).[24] In fact, the very idea that a person, i.e. a combination of a soul and a body, *could* be the logical subject of a singular judgement would lead straight into one of the forms of confused thinking that Descartes was explicitly intent on eliminating by a course of philosophical therapy. In effect, it would involve confusing or failing to distinguish between two substances which are 'really distinct' (cf. *Principles* I.60; CSM I: 213). We might call it a form of category-mistake. Hobbes was transparently guilty of this kind of confused thinking when he claimed that a human body does have the power of thinking (AT VII: 173; CSM II: 122). So too would be any modern philosopher who adopted Strawson's principle that 'the concept of a person is primitive' (1959: ch. 3). Only if you screen out the metaphysical foundation of his position do you arrive at the view that there is nothing to be said in favour of his different scheme of logical analysis (see pp. 188–91).

The defining feature of Descartes' Dualism is the doctrine that there are only two kinds of substances: material objects and rational souls. The only mental substances are minds. Thinking or thought is *essentially* a mode of a mental substance. 'No thinking without a thinker' is an axiom of his system (not a hypothesis or assumption). This principle is a constitutive element of *his* concept of the mind. Dropping it would replace his concept with a different one (just as dropping his exclusion of action at a distance would modify his concept of efficient causation). This metaphysical doctrine is inseparable from Descartes' conception of the logical forms of singular judgements. Nothing other than a mind (or soul) can be the logical subject of a judgement whose logical predicate is an incorporeal property.

The Cartesian Legend regularly contradicts this restrictive principle. Each person's inner world is taken to be a kind of counterpart of the world of extended (or material) things, both logically and epistemologically. The 'thoughts' of the inner world are the logical subjects of singular judgements just as the material objects of the sensible world are. Thus, for instance, the judgement expressed by the sentence 'The thought I just had is brilliant' (or, granted the Expansion Thesis, 'The pain in my foot is agonizing') is thought to have *the same logical form* as the one expressed by the sentence 'The paperweight on my desk is made of marble'. The distinction between qualitative and numerical identity is applied to 'thoughts' or 'ideas'. Thus, for example, it is claimed to be evident that no two persons can have *the same* thought, and even that one person cannot have *the same* thought twice.[25] An epistemological principle stands on this logical foundation: introspection is taken to provide cognitive 'access' to singular truths about *objects* in the internal world just as sense-perception provides 'access' to singular truths

24 But they may be internally related (cf. pp. 188–91)!

25 Mill claimed that all such phrases involve 'incorrect applications of the word "same"', and he added that 'great confusion of ideas . . . and many fallacies' are produced by failing to distinguish identity from undistinguishable resemblance in respect of the genus of 'feelings' (*Logic* I.iii.11). James insisted on the importance of recognizing that the same thought, idea, or conception can never recur (James 1890: I.480–1).

about *substances* in the external world. Individual thoughts are the 'objects of introspection' in the same way that individual material things are the 'objects of sense-perception'.

This reasoning divorces *Descartes*' logical analysis of judgements from *his* metaphysics (of substances and modes). At the same time, the Legend ties its logical analysis of judgements to *its* own metaphysics (of particulars, properties, and relations). It takes for granted that *Descartes* countenanced singular judgements whose logical subjects are *mental particulars* like pains, mental images, and theorems of geometry. (This is, as it were, the cash value of the Two-Worlds View.) But it makes no more sense to divorce Descartes' logic from his metaphysics than it does to divorce modern logic from modern metaphysics.[26] The logical notion of *referring* to something is intertwined with the metaphysical concept of a *particular* or an *individual*, and it seems widely agreed that to *be* is to be the *value of a variable* or a member of the *domain of quantification*. Certain differences in metaphysical systems are mirrored directly in the corresponding analyses of the logical forms of judgements. This principle applies to Descartes' metaphysics of substances and attributes. Careful examination of his reasoning bears out the thesis that, in his view, the *logical* subject of any singular judgement *must* be *a substance*. Hence (if you like) the only *particulars* are substances. To ascribe the Two-Worlds View to Descartes requires us to ignore the logical requirement that any logical subject of a judgement must be a substance;[27] and *this*, in effect, is to require us to disregard the *metaphysical* requirement that substances must exist independently of every other substance. There is no such thing as a 'merely metaphysical' difference about what counts as a particular. Expositors of the Cartesian Legend treat his metaphysical notions as free wheels, as things that you can safely ignore in evaluating his logic and epistemology. This piece of legerdemain is one of the decisive moves in conjuring up the Legend out of his texts.[28]

Indeed one might go further. Descartes repeatedly tackled the common error of confusing modes and substances, i.e. of failing to distinguish what is 'modally

26 Even if we today like to think that logic and metaphysics are insulated completely from each other. (There are different ways of interpreting 'metaphysics'!)

27 Leibniz held the closely related principle that 'all science deals with substance', from which he claimed to have proved 'that figure is a substance, or rather that space is a substance and figure something *substantive*' (*Lettres* 98).

28 The influence of the Two-Worlds View might be a good instance of what Wittgenstein described as the imposition of a dogma: 'The effect of making men think in accordance with dogmas, perhaps in the form of certain graphic propositions, will be very peculiar: I am not thinking of these dogmas as determining men's opinions but rather as completely controlling the *expression* of all opinions. People will live under an absolute, palpable tyranny, though without being able to say they are not free . . . . For dogma is expressed in the form of an assertion, and is unshakable, but at the same time any practical opinion *can* be made to harmonize with it; admittedly more easily in some cases than in others. It is not a *wall* setting limits to what can be believed, but more like a *brake* which, however, practically serves the same purpose; it's almost as though someone were to attach a weight to your foot to restrict your freedom of movement. That is how dogma becomes irrefutable and beyond the reach of attack' (*CV* 28).

distinct'. He suggested that mathematicians had misconceived what they investigated through taking numbers or shapes to be substances. They will achieve a clear and distinct understanding of these things provided they scrupulously avoid 'tacking on to them any concept of substance' and 'do not regard order or number as anything separate from the things which are ordered or numbered' (*Principles* I.55; CSM I: 211). Likewise he criticized advocates of 'real attributes' or 'substantial forms' for the same mistake of treating modes as substances. As a consequence of this confusion, they produced pseudo-explanations of the motions of material objects and blocked the way to apprehending the true principles of mechanics. One of the foundations of rational science is to acknowledge that the *power* to bring about a change in the motion of any matter must be a mode of a substance, not itself a substance.[29] No number, shape, distance, motion, causal power, colour, weight, pain, emotion and passion, thought, volition, desire, memory, etc. can be the logical subject of any judgement. Only a substance, corporeal or mental, can play that role. Consequently, from Descartes' point of view, the Two-Worlds View itself embodies confusion of things modally distinct.

To summarize, it is one pillar of Descartes' Dualism that any singular judgement must have a *substance* as its logical subject. The Cartesian Legend gives no place at all to this principle. Indeed, by adopting the Two-Worlds View, it *contradicts* this axiom and thereby brings down the whole of *Descartes*' system in ruins. That the rubble is uninhabitable is surely no criticism of the building's architect or of its design! The Two Worlds can't be viewed as an unactualized possibility within his dualism or as a further refinement of his conception. It must be treated as a different (and incommensurable) *Weltanschauung*. His thinking will continue to be misrepresented until the tyranny of the idea of 'two *worlds* of mind and matter' is broken. We must learn to express his dualism as he himself expressed it: 'two kinds of *substances*: material thing*s* and mind*s*'.[30]

RATIONAL SOULS AND SENTIENT MACHINES

We propose an alternative picture of how Descartes drew the mind–body boundary. We will argue that the key to his conception is not the now familiar contrast between consciousness and clockwork, but a now unfamiliar contrast between 'rational' and 'animal'. The contrast is between the mind or *rational soul* and the body whose 'functions' 'are just the ones in which *animals without reason* may be said to resemble us' (AT VI: 46, CSM I: 134, italics added; cf. AT XI: 200, CSM I: 107). It is made manifest in the contrast he himself drew between

29 This doctrine has obvious implications for the logical analysis of causal judgements. These *cannot* state relations to hold between two things, but *must* predicate of one thing an inherent (general) power. More accurately, it must consist of a conjunction of two correlative judgements, one predicating an active power of one thing, the other a passive power of the other thing (see pp. 173–5).

30 Cf. Watts, *Logick* I.ii.2: there are 'but two sorts of Substances in the World', namely '*thinking* or conscious Beings' and '*extended* and *solid* or *impenetrable* [Beings]'.

animal sentience (animal responses to sights, sounds, pain, hunger, etc.) and rational sentience (human articulation of 'sensations' or sense-based thoughts); equally, in the contrast between animal emotions and rational emotions ('the passions of the *soul*'), between animal desire and rational desire, etc. His understanding of these terms needs further clarification, but our initial naive understanding of them is sufficient at least to point our thinking in the right direction.

We attach great importance to two facts. First, he used the term 'mind' ('*mens*', '*esprit*') interchangeably with the terms '(rational) soul', 'intellect', and 'reason' ('*anima*', '*intellectus*', '*ratio*', '*âme*', '*entendement*', '*raison*'). Our reading is intended to highlight his claim that the essence of the mind is *thought*. Second, he considered the rational soul to be the bearer of moral responsibility (and freedom); it is immortal, and it provides the link between a mortal person and the resurrected person who faces God at the Last Judgement. These two points are essential to understanding what he meant by 'thought', 'modes of thinking', and 'operations of the soul', hence indirectly for grasping what he meant by '*conscientia*' (which includes moral conscience). We argue (on pp. 70–5) that Descartes made use of the term '*thought*' ('*cogitatio*' or '*pensée*') precisely because it had the connotations of rationality (including the possibility of being fully articulated in language: see pp. 108–9). His concern is with cognition and reasoning, with moral knowledge and practical deliberation, and with the pursuit of truth and virtue. His focus is on the activities and active powers of the soul, on the principles or rules that should regulate them. The same two points are equally crucial for understanding his denial that animals had minds or rational souls. It should then be evident that he denied them intellect and moral agency, not sentience. We argue (on pp. 91–100) that in Descartes' view both animals and human bodies are 'conscious',[31] or (more accurately) 'sentient', machines.

Minds as rational souls

Let's start by reviewing the passages which are commonly taken as evidence for the Expansion Thesis:

> (1) By the term 'thought', I understand everything which we are aware of as happening within us, in so far as we have awareness of it. Hence, *thinking* is to be identified here not merely with understanding, willing, imagining, but also with sensory awareness [*sentire*]. For if I say 'I am seeing, or I am walking, therefore I exist,' and take this as applying to vision or walking as bodily activities, then the conclusion is not absolutely certain. This is because, as often happens during sleep, it is possible for me to think I am seeing or walking, though my eyes are closed and I am not moving about;

31 But not *conscius*! *Conscientia* is a cognitive power of the rational soul, hence something that brutes must lack (see below, pp. 105–6). And not 'conscious' in the twentieth-century Anglo-American sense, since Descartes would regard this as a confused idea (see pp. 86–7).

> such thoughts might even be possible if I had no body at all. But if I take 'seeing' or 'walking' to apply to the actual sense or awareness of seeing or walking [*sensus sive conscientia videndi aut ambulandi*], then the conclusion is quite certain, since it relates to the mind, which alone has the sensation or thought that it is seeing or walking [. . . *ad mentem, quae sola sentit sive cogitat se videre aut ambulare*].
>
> (*Principles* I.9 (AT VIIIA: 7–8, CSM I: 195))
>
> (2) But what then am I? A thing that thinks. What is that? A thing that doubts, understands, affirms, denies, is willing, is unwilling, and also imagines [*imaginari*] and has sensory perceptions [*sentire*].
>
> (AT VII: 28; CSM II: 19)
>
> (3) I am now seeing light, hearing a noise, feeling heat. But I am asleep, so all this is false. Yet I certainly *seem* to see, to hear, and to be warmed. This cannot be false; what is called 'having a sensory perception' [*sentire*] is strictly just this, and in this restricted sense of the term it is simply thinking [*cogitatio*].
>
> (AT VII: 29; CSM II: 19)

We argued above (pp. 32–4) that Descartes was in the business of disambiguation in (1) and (3): he identified two legitimate or proper senses of '*sentire*', not a 'strict' and an etiolated (or secondary) sense. These two senses are what he distinguished under the general headings 'animal' and 'rational'. In the second of these senses, each expression falling within the scope of the generic term '*sentire*' signifies a 'mode of thinking', and these modes are properties that must inhere in a rational soul (*res cogitans*).

This sets us four immediate tasks.

1 The first is to spell out our own interpretation of the 'mental' or rational sense of '*sentire*', reported by '*It seems to me that* I see light' in (3) and described as 'the sense of seeing' ('*sensus videndi*') in (1). We need to explain precisely how this is to be contrasted with the 'bodily' sense, that is, animal sense-perception. (This explanation must meet the further constraint that it makes sense of the symmetry asserted in passage (1) between 'seeing' and 'walking'.)
2 Next we need to specify the range of expressions held to display the ambiguity between 'animal' and 'rational'. It is clear that he held a vast number of predicates applicable to human beings to be equivocal, including, of course, 'walking'.
3 We need to make clear what the justification is for the use of the term '*ambiguous*' for predicates describing sense-perception (e.g., 'sees light' or 'feels warmth').
4 Finally, we need to bring to light the philosophical, rhetorical, and therapeutic aims or motivations for his disambiguations.[32]

32 A much earlier version of the ideas presented on pp. 72–7 occurs in Baker and Morris (1993). Some of the material on pp. 77–87 was developed in K. Morris (1995).

Rational sense-perception

How then do we interpret 'It seems to me that I see light'? Passages (1) and (3) make a distinction between two meanings of 'seeing (light)'. In one sense this expression refers to something purely bodily, which animals too could exhibit; for now we will simply mark this sense with a subscript: 'seeing$_1$' (or 'animal seeing'). In another sense, it refers to something purely mental, namely having a thought with a particular content, which brutes (lacking souls) could not exhibit. We mark this sense with another subscript: 'seeing$_2$' (or 'rational seeing'). For a Thinker to see$_2$ (to see 'in the restricted sense') is for him to *think* that he sees$_1$. Descartes elsewhere described the contrast thus, when he criticized those who 'think that animals see just as we do, i.e. *being aware or thinking* they see [*hoc est sentiendo sive cogitando se videre*]' (AT I: 413; CSMK III: 61). These two senses have different criteria. The criteria for someone's seeing$_1$ light will relate to the situation of the person's body and its reactions to that situation. (Animals too can meet these criteria; see p. 99) But someone who makes the statement (voluntarily expresses the thought)[33] 'I see light' satisfies a criterion for seeing$_2$ light (seeing in the 'restricted' sense).[34] The criteria for 'seeing light' in these two senses may come apart: for instance, I can think that I see$_1$ light although (because I am dreaming) I do not.[35]

Of course, 'thinking that one sees$_1$ light' *might* be taken in one of two ways: it might mean simply having a particular thought (the content of a possible judgement) in one's mind, or it might mean actually making a judgement. Even if it were read in the first way, of course, it would still definitely be a *thought* (i.e. something cognitive and propositional, by contrast with the Legend's sense-datum reading). We, however, are inclined to take it in the second way; this would make the report of 'the sense of seeing' in passage (1) parallel, as it appears to be, to '*I judge that* I am touching the earth' ('*judico me terram tangere*') (*Principles* I.11; CSM I: 196): these reports play a parallel role as the premise for the *Cogito*.

It might be thought that this isn't a possible reading, for at least three reasons; yet none of these seem to be decisive. First, it might be felt that 'seeing in the restricted sense' was too 'automatic' to count as judgement, which is essentially a form of voluntary action. But arguably the point of calling judgement voluntary isn't that it involves a decision (arrived at through deliberation, say; the point is

33 Neither a parrot nor a sleeping person who utters the sounds 'I see light' satisfies the criteria for seeing$_2$ light.

34 It would surely be too stringent to insist on just *this* form of words ('I see light') and no other as an expression of 'rationally seeing light' (e.g., 'There is light', etc.), although we ignore this refinement in what follows. Note, however, that 'seeing light', 'hearing sound, 'feeling heat', and so on (what on p. 176. we call '"basic" sense-perception') are the only kinds of case of 'rational sense-perception' discussed by Descartes (further details on pp. 176–7).

35 This point presupposes accepting Descartes' idea that the soul can exercise all its functions in dreams. But the same contrast between the two senses of 'see' could be made independently of this (contentious) doctrine.

that it makes sense to ask someone to refrain from making it;[36] and that is clearly the case here, however the judgement comes about. Second, it might be suggested that 'It seems to me that I see light' (at least in (1) and (3)) reports a tendency or inclination to judge that I see light rather than an outright judgement (cf. Curley 1979: 191). Part of what makes this suggestion tempting is the fact that Descartes in these very passages invokes the possibility of being asleep: if I might at this moment be asleep, then I have reason to refrain from judging that I see_1 light. But this, while true, settles nothing. If I judge that I see_1 light, $hear_1$ noise, or $feel_1$ heat, and then consider the possibility that I might be dreaming, this might give me reason to withhold judgement henceforth (although I may or may not do so). But it can hardly alter the fact that I do (did just) so judge.[37] The question is whether 'It seems to me that I see light' is said after I have refrained from judging, if I do indeed do so (recording the fact that I am still tempted to judge), or simply after considering the possibility that my judgements might be false (recording the fact that I nonetheless just did so judge). We are not forced to read it in the former way. Third, Descartes' well-known account of the 'three grades of sensory response' might seem to go against our suggestion:

> The first is limited to the immediate stimulation of the bodily organs by external objects . . . . The second grade comprises all the immediate effects produced in the mind as a result of its being united with a bodily organ which is affected in this way. Such effects include the perceptions of pain, pleasure, thirst, hunger, colours, sound, taste, smell, heat, cold and the like . . . . The third grade includes all the judgements about things outside us which we have been accustomed to make from our earliest years.
>
> (AT VII: 436–7; CSM II: 294–5)

The second grade is often taken to be something mental but non-cognitive, e.g., a sense-datum, or a sensation with 'phenomenological qualities' (cf. Cottingham 1986: 128–9). But the passage doesn't exclude the second grade's being something cognitive, or even *judgements*, as long as these are contrasted in *content* with judgements 'about things outside us which we have been accustomed to make from our earliest years'.

Thus we see no powerful reason *not* to interpret $seeing_2$ (in passages (1) and (3)) as making the judgement rather than simply having the thought (the content of a possible judgement) that one $sees_1$ light, although either interpretation would make it something cognitive and propositional. According to our account, then,

36 Wittgenstein clarified the voluntary/involuntary distinction in respect of his remarking that mental images and aspect-seeing can be called 'voluntary' in contrast to sense-perception. He stressed that a voluntary action is something that we can sensibly tell somebody to perform or to desist from, hence, too, something that this person may (or may not) succeed in performing or desisting from in response to an order. It need not be something based on a prior decision or something that can be done 'at will'. (See *Wittgenstein's Lectures on Philosophical Psychology 1946–47*, London: Harvester, 1988, pp. 35–6, 334.)

37 We discuss this use of the perfect tense ('I have just judged . . .') at greater length on p. 110 n.134.

'It seems to me that I see light' ('I see_2 light') is understood to be equivalent to 'I judge that I see_1 light', and it reports the fact that I am making (or have just made) that judgement. The judgement *that* I judge (have just judged) that I see_1 light, etc. is an exercise of *conscientia* (the power to reflect on the operations of one's mind) which, in this particular case, 'cannot be false' (see pp. 115–18).

Parallel interpretations are to be offered for some parallel passages where Descartes discussed other instances of 'having a sensory perception' (*sentire*). For example, he asserted that '[feeling] pain in the strict [i.e. restricted] sense' does not occur in animals (AT III: 85; CSMK III: 148).[38] 'Feeling pain' is an instance of 'having a sensory perception', being the exercise of an internal sense (see below, pp. 124–38). It is here indicated to be ambiguous in just the way that 'seeing light' is. Note that it is '*feeling* pain', not 'pain', which is ambiguous, just as it was 'seeing light', not 'light', which has contrasting 'animal' and 'rational' senses; both 'pain' and 'light' refer unambiguously, if not entirely straightforwardly, to modes of extension (see pp. 128–34). 'Feeling pain' can refer to something purely bodily which can occur in animals as well as in human beings. It can also refer to the judgement that one $feels_1$ pain. This judgement is an instance of what Descartes here called 'feeling pain in the restricted sense' ('$feeling_2$ pain'), and exactly like 'seeing light in the restricted sense', this predicate stands for a mode of thinking and hence cannot be instantiated by a brute.

There is clearly more to be said about this 'restricted' sense of *sentire*-predicates; we can only make a few gestures in this direction here. Judgements which count as $seeing_2$ (and similarly for other instances of *sentire* in the restricted sense) are, in a *certain* sense, reflexive: to say that x $sees_2$ light is (roughly speaking) to say that x judges that x $sees_1$ light. But the two occurrences of 'x' designate, respectively, a rational soul (which makes the judgement that . . .) and a body (what is judged to see_1 light); there is clearly a difficulty in talking about such a judgement as 'reflexive': its resolution turns on the fact that mind and body are internally related (pp. 188–91).[39] Judgements reporting rational sense-perception are also 'present-tense'[40] (so 'I judge that I $felt_1$ pain *yesterday*' is not an instance of *sentire*). And they must refer to the perception of so-called 'secondary qualities' – what Locke said were 'usually called *sensible qualities*' (*Essay* II.viii.23) – rather than 'primary qualities'; so they are exemplified by my

38 This passage deviates from his usual standards of precision of expression. He regularly distinguished 'pain' from 'the sensation of pain', and we argue that this distinction is of fundamental importance to him. But here, having correctly picked out 'the sensation of pain' ('*le sentiment de la douleur*') as his topic, he twice used the term 'pain' ('*la douleur*') in place of the longer expression.

39 The judgement that *I* see_2 light (as opposed to the third-person version of that judgement) is an exercise of *conscientia* (see pp. 100ff.); it expresses a judgement that I (my rational soul) have a particular property, namely the property of *judging* that I see_1 light (i.e. the property of $seeing_2$ light). This further judgement is straightforwardly reflexive; the two 'I's (the one which judges, the other which is judged to see_2) are both the same (the rational soul).

40 This needs to be understood as the 'present of action'; not as an instant without any duration, but something more like 'the specious present' (see p. 110 n.134).

seeing light, hearing noise, feeling pain, etc., but not by my seeing size, shape, movement, etc.[41] The crucial point for present purposes, however, is that, though 'having sense-perceptions in the restricted sense' is having thoughts with a distinctive content, it is for all that a matter of having (genuine) *thoughts*. So Descartes' choice of the cognitive, 'propositional' term 'thought' ('*cogitatio*') to express the essence of the mind is straightforward and accurate even in the knowledge that he included sense-perception and Imagination among *modes of thinking*. The mind is the *rational* soul.

Can we now make some sense of the symmetry between 'seeing' and 'walking' in passage (1)? There is one important unclarity. It looks at first sight as though 'is walking', like 'is seeing', is offered as an instance of *sentire*. Can we make any sense of this? Some modern philosophers have argued for a distinctive form of sense-perception (variously called 'proprioception' or 'kinaesthesia') whose objects are the position and movements of parts of one's own body. But this seems irrelevant to (1), since what we require is to exhibit walking itself, not the putative having of kinaesthetic sensations of walking, as a form of *sentire*.

Another more attractive possibility might be to connect *sentire* in *this* context not simply with sense-perception but with the scholastic doctrine of the 'sensitive soul' (discussed below). This was clearly a doctrine with which Descartes was familiar, and walking, as a species of locomotion, was certainly viewed as one of the paradigmatic functions of the sensitive soul. This suggestion is not unproblematic: it would imply that Descartes' use of certain central terms (e.g., '*sentire*') was not wholly consistent; and there is the fact that in (1) *imaginari* is *not* included along with *sentire*, as it is in (2), even though Imagination was traditionally treated as a genus of functions of the sensitive soul. Neither of these objections seems clearly decisive.

On the other hand, the text does not force us to understand 'walking' as an instance of '*sentire*'. Indeed if we denied this, it would circumvent the appearance of redundancy in the two phrases 'sense [*sensus*] or awareness [*conscientia*] of seeing or walking' and 'has the sensation or thought that it is seeing or walking'. The term '*sensus*' is the noun corresponding to the verb '*sentire*'. So we could read the first phrase, perhaps a little unnaturally, as 'sense of seeing, or awareness of walking'; and the second, correspondingly, as 'has the sensation that it is seeing, or the thought that it is walking'. This reading would tie the term '*conscientia*' to the action of walking. This is striking, since Descartes took *conscientia* to be the *soul*'s knowledge of *its own* operations (see pp. 112–13). In this context, however, it cannot mean this, since that of which we are said to have *conscientia* here is

41 Descartes never used the term 'sensation' (*sentire*) in application to the sensory perception of shape or size, only to light, sound, colour, pain, etc. (For a discussion of some of the issues here, see, e.g., Ann Wilbur MacKenzie, 'The Reconfiguration of Sensory Experience', in Cottingham 1994.) Equivalently, the term 'sensation' is restricted to the thoughts concerning the 'proper objects' of the various senses (a point also made by Wilson (1994: 216)); for instance, 'light and colour [are] the only qualities belonging properly to the sense of sight' (AT VI: 130; CSM I: 167).

'walking as a bodily action'. But arguably *conscientia* works like 'judgement' (or 'thought'), which can refer either to the act of judging (or thinking) or to what is judged (or thought); in this case to refer to '*conscientia* of a bodily action' is to refer to an operation of the soul (not in *this* case further specifiable as an instance of *sentire*) *of which* we have *conscientia*.

But whichever reading we opt for (and there are advantages and disadvantages of each), the point of (1) is clear: both 'walking' and 'seeing' are described (in one sense) as 'bodily actions' and contrasted with another sense in which they count as 'modes of thinking'. In the first sense, they are modes of extension; in the second, they are properties of the soul. The phrase '*sensus sive conscientia videndi aut ambulandi*' (which will refer to '"seeing" or "walking" in the restricted sense', i.e. $seeing_2$ or $walking_2$) is evidently the nominalization of the verb phrase '*sentit sive cogitat se videre aut ambulare*', which thus refers to the thought *that I see* or the thought *that I am walking* (i.e. the thought or judgement that I am $seeing_1$ or $walking_1$).[42] Either judgement would provide an appropriate premise for reaching the conclusion 'I am'.[43]

The minimal interpretation of (1) must be that $walking_1$ is a bodily action, while $walking_2$ is a judgement that one is $walking_1$. (It may well be that $walking_2$ is also a volition.)[44] Such judgements (like *sentire*-judgements) will be 'present-tense' and in a *certain* sense reflexive: to say that x $walks_2$ is to say that x judges that x $walks_1$, but the two occurrences of 'x' designate, respectively, a rational soul (which judges that . . .) and a body (what is judged to $walk_1$).[45] Once again there is evidently a difficulty in talking about such a judgement as 'reflexive' (see pp. 188–91).

The claim that the predicate 'is walking' is ambiguous and refers in one sense to a thought or judgement is clearly Descartes' view. It is likely to strike us today as highly unnatural.[46] It will no doubt continue to do so until we appreciate

42 The French text supports this interpretation: '*si j'entends parler seulement* de l'action de ma pensée, ou *du sentiment, c'est à dire de la connoissance qui est en moy*, qui fait qu'il me semble *que je voy ou que je marche, cette mesme conclusion est* si *absolument vraye* que je n'en peux douter . . .' (AT IXB: 28).

43 The point Descartes made here is parallel to the point he made elsewhere (AT II: 38; CSMK III: 98) that 'I breathe' can function as a premise for the *Cogito* as long as it is understood to mean 'the feeling or the belief' that I breathe (i.e. the thought or judgement that I $breathe_1$).

44 Anything more than this minimal interpretation is speculative, but the following seems to be a natural extension. In many cases, especially in animal behaviour, $walking_1$ will be a goal-directed activity, exhibiting 'animal desire' ($desire_1$). In these cases, $walking_2$ would be the counterpart judgement that one is $walking_1$, and hence it would include a judgement about what goal is aimed at. Arguably, too, it is a *volition* which exhibits 'rational desire' ($desire_2$).

Note that this distinction between manifestations of animal desire and manifestations of rational desire is entirely different from the distinction between 'mere bodily movement' and action. This would undercut Williams' argument (Williams 1978: 291) that 'on the Cartesian account', 'when I move my arm at will, what I will is *that my arm move*'. What I will or judge is that I (my body) $move_1$ its arm.

45 Unless one sees such judgements as in some sense reflexive, the final sentence of (1) *must* be supposed to contain a solecism: 'relates to the mind, which alone has the sensation or thought that *it* is seeing or walking [se *videre aut ambulare*]'.

46 It is, however, far from clear why it should strike us as *more* unnatural than the parallel claim that 'is seeing' has a purely mental sense.

Descartes' motivation for insisting on an ambiguity (below) and until we attain a clearer understanding of his conception of voluntary action (see pp. 175–6).

'Sensitive predicates' and sensitive souls

Our second task was to explicate the range of ambiguities identified by Descartes. Passages (1) to (3) themselves suggest that he held a kind of ambiguity to affect a very wide range of terms referring to the 'functions' of animals (and humans). Didactic as this device is, it will aid clear discussion to tabulate a sample of the range of predicates applicable to human beings, both those which are ambiguous in his view and those which are not (see Table 1).

Table 1 A classification of predicates applicable to human beings

Predicates	*Tradition*	*Descartes*
'weighs ten stone' 'is in the drawing-room'	No souls required	Ascribable only to corporeal substances (C-predicates)
'is alive' 'is nourished'	Vegetative soul required	
'breathes' 'walks' 'sees light' 'feels pain' 'feels angry' 'remembers' 'expects' 'desires'	Sensitive soul required	Ascribed in ordinary language both to corporeal and mental substances; but since this is incoherent, these predicates *must* be ambiguous (S-predicates)
'thinks' 'judges' 'is courageous' 'is cowardly'	Rational soul required	Ascribable only to mental substances (R-predicates)

On our view, the predicates which Descartes held to be ambiguous are exactly those which the Aristotelian tradition identified as designating functions of the sensitive soul. Since our aim is to produce a representative sample of this set of predicates, not to give a precise delineation of its boundaries, a crude outline of this scholastic background should suffice. The Aristotelian tradition held that some properties of things did not require souls, but that many did. It depicted a hierarchy of living things. The lowest form are plants, having 'vegetative' souls which conferred the powers of nutrition and growth. Animals are a higher form of life, having 'sensitive' souls which conferred (in addition to nutrition and growth) the powers of memory, Imagination (desire and anticipation), sense-perception and locomotion. Human beings are at the top of the heap, having 'rational' souls which conferred, in addition to all the 'vegetative' and 'sensitive' functions, the powers of judging, willing, reasoning, and deliberating; possession of a rational soul is what makes a person free and morally responsible.

This Aristotelian hierarchy generates a fourfold distinction of the properties that may be predicated of human beings. Some of these properties are shared with lifeless matter: for example, height, weight, or spatial location. Some are shared with plants: for example, features of metabolism and reproduction; these are the 'vegetative functions'. Others are shared with animals: for example, feeling hunger, hearing sounds, feeling warmth, desiring to drink, walking, and searching for food; these are the distinctive 'sensitive functions'. Yet others are distinctive of humans and shared with no other living creatures: for instance, proving a geometrical theorem, making a judgement, acting courageously, deliberating about what to do, or planning a campaign of action; these are the distinctive 'operations of the rational soul'. Descartes' programme of philosophical disambiguation is directed at the third of the groups in this hierarchy of the properties of human beings. These are the functions traditionally ascribed to the sensitive soul, and they were regularly distinguished into a genus of passive powers (sense-perception) and a genus of active powers (locomotion).

Descartes redesigned this categorization of properties. He agreed with the tradition that many predicates applied only to corporeal substances (though he expanded this set to include the 'vegetative functions'); we label these 'corporeal predicates' or 'C-predicates'.[47] He agreed too that many other predicates (all those which the tradition ascribed to the rational soul alone) apply only to mental substances; these we have called 'rational predicates' or 'R-predicates'. His innovation concerns all and only those predicates which the tradition ascribed to the sensitive soul ('sensitive predicates' or 'S-predicates'). On his schematization, they apply both to corporeal substances (in particular animals and human bodies) and to mental substances (rational souls). But he held it to be impossible that the very same properties should be ascribed both to corporeal and to mental substances.[48] That would either require a corporeal substance to possess a mode of thinking or mental substance to possess a mode of extension (or both), and that is ruled out by a metaphysical axiom.[49] Consequently, those predicates which apply to both corporeal and mental substances *must* be ambiguous; in one sense

47 The terminology here obviously owes its inspiration to Strawson's (1959: ch. 3) M-predicates and P-predicates; we leave it to the reader familiar with Strawson to compare and contrast.

48 The scholastic tradition of logic acknowledged the possibility that some concepts could be classified as 'syncategoremata' (e.g., time, identity). Descartes apparently extended this idea to his own conception of 'categories'. We neglect this complication here.

49 Cottingham (1986) recognizes this; but instead of drawing the conclusion that these predicates must therefore be ambiguous, he deduces an internal tension within Descartes' dualism.

they are C-predicates, in another, they are R-predicates.[50] The Aristotelian tradition was mistaken in treating S-predicates as constituting a separate category over and above C-predicates and R-predicates even though it was correct in noting their peculiar status. Acknowledging the ambiguity of *every* S-predicate makes it possible to accommodate all properties of human beings within a rigorous dualistic schema of categories.

Table 1 visibly links our interpretation of his conception of the mind–body divide with the Aristotelian tradition; we see his alterations to these concepts as straightforward modifications to that tradition. In this respect, it differs sharply from the mind–body classification presented by the Legend. That categorization fails to mesh with the tradition in two important ways. First, the treatment of S-predicates is non-uniform: some (e.g., 'is walking') are excluded from the realm of the mental, others (e.g., 'sees light' or 'feels pain') are allocated unambiguously to the mental; this is what removes the possibility for making sense of the symmetry between seeing and walking in passage (1). Second, a range of traditional R-predicates are also excluded from the realm of the mental, namely predicates ascribing states of moral character (e.g., 'is courageous', 'is cowardly'). In fact, these are excluded completely from the Legend's categorization of properties of persons. This is what removes the possibility of making sense of his denial that animals have minds.

The ambiguity of 'sensitive predicates'

We have contended that Descartes argued for a distinction between two senses of each S-predicate, what we have called the animal sense and the rational sense. We have also described his project as 'disambiguating S-predicates'. But what right have we to speak here of '*ambiguity*'? Do S-predicates like 'sees light' or 'is walking' satisfy the criteria for calling an expression 'ambiguous'?

With one crucial proviso, we argue that these scruples are out of place. Working within the same Aristotelian framework, the Port-Royalists provide a clear precedent for the thesis that S-predicates are properly speaking 'ambiguous' or 'equivocal'.[51] They apparently took this doctrine from Descartes, and they rightly

50 Descartes sometimes marked the first sense of these ambiguous expressions by the term 'corporeal' or 'animal', resulting in phrases that must from the point of view of the Cartesian Legend look like monsters: 'corporeal imagination' (e.g., AT X: 414–15; CSM I: 42), 'corporeal memory' (e.g., AT X: 416, CSM I: 43; cf. AT III: 143, CSMK III: 151), 'animal joy' (*Principles* IV.190; CSM I: 281), etc., and he even asserted that the 'brutes' had a 'corporeal soul' (AT VII: 426; CSM II: 288)! The word 'idea' likewise exhibited a partially parallel ambiguity: in one sense it was clearly equivalent to 'perception' or 'thought' (in this sense ideas are what are clearly and distinctly perceived); in another it referred to the 'figures' 'which are traced in the [animal] spirits on the surface of the [pineal] gland' in the mechanical process of sense-perception (AT XI: 176; CSM I: 106).

51 For example, three senses of '*sens*' and '*sentimens*' ('sense' and 'sensation') are carefully distinguished, and the phrase 'deceived by the senses' is argued to be a form of nonsense generated by conflating these senses (*PRL* I.xi).

saw that the thesis of the systematic ambiguity of S-predicates is an *essential* component of his dualism.[52]

What then are his reasons for concluding that S-predicates are ambiguous? We drew attention to them in clarifying the two distinct senses of 'seeing light'. Descartes described two uses of this expression which meet the standard Aristotelian criteria for ambiguity as laid out in standard arguments for distinguishing two senses of the adjective 'light': viz. light in colour and light in weight.[53] (In fact it would be more strictly analogous to the case for distinguishing two senses of the term 'sharp' ('*oxus*'), that is as applied to a knife-blade and as applied to a note sounded on a lyre, because the term 'sharp' in these two senses is necessarily predicated of different kinds of subjects, just as Descartes' two senses of *sentire*-words are necessarily predicated of different kinds of subjects, namely animals or bodies and rational souls.) In each case, the two senses are logically independent of each other: the fact that the predicate is correctly applied to something in one sense doesn't entail that it is correctly applicable in the other sense. Animals and human reflex actions – actions performed when 'our mind is elsewhere' (AT I: 413; CSMK III: 62) – show, for example, that 'see$_1$ light' doesn't entail 'see$_2$ light', while hallucination (or deception by the senses) shows that 'see$_2$ light' doesn't entail 'see$_1$ light'.

Descartes thought that this case for the ambiguity of the predicate 'to see light' could be duplicated for every S-predicate.[54] We must bear in mind that the ambiguity of predicates falling within the genus '*sentire*' ('sense-perception') embraces not just 'hearing sound', 'feeling heat', 'tasting saltiness', etc., but also predicates connected with the two internal senses, such as 'feeling pain', 'feeling hungry', 'feeling angry', 'feeling afraid', etc. Parallel arguments hold for the wide range of predicates falling within the genus '*imaginari*', such as 'remembering', 'desiring', 'expecting', etc. Every such predicate has an animal sense and a contrasting rational sense. Finally, the same point holds of all predicates of movement/action. The schema for this argument is presented for the verb 'to walk' in passage (1). The ambiguity of all such predicates of 'locomotion' generates unfamiliar complexity in reconstructing Descartes' conception of voluntary action.

In all these cases, he usually made use of an idiom that he understood

52 But they had an imperfect understanding of it, as is evident from their classifying 'feeling pain' as designating something unambiguously mental (*PRL* I.ix).

53 Aristotle, *Topica* I.15.

54 To make this doctrine precise, we might need to invent some further refinements; or perhaps to rediscover some of the more sophisticated elements in the tradition of Aristotelian psychology. For instance, the most natural reading of the sentence '*x* saw (noticed) the Rembrandt hanging in the hall' might be to attribute a property that an animal could not exhibit even though the main verb 'see' is a paradigm of something expressing a form of sentience. It would be plausible for an Aristotelian to exclude this from the range of the 'functions of the sensitive soul', hence from the class of S-predicates. This would be analogous to the distinction drawn by Aquinas between human action driven by animal desires (thirst, hunger, lust) and voluntary action in pursuit of long-term, complex goals (e.g., desire to secure the salvation of one's soul); the first form of desire is a 'sensitive function', the second can only be an operation of the rational soul. We cannot pursue these complex issues here.

unambiguously to pick out the rational sense of the corresponding S-predicate: namely 'perception of . . .', 'sensation of . . .', or '*conscientia* of . . .'. This is now easy to overlook or to misconstrue. For instance, the rational sense of the S-predicate 'feel pain' is often expressed by the R-predicate 'have the sensation of pain' or 'have the perception of pain'; and the rational sense of the S-predicate 'walk' is expressed by the R-predicate 'have *conscientia* of walking' (cf. passage (1)). As a consequence, when Descartes denies that animals have the sensation of pain, he would *not* accept as correct the paraphrase 'Animals do not feel pain' (see also pp. 128–9).

Three points about this doctrine are noteworthy:

1 Each S-predicate has two meanings,[55] one standing for a property of the body (which could be expressed by a C-predicate), the other for a property of the rational soul (which could be expressed by an R-predicate). Consequently, Descartes' view is clearly that none of them can be classified as *unambiguously* a 'psychological concept' or 'mentalistic predicate', not even 'feeling pain' and 'feeling joy'.[56] Equally, none of them is unambiguously a 'bodily predicate', not even 'is walking' or 'is breathing'.
2 The two senses of each S-predicate enjoy, as it were, parity of esteem.[57] Each is a genuine property of certain substances. In the animal sense, each predicate designates a mode of extension; in the rational sense, a mode of thinking. It would be a serious misunderstanding to claim, for instance, that a dog only goes through the motions of feeling pain or seeing light, or that 'strictly speaking'

55 Below (pp. 173–6) we suggest that each S-predicate has a 'human' sense, in some sense 'in addition' to an 'animal' and a purely 'rational' sense. To decide whether this was a *third* sense of these predicates (i.e. that they were trebly ambiguous) would require both a more precise delineation of criteria for ambiguity than it would be pointful to provide here, and a more definite characterization of the conceptual relations between the human, rational, and animal senses than Descartes himself provided.

56 Cottingham (1978a: 558) claims that 'Descartes is in a philosophical mess' when he speaks of '*laetitia animalis*' ('animal joy'), because he denies that animals have minds, but '*laetitia*' ('joy') is 'an inescapably "mental" predicate' (p. 559). This is precisely wrong: there is a case for saying that 'joy' (at least in so far as it is linked to the second internal sense) is unambiguously a *corporeal* predicate, and 'feeling joy' is *not, unambiguously*, a 'mental' predicate. There is a further difficulty with emotion-words that sometimes generates misunderstanding: if we take the word 'passion' to mean 'emotion', hence to cover feeling anger and joy, then animals have passions in one sense of these terms. If we take it to mean 'passions of the soul', then clearly they do not.

57 There is a real danger of misunderstanding the *spirit* of Descartes' mechanistic view of animal behaviour, a misunderstanding which is apparent in many glosses of his treatment of *sentire*-words. His aim is often taken to be metaphysical and reductive: 'nothing but clockwork', 'going through the motions of reacting to stimuli' (cf. Grene 1985: 51: 'Sensing is either just motion, so is non-sentient, or it is thought', so that the *Bête-Machine* Doctrine is incompatible with the ascription of sentience to animals). But surely it is intended to be scientific and explanatory (i.e. non-reductive). In his view, animals are truly (and strictly speaking) 'sentient', but this doesn't eliminate the possibility of giving a complete explanation of their reactive behaviour in terms of the operation of physical mechanisms. (Gaukroger emphasizes that Descartes did not eliminate 'the traditional functions of the organic soul', but rather sought to explain or describe them in mechanistic terms (1995: 167). He wanted to explain 'animal cognition', not to explain it away (278–9).) There is a parallel point about his treatment of 'secondary qualities'. It is misrepresented when reformulated as a metaphysical doctrine (see pp. 129–34).

only a person feels pain or sees light. The truth is that a dog *really* feels_1 pain or sees_1 light, but that it *cannot* feel_2 pain or see_2 light – just as the knife-blade *really is* sharp in one sense, and *cannot* be sharp in the other (the sense in which a note sounded on a lyre can be sharp).

3 The two senses of each S-predicate are given separate explanations. In each case, the animal sense is clarified in terms of bodily structure and movement; Descartes held, in effect, that there are 'behavioural criteria' for applying any S-predicate in the animal sense. The rational sense of each predicate is explained on the basis of its animal sense according to a uniform pattern: '$x\ \phi_2$' means 'x thinks or judges that he ϕ_1'. There is no question here of requiring (or even admitting) any explanation of the rational sense of any S-predicate by some 'private ostensive definition'. On the contrary, all of these modes of thinking must be differentiated from each other in terms of the propositional content of what is thought, and the explanations of each of them must make this explicit. It is equally noteworthy that the 'restricted' (or rational) sense of any S-predicate is definitely *not* 'prior logically and epistemologically' to its animal sense. Rather, understanding its explanation presupposes an understanding of the corresponding animal sense of the same predicate.

Although S-predicates are, on Descartes' view, ambiguous according to the traditional (Aristotelian) criteria for judging ambiguity, they are not commonly reckoned to be equivocal even by competent speakers of Latin, French, or English. In this one important respect they differ from the usual paradigms of lexical ambiguity, and this needs to be considered carefully. But we should note first that Descartes was well aware of the fact that the ambiguities of S-predicates are generally unrecognized, had a clear explanation for this fact, and also (as we will see) held it to be very important. Our confusion is *deeply* entrenched in our thinking and *completely* disguised in ordinary speech.[58] As the Port-Royalists noted, 'when an equivocal name signifies two things which have no relation to each other', it is extremely unlikely that 'it can become the cause of any error, as no one with any common sense would be deceived by the ambiguity of the word *ram*, which signifies an animal, and a sign of the zodiac' (*PRL* I.11).[59] But the two meanings of 'is seeing' or 'is walking' do 'have relations to each other'. In each case the 'mental' meaning is a judgement to the effect that the state of affairs referred to in the 'bodily' meaning obtains. And thanks to our God-ordained

58 AT I: 81; CSMK III: 13: 'almost all our words have confused meanings, and men's minds are so accustomed to them that there is hardly anything which they can perfectly understand'.

59 They contrast this with the multiple ambiguity of the word 'soul', which they identified as a major source of confusion and fallacious reasoning (*PRL* I.xi). Their account adheres to Descartes' principle that 'the term "soul" is ambiguous as used of animals and of human beings' (AT III: 370; CSMK III: 181). He offered an explanation of the origin of this ambiguity: 'primitive man probably did not distinguish between, on the one hand, the principle by which we are nourished and grow and accomplish without any thought all the other operations which we have in common with the brutes, and, on the other hand, the principle by virtue of which we think. He therefore used the single term "soul" to apply to both' (AT VII: 356; CSM II: 246).

Nature (see pp. 168ff.), the truth or falsity of the judgements in each of these pairs are generally linked. (For example, *normally*, whenever it is true that I see_2 light (= I judge that I see_1 light), it is also true that I see_1 light, etc.) Failing to distinguish these two meanings is perfectly understandable, and indeed most people never do make the distinction, as this would contribute nothing to their welfare (see pp. 178–83). As a result, they habitually 'fail to distinguish' between mind and body, two substances that are really distinct.

But what are we to make of an 'ambiguity' which goes generally unrecognized? We have here an instance of a hidden ambiguity which it seems to be the *métier* of philosophers to discover. Others have revealed hitherto unnoticed equivocations in terms such as 'true' and 'false', 'see', 'cause', 'solid', 'is', 'meaning', 'proposition', 'know', 'length', and 'exist'. The alleged ambiguities in such expressions are taken to be none the less real for requiring skill, intelligence, and logical sophistication to discern. On the contrary, the worth of these disambiguations is thought to be proportional to the degree that common sense must be supplemented by rigorous arguments employing sophisticated tools of logical analysis. High technology, whether in the form of second intentions, quantification theory, or possible worlds, is supposed to make the conclusions of these arguments unassailable. However, it is characteristic of the verdict of any 'philosophical analysis' that it be essentially *contestable*. (This applies just as directly to Frege, Tarski, Quine, Kripke, Davidson, et al. as it does to Descartes.)

Twentieth-century philosophers don't contest Descartes' thesis that S-predicates are ambiguous for the simple reason that they are blind to it. But they do commonly attack his related thesis that personal pronouns, in particular the pronoun 'I', have two distinct meanings.[60] Descartes would undoubtedly have accused such philosophers of allowing themselves to be misled by ordinary speech into confusing two things which are in reality distinct (indeed 'really distinct'); they would fall among 'those who have not done their philosophizing in an orderly way':

> Although they may have put the certainty of their own existence before that of anything else, they failed to realize that they should have taken 'themselves' in this context to mean their minds alone. They were inclined instead to take 'themselves' to mean only their bodies. . .
>
> (*Principles* I.12; CSM I: 196)

Strawson's 'refutation' of Descartes seems a clear case of the fallacy of *ignoratio elenchi*.

The doctrine of the systematic ambiguity of S-predicates and the thesis of the ambiguity of personal pronouns (and proper names of persons) are strictly correlative. Neither seems amenable to being settled by collecting data about the

60 For example, Strawson castigates what he calls the 'Cartesian *error*' of seeing '"I" or "Smith" as suffering from type-ambiguity' (1959: 105, italics added). Descartes would no doubt castigate Strawson as making the error of supposing that 'he is one and the same being who thinks and who moves from place to place' (AT VII: 423; CSM II: 285)!

utterances of the English-speaking (or French- or Latin-speaking) peoples, by cataloguing linguistic or grammatical facts. (Both disputants are *agreed* about what the prevailing speech-patterns are.) Still less can it be appropriately addressed by asking native speakers whether or not they would classify the disputed predicates as 'ambiguous'. From Descartes' point of view, the fact that we don't ordinarily notice the ambiguities is news from nowhere: it is an exemplary instance of 'bad intellectual habits', which began in 'our childhood [when] the mind was so immersed in the body that although there was much that it perceived clearly, it never perceived anything distinctly' (*Principles* I.47, CSM I: 208; cf. *Principles* I.71, CSM I: 218–19).

The aims of disambiguation

Finally, we need to clarify Descartes' motivation for developing the doctrine of the systematic ambiguity of S-predicates. Two matters are relatively specific and easy to grasp; others may be more diffuse and speculative.

His analysis of S-predicates seems to be immediately connected with improvements to the tradition of Aristotelian psychology, and thereby to other important aspects of his metaphysico-scientific ambitions. (1) One immediate aim is to *narrow* the application of the term 'rational soul' so that it coincides with the traditional application of the term 'mind'. In other words, he wished to limit the functions of the rational soul to intellect and volition (see, e.g., AT III: 371; CSMK III: 182), thus excluding its performance of the 'vegetative' and 'sensitive' functions in human beings. (2) A second clear aim is to *extend* the range of mechanical explanation in order to embrace the whole list of properties traditionally applied to living things (including both animals and human bodies), i.e. what the tradition identified as the vegetative and sensitive functions (life, nutrition, growth, movement, sensation, sense-perception, memory, Imagination, and so on). To explain these functions mechanically is to obviate the need to talk of vegetative and sensitive *souls*.[61] In that sense, he could be seen as *expanding* the list of functions which the body ('unaided' by any soul) could perform.[62] This second goal is the guiding thought of the *Treatise on Man*:

> In order to explain these functions . . . it is not necessary to conceive of this machine [sc. the human body without a rational soul] as having any

61 This point holds in as much as the vegetative and sensitive souls were entities that belonged exclusively to Aristotelian biology. They were meant to explain functions of plants and animals that would otherwise be inexplicable. A parallel argument could not be effective against Descartes' notion of the rational soul. This concept is essentially tied to the concept of a moral agent, and that concept could not be made redundant by scientific advances in physiology, psychology, etc. (see pp. 202–4).

62 Our interpretation thus inverts the Legend's image of Descartes' conception of the mind–body divide. The Legend sees him as *extending* the scope of the mental (by reference to his scholastic predecessors) and *narrowing* the range of the bodily. No plausible motivation is offered for this innovation, presumably because it is seen by the Legend as his coming to recognize the truth of the matter. (As if only mistakes call for explanation!)

> vegetative or sensitive soul or other principle of movement and life, apart from its blood and its [animal] spirits, which are agitated by the heat of the fire burning continuously in its heart – a fire which has the same nature as all the fires that occur in inanimate bodies.
>
> (AT XI: 202; CSM I: 108)

The upshot of these two innovations was the demonstration that there was no longer any need to use the word 'soul' in any sense other than 'rational soul' (cf. AT VIIIB: 347, CSM I: 296; AT III: 370–1, CSMK III: 181–2). 'Mind' thus became equivalent to 'soul' (i.e. 'rational soul'), and mind and body became wholly distinct, the one being immaterial and unextended, the other being material and extended (hence mechanically explicable).

These results served two broader aims: (3) to demonstrate the possibility that the rational soul was immortal (since it was now shown to be really distinct from and hence separable from the human body) and (4) to license absolute freedom of scientific enquiry, confident that discoveries in mechanics could not overturn central theological precepts.[63]

Descartes' concern with S-predicates is linked to his scientific programme of subsuming biology and medicine within a comprehensive system of mechanics. His doctrine that these predicates are ambiguous has an equally direct philosophical motivation. He wished to exploit the familiar strategy of accusing his opponents of committing fallacies of equivocation, and nothing but exposing an ambiguity can serve this purpose.[64]

He was particularly keen to deploy this technique against empiricists, whom he regarded as the principal obstacle to the pursuit of science on rational principles. The disambiguation in passage (3), for example, is clearly aimed at them. For it is characteristic of empiricism to hold that what I have acquired 'either from the senses or through the senses' is 'most true' (AT VII: 18; CSM II: 12). This general prejudice, in Descartes' view, is the result of *confusing* (failing to distinguish) two meanings of expressions referring to sense-perception. In *one* of these meanings, what I have acquired through the senses is indeed 'most true'. I cannot, for instance, be mistaken in judging that I see_2 light (i.e. that I judge or have just judged that I see_1 light). But in this sense of '*sentire*', all sense-based judgements

63 Descartes explained this point to a Jesuit: 'the main reason why your Colleges take great care to reject all sorts of innovations in philosophical matters is their fear that these innovations may bring about some change in theology as well. That is why I want especially to point out that you have nothing to fear on this score so far as my own innovations are concerned . . . the views which, from my reflection on natural causes, seemed to me most true in physics were always those which are the most compatible with the mysteries of religion' (AT I: 455–6; CSMK III: 75).

64 Until this century, the primary critical method of philosophers was seen as revealing *fallacies* on the part of other philosophers; lists of fallacies formed an important part of most standard logic textbooks. The various fallacies listed in textbooks of Aristotelian logic provide, as it were, the normal forms of philosophical blunders. (Modern analytic philosophers have discarded some traditional fallacies, e.g., the fallacy of the undistributed middle, and introduced novel ones, e.g., fallacies of quantifier inversion or of treating existence as a predicate, and 'category-mistakes' à la Ryle.) What counts as a fallacy may be as contestable as what counts as ambiguous.

are reports of *cognitions* (viz. of having particular thoughts), and their truth is independent of the senses. In the *other* sense of '*sentire*', sense-based judgements (e.g., 'I see$_1$ light') are not 'most true'; on the contrary, they are frequently mistaken and can even, as a body, be called into doubt 'for powerful and well thought-out reasons' (AT VII: 21; CSM II: 15). The general justification of empiricism is an argument conflating these two distinct ideas. The indubitability distinctive of judgements making use of '*sentire*' in the restricted sense is illegitimately transferred to judgements recording instances of animal sentience. Consequently, the argument needed to support the empiricist programme of treating reports of animal sentience as the foundations of knowledge can, in this way, be exposed as a paradigm of the fallacy of equivocation (QED!).

Descartes might have brought the very same charge against twentieth-century Anglo-American philosophers who classify feeling pain, seeing light, feeling warmth, feeling angry, etc. as 'states of consciousness'. Descartes would have seen this concept of 'consciousness' as a *paradigmatically* 'confused idea' for two linked reasons.

First, it supposes that there is a single concept of 'seeing light' or 'feeling pain' which applies both to animals and to human beings, *and* which counts as an instance of thinking (*cogitare*). This is precisely the point that he challenged. In his view these expressions are (*must* be) *ambiguous*: there is *one* sense in which they apply both to animals and human beings and *another*, entirely different, sense in which they count as modes of thinking. The idea of consciousness current in philosophy of mind nonchalantly conflates what he took such pains to distinguish. Accepting it begs the question against him.

Second, many modern philosophers are inclined to say that there are two sorts of *criteria* for sentience: for example, for saying of someone that he feels a pain in his foot. On the one hand, you look at his 'non-verbal behaviour': he withdraws his foot from the source of the injury, he limps, he rubs the foot, and so on. On the other hand, you attend to his utterances (his 'verbal behaviour'): he *says* 'My foot hurts' or 'I've got a terrible stabbing pain in my left foot', and he thereby expresses a thought. These are treated as parallel (or comparable) forms of human behaviour in respect of being cited as alternative criteria for *the same thing*, namely another's having a pain in his foot.

But, in Descartes' view, these two sets of criteria are themselves of wholly different kinds; the first are animal actions, the second are rational voluntary actions (viz. speech). What are now taken to be alternative criteria for applying one and the same concept (e.g., 'feeling pain'), he treated as criteria for applying two different concepts. No doubt he would have deplored the modern philosophical practice of using the term 'behaviour' for both animal behaviour and for human speech. Descartes repeatedly cautioned us against the danger of confusing these two things. '[W]e must not confuse speech with the natural movements which express passions and which can be imitated by machines as well as by animals' (AT VI: 58, CSM I: 141; cf. AT V: 344–5, CSMK III: 374). The upshot of this common confusion is a serious misunderstanding: 'after the error of those who deny God, . . . there is *none* that leads weak minds further from the straight path of virtue than that of imagining that the souls of the beasts are of the same nature as ours' (AT VI: 59; CSM I: 141, italics added).[65] Here as elsewhere, he thought, the path to vice runs through error.

The technique of disambiguating S-predicates is also part of a more general and less polemical programme of philosophical therapy. In his view, most people in ordinary life fail to distinguish between animal and rational sentience. This confusion is liable to lead us into error, not only in theoretical reasoning, but also in practical deliberation. Clear thinking is important for virtuous conduct and human welfare. Being of this persuasion, Descartes took upon himself the moral mission of trying to persuade everyone, 'once in the course of our life' (*Principles* I.1, CSM I: 193; cf. AT VII: 17, CSM II: 12) to make a sustained effort to break bad intellectual habits. In this way, bringing home to us the ambiguity of S-predicates is integral to the overarching therapeutic purpose of his philosophizing.

Bodies as sentient machines[66]

The mind is the rational soul. The body can be characterized as possessing just those 'functions' in respect of which 'animals without reason may be said to resemble us'. There are two important aspects of this analogy. First, in his view, both the human body and non-human animals can be regarded as *machines*. This claim amounts to the thesis that all of their behaviour can be completely explained 'mechanically' (although this term too stands in need of exploration). Thus it implies that animals lack free will. Second, both the human body and non-human animals are *sentient*. (The concept of the 'sentient (or sensitive) body' was a commonplace in Descartes' time. Like the concept of the internal senses (see pp. 126–7) it has been so thoroughly lost today as to be virtually invisible.)[67] This point

65 Cf. Malebranche: the 'prejudice that beasts have a soul' 'is very dangerous in view of its consequences' (*Recherche* 353). Opponents of the *Bête-Machine* Doctrine argued the opposite, as ridiculed by Malebranche here: 'Let a Man but say in Company, with an Air of Gravity . . . *Really, the Cartesians are strange people; They maintain, That Beasts have no Soul. I am afraid in a little time they will say as much of Man*: And this will be enough to persuade a great many that this is a dangerous Opinion' (quoted in Gunderson 1964: 221).

66 A version of this subsection was presented under the title 'Descartes' Beastly Machines' at the Universities of St Andrews, Stirling, and Edinburgh in November 1994. We are grateful for the constructive comments we received on these occasions.

67 Galileo's claim that 'these tastes, odours, colours, etc. . . . are nothing but mere names for something which resides exclusively in our *sensitive body*', so that 'if the *living, sensing body* were removed, nothing would remain . . . but an empty name' (italics added; quoted in Hacker 1987: 3, 6) tends to be read by twentieth-century Anglo-American philosophers as the claim that tastes and colours are *in the mind*. E.g., Hacker sees Galileo's claim that sensible qualities are subjective (p. 7) as the origin of the idea that they are the offspring of the mind (pp. 2–3).

together with the first implies that sentience is mechanically explicable. We pursue these implications in turn.[68]

Mechanical explanation and free will

Some mundane uses of the word 'mechanical' (shared with seventeenth-century speakers) help at least to apprehend the thrust of the *Bête-Machine* Doctrine. Consider the idioms of 'playing the piano mechanically', 'reacting mechanically to another's suggestion', and 'thinking mechanically about behaviourism in writing an examination answer'. Here 'mechanical' is linked with such terms as 'automatic', 'habitual', 'regular', 'predictable', 'uniform', 'pedestrian', and so on (and contrasted with the terms 'intelligent', 'plastic', 'spontaneous', 'imaginative', etc.). Part of Descartes' contention that animals could be seen as machines is the simple and unscandalous claim that their behaviour was regular and that it lacked the sort of plasticity and spontaneity that characterizes the behaviour of human beings who are concentrating on the execution of demanding tasks, exploring different ways of achieving some result, or acting purposefully in pursuit of long-term goals. The human body could also be seen as a machine in respect of functions that don't involve the operations of the rational soul, paradigmatically in acting from reflex (e.g., sticking your hands out to break your fall when you trip unexpectedly) or in carrying out learned routines (e.g., in eating or tying a shoelace).

In this connection, Descartes noted that if there were machines which

> bore a resemblance to our bodies and imitated our actions as closely as possible for all practical purposes, we should still have two very certain means of recognizing that they were not real men. The first is that they could never use words, or put together other signs, as we do in order to declare our thoughts to others . . . . Secondly, even though such machines might do some things as well as we do them, or perhaps even better, they would inevitably fail in others, which would reveal that they were acting not through understanding but only from the disposition of their organs.
>
> (AT VI: 56–7, CSM I: 139–40; cf. AT IV: 573, CSMK III: 302–3)

This might be thought to suggest that there are movements which a body not united with a soul (likewise an animal) *could not* make. It seems clear that Descartes neither held nor could have held that view. On the contrary, he suggested that *any* human movement can be duplicated in principle by an animal or a machine.

68 There are large issues in this area about positive connections between sentience (in particular, susceptibility to pain) and morality, which cannot be explored here. We are today inclined to think that inflicting pain is (*prima facie*) intrinsically wrong, whereas it is not obvious that Descartes held this view. But a further aspect is the idea (explicit in some theodicies) that pain is punishment for moral wrongdoing. Malebranche used this to demonstrate that animals don't feel pain, since 'this would mean that under an infinitely just and omnipotent God, an innocent creature would suffer pain, which is a penalty and punishment for some sin' (*Recherche* 323).

In fact, many or most of them can be performed more accurately and more reliably by machines, just as 'a clock, consisting only of wheels and springs, can count hours and measure time more accurately than we can with all our wisdom' (AT VI: 59; CSM I: 141). It is possible to 'conceive of a machine so constructed that it utters words, and even utters words which correspond to bodily actions causing a change in its organs (e.g., if you touch it in one spot it asks what you want of it, if you touch it in another it cries out that you are hurting it, and so on)' (AT VI: 56; CSM I: 140). What is explicitly claimed to distinguish human movements from animal movements here is their global organization and plasticity. Hence one might see this passage as turning on a quantifier-shift: *any* human movement can be performed by a machine, but no machine can perform *every* human movement.[69] But even this claim cannot be interpreted as an infallible *empirical* test for distinguishing human beings from mere machines. It cannot be *logically* impossible for a machine to pass the 'Turing test'. There can be no limit to the complexity of a machine which could be created by God, hence the claim *cannot* be that it is logically impossible for God to make a machine capable of performing every movement that human beings can make.[70] What is absolutely ruled out is that a machine could 'declare its thoughts to others' or 'act through understanding'. (The monkeys in the basement of the British Museum could type out all the words of Shakespeare's sonnets. They could not thereby *write sonnets*, i.e. express thoughts.) A machine could utter words, but it could not *speak*.[71]

We are still inclined to contrast 'mechanical behaviour' with actions which exhibit attention, intelligence, and flexibility. But in Descartes' scheme, the term 'mechanical' is clearly contrasted just as directly with 'free, morally responsible and virtuous (or vicious)' as it is with 'intelligent and plastic'.[72] (Thus a machine could not make a promise, issue a legal verdict, or make a generous donation to charity.) This last point throws some unexpected light on his conception of 'modes of thinking'. He held the view that there is an opposition between mechanical explicability and free will,[73] and that talk about volition or free will is *moral* talk. 'The supreme perfection of man is that he acts freely or voluntarily, and it is this

69 Roughly this point is stressed by Gunderson 1964.

70 It is here asserted to be '*morally* impossible', and there is much to be said about this important locution (see pp. 183–8). We might speculate that the point *here* is that God, being benevolent, would not create machines which passed the Turing test, since that would make moral life impossible.

71 Our principal criticism of Leiber's otherwise excellent article (1988) is that he (likewise Gunderson 1964) runs together 'moral impossibility' and 'logical impossibility'. It is morally impossible that a machine could pass muster as a 'speaker'; but it is logically impossible that it could *speak*. There is no logically *infallible* empirical test of whether a creature is using language.

72 In the *Oxford English Dictionary*, 'machine' is contrasted with 'free, voluntary, and conscious'.

73 Modern discussions of 'free will vs. determinism' take place firmly in the framework of the Two-Worlds view, a framework established by Hume. It is doubtful that they can be fruitfully carried over without remainder to Descartes' doctrine of freedom, although attempts are periodically made either to assert or to deny that Descartes was an indeterminist. Also required is a more sensitive treatment of *Descartes*' conception of 'cause' than is usually given; Vere Chappell's discussion is good in this respect ('Descartes' Compatibilism', in Cottingham 1994).

which makes him deserve praise or blame'; consequently, it makes no sense to 'praise automatons for accurately producing all the movements they were designed to perform, because the production of these movements occurs necessarily' (*Principles* I.37; CSM I: 205). Mechanism excludes moral responsibility. Conversely, all of the voluntary actions for which the agent is *morally responsible* cannot (in principle) be mechanically explicable. They must be manifestations of the agent's *freedom*, and they are operations of the soul of which he must be *conscius*. Moral agency excludes mechanism. The functions of the body which *do* depend on the operations of the rational soul are all the bodily actions for which persons can be praised or blamed.

Descartes' concern with freedom and responsibility puts a wholly unfamiliar face on his 'notorious' doctrine that animals are machines. Most commentators recognize this as denying intelligence to animals, and many object just as strongly to his denial of *sapience* to animals as they do to his (alleged) denial of *sentience*. Some object on the grounds of 'ordinary usage', others on the basis of recent research on bonobo chimpanzees. It is now widely accepted as a *fact* that higher animals do have some (perhaps limited) capacity to *think*.[74] But for Descartes, to assert that animals can be viewed as machines or automata, that all their movements are mechanically explicable, is first and foremost to say that they do not have free will.[75] (It follows that they cannot think, since thinking is inseparable from the capacity to make judgements and judging is an operation of the will). To say that they do not have free will is to assert that, just like (lifeless) automata (*Principles* I.37; CSM: I 205), they cannot be praised or blamed for what they do. Indeed the Cartesian rational soul is what is supposed to be immortal, and whose fate in the afterlife depends on its moral character. The claim that animals do not think thus amounts to the claim that they do not have *immortal souls* – 'if they thought as we do, they would have an immortal soul like us. This is unlikely, because there is no reason to believe it of some animals without believing it of all, and many of them such as oysters and sponges are too imperfect for this to be credible' (AT IV: 576, CSMK III: 304; cf. AT V: 277–8, CSMK III: 366).[76]

74 We have had many lively interchanges with Brian Farrell on this point.

75 'As for animals that lack reason it is obvious that they are not free, since they do not have [the real and] positive power to determine themselves; what they have is a pure negation, namely the power of not being forced or constrained' (AT IV: 117; CSMK III: 234). They may have (or lack) the power to act in accord with their (animal) desires, i.e. to act$_1$ as they desire$_1$. But they can't act in accord with rational volitions, i.e. they necessarily lack the power to act$_2$ as they desire$_2$. Descartes here distinguished two concepts of freedom that are undoubtedly 'commonly confused'.

76 Note: 'unlikely'. Descartes would have willingly embraced Loeb's 'objection' that 'if animals have minds, his conclusions about immortality will apply equally to them' (1981: 114). What is metaphysically certain is not that animals do not think, but that the mind is distinct from the body: 'As for dogs and apes, even were I to concede that they have thought, it would not in any way follow from this that the human mind is not distinct from the body; the conclusion would rather be that in other animals, too, the mind is distinct from the body' (AT VII: 426; CSM II: 287): Gunderson (1964: 219) recognizes this.

On Descartes' view, *pace* Williams (1978: 287), the fact that 'the idea of an animal soul would encourage the absurd idea of animal immortality' is not 'external' to the fact that animals do not engage in 'conceptual thought'.

Descartes suggested that most people who insist that animals think can't really believe what they say. If you really took seriously the idea that animals could *think*, you would have to accord them all the moral rights and duties that are inseparable from having a rational soul.[77] You would be guilty of *murder* in killing a pig to eat. You would have a moral obligation to look after your pets' moral and religious education.[78] And so on. But your doing any of these things wouldn't be merely quixotic; you would clearly fall into a notorious form of heresy.[79] Hence, Descartes concluded, 'my opinion is not so much cruel to animals as indulgent to human beings . . . since it absolves them from the suspicion of *crime* [i.e. moral turpitude] when they eat or kill animals' (AT V: 279; CSMK III: 366, italics added).

Mechanical explanation and sentience

The second important implication of the *Bête-Machine* Doctrine is *not* that animals lack sentience (any more than the human body does!), but rather that sentience is mechanically explicable.[80] The *Treatise on Man* explicitly set out to demonstrate that all of the functions which were traditionally taken to require a vegetative or sensitive soul (life, nutrition, growth, movement, sensation, sense-perception, memory, Imagination) could be performed by an 'organic machine'. Fully to make sense of Descartes' doctrine, we need to understand his conception of a machine and of 'mechanical explanation'. Only then will we be in a position to grasp the claim that the 'sensitive functions' are mechanically explicable, i.e. to give some content to the animal or bodily sense of the ambiguous terms 'seeing', 'feeling', 'walking', etc.

It is clear that both the concept of a machine and the 'sociology' of machines have altered vastly since the seventeenth century. We need to recapture both aspects of the background to Descartes' use of the term 'machine'.

First and foremost, the class of objects which were then called 'machines' is very different in extension and in intension from the class of things so-called in the twentieth century. Many of these differences are entirely predictable: most of the objects to which we today apply the term 'machine' did not even exist then (or lacked any close analogues). Other differences may be surprising. Modern usage of 'machine' is fairly complicated and subject to many restrictions. We don't now apply the term 'machine' to all artificial devices designed for a

77 This implication is clearly debatable. Montaigne certainly separated these two issues in contending that animals do have the capacity to think.

78 There are those, of course, who bury their dead pets in pet cemeteries and those who publish obituaries of their dogs, horses, etc. But what follows from this? They may link this behaviour to some form of belief in animals' immortal souls, but probably not to any belief about their pets being rational moral agents.

79 Various versions of this heresy cropped up repeatedly among various communities in sixteenth- and seventeenth-century Europe. It was a significant social phenomenon, not fanciful hypothesis (cf. K. V. Thomas, *Religion and the Decline of Magic*, London: Weidenfeld & Nicolson, 1971).

80 Since consciousness is standardly seen as including sentience, the suggestion that the force of the *Bête-Machine* Doctrine was to deny consciousness to animals is thus 180 degrees off course.

particular purpose. We tend to contrast machines with engines, power tools, motors, generators, dynamos, boilers, and gadgets. We tend to limit 'machine' to devices that work by wires and cogs, pistons and gear-trains, i.e. 'mechanically' as opposed to pneumatically, hydraulically, or electrically; hence we exclude jacks working on Pascal's principle and telephones (but not computers!). And we tend to demand that machines must have certain kinds of outputs or products, not (usually) information, heat, electricity, etc., but motion or harnessable mechanical energy or medium-sized dry-goods.[81]

By contrast, seventeenth-century usage of the term 'machine' was far freer. Then vehicles, especially horse-drawn coaches and carts, and sometimes even sailing ships, were standard examples of 'machines'.[82] (In the same spirit, talk of 'flying machines' was common not long ago, and even today automobiles are referred to jocularly as 'machines', or more formally and somewhat archaically as 'motors'; none the less we don't tend to call modern aeroplanes machines, and certainly do not apply this word to horse-drawn coaches or sail-powered yachts.) More generally, the term 'machine' was applied in seventeenth-century usage to almost any human artefact that manifestly worked on 'mechanical principles'. For example, in response to Huygens' 'request for something on mechanics', Descartes wrote 'An account of the *machines* by means of which a small force can be used to lift heavy weights', which discusses pulleys, inclined planes, wedges, cog-wheels, screws and levers (AT I: 435ff.; CSMK III: 66ff., italics added).[83] 'Machine' covered mechanical clocks and astrolabes (despite absence of 'output'), the hydraulically operated garden statuary of Italianate water-grottoes (despite the absence of gear-trains and mechanical input), various forms of siege-engines and theatrical equipment, wind-driven or water-powered mills, etc. There was in his time nothing unnatural or strained about Descartes' having taken mechanical clocks and moving automata of Neptune or Diana as his paradigms of 'machines'.

On the other hand, there is something of great interest in the particular paradigms that he chose. This relates to the evolving 'sociology' of machines. The role and status of machines in everyday life in the seventeenth century was very different from their place today. This is *conspicuously* true of Descartes' own paradigms.

Consider clocks first. They are now commonplace; they are cheap, mass-produced, and indispensable to most people for adhering to schedules, calculating pay, tuning in to television programmes, etc. By contrast, clocks were *rarities* in

81 This idea of a machine is the one from which Turing *abstracted* in constructing the concept of a Turing-machine, that is something which goes through certain steps so as to transform something into something else.

82 For this reason, the simile of the pilot in his *ship* may be meant to belong together with the strategy of seeing the human body as a *machine*.

83 He evidently felt that the very idea that a small force could have large effects was something that most people found puzzling. His analogy between the pineal gland and a fountain-keeper is meant, in part, to remove this mystery.

the seventeenth century. Only a wealthy household, or even a wealthy town, could afford one. Others had to tell the time approximately and from a distance, relying on clocks placed on church towers or chateaux, or perhaps on sundials by day (when the weather was good); more usually people had to make do with estimates based on the occasional temporal landmark (e.g., the ringing of a bell in a distant church to mark noon or the sun's standing over a mountain locally called '*le Pic du Midi*'). Pre-pendulum clocks were very rare and expensive, typically ornate and imposing in size, intricately precision-engineered by hand, and requiring real expertise and much labour to build and decorate. In speaking of clocks, Descartes had in mind instruments that were magnificent in appearance and practically miraculous in their sophistication and accuracy. They were objects of *respect* (as the clock in Salisbury Cathedral still is).

The same point holds even more obviously of his other example: the complex automata that gradually spread into northern Europe from the much-admired Renaissance water-gardens of Italy. Although the whole idea might strike twentieth-century intellectuals as rather absurd,[84] these constructions (variously termed '*machinae*', '*automates*', and '*hydrauliques*') struck even the most sophisticated and well-travelled of Descartes' contemporaries as among the genuine 'wonders of the world'. They were quite literally *awe*-inspiring, almost *miraculous* ('*paene nova naturae miracula*'). There are many testimonies to the sentiment in travel-journals and topographical guides. Montaigne (in the implausible guise of the plain man?) marvelled at such garden machinery at Augsburg, Pratolino, and Tivoli during his travels of 1580–1. During Descartes' lifetime, many others recorded similar sentiments of admiration and wonder at '*la merveille*' of these hydraulic mechanisms. The skill of their creators was so great that 'there is nothing in the world that cannot be reproduced': statues of men and women can speak, move around, sing, and even play musical instruments, while figures of birds can fly and sing, those of dogs can growl, bark, and engage in fights with cats, etc.[85] Henri IV employed an Italian under the grandiloquent title '*intendant général des eaux et fontaines de France*' to ornament the royal gardens at Fontainebleau and Saint-Germain-en-Laye with similar 'machines'. These machines that could be seen 'in the gardens of our kings' (AT XI: 130) were 'admired by all those who saw them'.[86] These are the mechanisms with which Descartes compared the human body:

> [External objects stimulating the sense-organs and triggering off bodily movements] are like the visitors who enter the grottos of these fountains and unwittingly cause the movements which take place before their eyes.

84 Compare the 'special effects' in very early horror films like *King Kong* and *Godzilla*, which now strike those of us brought up on *Alien* and *Terminator* as uproariously funny; their original audiences found them terrifying.

85 A list of citations and references is available in AT XI: 212–15 (among the notes for *Traité de l'Homme*).

86 Further information and references are to be found at AT XI: 669.

> For they cannot enter without stepping on certain tiles which are so arranged that if, for example, they approach a Diana who is bathing they will cause her to hide in the reeds, and if they move forward to pursue her they will cause a Neptune to advance and threaten them with his trident; or if they go in another direction they will cause a sea-monster to emerge and spew water onto their faces; or other such things according to the whim of the engineers who made the fountains.
>
> (AT XI: 131; CSM I: 101)

This background is important for appreciating the spirit of Descartes' revolutionary *Bête-Machine* Doctrine. He compared animals with certain mechanisms that were expressly chosen because they were then the objects of admiration and wonder. Ignorant of his intentions, twentieth-century readers are apt to sense something derogatory in the term 'machine', and modern commentators are liable to paraphrase his doctrine as 'Animals are *mere* machines'. This minute addition makes a BIG difference.

Descartes took for granted certain general implications of the term 'machine', implications still present in twentieth-century usage. First, machines must be *artefacts*: they must be fabricated or constructed on the basis of designs or blueprints. Second, a machine must have a goal-oriented function. It must be designed to serve certain purposes and to supply certain needs, for instance, to produce glass bottles, to milk cows, to fill bottles with milk, or to tell the time. Third, a properly functioning machine must act with perfect regularity or uniformity: the same input must produce the same output. In making our body like a machine, God 'wanted it to function like a universal instrument which would always operate in the same manner in accordance with its own laws' (AT V: 163; CSMK III: 346). Failures in functioning are a criterion for mechanical breakdown. Finally, a machine must operate *mechanically*; its functioning must be wholly explicable by the laws of mechanics. All four of these commonplaces are important for understanding the *Bête-Machine* Doctrine.

Generic as the seventeenth-century use of the term 'machine' was, Descartes' inclusion of animals under this heading amounted to a partial redefinition. His 'revisionist' conception began from the fixed points that machines are constructed, purpose-oriented, regular, and 'mechanical'. But he drew out the implications of these truisms in accord with his own distinctive theological and scientific framework and goals.[87] In a nutshell, he included *God* among the artificers of

87 The Legend finds the question of motivation difficult. Why should it be important to Descartes to deny that animals were 'conscious'? That the *Bête-Machine* Doctrine was of immense importance to him cannot be doubted by anyone who reads his correspondence; he adverted to the topic time and again, and even stated that 'after the error of those who deny God . . . there is none that leads weak minds further from the straight path of virtue than that of imagining that the souls of the beasts are of the same nature as ours' (AT VI: 59; CSM I: 141). Can we seriously suppose that his doctrine was grounded in a simple mistake (e.g., confusing consciousness with self-consciousness), that were his mistake to be pointed out to him he would willingly just give it up?

machines, and he expanded the *scope* of mechanical explanation to cover much that his predecessors felt they required souls to explain.[88] We need to keep both of these points clearly in view to grasp *his Bête-Machine* Doctrine.

First, the very idea of seeing animals as machines invokes the Argument from Design. This 'aspect' is visible only from the perspective of regarding animals as the products of God's handiwork, as His creations. As we have seen, even such human artefacts as clocks and hydraulic automata are to be viewed as objects of wonder and admiration. *Any* machine made by God must be infinitely *more* marvellous and awe-inspiring. That this is the point of calling animals or the human body 'machines' is made explicit: the human body is to be regarded 'as a machine which, having been *made by the hands of God*, is *incomparably better ordered* than any machine that can be devised by man, and contains in itself movements more wonderful than those in any such machine' (AT VI: 56, CSM I: 139, italics added; cf. AT XI: 120, CSM I: 99). He even added this argument: 'since art copies nature, and people can make various automatons which move without thought, it seems reasonable that Nature [i.e. God] should even produce its own automatons, which are much more splendid than artificial ones – namely the animals' (AT V: 277; CSMK III: 366).

The logical point, that the *Bête-Machine* Doctrine requires God as the Artificer, has two implications, one moral, the other theological. First, this point has the power to defuse the common criticism that his doctrine is morally outrageous. It would be a serious form of wrongdoing to smash up the products of another's labour and skill; not mere vandalism to destroy a clock, but rather an injury to the clock-maker (in a different sense, to the whole village in the case of a church clock). (We today might react with similar outrage to vandalism of an Old Master's painting.) The wanton harming or destruction of animals would be an even more heinous crime – nothing less than doing an injury *to God*. A serious misunderstanding is involved in the widespread objection that Descartes' *Bête-Machine* Doctrine makes the torturing of brutes morally blameless.[89] But second,

88 In fact he saw these points as connected: it isn't that his contemporaries would have baulked at the idea of God as a great Artificer, but they didn't draw the correct consequences from this, i.e. that the material world must operate on a few simple and universal principles which were intelligible to the human intellect, properly employed. God 'has laid down these laws in nature just as a king lays down laws in his kingdom. There is no single one that we cannot grasp if our mind turns to consider it' (AT I: 145; CSMK III: 23).

89 Many modern defenders of animal rights quote a single 'eyewitness account' (by Fontaine) of the actions of 'Cartesian' physiologists: 'They administered beatings to dogs with perfect indifference, and made fun of those who pitied the creatures as if they felt pain . . . . They nailed poor animals up on boards by their four paws to vivisect them and see the circulation of the blood which was a great subject of conversation' (quoted by Leiber 1988: 313). Leiber points out that 'Fontaine's *Memoires de Port-Royal* . . . were written, according to his editors, a long time after the events described and with many chronological mistakes – and all this by a man who held Cartesianism to be scientific blasphemy' (314). Moreover, even were the eyewitness account accurate, no one can read Descartes' correspondence without being struck by the degree of animosity which his various doctrines inspired among his contemporaries, and by their willingness to distort his doctrines in order to discredit him.

he wanted to urge the view that those who *denied* that animals were mechanically explicable were detracting from God's power and immutability:

> The number and orderly arrangement of the nerves, veins, bones and other parts of an animal do not show that nature is insufficient to form them, provided you suppose that in everything nature acts exactly in accordance with the laws of mechanics, and that these laws have been imposed on it by God.
>
> (AT II: 525; CSMK III: 134)[90]

The second point was that Descartes sought to *extend* the range of application of *mechanical* explanation beyond its then-accepted range. The *Treatise on Man* explicitly set out to demonstrate that all of the functions which were traditionally taken to require a vegetative or sensitive soul could be performed by an 'organic machine'. On this basis, he drew the conclusion: 'In order to explain these functions . . . it is not necessary to conceive of this machine as having any vegetative or sensitive soul or other principle of movement and life, apart from its blood and its [animal] spirits' (AT XI: 202; CSM I: 108). Physiology has no need for this traditional theoretical apparatus. In particular, 'everything [in animals] which we call Natural appetites or inclinations is explained on my theory solely in terms of the principles of mechanics [*par les seules regles des Mechaniques*]' (AT III: 213; CSMK III: 155*).

Descartes, of course, had a particular conception of the nature of such 'mechanical' explanations, namely that they need only invoke 'geometrical' properties or 'modes of extension'. (This doctrine is not well understood in the literature, but we cannot discuss it in detail here.) The main point needed here is that the parameters of physical explanation are fixed within his physics; in particular, the sole cause of the motion of matter is the impact of other moving matter. Where the matter which produces motion is not perceptible, it must be very refined and aethereal (e.g. animal spirits, 'globules of the third kind'). It was pleonastic, in his usage, to say that efficient causation among corporeal objects is mechanical; no causal explanation could be deemed complete until the underlying mechanism has been brought to light.[91] His vision (or programme) of extending the scope of mechanical explanation has affinities with the modern prejudice that physical explanations underlie all phenomena (that quantum mechanics is the lowest common denominator of all scientific explanations, and that other explanations, for example, in chemistry or biology, are simply place-holders for

90 Cf. Malebranche: 'Let us recognize that in His limitless wisdom He placed in all the animals every principle necessary for the preservation of their life and for the propagation of their species . . . . We shall not then indiscretely limit the wisdom of the Creator . . . by our tendency to judge that what we cannot comprehend is absolutely impossible for Him' (*Recherche* 353).

91 Our concept of efficient causation has crucially shifted (see pp. 145–52), and so too has the scientific conception of what counts as 'mechanical explanation'. The scope of mechanics no longer embraces all physical forces and interactions: electricity, magnetism, chemical reactions, and nuclear forces are now treated as definitely non-mechanical.

a complete quantum-mechanical explanation to be worked in the scientific millennium).[92]

In calling animals machines, Descartes committed himself to a programme of giving a particular kind of physical explanation of the motions of their bodies. One consequence of this difference in conceptual framework is that the rhetorical weight of the term 'animate' may not strike us today. First, Descartes, in rebellion against the tradition, regarded living beings (apart from man) as *inanimate*, i.e. as lacking a *soul* (*anima*).[93] We now, by contrast, use the term 'inanimate' of inert or lifeless matter and contrast it with animate matter, i.e. plants and animals; but we don't mean thereby to ascribe souls to them. Second, Descartes had a picture of a unified science of matter; hence he saw no reason at all to differentiate between living and lifeless matter in respect of the possibility of a complete explanation of behaviour (movement) by reference to general principles of physics. In this framework, to call animals 'inanimate' is simply to regard them as physical systems, as within the scope of scientific explanation, by contrast with those aspects of human behaviour which manifest the operations of the soul; all of this behaviour is in principle outside the scope of scientific explanation and within the scope of moral appraisal. But in calling animals 'animate' we don't today mean to exempt their behaviour from the scope of possible scientific explanation or to ascribe virtues and vices to them.

Descartes' doctrine of the scope of mechanical explanation was clearly revisionist; the analogies he drew between animals and machines were as shocking to his contemporaries as they are to us today.[94] But they found it shocking because they were persuaded that seeing light, feeling pain, the powers of nutrition and locomotion, and life itself all required a *soul*. This conviction is importantly alien to our twentieth-century way of thinking, in a number of respects. At least part of the modern resistance to the *Bête-Machine* Doctrine surely lies, very simply, in the fact that in our (modern) view, there is no such thing as (nothing counts as) an *organic* or a *living* machine: these expressions are conceptually awry.[95] This is light-years away from the reasons that Descartes' contemporaries baulked at

92 There are obviously asymmetries between his vision and the parallel modern one. His idea was essentially tied to theological and moral doctrines (the Argument from Design, concern with moral welfare and the salvation of souls, etc.); and it suggested an absolute or metaphysical limit on the possibility of scientific explanation (viz. the operations of the rational soul). We might say that science played a different role in the economy of his thinking than it does in twentieth-century thought (see pp. 201–7).

93 This implication was controversial even in his day, indeed frequently contradicted, both then and later. Leibniz, for instance, took sentience and life to require the presence of a soul, and he therefore rejected Descartes' doctrine (*Lettres* 342).

94 Cf. Arnauld: 'there are some very true things' against which people are 'prejudiced': many people are 'shocked' when told that 'animals are only automata' (*Ideas* ch. 11); indeed 'there are very few people who can believe that what animals do they do unknowingly, merely by modifications of extension' (ch. 23).

95 Alternatively, we see the notion of a 'living machine' as ruled out by the alleged fact that life evolved *naturally* and that this is seen as incompatible with the conceptual truth that machines are artefacts. Descartes' contemporaries would not share this latter worry: the concept of a 'natural machine' is simply the concept of a machine made by *God* as opposed to a human artificer.

these ideas. (Likewise, our twentieth-century worries about 'machines which digest' or 'machines which breathe' will not be because we suppose these functions to require a soul.) Modern qualms about 'sentient machines' – machines which feel pain or see light – are similarly not grounded in the presupposition that sentience requires a soul; none the less, the phrase 'sentient machine' may now seem closely akin to expressions that are straightforwardly self-contradictory – for reasons that would not have made sense to him (see below). Finally, the fact that animals have the power of locomotion is no part of modern resistance to the *Bête-Machine* Doctrine, whereas Descartes' contemporaries supposed this to be an insuperable objection since this power too was deemed to require a soul.

Descartes' attempts at philosophical 'therapy' were, concomitantly, aimed at addressing the 'prejudices' of his contemporaries. He felt that these prejudices stood in the way, *inter alia*, of progress in medicine: 'if only [he lamented] we had spent enough effort on getting to know the nature of our body, instead of attributing to the soul functions which depend solely on the body' (AT XI: 224; CSM I: 314). His concern in this particular work was principally with such 'vegetative' functions as nutrition and reproduction, and with the 'sensitive' power of locomotion, all of which his contemporaries 'attributed to the soul'. He identified three reasons for this, and sought to tackle each of them. The first was the fact that since childhood, 'we have all found by experience that many bodily movements occur in obedience to the will, which is one of the faculties of the soul, and this has led us to believe that the soul is the principle responsible for all bodily movement' (AT XI: 224; CSM I: 314). To accept this was to accept that none of the operations or behaviour of the human body could be given mechanical explanations – disastrously for medicine, in his view. He tackled it by the technique of disambiguation (cf. pp. 84–7): he called attention to an 'ambiguity' in the expression 'principles of movement': there are 'those [movements] which are performed in us with the help of the mind' and 'those which depend merely on the flow of the animal spirits and the disposition of the organs' (AT VII: 229–31, CSM II: 161–2; cf. *PRL* I.xi). (Confusion between these two distinct things is what leads us to 'imagine' that the first as well as the second 'principle of motion' are to be found in the brutes. This amounts to another instance of the fallacy of equivocation in pre-philosophical thinking.)

A second reason was our 'ignorance of anatomy and mechanics': 'in restricting our consideration to the outside of the human body, we have never imagined that it has within it enough organs or mechanisms to move of its own accord in all the different ways which we observe' (AT XI: 224; CSM I: 314). He also saw that people were relatively unfamiliar with the detailed functioning of 'automata' or self-moving machines. He therefore expended much energy in describing the anatomy of the human body and in explaining, with admirable clarity, how precisely various 'automata' worked (e.g., the hydraulically operated Italian statues of Diana and Neptune, cf. AT XI: 131–2; CSM I: 100–1); and he aimed to 'give such a full account of the entire bodily machine that we will have no more reason to think that it is our soul which produces in it the movements which we know by experience are not controlled by our will than we have reason to think that there is a soul in a clock which makes it tell the time' (AT XI: 226; CSM I: 315). A final reason for ascribing these things to the soul was 'our belief that no movement occurs inside a corpse, though it possesses the same organs as a living body, and lacks only a soul' (AT XI: 224; CSM I: 314), from which we infer that 'it is the soul which produces' the movements (AT XI: 225; CSM I: 315). To tackle this source of prejudice, Descartes argued that the difference between a living body and a corpse is analogous to the difference between a watch when it is functioning properly and when it is broken (*Passions* I.6; CSM I: 329–30). With this battery of arguments, he tried to expose the confusions and fallacies that underlay the contemporary prejudice that the soul must be responsible for life and locomotion in animals.

But what about 'sentient machines'? Here too, of course, Descartes addressed the 'prejudices' of his contemporaries. And he attempted to overcome *their* particular obstacles to supposing that machines could feel hunger or see light. One large obstacle was, again, their confusion of two senses of ambiguous expressions ('seeing light', 'feeling pain', 'being angry', etc.), for which the 'therapy' is disambiguation (see pp. 84–7). But the other major obstacle was that they did not see how a machine could *respond to stimuli*: 'how the external objects which strike the sense organs can prompt this machine to move in numerous different ways' (AT XI: 141; CSM I: 101). (The point might be put by saying that they did not see how a machine could be 'sensitive', i.e. *responsive*.) The cure for this, like the cure for the belief that machines could not be self-moving, was knowledge of anatomy and of the operation of actual machines that did respond differentially to stimuli.[96] Thus the sense in which instances of '*sentire*' apply to machines is a sense in which such expressions designate (the 'input' half of) fine-grained differential responses to stimuli (from both inside and outside the 'machine') mediated by the internal structure and workings of the machine.

A likely modern response to this account of 'sentient machines' is disappointment. You might feel that the sense in which machines can be said to 'see' and 'feel pain' is, after all, an impoverished sense. To say of a 'machine' (say, an animal or a human body) that it 'feels pain' seems to be *just* to say that it reacts to injury of, say, its foot by pulling its foot away from the source of the injury; to say of a sheep that it 'sees' a wolf and 'feels fear' at the sight of the wolf is *just* to say that 'the "light reflected from the body of a wolf onto the eyes of a sheep"' arouses 'the movements of flight in the sheep' (AT VII: 230; CSM II: 161). So-called 'sentient' machines merely 'go through the motions' of what is called 'feeling pain' or 'feeling fear'; where are the 'subjective experiences' and 'raw feels' and 'phenomenological qualities'? How can we purport to be talking about

96 Researchers in robotics have recently come to be impressed with the sheer technical difficulty of the engineering problems involved here. 'People tend to underestimate the astonishing nature of the simple things animals and humans do, like eye-hand coordination' (Roberto Cipolla, a robotics engineer, quoted in *The Times Magazine*, 20 November 1993, p. 42).

sentience if there's no 'What's it like?'? (Isn't the crucial thing about pain that it's *awful*?)

Without entering into these murky waters, we would urge two questions. First, how are you going to explain to Descartes what exactly it is that this picture leaves out? 'Subjective experiences' are commonly supposed to be both 'ineffable' and 'mental'; 'phenomenological qualities' are commonly viewed as inexpressible properties of experiences. If this is the sort of item you have in mind, you are talking about something which is from his point of view multiply nonsensical quite independently of the question of its application to 'animals without reason'; it is not only 'thoughtless brutes', but human beings with rational souls, that are 'geometrically excluded' from having a 'What's it like?' There is in his framework no such thing as (nothing *counts* as) an inexpressible form of *thinking*, nor are there mental properties of anything other than rational *souls*.

Second, why are you so eager to apply the word 'mere' to sensitivity and responsiveness? Descartes and his contemporaries would have found it wholly natural to link 'sentience' or 'sensitivity' to health (and hence welfare; see pp. 136–8 and 178–80). A large part of his enthusiasm for the *Corps-Machine* Doctrine was its potential benefits for medicine.[97] He had long dreamed of discovering 'a system of medicine which is founded on infallible demonstrations' (AT I: 105; CSMK III: 17); indeed, he went so far as to say that 'The preservation of health has always been the principal end of my studies' (AT IV: 329; CSMK III: 275). In breaking a series of conceptual connections that were crucial to Descartes, especially in divorcing pain, hunger, thirst, seeing, fear, anger, and so on from *welfare*, modern philosophers have arguably trivialized these concepts. Perhaps modern emphasis on the 'awfulness' of pain is a vain attempt to recapture something of the idea of its being *damaging* or *injurious*. Some of these issues will be pursued in Chapter 5 (especially pp. 216–18).

SELF-KNOWLEDGE

Conscientia

'The concept of consciousness (*Bewusstsein*) is the true philosophical Proteus . . . . It takes on an incessantly shifting meaning' (Cassirer). 'By common consent',

97 This enthusiasm was fully shared by Boyle. 'I do not only *acknowledge*, but *teach*, that the Body of a Man is an incomparable *Engine*, which the most wise *Author* of Things has so skillfully fram'd' (*A Free Enquiry into the Vulgarly Receiv'd Notion of Nature*, London, 1685, 220). Boyle saw it as a *radical* doctrine to call the body a machine: not a scandal, but the gateway to truly scientific medicine. Much more recently, T. H. Huxley wrote a paean to Descartes in an essay called 'On the Hypothesis that Animals are Automata, and its History' (in his *Method and Results*, London: Macmillan, 1894): 'The spirit of [*Traité de l'Homme*] is exactly that of the most advanced physiology of the present day; all that is necessary to make them coincide with our present physiology in form, is to represent the details of the working of the animal machinery in modern language, and by the aid of modern conceptions' (pp. 184–5). In Huxley's view, the *Corps-Machine* hypothesis is one of the first-magnitude stars in the galaxy of scientific achievements.

Descartes played a pivotal role in its evolution. Indeed he allegedly introduced 'the modern concept of consciousness'; he cut *conscientia* free from its traditional association with moral knowledge, and he made it the defining feature of the mind by equating *conscientia* with *cogitatio* (e.g., *Principles* I.9; AT VII: 176).[98] This interpretation is admittedly difficult to support with much textual evidence because Descartes himself made scant use of the terms '*conscientia*' and '*conscius*'.

We sketch a different picture. We make out a case that Descartes' conception of *conscientia* is in most respects very close to the scholastic one, and that crucial aspects of this tradition were understood by his successors (Arnauld, Malebranche, Locke, and Leibniz) to persist in his thinking. We argue that failure to appreciate this point is a source of radical misunderstanding; indeed it is essential to the case for convicting him of inventing the 'Myth of Introspection'.

This section falls into three parts. We first sketch in some of the most salient features of the scholastic notion of *conscientia* and some relevant fragments of the wider Aristotelian background. Next we pinpoint two features that differentiate Descartes' conception of *conscientia* from that of the scholastic tradition. Finally, we contrast his conception with modern notions of 'consciousness' and so-called Cartesian Introspection.

Inherited wisdom

The general notion of *conscientia* in Aristotelian psychology is quite complex, rather variable, and now completely obsolete. Even in Descartes' day it was tied up with a range of concepts that have undergone very substantial evolution over the last four centuries, and this creates real difficulty in getting a proper fix on it. What we offer here is a quick tour of some of the highlights of this conception, not a comprehensive in-depth analysis.

We must start from a point about terminology. The terms '*conscius*' and '*conscientia*', though infrequently used, are much more problematic in Descartes' texts than one might expect. '*Conscius*' is normally rendered by the cognate term 'conscious', '*conscientia*' by 'consciousness' or 'inner awareness'[99] (not by 'conscience'). In one respect, this translation captures an important aspect of the grammar of the two Latin terms, namely that '*conscius*' is the adjective directly corresponding to the noun '*conscientia*' just as 'skilful' corresponds to 'skill'.

98 These opening comments are taken from the *Wörterbuch*, I.888– 90. Compare: 'The employment of the word *conscientia*, of which our term consciousness is a translation, is, in its philosophical signification, not older than the philosophy of Descartes. Previously to him this word was used almost exclusively in the ethical sense expressed by our term *conscience* .... Thus, in the philosophy of the West, we may safely affirm that, prior to Descartes, there was no psychological term in recognized use for what, since his time, is expressed in philosophical Latinity by *conscientia*' (Sir William Hamilton, *Lectures on Metaphysics*, Edinburgh and London: Blackwood, 1882, pp. 196–7). Curiously, however, Hamilton distinguished consciousness from the knowledge which the intellect has of its own operations, because he distinguishes sense from intellect (p. 198).

99 CSM use this expression also to translate the phrase '*cognitio interna*' (AT VII: 422).

(The same parallelism held in *seventeenth-century* English, where 'conscience' served as the abstract noun corresponding to the adjective 'conscious'.)

The problem is that the usual translations into English are almost bound to produce misunderstandings or confusions among modern readers. The word 'consciousness' dissociates '*conscientia*' from *moral* sensibility in the minds of modern English-speakers, whereas both '*conscius*' and '*conscientia*' (as well as 'conscious' and 'conscience' in English) were paradigmatically used in texts of the sixteenth and seventeenth centuries to signify moral self-knowledge.[100] The native habitat of '*conscientia*' was at that time discussions of moral agency, responsibility, virtue, and vice. Conversely, the word 'consciousness' risks importing into Descartes' texts all of the rich and varied connotations of its modern use in philosophers' English. In particular, it suggests that immediate experiences (or non-cognitive items in the stream of consciousness) such as pain, hunger, fear, and joy are paradigmatic objects of *conscientia* (i.e. things *of* which someone may be *conscius*), whereas we will show that '*conscientia*' in Descartes' texts excludes all forms of animal sentience. On his view, brutes are definitely not *conscius*, but they do share with human beings many of the things now called 'states of consciousness'. This doctrine becomes self-contradictory only if '*conscius*' is translated by the term 'conscious'. To forestall such misunderstandings, we practise the austere policy of not translating these terms at all.

This cautious procedure has close affinities with sophisticated philosophical practice in Descartes' own day. These two terms were then acknowledged to have a quite specialized or 'technical' use in scholastic writings. This is evident from Arnauld's incorporating the Latin terms '*conscius*' and '*conscientia*' into his own French texts, commenting on the lack of any French expressions that carried the appropriate connotations.[101] The earliest French translation of Locke contained the gloss that his term 'consciousness' was to be understood to be synonymous with the scholastic term '*conscientia*'.[102] Leibniz later coined the terms '*apperception*' and '*consciosité*' to translate '*conscientia*' into French. If the same intellectual background informs Descartes' use of the terms '*conscius*' and '*conscientia*', then we need some method to make this conspicuous to our readers, and we have preferred to follow Arnauld's tactics rather than Leibniz's.

Even cursory investigation into linguistic archaeology provides a useful orientation for considering the scholastic notion of *conscientia*. There are two important aspects of this concept that have developed into two separate concepts in modern English, namely 'consciousness' and 'conscience'.[103] The first is

100 This is conspicuous in Locke's celebrated discussion of the identity of a person. Having appealed to 'consciousness' of present and past thoughts and actions as the criterion for individuating a person, he emphasized that identity of persons is a 'forensic' concept. It is essentially bound up with moral responsibility for thoughts and actions. Each person is answerable, on the Day of Judgement, for everything of which he is *conscious* (*Essay* II.xxvii.18, 22, 26).

101 Arnauld, *Ideas* ch. 2.

102 Note by A. C. Fraser appended to *Essay* II.xxvii.11.

103 German has a roughly similar distinction between '*Bewusstsein*' and '*Gewissen*'.

concerned with awareness or self-knowledge, the second with moral sensibility or knowledge of right and wrong in action. The concept of *conscientia* essentially involves *both*.

The first aspect is made prominent in the standard scholastic definition of *conscientia* as the soul's knowledge of itself and its operations (*scientia sui et suarum operationum*).[104] This constitutes a large part of what philosophers now call 'self-knowledge' or 'self-consciousness'. Even prior to investigating what is to be understood by 'operations of the soul', this definition suggests that *conscientia* embraces self-knowledge in respect of all the ('mental') acts that are integral to cognition and reasoning: for instance, entertaining a thought, making a judgement, deliberating, calculating, and exploring the implications of a theory or set of principles. That much is certainly correct.

In fact, even under this definition there are two distinct uses of '*conscientia*' (and '*conscius*'). On the one hand, there is an absolute use: man is defined as 'the *conscius* animal' ('*animal conscium*'). Likewise *conscientia* appears in lists of the attributes of the soul. Indeed, like rationality or reason (*ratio*), *conscientia* is taken to be an *essential* power of the (rational) soul. In this use, there are no such things as differing degrees of *conscientia*, absence or lack of *conscientia*, or any specifications of what someone is *conscius of*. ('Rational' has a similar use in the scholastic definition: 'Man is the rational animal [*animal rationale*]'.)[105] On the other hand, there is a relative use of these terms; here particular things are specified (or presupposed) *of which* someone has more or less extensive knowledge or *about which* he is ignorant at the moment. (Here '*conscius*' is used with a noun phrase in the genitive case or with an indirect statement in Latin.) Someone may, for instance, be *conscius of* telling a lie or of feeling angry, he may lack *conscientia of* most of his own vices, or he may be *conscius that* he has left some duty undone. In this use, there may be different degrees of *conscientia*, and somebody may no longer be *conscius* of something of which he was previously *conscius*. ('Rational' has a similar use in the observation 'He is very rational in economic matters, but not at all rational in affairs of the heart'.) Actual instances of self-knowledge (e.g., my *conscientia* of my sins) are manifestations of the capacity to attain self-knowledge (viz. my being *conscius*), but both are properly called '*conscientia*'.

The second aspect of the concept is prominent in Aquinas' celebrated treatment of *conscientia*. He defined this general power as 'the application of knowledge to acts' ('*applicatio scientiae ad actum*') (*ST* I/II.19.5). He gave a more detailed threefold analysis: it is the power of acknowledging what we have done and not done, of judging what we are to do and what we are not to do, and of judging of something we have done whether it was well done or not well done (*ST* I.79.13c). On this view, *conscientia* concerns the moral appraisal by an agent of *his own*

104 Cited as a standard formula in Arnauld, *Ideas*, ch. 2. There are clear echoes in Descartes' texts; for example, AT VII: 246 (CSM II: 172).

105 The questions 'How rational?', or 'What about new-born infants?', directed at *this* view, make as much sense as the White King's question 'How can you see *nobody* on the road?'

actions, past, present, and future.[106] (Hence it is a form of self-knowledge.)[107] It is the ability to distinguish right from wrong in respect of particular actions; and having this general power (the capacity to acquire this ability) is evidently an *essential* part of being a *moral agent*. This ability is realized by somebody to the extent that he makes correct judgements about the moral value of his own actions, and in respect of past or present actions, these evaluations presuppose knowledge of what he is doing or has done.

It is crucial to grasping the scholastic concept of *conscientia* to realize that these two aspects are closely linked, not independent of each other. On the one hand, *voluntary actions*, whether mental or bodily, are paradigms of operations of the soul; I am *conscius* of what I am now doing, what I have done more or less recently, and of what I am going to do (as it were, at least of the trajectory of my current activities). For example, I am *conscius* that I am now walking from Woodstock to Oxford, that I am being dilatory in paying a bill for books, that I did not protest when the grocer undercharged me for tomatoes, or that I am going to stucco the wall once I have mixed the concrete. These are straightforward instances of my having what is called 'knowledge of the *operations of my soul*'. On the other hand, states of *moral character* (virtues, vices, moral freedom, and being subject to moral constraints) are paradigms of 'modes of thinking' (or 'states of mind'). They are treated as being self-evidently properties of the rational soul. As a consequence, the power of *conscientia* is exemplified when someone makes correct, well-founded judgements about his own moral character. For instance, a paradigm of having *conscientia* might be my judgement that I am arrogant, rash, courageous, or pusillanimous; or I may fail to be *conscius* of irascibility or intemperance. These are all straightforward instances of my having (or lacking) 'knowledge of *modes of thinking*'. Though scholastic accounts of *conscientia* may focus on one aspect or the other, they take it for granted that these two aspects are inseparable.

We are now very apt to fail to notice or to appreciate this point. We can scarcely imagine that anybody could count voluntary actions as paradigmatic 'operations *of the soul*' or treat virtues and vices as basic 'modes *of thinking*'.[108] What we need to do is constantly to remind ourselves of the crucial place of *conscientia* in the 'Moral Order'. The responsibility of every person for his own actions (especially his responsibility to God on the Day of Judgement) is intelligible only on the supposition that an agent has the capacity to know what he is doing, hence what he has done (not simply what he is trying to do or what his intentions were). *Conscientia* is essential to '*moral* identity'.[109]

After this preliminary stage-setting, we now fill in a few more details of the scholastic conception of *conscientia*. We focus on nine ideas that Descartes took

106 Ryle notes the same point about the 'syntax' of the word 'conscience' in modern English (*Collected Papers*, London: Hutchison, 1971, vol. 2, p. 185).

107 On this conception, *conscientia* is restricted to casuistry or applied ethics; it does not include knowledge of general moral principles, though it may presuppose knowledge of them.

108 Or as paradigms of 'states of *mind*' or '*mental* qualities' (cf. Mill, *Logic* I.iii.14, I.v.7).

109 Leibniz, *Essais* 236.

over from the tradition. At the same time, we offer some provisional evidence for the claim that he did build his own ideas upon them.

First, consider the absolute use of '*conscientia*':

1 The idea that a person is essentially the union of a mind (rational soul) with a body underpins the familiar scholastic definition of man ('*homo*') as 'the rational animal' ('*animal rationale*'). Because *conscientia* is logically inseparable from being rational (i.e. having a rational soul), an alternative real definition of man is 'the *conscius* animal' ('*animal conscium*').[110] Similarly, given Descartes' commitment to the doctrine that somebody cannot be thinking something without being *conscius* that he is so thinking, his characterization of the soul as '*res cogitans*' is equivalent to calling it '*res conscia*' (cf. AT V: 149; CSMK III: 335).[111] Possessing *conscientia* is a cognitive power that belongs to the *essence* of the rational soul. (In this respect it differs from such 'faculties' as sense-perception and Imagination, since I can clearly and distinctly perceive that I might lack them; see *Meditation* VI.) Descartes acknowledged this point in his definition of 'thinking': the phrase '*nobis consciis*' ('we being *conscius*') states a necessary condition for counting as a mode of thinking (*cogitatio*) anything which 'happens within us' (*Principles* I.9).

Since having *conscientia* is essential to the rational soul, it is something innate and inalienable in human beings. It cannot be acquired in the course of maturation or lost as a result of disease, injury, or ageing. It has no degrees: every soul *must* be *conscius* at all times. In all these respects, *conscientia* differs essentially from the cognitive capacity that many twentieth-century philosophers call 'self-consciousness'.[112]

2 As an essential attribute of the soul, *conscientia* is to be understood, at least roughly, as the capacity for having or acquiring a kind of knowledge, namely knowledge of the operations of one's soul. (Correspondingly, its absence in animals indicates a *cognitive* incapacity.) Pinning down this cognitive capacity depends on ascertaining precisely what is included under the phrase 'operations of the soul'. Even within the scholastic tradition, this varied somewhat from

110 Arnauld alluded to this equivalence (*Ideas* ch. 2).

111 This equivalence no more demonstrates that Descartes equated thinking with consciousness than the equivalence of '*animal rationale*' with '*animal conscium*' shows that scholastic thinkers identified reason (*ratio*) with consciousness!

Leibniz noted Descartes' commitment to this equivalence: '*Princeps Cartesius admonuit quid simus mentem scilicet seu Ens cogitans seu conscium sui*' (quoted in *Wörterbuch* I.890). The same equivalence in evident in Locke: '*Self* is that conscious thinking thing' (*Essay* II.xxvii.17). It long remained a standard ingredient in the conception of the soul: 'Among *Substances* some are *thinking* or conscious Beings, or have a Power of Thought, such as the *Mind of Man, God, Angels*' (Watts, *Logick*, I.ii.2).

112 In particular, it is usually affirmed that self-consciousness presupposes the mastery of a language (e.g., Kenny 1989: 9, 23); hence it must be lacking in infancy.

philosopher to philosopher. It was, however, standard to include all of the voluntary actions of moral agents which manifest reason, whether these actions be mental acts (like suspending judgement) or bodily actions (like walking to work or expressing a thought in speech or writing), whether they be present or past.[113] Given the supposition that the functions of the rational soul subsume the functions of the lower forms of souls (sensitive and vegetative), it is common to include too all forms of sentience and locomotion. Thus Aquinas included all forms of sense-perception (*sentire*) and spontaneous movement as well as all forms of thinking (*cogitare*). Finally, given the pivotal role that *conscientia* plays in discussions of moral deliberation and responsibility, it must be taken to include the possibility of self-knowledge in respect of the *moral* qualities of one's actions and of one's own states of character. Possession of *conscientia* is what makes human beings *moral agents*.[114] (Likewise, its absence in brute animals excludes the possibility of their being moral agents, i.e. of their committing sins, having virtues or vices, feeling guilt or remorse, or enjoying happiness or misery.)[115] In the scholastic tradition, the moral order demands that free and responsible rational agents have a *cognitive* capacity that encompasses the possibility of knowledge of *past* voluntary *actions* and of *moral character*. In these respects, *conscientia* differs radically from any concept that occurs in twentieth-century philosophical discussions of self-consciousness and introspection.

Conscientia may also be described as the power of the mind to *reflect on* its own thinking, or as the capacity for 'reflection' ('*reflectio*') or 'reflective knowledge' ('*scientia reflexa*'). Descartes may himself have considered *conscientia* (*cognitio interna*) the precondition for having reflective knowledge (AT VII: 422; CSM II: 285).

Now we turn to the relative use of '*conscientia*' and '*conscius*', i.e. the use of these terms with complements of the form 'of . . .' or 'that . . .'.

1 First and foremost, having *conscientia* is possessing *knowledge* (*scientia*)[116] whose scope is the soul and its 'operations' ('*operationes*').[117] This form of knowledge, like geometry or metaphysics, is distinguished from other kinds of knowledge by its subject-matter. Like all forms of knowledge, it is conceived to

113 It is an essential property of voluntary actions that I can be *conscius* of them and reflect on them (Leibniz, *Essais* 173).

114 This point is prominent in Locke's treatment of personal identity and his definitions of Person (*Essay* II.xxvii.9) and of Self (*Essay* II.xxvii.17), where 'consciousness' is the key to linking acts and thoughts together into the life or career of a single moral agent.

115 Compare Reid: 'Conscience is peculiar to man. We see not a vestige of it in brute animals . . . . [If they had this capacity], it would follow, that some brutes are moral agents, and accountable for their conduct . . . . But they cannot be immoral; nor can they be virtuous' (*Essay* III, Part III, Ch. VIII).

116 This identification is indicated in a famous passage where Augustine declared that each person knows his own faith '*certissima scientia, et clamante conscientia*' (*De Trinitate* I) (quoted by Arnauld, *Ideas* ch. 24).

117 Locke defined the closely related power of 'reflection' as the '*Perception of the Operations of our own Minds* within us' (*Essay* II.i.4).

be a disposition or capacity, not a performance or action.[118] It is a power comparable to knowing the Greek alphabet or the five-times table; or perhaps to remembering an incident or a conversation. This knowledge, like any other, may be more or less extensive. *Conscientia* is exhibited by anybody to the extent that he articulates true judgements about the 'operations of his soul'.[119] Knowledge of any kind may exist even when it is not being formulated by the knower. In particular, just as I may know the Greek alphabet or the five-times table when I am not saying it over aloud or to myself, so I may know that I have the thought that God is omnipotent without saying to myself that I have this thought, and I may know that I have just played through a Mozart sonata even though I don't now engage in any interior soliloquy. Knowing about one operation of my soul no doubt requires the *possibility* of performing another operation of my soul, but it doesn't consist of my *doing* two things at once.

This point is vital to making sense of the idea that *conscientia* is 'reflexive'. For instance, if I have the thought that God is omnipotent, then I must have the *capacity* to judge that I have the thought that God is omnipotent, likewise to judge that I have judged that I have the thought that . . ., and so on, *ad infinitum*. These are all distinct thoughts, and each of them is a potential object of *conscientia*. Descartes alluded to this point in noting that the soul 'has the power to reflect on its thoughts *as often as it likes*' (AT V: 149; CSMK III: 149, italics added). In fact, it seems to be a standard scholastic contention that there is a restrictive sense of 'operation' which justifies the principle that the soul must be actually (not just potentially) *conscius* of any of its *operations*. In this usage, 'operations' are distinguished from 'powers' (AT VII: 232, 246; CSM II: 162, 171–2). In Descartes' system, this takes the form of the axiom that I must be *conscius* of thinking something at the time of so thinking (AT VII: 232, 246, CSM II: 162, 171–2; cf. AT V: 221–2, CSMK III: 357). Provided that knowing something is properly conceived as a capacity, not a performance, this axiom doesn't threaten to launch a vicious infinite regress. Of course, making a judgement is a paradigm case of thinking (*cogitatio*), so that it follows from this axiom that I must be *conscius* of making this judgement. But, if Descartes conceived my making a judgement as my saying something to myself, then it would be *obviously absurd* to take the *conscientia* that is essential to making a judgement to consist necessarily in my making a second distinct judgement whose content is the thought that I have made the first judgement.[120] There is no antinomy lurking in the original

118 The distinction between actuality and potentiality is fundamental to philosophy in the Aristotelian tradition. In this context, it clearly persisted. Leibniz stressed that 'thoughts are actions, whereas items of knowledge . . . are tendencies or dispositions; and we know many things which we scarcely think about' (*Essais* 86).

119 This point is presented as a *criticism* of the Cartesian view of the mind! 'To be . . . conscious of a pain, a mood, or of thinking does not belong to the category of perceptual awareness, let alone to "inner perception", but to the categories of capacity, in particular to say how things are with one . . .' (Hacker 1990: 55).

120 The proposition that I must be *conscius* of having a thought at the moment of having it is to be compared with the judgement that the moon is visible to me here and now, not with the judgement that I notice the moon at the present moment.

scholastic principle that I must be *conscius* of every operation of my soul or in Descartes' variant that I must be *conscius* of thinking something at the time of so thinking.[121]

2 What count as instances of *conscientia* depends on precisely what is included under the phrase 'operations of the soul'. There are some variations in how this is understood by different philosophers, and a contrast between a wider and a stricter sense of 'operation'. Despite these complexities, there was an indisputable core consisting of 'reasoning, judging, volition, and knowledge' as well as 'compounding, comparing, and abstracting ideas' (Locke, *Essay* II.xix.2, II.xi.14). In addition, there was a general scholastic consensus that 'operations of the soul' included the exercises of its 'active powers', i.e. voluntary actions.[122] Hence the ability to recall one's own past actions and to assess their moral value is a central form of *conscientia*,[123] and it seems generally to encompass as well the ability to assess one's own moral character, especially virtues and vices.[124] Paradigm instances of *conscientia* are accurate confessions of past sins or clarifications of what one is currently doing as well as just appreciations of one's character. (These items never occur on lists of items allegedly known through introspection.)

3 *Conscientia* is manifested in the articulation of true judgements about oneself (more accurately, about one's soul). It is not realized in the possession of some kind of inarticulate data which are comparable to sense-impressions or immediate perceptual experiences.[125] It is not a form of 'knowledge by acquaintance',[126] but a kind of *scientia* or 'knowledge of truths'. (Hence it is out of the question that *conscientia* can be exhibited by a dumb animal.) In this respect, it is comparable to faculties of (rational) sense-perception, i.e. to the capacity of a person to make

121 Arnauld used the term 'implicit' to qualify the 'reflection' which must accompany every thought (*Ideas* ch. 2).

122 Malebranche attested to this consensus by dissociating himself from it. He denied that inner sense or *conscience* encompasses the voluntary movement of the arm, affirming that it embraces only the sensation (*sentiment*) of this movement (*Eclaircissements* XV, *VIme Preuve*).

123 This tradition persisted, for example, in this definition: 'The word conscience properly signifies, that *knowledge* which a man has within himself of his own thoughts and *actions*' (Swift 1745, italics added; cited by the *OED* s.v. 'Conscience').

What we learn by 'inward Consciousness' includes such propositions as 'I think before I speak', 'I desire large knowledge', 'I suspect my own practice', 'I studied hard today', 'My conscience bears witness of my sincerity', 'My soul hates vain thoughts', 'Fear is an uneasy passion', and 'Long meditation on one thing is tiresome' (Watts, *Logick* II.ii.9).

124 'Through this inner sense [*sentiment intérieur*] of their own sins [*désordres*], [men] know that they are deserving of hell' (Malebranche, *Recherche* IV.12).

125 For example, Humean impressions of reflexion.

126 'When I see the sun, I am often aware of my seeing the sun; thus "my seeing the sun" is an object with which I have acquaintance . . . . This kind of acquaintance, which may be called self-consciousness, is the source of all our knowledge of mental things' (Russell 1912: 49–50).

true judgements about the sensible properties of things around him (or, in Quine-speak, to report accurately what 'impinges on his sensory surfaces'). On the scholastic view, the concept of *conscientia* is essentially tied to the possibility of articulating judgements.[127]

This has the immediate corollary that *conscientia* is not essentially 'private'; it is not knowledge of something that only I can know anything about, or that I cannot share with another. Rather, being '*conscius* of' something is closely akin to 'being privy to' it. Whatever I am *conscius* of I could in principle fully and perfectly articulate, hence divulge to others, and another's knowledge need be in no respect inferior to my own.[128] Far from being 'logically private', *conscientia* must be essentially communicable.[129]

4 *Conscientia* is inseparable from 'operations of the soul' (in the strict sense); i.e. it belongs to the essence of an 'operation' that the soul is *conscius* of every one of its operations.[130] In Descartes' texts, this axiom takes the form of building *conscientia* into the definition of 'thinking' (*cogitatio*): 'what happens within us' falls under the term 'thinking' only in so far as we have *conscientia* of it (*Principles* I.9).[131] In his view, *conscientia* belongs to the concept of thinking (*cogitatio*)[132] just as truth and falsity belong to the concept of a judgement (AT VII: 37; CSM II: 26). He took himself to be defending a standard scholastic doctrine in rebutting objections to his axiom that I must be *conscius* of thinking something at the time of so thinking (cf. AT VII: 232, 246).[133]

5 Scholastic thought generally treated being *conscius of* something as a *time-relative* cognitive capacity. Descartes clearly held this view. He defended this

127 This is true even though a pre-linguistic infant must have *conscientia* of the operations of its soul. An infant is conceived as having a capacity which it has had no opportunity to manifest. (It might be better to picture *conscientia* as a capacity to acquire the capacity to articulate judgements.)

128 This is inherited from the wider use of '*conscius*' in classical Latin: then, among paradigms of things of which one may be *conscius* are *a friend's* financial or family affairs and a *multi-person* plot to assassinate the head of state.

129 Contrast Kenny 1966: 360.

130 This might take various forms. Leibniz later defended the doctrine that the moral agent must be *conscius* of every one of his voluntary actions over the whole of his lifetime even if he was unable to recollect some or all of them (*Essais* 239–40).

131 Leibniz exploited this conceptual connection in arguing that animals must be denied any form of thinking *because* they are known to lack *conscientia* (*Essais* 173, cf. 134).

132 Locke expressed the same idea: 'that consciousness which is *inseparable from* thinking, and, as it seems to me, *essential to* it; it being impossible for any one to perceive without *perceiving* that he does perceive. When we see, hear, smell, taste, meditate, or will anything, we know that we do so . . . . since consciousness always accompanies thinking' (*Essay* II.xxvii.11, first two italics added).

133 Compare Locke's claim that there is no such thing as having an *idea* without being conscious of it (*Essay* II.i.11–12).

principle: *at the time of* thinking something,[134] I must be *conscius* of so thinking,[135] but I may later forget what I was thinking earlier and thereby lose this *conscientia*. Given that *conscientia* is a form of knowledge and that knowledge of any kind is a capacity to make judgements, this principle can be rephrased: *at the time of* thinking something, I must have the capacity to say what I am thinking, but I may subsequently, sooner or later, lose this particular cognitive capacity through lapse of memory. This point holds for all forms of thinking, including rational sense-perception and rational action: for example, 'seeing' and 'walking' in the rational sense (*Principles* I.9). Being *conscius* of something is exemplified by someone who explains what he is now doing or who recounts one of his own past exploits. Ascriptions of *conscientia* require specific abilities to make true statements.[136]

6 *Conscientia* is knowledge *of the soul* and its attributes (or its operations).[137] It is *self*-knowledge, and it is confined to attributes of the *soul* (as opposed to properties of the body). Consequently, it must be manifested in making true singular judgements about the soul's operations. The fact that the scholastic tradition used the formula '*scientia* sui *et suum operationum*' suggests that the normal form of these judgements would be first-person judgements in which operations of the soul are predicated of the subject (or agent). This would surely be plausible for manifestations of *conscientia* in the form of confessions of sins, admissions of responsibility, or attributions of virtues. The moral dimension of *conscientia* is focused on God's meting out other-worldly rewards and punishments to *agents*.

In Descartes' thinking, this agent-centred aspect of *conscientia* is given a more rigid form. Given that modes must inhere in substances, and given that any singular judgement must have a substance as its logical subject, the logical form of any judgement that exhibits my *conscientia* must be that *I* (the soul) have a

134 This phrase needs to be clarified. Arguably Descartes conceived the present moment to be temporally extended and to be differentiated from the past by virtue of the fact that our knowledge of what is present is independent of memory. If so, there is a serious risk of distortion by following Mill and introducing a distinction between 'introspection' and 'retrospection' on the following specifications: 'a fact may be studied through the medium of memory, *not at the very moment* of our perceiving it, *but the moment after*; and this is really the mode in which our best knowledge of our intellectual acts is generally acquired. We reflect on what we have been doing when the act is past, but when its impression in the memory is still fresh' (quoted in Hacker 1990: 55, italics added).

135 Similarly, Locke held that it is absurd to suppose that someone could think without being 'conscious' that he is thinking, or that we can have an idea and not be conscious of it (*Essay* II.i.10–11). Indeed, he went so far as to claim that 'thinking consists in being conscious that one thinks' (*Essay* II.i.19). This is comparable to Descartes' identification of willing something with the perception of willing it as 'really one and the same thing' (*Passions* I.19; CSM I: 336).

136 Compare so-called 'event-memory': this is exemplified in the ability to make a fairly open or indefinite range of statements about a particular episode in one's past (as opposed to recounting a narrative that one has learned by rote).

137 Aristotle had argued that the soul is not only the knower, but also an object of knowledge (*noeton*) to itself (*De Anima* 430a2–9).

mode of thinking.[138] Instances of *conscientia* might be my correctly judging 'I want$_2$ a drink', 'I have the thought that God is omnipotent', 'I have just judged that I see light', 'I am rifling the alms box', or 'I am very stingy'. In all cases, *conscientia* must be expressed in *I*-thoughts.[139] I can't make a true judgement about any mode of thinking 'that I find within me' unless I think that this mode of thinking is a property of myself (i.e. my soul). For this reason, I-thoughts must be the minimal moves in the language-game of exhibiting *conscientia*.[140] Even if this doctrine about logical form in this fully developed state is original to Descartes, it seems to follow the trajectory of the traditional doctrine that *conscientia* is knowledge *of the soul* and its operations.

7 The idea that any sincere claim to self-knowledge must be infallible is no part of the scholastic conception of *conscientia*.[141] This idea is altogether implausible once we recognize that *conscientia* embraces knowledge of the past as well as the present, dispositions and abilities as well as performances, voluntary bodily actions as well as such 'mental acts' as making judgements or entertaining hypotheses, and the moral evaluation of voluntary actions and states of character. In addition, the claim of infallibility is explicitly denied (for instance, by Aquinas). Indeed the whole idea of first-/third-person asymmetry is inapplicable to the subject-matter of *conscientia*.[142] In a wide range of cases, my claims to *conscientia* are subject to correction by others,[143] and in some cases others may be in a better

138 Contrast the explanation that Descartes' doctrine that the first-person pronoun refers to *res cogitans* is a dire confusion resting on misconstruing the grammar of reflexive pronouns (Hacker 1986: 282)!

139 Contrast with this the objection that Descartes' report of 'internal perception', viz. *Cogito*, rests on 'the false assumption that the . . . subject constitutes part of every experience of consciousness' (Schlick 1974: 160–1).

140 Descartes was aware of, and dismissed, empiricists' objections that we can have no idea of the soul. He held that there *can* be *no* such thing as a sense-impression of one's own (or another's) soul. (Hume demoted this *metaphysical* principle to the status of a negative empirical generalization. Correlatively, he developed the anti-Cartesian doctrine that self-knowledge consists of reports of 'ownerless' experiences.)

141 Infallibility later became part of the notion of 'conscience'. For instance, Malebranche contrasted it with the external senses in precisely this respect: 'our internal sense [*sentiment intérieur*] never deceives us' (*Recherche* III. 10).

This must be distinguished from the grammatical claim that 'to be *conscius* of' is a success-verb like 'remember' or 'see'. There is no such thing as my being *conscius* of thinking something that I am not thinking (or of being *conscius* of doing something that I am not doing), any more than there is of my remembering an event that didn't happen or seeing a dagger when there is none to be seen.

142 This form of knowledge does not concern matters about which 'the subject is in a position of special authority' (Kenny 1966: 360). Any asymmetry is one of degree, not of kind. This is roughly the conception of self-knowledge advocated by Ryle in his criticism of the myth of introspection (cf. 1949: ch. VI).

143 Descartes clearly endorsed this position. Indeed, given our knowledge (by the Natural light) that the soul must always be thinking, we have conclusive reason to reject anyone's judgement that he has passed through a period of thoughtless existence (e.g., on his waking from dreamless sleep, cf. AT III: 423, 478–9; CSMK III: 189, 203).

position than I am myself to ascertain some of the 'operations of my soul' or my 'modes of thinking'.

The general fallibility of claims to *conscientia* is two-sided. Someone's sincere disavowal that he is *conscius* of something no more establishes an impregnable negative truth than his claim to be *conscius* of something establishes a positive one. Again this is especially clear in respect of *conscientia* of one's own present and past voluntary actions. Amnesia is a severe deficiency relative to normal cognitive capacity in respect of past actions, but it doesn't eliminate responsibility for *all* one's past actions (i.e. it doesn't wipe clean one's moral slate, as it were). This point is crucial to the Christian doctrine of moral responsibility: sincere memory lapses will not provide any defence on the Day of Judgement against condemnation for all the sins of one's whole life.[144]

Cartesian conscientia*: continuity and change*

Descartes' conception of *conscientia* can best be clarified by comparing and contrasting it with the notion that was developed in the scholastic reworking of Aristotelian psychology. We think that modern Anglo-American discussions of his dualism have failed to grasp his system of thought through ignorance of this background.

Despite the infrequency of his using '*conscientia*' or '*conscius*', it seems clear that his conception shows striking similarities with its precursor. Many of these are obvious once we see that he usually used the term 'thinking' ('*cogitatio*') as the equivalent of the scholastic phrase 'operation of the soul' ('*operatio animae*').

Others are clear, though modern readers tend to be blind to their real significance. We single out three ideas that are prominent in our account of the scholastic background.

First, *conscientia* is taken to embrace powers, dispositions, or abilities of the soul, not just acts or performances. Descartes noted that an infant is not *conscius* of having the power of thinking (AT VII: 214; CSM II: 150); this observation suggests that he thought that most adults have *conscientia* of their having this power. That conclusion is reinforced by other remarks. He held that any person of sound mind would be *conscius* of being the union of mind and body, and he suggested that this *conscientia* includes knowledge that the mind has the power to move the body.[145] He further thought that each person must be *conscius* of being free, in particular of having complete freedom to make judgements or to

144 Locke argued that this doctrine of unqualified responsibility requires the support of the principle that God will, on the Day of Judgement, revive consciousness (i.e. active memory) of all one's past actions (*Essay II.xxvii.22*). Leibniz dissented from this argument, though he agreed that there must be some sense in which an agent is *conscius* of all his past actions (*Essais* 243–4, cf. 239).

145 '. . . *mentis cum corpore unio, cuius sane mens* conscia *est*. . . . *Quod mens* . . . *corpus possit impellere* . . . certissima & evidentissima experientia *quotidie nobis* ostendit' (AT V: 222, emphasis added).

suspend judgement.[146] In all these cases, *conscientia* of the powers of the soul is a foundation of metaphysical and moral knowledge, not some sort of impression that might turn out to be unjustified.[147]

Second, *conscientia* is taken to encompass voluntary actions of agents who act on the basis of reasoning, deliberation, and volition. It embraces all actions of which the principles are thoughts or volitions,[148] but not mere 'animal movements'. In other words, it includes cases of self-predication of the rational senses of S-predicates of locomotion. This much is clear from the puzzling discussion of walking in *Principles* I.9: there must be a sense of 'walk' in which it makes sense to speak of '*conscientia* of walking' ('*conscientia ambulandi*'), and equally this sense of 'walk' must be a mode of thinking predicated of the rational soul or mind, since the final sentence includes the sub-sentence '*mens cogitat* se *ambulare*' (emphasis added).

There are other indications of this doctrine. One is his treatment of the objection that brutes may think because they must be *conscius* of their movements just as we humans are (AT VII: 414; CSM II: 279): Descartes didn't reply that the observation about humans is incorrect, but rather that attributing *conscientia* of their spontaneous movements to animals begs the question whether they can think (AT VII: 426; CSM II: 288). Another is his famous contention that having a volition and being *conscius* of having it are one and the same thing (*Passions* I.19; CSM I: 336): since this applies to all volitions, including those 'actions which terminate in the body' (*Passions* I.18; CSM I: 335), it may subsume the thesis that we have *conscientia* of voluntary bodily actions (unless there is some conclusive independent argument that this thesis is inadmissible). The central place of voluntary actions in the scholastic conception of *conscientia* has surprisingly strong echoes in Descartes' texts.

146 '*Jam autem nos intime conscii sumus nostrae libertatis, et nos ita posse cohibere assensum, cum volumus*' (AT IV: 159). Malebranche agreed in holding that a person has an (intermittent) infallible inner sensation of being free (*sentiment intérieur de notre liberté*) (*Recherche* III. 10).

147 Compare Spinoza's criticism of the idea of being *conscius* of being free: a conscious stone might have a feeling of being free as it fell to the ground under the influence of gravity. The impression that human agents have of being free has no superior cognitive status, in his view.

148 At first sight, this claim is flatly contradicted. 'I use the term ["thought"] to include everything that is within us in such a way that we are immediately [immediate] *conscius* of it . . . . I say "immediately" so as to exclude the consequences of thoughts; a voluntary movement [*motus voluntarius*], for example, originates in a thought but is not itself a thought' (AT VII: 160; CSM II: 113). But careful reflection suggests that he intended to single out by the qualification 'immediately' a sub-domain from a wider domain of things of which we are indeed *conscius*, and this legislation which expressly narrows the application of 'thinking' is undertaken for the purpose of validating the *Cogito*. This sub-domain consists of operations of the soul ('modes of thinking') about which our judgements are indubitable. The wider domain also consists in what are called 'modes of thinking' (in a less restricted sense of 'thinking'), and it includes voluntary actions.

This disambiguation of 'modes of thinking' is paralleled by distinguishing a narrower from a wider sense of 'modes of extension'. The narrower one includes only mechanical (or 'geometrical') properties of corporeal substances, while the wider one includes sensible qualities (colour, light, taste, etc.) and dispositions (fragility, viscosity, etc.).

Third, the principle that someone must be *conscius* of thinking something *at the time* of so thinking might suggest that *conscientia* must be limited to the *present* (as introspection is supposed to be). But Descartes' defence of the axiom that the soul must always be thinking makes it clear that he took *conscientia* to extend over the past as well as the present. The presupposition of his opponents seems to be that *conscientia*, like other forms of cognition, tends to persist. On this view, if I were *conscius* in the middle of last night that I was then thinking something, I would still be *conscius* in the morning of having so thought at that time. Yet after a night of uninterrupted dreamless sleep, I will deny that I did any thinking in the middle of the night. Therefore, if I had been thinking then, and I have no *conscientia* now of having done so, this supports the conclusion that I was not then *conscius* of doing so. Unless it makes sense for me to have *conscientia* of what I have (or have not) done in the past, the objection is hard to motivate. So too is Descartes' response, namely that it is more reasonable for me to judge that I have forgotten the thinking I did in the middle of the night than to deny the axiom that the soul must be *conscius* of thinking something at the time of so thinking (AT III: 478–9; CSMK III: 203).[149] In fact, if we bear in mind that *conscientia* is a form of knowledge with a distinctive scope, then it will seem altogether natural that it extends over past 'modes of thinking'.

Our stressing the many points of continuity between Descartes' ideas and the scholastic tradition is not meant as a denial that there are some crucial innovations in his conception of *conscientia*.[150] We focus on two. Both make direct contact with the earlier tradition, and both are directly motivated when seen as imaginative and intelligent modifications of it. The task of clarifying these motivations is a crucial part of making sense of his conceptual innovations. The first is his redefinition of the 'operations of the soul' expressly to exclude all forms of *animal* sentience (and *animal* locomotion). This is directly linked with his doctrine that all S-predicates are systematically ambiguous. The second is his introduction of the doctrine that everyone has infallible *conscientia* of their own present acts of making a judgement (and of withholding assent from a thought). This is directly linked with a moral doctrine of central importance: everybody enjoys *complete freedom* to affirm or deny a thought or to suspend judgement, and therefore each of us has a completely *unqualified responsibility* for what we think.

149 Locke criticized this reasoning. He argued that we should reject Descartes' principle that the soul is always thinking. It is 'much more probable [*sic*] that it [the soul] should sometimes not think, than that it should often think, and that a long while together, and not be conscious to itself, the next moment after, that it had thought' (*Essay* II.i.18, cf. II.i.14). This argument too accepts that someone may be (indeed usually is) 'conscious' of his recent *past* thinking.

150 Others have claimed that his most important innovation is purging *conscientia* of all of its moral connotations and making it a purely 'anthropological concept' (*Wörterbuch* I.890). In our view, the burden of proof falls on advocates of this position; the case is not established by absence of sustained discussion of self-knowledge in respect of the moral evaluation of actions and character.

Distinctive of Descartes' 'psychology' is the narrowing of the 'operations of the (rational) soul' by the reasoned exclusion of the functions of the vegetative and sensitive souls. All these 'functions' in human beings are to be given purely mechanical explanations. (The same explanation also embraces sense-perception and locomotion in animals.) As a direct consequence, the traditional concept of *conscientia* is decisively narrowed. In making any judgement in which I predicate the animal sense of an S-predicate of myself (e.g., in judging 'I see_1 light' or 'I $fear_1$ the bonfire'), I cannot be manifesting *conscientia* since the logical subject of the judgement is the body, not the *soul*. Descartes thus reinterpreted the definition of *conscientia* as 'knowledge of the soul and its operations'. This stipulation is now understood to exclude all self-predications of the animal senses of S-predicates. What it leaves to *conscientia* are all and only those properties of persons which essentially involve reasoning, intelligence, freedom, and moral responsibility. Self-knowledge about these matters alone qualifies as *conscientia*. (Self-knowledge about states of animal sentience, Imagination, or movement is grouped together with other forms of knowledge about one's body, e.g., the capacity to make true judgements about one's health, weight, co-ordination.)

The other main innovation is the doctrine of the infallibility of self-knowledge in a *strictly limited* sub-domain of the operations of the soul. Although the wide scope of *conscientia* makes the very idea of its universal infallibility absurd, there may nevertheless be kinds of claim to self-knowledge where the Thinker's word carries special authority. In fact, Descartes' texts isolate just such a special set of judgements about modes of thinking about which the Thinker himself *cannot* be mistaken:

> I am now seeing light, hearing a noise, feeling heat. But I am asleep, so all this is false. Yet I certainly *seem* to see, to hear, and to be warmed. This *cannot be false*; what is called 'having a sensory perception' [*sentire*] is strictly [*proprie*] just this, and in this restricted sense of the term it is simply thinking.
>
> (AT VII: 29; CSM II: 19, italics added)

This point is echoed in the corresponding passages in the *Principles*:

> if I take 'seeing' and 'walking' to apply to the actual sense or awareness of seeing or walking [*Sed si intelligam de ipso sensu sive conscientia videndi aut ambulandi*], then the conclusion is *fully certain* [*plane certum*], since it relates to the mind, which alone has the sensation or thought that it is seeing or walking.
>
> (*Principles* I.9 (AT VIIIA: 7–8; CSM I: 195*), italics added)

Finally, in presenting his reasoning *more geometrico*, he singled out a sub-domain within what are called 'modes of thinking' by adding the qualification 'immediately' to the term '*conscius*', and his intention is to focus on instances of thinking that can serve as premises for the *Cogito* (AT VII: 160; CSM II: 113).

The real difficulty is to ascertain exactly what are the contents of the judgements which he declared to be indubitable.[151]

We are now in a position to clarify this point. *Meditation* II couples the claim that a restricted set of sense-based judgements is immune to error with the singling out of the restricted sense of *sentire*. We have explained the contents of these judgements to be 'I have the thought that I have (just now) made certain judgements'. In daily life, with no hesitation at all, I make such judgements as these: 'I see light', 'I feel heat from the fire', etc. But, having now learned (from the reasoning presented in *Meditation* I) that I have solid reasons to call each and every one of these sense-based judgements into doubt, I reflect on my habitual judgements and notice the fact that I have just made them. By my power to reflect on my own thinking (i.e. *conscientia*), I can say 'I have (just) judged that I see light', or, what Descartes took to be equivalent, 'I judge [*judico*] that I see light' or 'I think [*puto*] that I see light' (cf. *Principles* I.9, 11). This is a distinct judgement from the original dubious claim 'I see light',[152] and its logical predicate is what Descartes called 'seeing' in the restricted sense. This judgement seems evidently immune from any risk of error. Whether or not it is true that I have eyes to be affected by light or that there is light to be seen, I have made the everyday sense-based judgement 'I see light'. So if I now express the judgement 'I judge/judged that I see light', how could I possibly go wrong? Our suggestion, then, is that Descartes here singled out judgements whose content is that the Judger has *made a* particular sense-based *judgement*. All judgements of this class clearly meet the general necessary condition for *conscientia*: they predicate a mode of thinking of the rational soul. The parallel passages in the *Principles* strongly confirm this interpretation.

In fact, the restriction to judgements about having made *sense-based* judgements can be dropped. Descartes' doctrine is the general principle that a person cannot be mistaken in his own (sincere) judgements that he has particular 'perceptions' or that he makes/has made particular judgements. This is a strictly circumscribed principle: only a single mode of thinking is accorded a special cognitive status, namely the mental act of judging something to be true.[153] (Knowledge of my own volitions is a special case under this heading.) Even if in making a particular judgement I may be mistaken about the truth of what I judge

151 A supplementary question is what he understood by the term 'indubitable' (as well as the expressions 'quite certain', 'cannot be false', 'immune to error', etc.). We think that *Meditation* I makes clear his commitment to the idea that doubt requires grounds, so that 'indubitable' must mean 'impossible to *call into* doubt', not 'logically impossible to doubt'. His concern is to establish what it is *rational* to treat as beyond doubt, not to isolate thoughts which it would be nonsensical or self-contradictory to doubt. But we cannot investigate this issue further here.

152 This point is *not* self-evident, especially within the framework of syllogistic logic. The utterance 'It seems to me that I see light' might be taken to make no judgement at all (perhaps, positively, to express an appearance or '*phantasia*') or to make the very same judgement as 'I see light' (though these sentences differ 'modally'). Descartes may have been responsible for redefining 'judgement' (and hence also 'thought' or 'perception') in just this respect. We can't here explore this important issue any further.

153 This is common to all the forms of thinking called 'the operations of the will, the intellect, the imagination and the senses' (AT VII: 160; CSM II: 113).

to be true, I can never be in error if I make the judgement that I am making (or have just made) this judgement.[154]

This principle interlocks with the axiom that, whenever I think something, I must be *conscius* at that time of so thinking. That axiom states the presupposition of the pattern of argument exemplified in *Meditation* II. Because all instances of rational sense-perception, Imagination, and voluntary action involve making judgements, they are all cases of thinking or having thoughts ('perceptions'). My having *conscientia* guarantees that I must always have the *capacity* to attain reflective knowledge of these operations of the soul, hence to 'perceive' that I have them. Therefore, in every case, I can make the judgement *that* I have a particular thought, and because I cannot be mistaken about this judgement, I can by the power of reflection always obtain an indubitable premise for the *Cogito*. This is precisely the manoeuvre that Descartes carried out to isolate the judgement 'I see$_2$ light'. My knowledge that I *seem* to see light is an instance of *conscientia*, and it is infallible because it is a judgement whose content is that I have just performed an act of making a judgement. Nothing less than his axiom connecting thinking with *conscientia* would suffice for his argument, and nothing more is required.

The doctrine of the *restricted* infallibility of *conscientia* has a clear *moral* motivation in Descartes' thinking. It is essential to making sense of his principle that, in respect of making judgements, each person enjoys complete freedom. (My own judgements are the only acts that lie *wholly* within my power.) Being perfectly free in making judgements (and withholding assent), I am also fully responsible for *all* the judgements I make over the whole of my lifetime. Or, somewhat more leniently, I am responsible for all the *principles* on which my judgements are based.[155] We humans will all be answerable to God on the Day of Judgement for any wilful misuse of our God-given intellects. (The instrument is as perfect as possible: that is what *Meditation* IV is meant to put beyond doubt. We can in principle avoid error by withholding assent from any idea not clearly and distinctly perceived; and we can arrive at knowledge of everything that can be known by building up carefully from ideas that we do clearly and distinctly perceive.) 'The fact that we fall into error is a defect in the way we act, not a defect in our Nature' (*Principles* I.38; CSM I: 205).

This moral vision makes sense only if freedom is correlated with the possibility of knowledge about the things for which I am to be held responsible (what I am now doing and what I have done). If it is just for God to hold me responsible for my judgements, He must have endowed me with the capacity to judge correctly what I am judging/have just judged.[156] It must be part of my Nature as a thinking

154 Some modification might be required if we took seriously the objection that I might be mistaken in thinking that what I said (or said to myself) makes sense. We ignore this complication.

155 Hence I have a *moral duty*, at least once in my lifetime, to examine these principles (AT VII: 17; CSM II: 12).

156 And the capacity to ascertain the principles on which my judgements are based (cf. AT VII: 18; CSM II: 12)! This point might suggest that *conscientia* must include the potential to explain why (i.e. on what grounds) I make/have made this judgement.

thing that, if I make a judgement, then I *must* be *conscius* of making/having made this judgement;[157] I must be capable of framing the reflective judgement 'I judge (or think) that . . .' (even if I fail to articulate it).[158] Nothing less would make sense of what Descartes took to be the *Christian* doctrine that, on the Day of Judgement, God will hold each soul responsible for all of its *judgements*. This is a necessary feature of the 'moral order'.[159] Unqualified responsibility requires the possibility of *perfect* knowledge. There must be no possibility of my having made a judgement when I judge in good conscience (*sic*!) that I have not done so and no possibility of my having failed to make a judgement when I judge in good conscience that I have done so. Nothing less than this epistemological guarantee (or *moral certainty*) would make sense of Descartes' moral crusade, and nothing more comprehensive is required.[160]

Conscientia, *consciousness, and introspection*

Our analysis depicts Descartes' conception of *conscientia* as an intelligible development of scholastic thought. It shows many points of continuity with the inherited wisdom of his day as well as two points of clearly motivated disagreement. We offer textual documentation for our case, and we argue that clarifying his conception of *conscientia* throws light on many other matters.

We now aim at some further clarification by drawing out some important implications of his conception of *conscientia* which differentiate it sharply from notions that are expressed (neither uniformly nor clearly) by the terms 'consciousness', 'self-consciousness', and 'introspection'.

It seems certain that *conscientia* is self-knowledge in respect of modes of *thinking*. But identifying modes of thinking with what are now called 'states of consciousness' misrepresents the scope of this knowledge. It excludes some things

157 The nature of the necessity involved in this claim is to be clarified in terms of the distinctive necessity that is characteristic of 'our (God-given!) Nature' (see below, pp. 183–8).

Leibniz built a more general requirement of infallibility into 'the moral order': namely 'a present or immediate memory, the memory of what was taking place [past actions] immediately before – or in other words, the consciousness or reflection which accompanies inner activity – *cannot Naturally* deceive us' (*Essais* 238, italics added).

158 Aquinas noted this presupposition of freedom: 'Judgement is in the power of the person judging to the extent that he can make a judgement about his own judging . . . . But only reason can make a judgement about its own judgement, which reflects upon its own action . . . . Hence the basis of all freedom is built on reason' (*Quaestiones Disputatae de Veritate* V. 24.2).

159 This requirement of rational morality is made perfectly explicit by Leibniz (*Essais* 245–6). The more general analogue, applying to all voluntary action, is frequently treated as a precondition for the intelligibility of God's holding each of us responsible for all of the acts of an entire lifetime, e.g., by Locke (*Essay* II.xxvii.22, 26).

160 This interpretation is the diametrical opposite of the one given in Gaukroger 1995. He argues that there is a 'self-reflective or self-conscious awareness that accompanies *many* acts of human cognition' (p. 325). This 'awareness of one's own mental states is the key to the difference between creatures with a mind and automata, and [without it] the characteristic features of human mental life would not be possible' (p. 350). Although 'we need to be aware of our mental states *if* we are to make judgements about them', it is mistaken to argue that there is any 'need for the mind to have the capacity to be aware . . . of its *judgements*' (p. 461, n.193, all italics added).

that Descartes definitely included: in particular, voluntary actions,[161] and states of intellect and character (e.g., intelligence, perceptiveness, freedom, virtues and vices). Conversely, it includes some things that Descartes excluded: in particular, all forms of animal sentience, including the objects of the two internal senses (e.g., pain, hunger, thirst, fear, anger, and joy), and animal Imagination (e.g., mental images and animal desires). These are radical (BIG!) differences between two distinct concepts. If the soul and its operations comprise all and only those things of which it makes sense to say that someone is *conscius*, then what Descartes called the mind (*mens, esprit*) is definitely not the subject-matter of twentieth-century philosophy of mind, and he definitely did not propound his dualism as a solution to what is now called 'the mind–body problem'.

This has an important corollary: it immediately undermines one indirect argument for Descartes' term 'thinking' (*cogitatio*) to cover all states of consciousness. Neglect of the doctrine of the systematic ambiguity of S-predicates leads to a misunderstanding of his conception of *conscientia*. In their rational (or 'restricted') sense, each of these predicates is used to signify a mode of thinking. As a consequence, *when used in this way*, each of them predicates a mode of thinking of a rational soul, and in the case of self-predication of these properties, a Thinker's making true judgements of this form is a manifestation of *conscientia* (e.g., in judging 'I see$_2$ light' or 'I fear$_2$ the bonfire'). This point is perfectly straightforward since the rational sense of any S-predicate is used to state that the subject of the judgement has an articulate thought and this judgement evidently reports an 'operation' of the rational soul. But, if we don't respect the doctrine of the systematic ambiguity of S-predicates, we seem sure to conflate this unremarkable thesis about the scope of *conscientia* with the very different thesis that *animal* sentience in humans falls within the scope of this same cognitive capacity. This conclusion might then be taken to support the claim that Descartes extended the term 'thinking' to embrace the functions traditionally ascribed to the sensitive soul, in particular all forms of (animal) sentience and (animal) Imagination.[162] This seductive line of reasoning is a *non sequitur*: such a derivation of the 'Courtesy Thesis' (see p. 15) commits the fallacy of equivocation by failing to distinguish the two senses (animal and rational) of each and every S-predicate. As a result, it mistakes Descartes' narrowing of the scope of Aristotelian *conscientia* for a widening of the scope of traditional notions of the mind (*ratio*)!

Likewise, introspection is definitely a different concept (or pseudo-concept?) from *conscientia*. In fact, this putative power *infallibly* to apprehend the ghostly

161 This has important implications for delineating Descartes' conception of an agent's cognitive relation to his own body. In particular, this cannot be described correctly as a matter exclusively of sense-perception by the external senses. Cartesian Dualism misrepresents his conception by claiming that one's own body is unequivocally part of the 'External World'.

162 It is noteworthy that S-predicates of locomotion (or, more generally, bodily movement) are not treated in a parallel way by modern commentators. This generates some embarrassment: for instance, the difficulty of making sense of the parallelism between seeing and walking in *Principles* I.9.

episodes that take place on the boards of one's private mental stage is twice removed from the cognitive power called '*conscientia*'.

First, the notion of introspection is self-evidently absurd unless its objects are strictly limited to (present) states of consciousness. There is nothing 'essentially private' about voluntary actions or states of character, and there is little inclination in these cases to make claims about 'privileged access' or 'one's own word carrying special authority'. *Conscientia* may differ from knowledge of others' modes of thinking in degree (or extensiveness), but there is no essential difference in kind.

Second, introspection incorporates a perceptual model of self-knowledge: it is supposed to be one's means of access to items in one's inner or mental world just as the senses of sight, hearing, etc. give access to items in the outer or material world.[163] This presupposes a conception of sense-perception that Descartes did not have,[164] and then it refashions his conception of *conscientia* on this inappropriate model.

Introspection, like sight, is usually conceived as a form of knowledge by acquaintance with objects which must be distinguished from articulate thoughts or judgements;[165] paradigms are taken to be pains, hunger pangs, or transports of anger or joy. These are all *things* with which we are 'directly presented'.[166] Both self-knowledge and knowledge of the external world are taken to be something more complex, namely judgements based on the data of 'immediate experience', and the logical forms of these judgements are taken to be parallel.[167] Both introspection and sight are more primitive than the capacity to make judgements, and both are shared by humans with higher animals. The analogy between these two faculties is encapsulated in calling introspection 'inner *sense*'.

This analogy is something that Descartes did not accept *in this form*, indeed one that he could not have. The analogy that he saw is radically different. In his view, there can be no such thing as *conscientia* in a brute, and any parallelism

163 This conception crops up frequently. James Mill noted it in Reid's notion of 'consciousness' (*Analysis of the Phenomena of The Human Mind*, Longman Green Reader & Dyer: London, 1869, I.227). Shoemaker attributes this model to Descartes and suggests that it underlies his conception of thoughts as 'mental *objects*' (*Self-knowledge and Self-Identity*, Ithaca: Cornell University Press, 1963).

164 In fact, one that introduces the 'pseudo-ideas' that Arnauld so vigorously attacked in the work of Malebranche and castigated as a deviation from Descartes' view.

165 Both points are evident in Russell. He highlighted the notion of acquaintance in this context (1912: 49–50: quoted above, n. 126), and he argued that knowledge of truths is more complex than, and must be grounded in, knowledge by acquaintance (pp. 42, 46–7).

166 Arnauld attacked this non-Cartesian account of perception in Malebranche. In his view, Malebranche erred in taking ideas to be 'real beings', 'spiritual beings' distinct from the bodies they represent, entities 'which our mind must envisage before it forms perceptions', and objects 'actually distinct from our mind' as well as from the objects sense-perceived. There *cannot* be any such intermediaries in rational sense-perception (*Ideas* ch. 4, 26–7).

167 Sometimes the basic form is taken to be relational: 'I see Socrates' and 'I have the sensation of pain in the foot' express binary relations. More commonly the subject-term 'I' is suppressed in logical analysis: then 'Here-now the colour red' is comparable to 'Here-now the sensation of pain'.

between *conscientia* and sense-perception must concern *rational* sense-perception (not animal sentience). Both of these are *cognitive* powers of the rational soul, and any exercise of these powers must involve having (articulate) *thoughts*, and making *judgements* (or suspending judgement). Any judgement exhibiting either form of knowledge must have the rational soul as its logical subject: no other possibility is conceivable within Descartes' logico-metaphysical framework.

In his philosophical analysis of *conscientia*, as in that of (rational) sense-perception, there is no logical space for any kind of 'knowledge by acquaintance' with more primitive, essentially inarticulate, mental intermediaries.[168] Nothing would be made more intelligible by introducing any such pseudo-ideas; hence this possibility can be excluded on the basis of the axiom that God always works in the most economical manner. All forms of rational sense-perception might be called *primitive* cognitive powers. They are part of our Nature as the union of mind and body. The only possible way of making any sense at all of the correlation of *motions* in the sense-organs with *thoughts* is God's having so instituted our Nature. For a parallel reason, *conscientia* must be a *primitive* power. In any instance of its exercise, one thought is correlated with a logically independent thought, i.e. with a thought with which it has 'no intelligible resemblance'. For example, when I make the judgement 'I see light', I manifest *conscientia* in making the distinct judgement 'I judge/have just judged that I see light'. Here too the only possible way of making any sense at all of such systematic non-logical relations of thoughts is to make reference to what God has ordained. (The elements in this reasoning are explained more fully on p. 172 below.) In both cases, no further explanatory machinery could eliminate the need to invoke God's intervention at some stage, so that it could do nothing other than making matters more complex (QED).

In some other respects, *conscientia* is not parallel even with rational sense-perception, and in these respects, it is essentially different from introspection. On Descartes' conception, sense-perception (*sentire*) is necessarily confined to the (specious) present; past-tense and future-tense sensory judgements are allocated to the distinct faculty of Imagination. Thus *conscientia* is essentially different here, since it makes sense for somebody to be *conscius* of his own *past* modes of thinking (and acting). Moreover, there are some sense-based judgements that apparently incorporate 'substantial attributes': for example, 'I see Socrates' plausibly has the same logical form as 'I hit Socrates'.[169] It is clear that there is no analogue for judgements exhibiting *conscientia*. The phrase 'the thought that God exists' or 'the sensation of having a pain in the foot' is definitely not the name of an incorporeal *substance*, so that the judgements 'I have the thought that God exists' and 'I have

168 This has the corollary that it may be a fundamental mistake to ascribe to Descartes the view that the foundations of knowledge are to be found in immediate subjective *experience* (for example, if we referred to Russell's concept of experience).

169 We ignore the question whether the animal and rational senses of 'see' (and other S-predicates) differ in this respect. Some commentators dispute whether Descartes could account for the 'world-involvingness' of thought.

the sensation of having pain in the foot' cannot be treated as instances of substantial predication. This point is overlooked by arguments that pin the Two-Worlds View on him on the grounds that *he* (mistakenly!) accepted that *conscientia*-judgements had the same form as the relational perceptual judgement 'I see Socrates'. The Legendary picture is that he took *conscientia* to stand to objects in the inner world as the senses stand to objects in the external world!

We could sum up this discussion by claiming that the perceptual model built into the concept of introspection does not fit Descartes' conception of *conscientia*. On the one hand, it pays no heed to radical differences between rational sense-perception and *conscientia*. On the other hand, it completely misrepresents his complex analysis of sense-perception itself.

In fact, the very idea that *conscientia* is seriously *analogous* to sense-perception (as it were, a form of 'inner *sense*') contains a more subtle distortion. It shifts attention from actions (operations of the mind) to happenings (what passes before the mind), from agents (who attend to things, make judgements, reason and deliberate) to spectators (who find that they have acquired beliefs, expectations, and habits of associating ideas from the steady accumulation of sense-experiences). On Descartes' view, action is a crucial part even of the 'passive' power of the soul to be acted on by the body; making a judgement is an essential component of any instance of (rational) sense-perception,[170] and this is an *act* which lies wholly within our power and for which we are fully responsible. Other operations of the soul are even more obviously actions: striving for clear and distinct perceptions, analysing an issue into component problems and working out rigorous solutions to them, calculating, deliberating about what is to be done, etc.[171] The soul is conceived to be essentially *active*.[172] *Conscientia* is primarily an *agent's* knowledge of his own *actions*, and it is exercised actively in making reasoned judgements about the soul's own operations.[173] By contrast, 'reflection' (in Locke and Hume) is primarily a person's awareness of what *happens* in his own mind, of the experiences that befall him, or of what is *given* (what Bergson called '*les*

170 This point about judgement is emphasized in a modern attack on the 'Myth of the Given', though it is associated with a conception of experience that Descartes would have rejected: 'We would not be able to suppose that the capacities that are in play in experience are conceptual . . . unless they could also be exercised in active thinking . . . . Minimally, it must be possible to decide whether or not to judge that things are as one's experience represents them to be. How one's experience represents things to be is not under one's control, but it is up to one whether one accepts the appearance or rejects it' (McDowell 1994: 11).

171 In the construction of mechanics according to Cartesian canons, reasoning has far greater importance than one might expect, the gathering of sensory data less. This is an important consequence of freeing ourselves from the prejudice that what is known from and through the senses is most true (AT VII: 18; CSM II: 12).

172 Although Aquinas employed the phrase 'agent intellect' ('*intellectus agens*') for a more specific purpose, we might well appropriate it for characterizing Descartes' conception of the soul.

173 So understood, *conscientia* is indeed what underpins the *Cogito* and constitutes a crucial part of the foundations of knowledge. (In having the sensation of pain, I am *conscius* of having this sensation; but having the *sensation* of pain is to perform the *action* of making a sense-based judgement.) Other elements in the foundations of knowledge are principles that we clearly and distinctly perceive by the Natural light, and this knowledge does not fall within *conscientia*.

données immédiates de l'expérience').[174] It is a matter of having impressions of impressions, and it requires little or no activity (at most, perhaps, directing one's attention). Surely a change of attitude is involved, as well as a shift of terminology.

This point is linked to two correlative differences between the British empiricists' notion of reflection and Descartes' concept of *conscientia*. Both differences indicate decisive shifts in the focus of philosophical investigations.

First, empiricists consider reflection as one of the two sources of ideas (or concepts), the other being the (external) senses. Reflection must supply all the impressions (experiences) from which simple ideas of anything imperceptible must be derived – for instance, the ideas of belief, volition, and thinking.[175] For this purpose, reflection must be thought closely to resemble sense-perception: closely enough so that the possibility of pinpointing an internal impression (e.g., a sentiment of belief) can be treated as vindicating the empiricist claim that everything in the intellect must have its origins in *the senses*. Moreover, since the senses are cast in the role of supplying the materials for fashioning the building-blocks of judgements ('ideas', 'notions', or 'concepts'), sense-*impressions* are taken to be essentially non-propositional or inarticulate.

Descartes quarrelled with this whole framework of thinking, root and branch. He dissented from the principle that simple ideas must originate in sense-experience, and he never appealed to *conscientia* (or reflection!) to supply the materials for framing judgements. Unlike the empiricists, he had no reason to claim symmetry between *conscientia* and sense-perception.

Second, the empiricists divorced the concept of reflection from the notion of *moral agency*.[176] Indeed they held that the Self is not given in experience, and that the simplest form of judgement grounded in reflection is the report of the occurrence of an ownerless impression. On this view, reflection clearly has no role in building the body of self-knowledge that alone makes sense of the idea of treating a person as a free and responsible agent. For this purpose, what we need is knowledge of our own present and *past* thoughts and *actions*. If this cognitive power is called 'reflection' (and its exercise 'reflective knowledge'), then it must embrace articulate (propositional) knowledge of what *the agent* is doing and has done.[177] It must consist of correct *I*-thoughts. This is precisely how Descartes

174 In defining Reflection as 'the perception of the operations of our own mind within us', Locke explicitly cancelled the implication that the term 'operations' be limited to 'the *actions* of the mind about its own ideas', admitting under this term 'some sort of *passions*' as well (*Essay* II.i.4, italics added). He added a similar gloss to the term 'perception', which is 'by some called thinking in general. Although thinking, in the propriety of the English tongue, signifies that sort of operation in the mind about its ideas, wherein the mind is *active* . . . . [I]n bare naked perception, the mind is, for the most part, only *passive*; and what it perceives, it cannot avoid perceiving' (II.ix.1, italics added).

175 For example: 'What perception is, every one will know better by *reflecting* on what he does himself, when he sees, hears, feels, &c., or thinks, than by any discourse of mine. Whoever *reflects* on what passes in his own mind cannot miss it' (Locke, *Essay* II.ix.1–2, italics added).

176 Arguably in Hume's account of personal identity, the very idea of moral agency is lost altogether.

177 Locke generally (though not uniformly, cf. *Essay* II.xxvii.11) used 'reflection' in accounting for the origin of ideas, but 'consciousness' in developing his notion of a person as a moral agent. His distinguishing these concepts alters the logical geography of both terms in *his* language.

conceived of *conscientia* (or reflection). *Res cogitans* is not an idealized observer or spectator, but the free and responsible agent making use of his powers. *Conscientia* is an essential part of his God-given Nature, and it secures the possibility of an agent's making true judgements about his own actions and their moral worth. *Conscientia* shows that thinking is as directly related to action, deliberation, and welfare as it is to knowledge, demonstration, and truth.[178] We have a moral duty to make the right use of reason, and we cannot secure our own welfare unless we perceive things clearly and distinctly enough. Failure to appreciate this moral dimension of his intellectual campaign seems to be the most severe form of blindness among Anglo-American interpreters of Descartes.[179] The assimilation of *conscientia* to the empiricists' notion of reflection is the diagnostic symptom of this disease of the understanding.

Finally, we must note that *conscientia* cannot be identified with what is now commonly called 'self-consciousness' in philosophy of mind. In its absolute use, '*conscientia*' names an essential, innate, inalienable, and invariant cognitive power; hence there is no such thing as a person who is not *conscius*. The term 'self-conscious' admits of no parallel use. In its relative use, '*conscientia*' denotes a body of true judgements that a person makes about his own thoughts and actions. In the case of each person, each of these judgements is a singular judgement that predicates a property of one and the same rational soul; its logical subject is an incorporeal substance, a thinking *thing*. Most modern analyses of self-knowledge contradict this doctrine in one way or another, dismissing the Cartesian Ego as a logical fiction.[180] If doctrines about the logical analysis of apparent I-thoughts are built into the conceptions of *conscientia* and of self-consciousness, then these two things are *essentially* different.

So Protean is the concept of consciousness that it seems a good working hypothesis to assume that another's concept is another concept. Beyond any doubt this method is appropriate for any twentieth-century philosopher who investigates Descartes' notion of *conscientia*.

The internal senses

That Descartes held that there were internal as well as external senses is not a matter of speculation, nor is it hidden away only in the obscurest of texts. The

178 S. Hampshire (*Thought and Action*, London: Chatto, 1960) makes this parallelism the basis of an attempt to draw together various ideas that are often treated by modern philosophers in isolation from each other. Descartes' project had similar ambitions.

179 'The Project of Pure Inquiry' goes wrong on the title page. The widespread idea that *Meditation* IV is tangential or peripheral to the whole work is *fundamentally* mistaken.

180 Here is a paradigm: '"I think" is [Descartes'] ultimate premise. Here the word "I" is really illegitimate; he ought to state his ultimate premise in the form "there are thoughts". The word "I" is grammatically convenient, but it does not describe a datum. When he goes on to say "I am a *thing* which thinks", he is already using uncritically the apparatus of categories handed down by scholasticism' (Russell 1946: 589).

concept of the internal senses plays a vital but generally unnoticed role in a well-known and much-discussed passage in *Meditation* VI:

> Later on . . . I had many experiences which gradually undermined all the faith I had had in the senses. Sometimes towers which had looked round from a distance appeared square from close up . . . . In these and countless other such cases, I found that the judgements of the external senses were mistaken. And this applied not only to the external senses but to *the internal senses* as well. For what can be more internal than *pain*? And yet I had heard that those who had had a leg or an arm amputated sometimes still *seemed to feel* pain intermittently in the missing part of the body [*se sibi videri . . . dolorem sentire*]. So even in my own case it was apparently *not fully certain* that a particular limb was hurting, even if I felt pain in it.
>
> (AT VII: 76–7; CSM II: 53*, italics added)

The question about how to interpret this passage might seem peripheral, but it is of the greatest importance, at least in part because the Legend takes pain to be a *paradigm* Cartesian thought (*cogitatio*) or 'state of consciousness'.

The passage has a number of clear implications. First, pains are apprehended by a form of sense-perception (*sentire*). Second, the amputee's feeling a 'phantom pain' in his amputated limb is an instance of 'deception by the senses' (more accurately, of false sensory judgement) which is strictly comparable to mistaking the shape of a tower seen in the distance.[181] Third, judgements based on the internal senses are no less fallible than judgements based on the external senses; so it is 'apparently not fully certain' that my limb is hurting.[182] Finally, there is scope for making a distinction in respect of what is apprehended by the internal senses between how things *seem* to be and how they *really* are.

All of these points are evident in this one text. If a modern commentator were in serious doubt about whether Descartes used the term 'the internal senses' ('*sensus interni*') literally or metaphorically here, he could set this doubt aside by examining the full-dress account of sense-perception in *Principles* IV. There Descartes described in some detail both the sense-organs and the physiology of the workings of the internal senses. He also made it clear that some animals have the same internal senses that are possessed by human beings (*Treatise on Man*). (Here it must be said that Descartes used different criteria in different places for picking out the internal senses, although in either case, 'internal' and 'external' are relative to the person's own body. In *Principles* IV.190 (CSM I: 280), the

181 This form of 'deception by the senses' seems not to be a staple item in the tradition of ancient scepticism. For example, it is absent from the texts of Sextus Empiricus.

182 One might add that judgements based on the internal senses are no *more* fallible than those based on the external senses. If the point of the phantom pain case is to illustrate a false internal-sense-based judgement that I have a pain in my foot, then there presumably are circumstances (e.g., when made by a non-amputee) in which that judgement would be true. This point is worth pressing: if Descartes held it to be logically or metaphysically impossible for pain to be in a limb (as seems to be implied by the Legendary view that pains are mental), *anyone* (not just an amputee) who judged that his limb was painful would be saying something *necessarily* false.

terms 'internal' and 'external' apparently had to do with the underlying *mechanisms* of the senses. The internal senses were constituted by nerves that extended to the '*interior* parts' of the body (the stomach, throat, heart, diaphragm, etc.), as opposed to the *peripheral* parts of the body (the skin, the tongue, the nose, the ears, or the eyes) to which the nerves constituting the external senses extended. And here pain seems to be associated with the sense of touch rather than with an internal sense (*Principles* IV.191; CSM I: 282). In the *Passions* I.23–4 (CSM I: 337), the 'internal/external' distinction appears to be based on whether we refer our 'perceptions' 'to our body' or 'to objects outside us', and by this criterion (as in *Meditation* VI), pain is an object of an internal sense. Despite this ambivalence, there is no doubt that he held that there are internal senses and that he thought one's apprehension of one's own pain to be a form of *sense*-perception; and usually he counted it as a form of *internal* sense-perception.) In *Principles* I, he regularly considered 'sensations of colour' and 'sensations of pain' in tandem, not because (as is sometimes suggested) he was taken in by the phrases '*feeling* pain', '*feeling* angry', etc., or because he failed to notice the disanalogies between tactile perceptions (of heat, texture, shape, etc.) and having bodily sensations or emotions, but because it was his fully worked-out view that these were parallel exemplifications of *sentire*.[183]

This conception of pain as an object of sense-perception is alien to twentieth-century Anglo-American philosophers. (So alien, indeed, that modern commentators fail even to see its main elements in this text.)[184] But Descartes' conception of the internal senses is something he took for granted. It is an integral part of the framework of Aristotelian psychology which he inherited. This notion has never wholly disappeared from the French tradition, although it has certainly altered over time.[185] It was still discussed this century by French phenomenologists, notably Merleau-Ponty (1962: Part I.2), who was critical of the perceptual model for one's awareness of one's own body.[186] In contrast, Anglo-American philo-

183 'I am convinced that hunger and thirst are felt in the same manner as colours, sounds, smells, and in general all the objects of the external senses, that is, by means of nerves stretched like fine threads from the brain to all the other parts of the body' (AT IV: 326; CSMK III: 274).

184 Neglect of his doctrine about the internal senses is surely one of the least contestable instances of lack of scholarly accuracy in interpreting his texts.

185 James attested to a different conception prominent among some continental psychologists: they tied the phrase 'internal perception' to the perception of time (1890: I 605), while treating pain, hunger, and thirst not as perceptions, but as aspects of the will (1890: II 549ff.). Malebranche contrasted the external senses with what he called '*sentiment intérieur*', but limited this to modifications of the soul. Maine de Biran's term '*sens intime*' referred to the sense-perception of muscular effort, and this notion was introduced as part of an anti-Cartesian polemic.

186 On the grounds that it could seem to make each person's relation to his own body too much like his relation to external objects. Merleau-Ponty was well aware that Descartes and others who talked about internal senses did everything they could to subvert the apparent implication that one's own body was an external object (see below). His complaint is rather like Wittgenstein's: 'The concept of the "inner picture" is misleading, for this concept uses the "*outer* picture" as a model; and yet the uses of the words for these concepts are no more like one another than the uses of "numeral" and "number". (And if one chose to call numbers "ideal numerals", one might produce a similar confusion.)': *PI* II 196.

sophy seems long ago to have 'lost' the concept of the internal senses; there is scarcely a trace of it even in Locke.[187] Without a clarification of this notion, however, there is no hope of attaining a sound understanding of *Descartes'* conception of pain. The same point holds for a wide range of so-called 'Cartesian thoughts'.[188] Bodily appetites (thirst, hunger, etc.) are also, in his view, objects of perception by one internal sense (*Principles* IV.190, CSM I: 280–1; cf. *Passions* I.24, CSM I: 337).[189]

The internal senses are part of the traditional 'package' of functions of the sensitive soul. They had a long and somewhat variable history within Aristotelian psychology, and Descartes was well versed in some parts of this tradition. In particular, he was familiar with the doctrine of Aquinas, who identified *four* 'interior senses' in addition to the five 'exterior senses' of sight, hearing, smell, taste, and touch; these are the 'common sense', Imagination, memory, and the *vis aestimativa* (literally, capacity of appraisal) by which, for example, danger or utility are perceived. Aquinas held these senses, like the external senses, to be possessed by animals as well as by human beings; they were termed 'senses' precisely because he regarded them as functions of the sensitive soul.

Descartes accepted and exploited the idea of the 'internal senses', but he allocated the functions of the sensitive soul differently from Aquinas, and this resulted in a different carving-out of the sphere of the internal senses and in different principles of individuation. He had a predominantly *physiological* motivation. His innovations were integral parts of his attempt to produce *mechanical* explanations for all the functions of the 'sensitive soul'. (Note that his conception therefore involves a fundamental change in the concept of a sense-modality. No longer are senses to be defined as functions conferred by a sensitive soul.)

In outline,[190] Descartes eliminated three of Aquinas' four internal senses and split the last one into two. He tended to count memory as a species of Imagination,

187 There are occasional attempts on the part of psychologists and philosophers to introduce or reintroduce 'internal senses' of one sort or another. By and large, philosophy of mind marches on undisturbed: philosophers carry on talking about 'the five senses'. (Hence our knowledge of the states of our own body is simply left in limbo.) Moreover, the attempts which are taken most seriously (e.g., attempts to get 'proprioception' and 'kinaesthesia' included on the official list of senses, e.g., by Armstrong 1984) are interestingly different from Descartes' internal senses: knowledge of the position of one's limbs hasn't the direct link with *welfare* that his internal senses had.

188 Not for all of them, of course. In particular, mental images, memories, expectations, desires, etc. (at least in simple forms) are exercises of the Imagination, not of the senses.

189 Although there are many further complications about his conception of the passions of the soul, any account of them must surely begin from his doctrine that feeling anger, joy, fear, etc. are all instances of sense-perception (*sentire*) by another internal sense (*Principles* IV.190; CSM I: 280–1).

190 It is not clear that Descartes was always wholly consistent in the way he carved things up. But many of the difficulties in constructing his doctrine are a product of the fact that all of the *exercises* of Aquinas' interior senses, being (*per* the tradition) functions of the sensitive soul, were designated by 'S-predicates', which were according to Descartes ambiguous. For our purposes *here*, it is only the 'animal' senses which are relevant. Hence, for example, 'memory is no different from imagination – at least the memory which is corporeal and similar to the one which animals possess' (AT X: 416; CSM I: 43).

and (*pace* Kenny 1989: 10) he distinguished Imagination from sense-perception because he held that it did not involve a sense-organ.[191] (Clearly this alteration involved a conceptual innovation regarding what counted as a sense-organ.)[192] The 'common sense' is referred to the pineal gland's function in co-ordinating the 'inputs' from the various senses (AT XI: 176–7; CSM I: 106). This purge leaves only the *vis aestimativa* by which potential harm and benefit are perceived. This 'internal sense' Descartes bifurcated, again for physiological reasons. He thought there to be seven sets of nerves involved in sense-perception, 'of which two have to do with internal sensations and five with external sensations' (*Principles* IV.190; CSM I: 280); so he distinguished between the 'natural appetites' (connected with the first internal sense) and the emotions (connected with the second) on the grounds that they involve different sets of nerves.[193] Despite this innovation, Descartes took over from Aquinas' notion of the *vis aestimativa* the idea that the objects of his two internal senses (pain, hunger, thirst, fear, anger, joy, etc.) are intrinsically connected with *health* or *welfare*.

Descartes regarded the internal senses as sense-modalities. The internal senses are distinguished from the external ones in virtue of the fact that their objects are properties of the percipient's body rather than things or properties of things outside the body. In this context, the terms 'internal' and 'external' have a *literal* meaning, and both are applicable to beings without minds (machines or animals), unlike the term 'inner' in the phrases 'inner world' or in Kant's phrase 'inner sense'. Both the 'genus' and the 'differentia' of the internal senses have important consequences for understanding Descartes' conception.

The internal senses as senses

Expressions like 'feeling pain', 'feeling thirst', and 'feeling angry' are all predicates falling within the genus *sentire* (sense-perception), and like all other S-predicates, they are systematically ambiguous between designating 'functions' of

191 Although Imaginings were 'caused by the body', they do not 'depend on the nerves' (*Passions* I.21; CSM I: 336).

192 Kenny (1993: 39) criticizes Aquinas' claim that Imagination was a sense on two counts. First, 'the imagination has no organ in the sense that sight has an organ', and second, 'it is not possible to be mistaken about what one is imagining as it is possible to be mistaken about what one is seeing'. Both these criticisms are question-begging. *Ad* the first, one might ask whether touch has an organ *in the sense* that sight has an organ. The concept of a sense-organ is itself flexible and controversial; Descartes, as we have seen, denied that Imagination has a sense-organ, but the only conclusion one can come to is that he had a different conception of a sense-organ than did Aquinas. *Ad* the second, one might ask whether *Aquinas* held that Imagination is infallible (as Descartes clearly did not). Did either of them have the same concept as the modern concept of 'imagination'?

193 Thus there was a wide range of internal states of the body perceived by the internal senses. But neither Aquinas nor Descartes numbered among the objects of the internal senses posture, movement, balance, muscular effort, or fatigue. Descartes neglected the possibility of feedback mechanisms in automata or brutes; and rational agents' knowledge of their own voluntary actions falls under *conscientia*, not sense-perception (*sentire*).

the body (or modes of extension) and 'operations of the soul' (or modes of thinking). In one sense, they refer to thoughts or judgements. Descartes' usual term for these judgements, i.e. for feeling$_2$ pain, hunger, and so on, is 'sensation'. This is commonly misunderstood. For example, 'these sensations of hunger, thirst, pain and so on are nothing but confused modes of thinking' (AT VII: 81; CSM II: 56) is regularly paraphrased as 'Hunger, thirst and pain . . . are confused modes of thought'.[194] That is, the words 'sensation of' are omitted, no doubt for the reason that we now tend to say that 'pain', 'hunger', and 'thirst' name species of the genus 'sensations'.[195] But expressions like 'sensation of hunger' and 'perception of pain' are far from pleonastic. (They are no more so than the expression 'sensation of colour' which is frequently juxtaposed with 'sensation of pain'.) In this context, they clearly refer to the rational meaning of the expressions 'feeling hunger' and 'feeling pain'; the sensation of hunger or pain is the *thought* or *judgement* that one feels$_1$ hunger or pain.[196] Pain or hunger is what one judges oneself to feel$_1$ (and what one does in fact feel$_1$ if one's judgement is true).

In the other sense – the sense that is directly relevant for present purposes – these S-predicates refer to activities of the body which we share with animals. Higher animals at least have comparable sets of nerves; they respond to being burnt or injured, for instance, by withdrawing the injured limb and subsequently exhibiting avoidance-behaviour or anxiety. They respond to clear and present threats to welfare, for instance, by taking flight. They perceive bodily needs for food and drink, and they take appropriate steps to secure what they need, etc. So it is perfectly clear that they are sentient in all these respects, i.e. that they have internal senses. 'Feeling$_1$ pain' and 'feeling$_1$ hunger' must be modes (properties) of the sentient or sensitive body (cf. also pp. 91–100).

A central implication of the fact that the internal senses are *senses* is that they have particular sense-organs. And causal, i.e. mechanical, interaction with sense-organs is part of the *concept* of sense-perception, on Descartes' view. 'What is perceived' by any of the senses, external or internal, must interact mechanically with a sense-organ, bringing about a change in the local motion of some of its parts, and thus must itself be a mode of extension that can be fully characterized in terms of its mechanical properties (or powers) (cf. Locke, *Essay* II.viii.11). But the expression 'what is perceived' or 'object of sense-perception' is multiply ambiguous. Minimally, we have to distinguish 'what interacts with the

194 Kenny 1968: 222; cf. Cottingham 1993: 74–5.

195 A similar move is sometimes made with the expression 'perception of (e.g.) pain', so that 'when someone feels an intense pain, the perception he has of it is indeed very clear, but is not always distinct' (*Principles* I.46; CSM I: 208) is paraphrased as 'a pain "in" the foot' is a 'confused conceptual thought' (Williams 1978: 286).

196 Descartes regularly used the expressions 'having the sensation or perception of pain', 'having the sensation of anger', etc. to refer to the 'restricted' (or rational) sense of these S-predicates. He seldom used 'pain', 'hunger', and the like for this purpose. But his usage is not absolutely consistent, for example, when he wrote that 'in my view pain exists only in the understanding' (AT III: 85; CSMK III: 148).

sense-organs' ('causal objects') from 'proper objects'.[197] The 'causal objects' of the senses must be modes of extension; in the case of sense-perception by an internal sense (feeling$_1$), one state or condition of the body (or some part of the body) must mechanically cause a change in some other state or condition of the body (or of some part of the body). But the '*proper* objects' of the first internal sense are pain, hunger, and thirst, just as the 'proper objects' of the sense of sight are light and colour (cf. AT VI: 130; CSM I: 167). The question is: how do these two senses of the expression 'object of sensory perception' connect? We will argue that they can be identified. Hence it will follow that pain, thirst, etc. are properties of the body or modes of extension. (Likewise, colours, tastes, sounds, etc. must be modes of extension.)

This point needs careful handling, however. Descartes insisted repeatedly that 'we cannot find any intelligible resemblance between the colour which we suppose to be in objects and that which we experience in our sensation [*illum quem experimur esse in sensu*]' (*Principles* I.70 (AT VIIIA: 34; CSM I: 218). Again, people commonly make an 'obscure judgement' 'concerning the nature of something which they think exists in the painful spot and which they suppose to resemble the sensation of pain [*simile sensui doloris*]' *Principles* I.46 (AT VIIIA: 22; CSM I: 208). The interpretation of these remarks is a notorious locus of difficulties. They are often cited as decisive evidence that he conceived of ideas as mental images, and they are generally taken to reinforce the thesis that he thought colours, pains, etc. to be subjective or mental things or properties. Without entering into these debates, we wish to propose a less naive understanding of the term 'resemble'. This seems particularly appropriate in view of the fact that debates about resemblance were one of the staple items of Aristotelian and scholastic epistemology. No naive reading of 'resemble' even begins to make sense of traditional arguments about whether the knower must resemble what he knows, or whether someone's knowledge must resemble what it is knowledge of.

The expression 'intelligible resemblance' is pleonastic in Descartes' usage (see p. 147).[198] Modes of extension have an 'intelligible resemblance' to each other, so that mechanical causation is 'intelligible'; but modes of thinking and modes of extension do not, so that mind–body interaction is 'unintelligible'. It might be

197 And there are other senses in which we might talk about 'what is perceived'. We might, for instance, connect 'what is perceived' with the answer to the question 'What do you perceive?' (Answers might include 'I see a green tree', 'I hear Verdi's *Requiem*', 'I feel hungry *for a cherry pie*', or 'I feel thirsty *for a cold lager*'.) 'Proper objects of the senses' are what we call below '"basic" sense-perceptions'; but answers to the question 'What do you perceive?' will typically refer to 'non-basic' sense-perceptions.

Further related complications arise for the emotions, although we cannot discuss these here: for example, what I fear may be a loud bang, or equally *that* the chimney may collapse in the night if the wind goes round to the north-east.

198 Wilson (1994) too connects 'resemblance' with 'intelligibility'; she also connects 'non-resemblance' with 'confusion', as we do. However, her explanations of both connections differ from ours.

tempting to see the claim that there is 'no intelligible resemblance between the colour which we suppose to be in objects and that which we experience in our sensation' or between 'the nature of something which we think exists in the painful spot and the sensation of pain', as special cases of the lack of 'intelligible resemblance' between modes of extension and modes of thinking.[199] But this cannot be the right reading, since Descartes was here (*Principles* I.70) *contrasting* these 'secondary qualities' with the 'primary qualities', and there can hardly be any *more* 'intelligible resemblance' in this sense between the square shape of the table (a mode of extension) and my *thought* that the table is square!

The claim must rather be that the 'colour we suppose to be in objects' or 'what exists in the painful spot' is a mode of extension capable of interacting with our sense-organs, whereas the colour 'which we experience in our sensation' (which bears no 'intelligible resemblance' to this) is not. That is, 'colour as it is' and 'colour as we think of it' do not 'resemble' each other in the way that modes of extension do. Minimally this must be related to the fact that we don't think of colour as a mode of extension, i.e. as a property of the sort that could mechanically interact with our sense-organs. Nobody, when asked to explain what the term 'red' means, would make reference to local motions on the surface of a corporeal thing. Many would object that this is certainly *not* what they *mean* by 'red'. All this is surely correct, and constitutes a plausible minimal interpretation of Descartes' point here.

His point might be somewhat more sophisticated. It might have to do with a kind of *logical* resemblance, amounting to a denial that there is a logical isomorphism between sensible properties and modes of extension. Here is a possible account: having a particular shape, having a particular size, moving in such and such a direction, and so on, are all properties which are logically independent of each other, and we are inclined to think of being painful and being coloured as further *independent* properties of corporeal objects.[200] If they were as we conceive of them in this respect, then they could not causally (i.e. *mechanically*) interact with our sense-organs, so they would be imperceptible.[201] Consequently, they cannot be *independent* modes of extension. (Our habitual inclination to think of them as independent might be part of what underlies Descartes' repeated assertion that the 'sensations' of colour, pain, hunger, and so on, are 'confused thoughts': see pp. 180–3.) On either the simpler or the more sophisticated account, then, pain and colour (the proper objects of our senses) *are*

199 This is in effect how Cottingham sees it (1986: 138ff.).

200 Harré (1964: 93–104) makes some interesting suggestions along these general lines.

201 This is also part of his argument against 'real qualities' (cf. AT VII: 434; CSM II: 293): these are not thought of as modes (and *a fortiori* not modes of extension), thus they could not causally interact with sense-organs and so could not be perceived.

modes of extension (the causal objects of our senses), though our ideas of these properties are 'commonly confused'.[202]

But this conclusion might appear to be contradicted by certain well-known passages:

> all of us have, from our early childhood, judged that all the objects of our sense-perception are things existing outside our minds and closely resembling our sensations .... Thus, on seeing a colour, for example, we supposed we were seeing a thing located outside us which closely resembled the idea of colour that we experienced within us at the time.
>
> (*Principles* I.66; CSM I: 216)

> The same thing happens with regard to everything else of which we have sensory awareness, even to pleasure and pain. For, although we do not suppose that these exist outside us, we generally regard them not as being in the mind alone . . . but as being in the hand or foot or in some other part of the body. But the fact that we feel a pain as it were in our foot does not make it certain that the pain exists outside our mind, in the foot, any more than the fact that we see light as it were in the sun, makes it certain the light exists outside us, in the sun.
>
> (*Principles* I.67; CSM I: 216–17)

Both passages are often cited to support the thesis that Descartes treated pain, colour, etc., as *mental* entities or objects in the 'inner world'. Surely, it might be said, the claim here is that colour and pain are 'in the mind alone,' that they do not 'exist outside the mind'.[203]

202 Cf. Arnauld: 'Two Cartesians are walking together. "Do you know," says one of them, "why snow is white, why charcoal is black, and why corpses are putrid?" "These are foolish questions," the other replies, "for snow is not white, nor charcoal black, nor corpses putrid; it is your soul that is white when you look at snow, and which is black when you look at charcoal, and which is putrid when you are near a corpse." I assume they both agree on the essentials of the doctrine; but I ask who expresses it better, and I maintain that the former does . . . it was due to our making language match the intentions of the Author of Nature that we call bodies white, black, or putrid, since it is in relation to bodies and not in relation to itself that our soul takes on different modifications' (*Ideas* ch. 23).

Although Margaret Wilson (as so many others) at one time ascribed to Descartes the view that 'there is really no such thing as color in the rose or pain in the foot' (1978: 217), she has recently defended a position somewhat similar to ours, in 'Descartes on the Representationality of Sensations' (in M. Kulstad and J. Cover (eds), *Central Themes in Early Modern Philosophy*, Indianapolis: Hackett, 1990).

203 On this view, colours, tastes, smells, etc. are 'in the mind', in some sense. This doctrine too has a long pedigree, and it may well originate in this very passage of the *Principles*, through the good offices of Malebranche: 'We are deceived not by our senses but by our will, through its precipitous judgments. When, e.g., we see light, it is quite certain that we see light; when we feel heat, we are not mistaken in believing that we feel heat . . . . But we are mistaken in judging that the heat we feel is outside the soul that feels it' (*Recherche* I.v).

The question is what is meant by the phrase 'existing outside our mind'.[204] Tempting though it evidently is, Descartes' expression 'has no existence outside our mind or thought' *cannot* be taken simply as a circumlocution for 'is mental' or 'is a mode of thinking'.[205] He introduced this phrase in this way: 'All the objects of our perception we regard either as things, or affections of things, or else as eternal truths which *have no existence outside our thought*' (*Principles* I.48; CSM I: 208, italics added). Here 'what has no existence outside our thought' is the foil of the phrase 'things or affections of things' (i.e. of substances and modes of substances).[206] (It is, in effect, a reformulation of the logical axiom that nothing other than substances and modes can be components of singular judgements.) Thus *all* substances and *all* modes of substances can properly be said to 'have an existence outside our thought', even if they are mental or incorporeal.[207] These passages therefore cannot be read as suggesting that pain and colour are mental; the issue is whether they are either substances or modes.

Descartes' specific concern here, in fact, is with whether they are *substances* ('*things* [*res*] existing outside our minds'). Evidently he held that people were tempted to think of pains and colours as *things* (particulars, substances) and wished to scotch that temptation. This so far leaves open the question of whether they are *affections* of things. But it seems clear that he held that colour and pain do 'have an existence outside our thought', even though they are not *things* which have an existence outside our thought: 'when we say that we perceive colours in objects,

204 Watts indicated part of the complex background behind the use of this phrase. He treated the distinction 'real/mental' as one of the principal divisions of modes, and he linked this use of 'mental' with the scholastic terminology of '*Entia rationis* or *second Notions*': these have 'no real Being, but by the Operation of the Mind' (*Logicke* I.ii.4).

205 One of the few commentators who recognizes this is J. Morris (1980: 383 n. 64).

206 Locke employed a similar locution for the same purpose. He declared that relations (and mixed modes) have 'no other reality but what they have in the Minds of Men' (*Essay* II.xxx.4). This seems to be equivalent to the remark that a relation is 'not contained in the real existence of things, but something extraneous and superinduced' (II. xxv.8).

Russell makes a parallel use of the phrase 'entities whose being is not merely mental' when he offers a proof that universals have being independently of their being thought of. Any relation, he argues, 'like the terms it relates, is not dependent upon thought, but belongs to the independent world which thought apprehends but does not create' (1912: 97–8). The same sort of being belongs to all mental particulars, in his view, and these include thoughts, feelings, and minds (1912: 100).

The French version of the *Principles* generates potential for confusion in English translations by describing substances and modes as 'all the *things* which have some existence' ('*toutes les choses qui on quelque existence*') (*Principles* I.48 (AT IXB: 45); see CSM I:208, n.1). The danger arises from the fact that both '*chose*' and '*res*' are normally translated into English as 'thing'. But Descartes fairly regularly used '*res*' to refer to substances in *contrasting* substances with their affections, whereas he used the term '*chose*' (or even the phrase '*chose qui a quelque existence*') to cover both 'things (substances) and the affections (or modes) of things', i.e. as the foil for whatever '*n'est rien hors de nostre pensée*'.

207 So, paradoxical as this might sound at first hearing, minds ('intellectual or thinking things') and their modes ('perception, volition, and all the modes both of perceiving and willing') 'have an existence outside our mind or thought'! To compound the potential for confusion, in a letter Descartes used the expressions 'modes of things themselves' and 'modes of thinking' to refer respectively to modes and attributes (whether of minds or of bodies). In this usage, 'love, hatred, affirmation, doubt, and so on are true modes in the mind', i.e. 'modes of things' *rather than* 'modes of thinking' (AT IV: 349; CSMK III: 280).

this is really just the same as saying that we perceive *something* [*aliquid*, not *res*] in the objects whose nature we do not know' (*Principles* I.70; CSM I: 218, italics added). If so, then it follows that they are affections (modes) of things, that is, of corporeal things, as we have already concluded.

Note therefore that 'pain', 'thirst', and 'colour' in a certain sense will drop out of the picture altogether. These sound as if they ought to be names for particulars (hence substances), but they are not. The objects of the internal senses are modes of the body or of parts of the body, and these might more naturally be expressed adjectivally, for example, as 'being painful' (a property of a limb) and 'being dry' (a property of the throat; cf., e.g., AT VII: 76; CSM II: 53); or perhaps 'having a painful foot' or 'having a dry throat' (properties of the whole body). In a similar way, we might think, talk of colour would be less misleading if re-expressed in talk of 'being coloured'.

This conclusion, it might be noted, casts a new light on the idea of 'pain-location'. Those who take Descartes to regard pain as a mental state (a 'state of consciousness') take him to suppose that there is something conceptually awry with the idea that pain (something mental, hence non-extended) has a bodily location. Pains can only be 'in' limbs, not *in* them (Williams 1978: 286).[208] Now, there is indeed something odd from Descartes' point of view in talking about the bodily location of a pain, *not* because pains are *mental* particulars but because they are *not particulars* (i.e substances) at all; for (spatial) location can be a property only of a particular. But it is none the less wholly unproblematic to say that I have a pain *in* my foot; the logical form of my utterance might be made perspicuous in the paraphrase 'My foot has the property of being painful' or perhaps 'My body has the property of having a painful foot'; that is what it *is* for 'a pain' to have 'a bodily location'.

The internal senses as 'internal'

The internal senses are distinguished from the external ones by virtue of the fact that their objects are (not just properties of the human body but) properties of

208 Indeed it is sometimes supposed that he is making just this point in calling the 'the sensation of pain' a 'confused thought' (Malcolm 1977: 48; Wilson 1978: 209). Of course, the insistence on '"in"' as opposed to 'in' is no doubt reinforced by his frequent description of pain as (e.g.) '*tanquam in pede*'; this is usually translated as 'as if in the foot' or 'as it were in the foot', and these phrases are understood to be counterfactual. This interpretation is not obligatory. Compare: 'If you see somebody loitering outside your house, treat him as if he were a burglar' (he might be!).

The conjunction of the two Legendary views that pains are to be identified with sensations of pain and that sensations of pain are non-cognitive is sometimes held to yield a difficulty: namely how a pain can even be 'as it were in the foot': 'how a sensation can represent its location in the mind' (Lott 1986: 247). (*Sic*! What is the referent of 'its' supposed to be here?) And it is usually held that, according to Descartes, 'sensations can have an intrinsic quality of location' (p. 247): 'each sensation has a specific quality of location and enters consciousness as an "in-the-foot", "in-the-elbow", etc. sensation' (p. 248). (This view is commonly seen to be problematic.) But, as we have argued, pain is not to be identified with the sensation of pain. And the sensation of pain is a thought or judgement. Is there a serious question about 'how the judgement "I have a pain in my foot" or "My foot hurts" can represent the pain as being in the foot'?

one's *own* body, as opposed to properties of things outside the (one's own) body. The causal chain (or mechanism) must lie wholly within the body.[209] *Which* properties of the body are perceived by internal senses is also important. It was essential to the Aristotelian framework that the concepts of pain, hunger, thirst, fear, anger, and joy – the objects of the *vis aestimativa* – are intrinsically connected to the concept of bodily welfare or health. Both these points are of great importance for understanding Descartes' conception of the substantial union between mind and body (amplified on pp. 163ff. below). Together, these two points begin to give some concrete content to his famous description of his own body as 'the body which by some special right I called "mine"' (AT VII: 76; CSM II: 52) and to the contrast he drew between himself and the sailor in his ship. They are also prerequisites for making sense of his lengthy discussion of dropsy in *Meditation* VI.[210] Clearly the very fact that (soulless) animals too have internal senses implies that these senses cannot be the *whole* story behind the substantial union of soul and body. Nevertheless they are a vital and frequently missed part of the story.

First, then, the scope of the internal senses is essentially confined to properties of one's *own* body.[211] Now this fact, together with the fact that the properties perceived by the internal senses are 'special sensibles', yields something like a first-/third-person asymmetry in regard to our knowledge of some states of the body. (Obviously epistemological properties are only applicable to human beings with rational souls, not to animals; none the less, this fact signifies a special role for the internal-sense-related S-predicates ('feeling pain', 'feeling hunger', and so on).) On the one hand, I may $feel_1$ a pain in my foot without $feeling_2$ it (judging that I $feel_1$ pain), in the same way that you can $feel_1$ a pain without my judging that you do; this might be an appropriate description of a case in which my mind is distracted from the painfulness of my foot by the charming conversation of my companion. Again, I may $feel_2$ a pain in my foot without my $feeling_1$ it, as in the phantom pain case, just as I may mistakenly judge that you $feel_1$ pain. On the other

209 The emotions raise a complication. The object of fear – for instance, a wolf emerging from the forest – may be perceived by an external sense (e.g., sight or smell), but the fear itself is perceived by an internal sense. We can't pursue this point here.

210 Most commentaries don't even attempt to do so; remarkably, the usual discussions of *Meditation* VI simply stop (at best) after the 'sailor in a ship' passage.

211 This may seem puzzling: if my body is a machine and so is yours, surely with appropriate 'rewiring' we could be hooked up together in such a way that my internal sense responds to states of your body (cf. Armstrong 1984). In this way, I could $feel_1$ your pain, i.e. pain in your body. But this argument is question-begging. On the face of it we are no more *forced* to accept this description than we are forced to say that 'touching' objects with the tip of a cane, or 'seeing' objects through a periscope, count as touching or seeing. Although there is, let us say, a continuous causal chain going from the object to my hand or eye, we might stipulate that touching something requires its being in contact with part of the body or that only what is in someone's line of sight can be seen by him. We might likewise stipulate that only properties of one's own body can be perceived by the internal senses, i.e. nothing else will be *counted* as an instance of perception by the internal sense. (Of course all of these stipulations *could* be seen as question-begging. Somebody might ask, 'Which body is *my* body?', but equally 'What counts as "contact"?' and 'What counts as "being in the line of sight"?')

hand, pain being a special sensible, it can only be $felt_2$, i.e. it cannot be $seen_2$ or $heard_2$. And only I can $feel_2$ my pain (although you can, of course, judge that I $feel_1$ pain, your judgement is not an instance of *sentire* because it lacks the requisite reflexivity – see p. 74.). Thus I have both 'asymmetrical' and 'superior' 'access' to the pain in my foot. So the thought I express when I say 'My foot hurts', although it is a judgement about a property of my body, exhibits *some* first-/third-person asymmetries. Indeed we might even say that such conditions of the *body* look like good candidates for Cartesian Privacy (even if not for Cartesian Transparency) – rather better candidates than *thoughts*![212]

One's own body is thus, logically and epistemologically speaking, not just one object among others, perceived (like any other object) only by the external senses. It has a special status *vis-à-vis* oneself. 'I felt all my appetites and emotions *in*, and for the sake of it' (AT VII: 76; CSM II: 52*, italics added).[213] The internal senses with their characteristic epistemological asymmetry are crucial for making sense of Descartes' phrase 'the body which *by some special right* I call "mine"' (AT VII: 76; CSM II: 52, italics added).

Our second point was that the objects of the internal senses are *essentially* connected with the organism's bodily welfare or ill-fare. The person's own body is not simply logically and epistemologically special, but *prudentially* (and, as we will see, *morally*): 'I felt all my appetites and emotions in, and *for the sake of* [*pro*] it' (AT VII: 76; CSM II: 52*, italics added). This is a striking feature of the internal senses, and it colours Descartes' whole conception of pain, hunger, thirst, etc. 'There is nothing that my own Nature teaches me more vividly than that I have a body, and that when I feel pain there is something *wrong* with the body, and that when I am hungry or thirsty the body *needs* food and drink, and so on' (AT VII: 80; CSM II: 56*, italics added). (Compare Locke: everyone 'sympathizes and is concerned for' 'the limbs of his body', a 'sympathy and concern' which ceases when the limbs are cut off: *Essay* II.xxvii.11.) My body, we might say, is that body whose health is part of *my* welfare. However much I care about you, your leg's hurting is not connected with my welfare in the same way that my leg's hurting is; and the response appropriate to your leg's hurting (viz. withdrawing it from the source of pain, etc.) is not available to me in the way in which it is available to you.

This point sheds some light on the celebrated 'sailor in a ship' passage. 'Nature' is said to teach me 'by these sensations [*sentire*] of pain, hunger, thirst and so on, that I am not merely present in my body as a sailor is present in a ship, but that I am very closely joined and, as it were, intermingled with it, so that I and the body form a unit' (AT VII: 81; CSM II: 56). This all-important 'teaching' of Nature seems to be specifically connected with the *internal* senses. An obvious and

212 This is in part what led us to suggest that Cartesian Introspection was the artefact of a commentators' *confusion* between *conscientia* and the internal senses.

213 This is surely intended to be an essential truth, not an accidental one. But it must be so understood that it is not incompatible with an amputee's having a phantom pain.

important point of contrast between my being united with my body and the sailor's being lodged in his ship is the fact that I perceive states of my body with my internal senses, whereas the sailor perceives states of his ship only with his external senses. He hasn't got special senses which inform him about his ship's 'health', whereas I have special senses which inform me about my body's health. In Descartes' view, this fact is closely linked to another: my body's well-being is (part of) *my* welfare, whereas the 'health' of the ship (if that makes sense), although clearly contingently bound up with the welfare of the sailor, *is not* (part of) his welfare. One crucial but surprising aspect of this is the idea that my body's *health* is essential for my (my soul's) freedom and hence its *moral* well-being: 'although when thriving in an adult and healthy body the mind enjoys some liberty to think of other things than those presented by the senses, we know there is not the same liberty in those who are sick' (AT III: 424; CSMK III: 190). These matters will be explored further below (pp. 178–80).

Finally, a large part of *Meditation* VI is concerned with the condition called dropsy, in which a patient feels a terrible thirst but drinking is positively harmful to him. Without recognizing both that thirst (or dryness of the throat) is a condition of the body perceived by an internal sense and that the internal senses are intrinsically linked to bodily health, we cannot begin to make sense of the issues here. Like the case of phantom pain, dropsy constitutes a case of 'deception by the senses' (AT VII: 145; CSM II: 104), that is, it involves an inclination to make false internal-sense-based judgements. (It is a particularly worrying case, morally and theologically speaking, because God can apparently be blamed for implanting this deceptive inclination.) But what exactly is the *content* of the false sense-based judgement? According to Descartes, dropsy in a human being involves *error* because the person 'is thirsty at a time when drink is going to cause [him] harm' (AT VII: 85, CSM II: 59; cf. AT VII: 143, CSM II: 102). But where is the *error*? Surely (we might say) his judgement that he is thirsty is *true*! But we need to see that *this* judgement itself winds together a number of different judgements which are 'commonly confused'. Thirst itself, as a bodily phenomenon, is normally mechanically connected, on the one hand, with the body's need to drink, and, on the other, with the appropriate liquid-seeking behaviour; it is this and similar mechanical connections that manifest the health-relatedness of the internal senses. Via 'our Nature', these mechanical links get mirrored in confused thoughts, so that I tend to confuse the judgement that I $feel_1$ thirsty with the judgement that drinking will do my body good (and that I ought to seek liquid). If I have dropsy these latter sensory judgements are false; so we might say that the 'package-judgement' that I am thirsty is itself false. Hence the confused sensation of thirst counts as an instance of deception by the senses. (This confusion, with the attendant liability to erroneous internal-sense-based judgements, is intelligible only because of the intrinsic connection between the internal senses and health: see below, pp. 180–3)

The Cartesian Legend is most conspicuously at odds with Descartes' Dualism in its treatment of pain. And nowhere is this clearer that in its neglect of the internal senses. This single omission bears a part of the blame not only for the Expansion Thesis (since one could suppose pain, thirst, anger, and fear to be *thoughts* only on condition that one failed to recognize that they were objects of internal senses), but also for the doctrine of Cartesian Introspection (which is arguably grounded in a failure to distinguish *conscientia* from the internal senses), and even for the view that animals are insentient machines (which could not be maintained if one acknowledged that they felt_1 pain and fear). But this neglect also undermines any possibility of making sense of Descartes' conception of the substantial union of mind and body. The two doctrines, that the internal senses, in effect, give us 'privileged' (if not incorrigible) access to conditions of our own bodies, and that they inform us about our body's health (itself vital for our soul's moral welfare), are essential elements of the background for understanding the contrast he drew between human beings and sailors lodged in ships. The Legend's conception of pain makes no contact with Descartes' account, and yet the Legend offers pain as *the paradigm* of a Cartesian thought (*cogitatio*)[214] and as the point at which Wittgenstein's 'private language argument' allegedly gets its teeth into the jugular of *Descartes'* conception of the mind. On the contrary: the details of his treatment of pain provide a *paradigm* of the divergence of Cartesian Dualism from Descartes' Dualism. A bit of scholasticism, namely clarifying his notion of the internal senses, might clear the ground of all these houses of cards.[215]

GOD AND 'OUR NATURE AS UNION OF MIND AND BODY'

Causing and occasioning

Let's start by reconsidering the alleged tension between the two idioms of 'causing' and 'occasioning' in Descartes' account of the relation between mind and body. *Prima facie* both are firmly entrenched in his account of the substantial union.

On the one hand, he declared that among our 'primitive notions' we find the notion 'of the soul's power to move the body and the body's power to act on the soul and cause its sensations and passions' (AT III: 665; CSMK III: 218). He frequently used such expressions as 'produce', 'make', and 'cause' in characterizing these: a certain motion in the part of brain to which the nerves from the foot are attached 'produce[s] in the mind a sensation of pain as occurring in the foot' (AT VII: 87; CSM II: 60*), and 'a given motion in the brain must always produce the same sensation in the mind' (AT VII: 88; CSM II: 61). Again, 'when we

214 'The difference between the two [Aquinas and Descartes] comes out clearly in the case of pain' (Kenny 1966: 353).

215 Compare: 'Where does our investigation get its importance from, since it seems only to destroy everything interesting, that is, all that is great and important? (As it were all the buildings, leaving behind only bits of stone and rubble.) What we are destroying is nothing but houses of cards (*Luftgebäude*)' (Wittgenstein, *PI* §118).

want to walk or move our body in some other way, this volition makes the gland drive the spirits to the muscles which serve to bring about this effect' (*Passions* I.43; CSM I: 344); 'if we want to adjust our eyes to look at a far-distant object, this volition causes the pupils to grow larger' (*Passions* I.44; CSM I: 344). It seems beyond question that he made regular use of various unambiguously *causal* idioms in characterizing the relation of mind and body, even if he did not go so far as using the technical terminology of 'efficient causation'.

On the other hand, he evidently took some pains to avoid using the term 'cause' on many occasions. In the *Optics*, he repeatedly described aspects of human vision by the cumbersome phraseology that a condition of the eyes (or the pineal gland) 'gives occasion to the soul to form the idea of . . .' (e.g., colour or light). In all forms of human sense-perception, movements in sense-organs occasion the soul's having thoughts. The evidence for occasionalism in human voluntary action is scanty, since he had little in the way of sustained discussion of voluntary action. But there is an apparently powerful indirect argument. Descartes can scarcely have been unaware that the very idea that the mind might originate, generate, or produce the motion of matter at least *seems* inconsistent with one of the axioms of his mechanics, known to us by the Natural light: namely that matter can be set in motion *only* by the impact of other moving matter.[216] This principle apparently eliminates the logical space for what Ryle calls the Myth of Volitions, namely the most natural reading of the claim that voluntary human action is to be defined as bodily movements *caused* by volitions. An occasionalist account of voluntary action seems the only alternative to convicting Descartes of self-contradiction.

Despite the presence of both idioms in his texts, some interpreters simply ignore one or the other of them in paraphrasing his doctrine. Perhaps because occasionalism now lacks intuitive appeal or theoretical interest, it is standard to present Descartes as unambiguously a causal interactionist. Philosophy of mind now takes two-way mind–body causation to be a *defining feature* of Cartesian Dualism: this position is understood to entail some version of the causal theory of perception and some causal characterization of voluntary action. Occasionalist idioms in his writings make little impression on *today*'s exponents of the Legend.

This might seem surprising in view of the fact that others have, with apparently equal right, drawn the opposite conclusion from the same body of textual evidence. A different consensus reigned among English-speaking philosophers a century ago, who took Cartesian Dualism obviously and unambiguously to entail a version of occasionalism.[217] On this interpretation, as expounded by James and

216 We explore this argument further below, pp. 156–8.

217 Contrast Loeb (1981: 134): in 'one of the most curious episodes in the history of the history of philosophy, S. V. Keeling, convinced that there would have been a blatant incoherence in Descartes' position had he held [that mind and body causally interact], maintains, in what is otherwise a scholarly classic, that Descartes denied that . . . mind and body causally interact'. (Keeling held that 'Descartes was (in some sense) an occasionalist' (p. 135).) But this interpretation was at one time a commonplace!

Russell,[218] Descartes was committed to denying the very *possibility* of any *causal* interaction of mind with matter, holding instead that these two streams of events are kept marching in step by God's constant interventions.

More perceptive modern interpreters take themselves to confront an interpretative *dilemma*. Noting *both* idioms, they take it to be indubitable that Descartes apparently committed himself to a pair of distinct general theories which are mutually incompatible. They presuppose that nobody can say both '*x* causes *y*' and '*x* occasions *y*' without contradicting himself.[219] This dilemma calls for some more sophisticated response. One is to say that he really did vacillate between two incompatible doctrines.[220] Another is to argue that the commitments to causal interaction and to occasionalism must be hedged round with sufficient qualifications and refinements to remove some or all of the apparent conflict.[221]

For the moment, we wish simply to understand the dilemma more clearly. We will argue that the perceived tension in Descartes' doctrine is extrinsic, not intrinsic. It is generated by a combination of the forms of reasoning and the conceptual apparatus that interpreters bring to bear on his ideas, not by the specimen itself that they put under the philosophical microscope to dissect. By achieving greater clarity about these preconceptions, the dilemma itself can be dissolved or made to disappear completely.

To a first approximation, we suggest that Descartes used the terms 'cause' and 'occasion' ('give occasion to') *interchangeably* in discussing the relation between mind and body. They are *roughly* synonymous *in this context*.[222] We might signal

218 James (1911: 194–5): 'Descartes led the way [to occasionalism] by his doctrine that mental and physical substance, the one consisting purely of thought, the other purely of extension, were absolutely dissimilar . . . . [Hence] any such causal intercourse as we instinctively perceive between mind and body *ceased to be rational*. For thinkers of that age, "*God*" was the great solvent of all absurdities' (italics added).

Russell thought that Descartes was 'on the whole . . . certainly not an occasionalist' because he mistakenly thought that the mind could influence the motion of matter by altering the direction but not the quantity of motion. 'Descartes would have been more consistent if he had been an occasionalist', and 'he shows a tendency to occasionalism now and then' (Bertrand Russell, *Collected Papers*, London: Allen & Unwin, 1983, I.154, 177, 180). In short, Descartes was not, strictly speaking, a Cartesian! (Cf. Russell 1946: 583–4.) For the 'Cartesian school' adhered to the doctrine of 'the reciprocal causal independence of mind and matter' (Russell 1921: 35–6).

219 It seems to be one of the fixed points in the grammar of '*x* occasions *y*' (and its variants such as '*y* happens on the occasion of *x*') that statements of this form are inconsistent with the statement '*x* is the efficient cause of *y*'. This holds for Hume, James, and Russell as much as for Descartes and Malebranche.

220 For example, Gaukroger (Introduction to Arnauld, *Ideas*, 4): Malebranche and Arnauld developed different 'conflicting strands of thought in Descartes' in respect of sense-perception. By contrast, Descartes 'would have rejected an occasionalist construal of the mind/body relation' in respect of voluntary movement (Gaukroger 1995: 390).

221 For example, Garber argues that Descartes' principles of motion in *Principles* II.36 and 40 are to be understood as 'leaving open the possibility that there may be incorporeal causes of . . . motion' (1992: 303).

222 It would be more accurate to claim that simple causal idioms (e.g., 'produces') are, in this context, to be understood as abbreviations for the formulation 'is ordained by Nature to make' or 'Naturally causes', and that this whole phrase is synonymous with 'gives occasion to' (see below).

this equivalence by making use of the phrase 'occasional cause'.[223] The two-way interaction of mind and body could be expressed in this idiom: in having the perception of the colour of an apple, local movements in the eyes are the *occasional cause* of having a sense-based thought, and in walking down the street to post a letter, an action-directed thought (or volition) is the *occasional cause* of observable bodily behaviour or movement. As a consequence, we argue that there is no collision between occasionalist and interactionist formulations in Descartes' texts.[224] To anticipate our conclusions, the causal idioms used to characterize mind–body interaction ('acts on', 'makes, 'produces', etc.) are to be understood uniformly to bear the qualification 'Naturally' (where this refers to 'our Nature as union of mind and body'), and the terms '(Naturally) cause' and 'occasion' do not exclude each other in the grammar of *his* language, unlike the terms '(efficiently) cause' and 'occasion'.[225] Critics who accuse him of inconsistency in his discussions of interaction commit the fallacy of equivocation themselves. In fact, they conflate 'Natural causes' with 'efficient causes'.[226] To forestall this misunderstanding, Descartes might best be described as an 'Occasionalist Interactionist'.

All these remarks are approximate and provisional. They are signposts which need to be placed in the right position to serve any real purpose. The principal problem is that both '(efficient) cause' and 'occasion' can be, indeed have actually been, understood in very different ways; hence too the contents of the doctrines labelled 'causal interactionism' and 'occasionalism'. Indeed, it might even be said that these two notions are strictly correlative, so that neither can change independently of the other. This imposes two different requirements on further clarification. First, we need to work out how *Descartes* meant *his* use of the terms 'efficient cause' and 'occasion' to be understood; this must be done primarily from careful reading of his texts. Second, we need to give some attention to the subsequent evolution of both of these correlative concepts, since all later understanding of his ideas is filtered through this medium. Both 'cause' and 'occasion' have undergone important shifts in meaning since the seventeenth century, and this series of gradual (and motivated) modifications of these concepts accounts for a large part (though not all) of the considerable variation in the interpretation of Descartes' doctrine over nearly four centuries.

223 The phrase is slightly anachronistic since it was apparently coined by Malebranche (*Recherche* VI.ii.3).

224 Loeb's (1981: 136ff.) strategy has some similarities to ours. But he mistakenly ascribes to Descartes a Humean conception of causality, neglecting the crucial role of God in Descartes' account.

225 Malebranche used the phrase 'natural cause' as an equivalent of 'occasional cause' (*Recherche* VI.ii.3).

226 There is some real irony in the suggestion that 'Descartes had a definite, *unambiguous* answer' to the question of the relation between mind and body, namely 'that they are *causally* related' (Dicker 1993: 218, first italics added).

Occasionalism

Perhaps the most salient feature of the term 'occasionalism' as it is used by philosophers over the years is the implication of divine intervention. If one thing is said to 'occasion' another, then God must play an essential role in the production of the second thing whenever the first occurs. But for the grace of God, the second would not have occurred even if the first did (to mimic one of Hume's definitions of 'cause').[227]

Now there is no doubt whatever that God plays an essential role in *Descartes*' analyses of the notions which characterize the substantial union of the mind and body: that is, in all forms of sense-perception and Imagination (*sentire* and *imaginari*), and all forms of action that manifest the 'functions' of the soul. This role is mediated, however, by what Descartes called 'our Nature' (in a restricted or limited sense). (For a fuller discussion see below, pp. 168–72.) There is a general sense: 'by my own Nature . . . I understand nothing other than the totality of things bestowed on me by God' (AT VII: 80; CSM II: 56). This is contrasted with what he called 'my Nature' in the 'limited sense': this consists exclusively of 'what God has bestowed on me as a combination of mind and body' (AT VII: 82; CSM II: 57). In vision, say, local movements in the eye which are caused by external objects are '*ordained by Nature*' to make our soul have 'sensations' of the object seen (AT VI: 130; CSM I: 167, italics added). More generally, all of 'the sensory perceptions *given me by Nature* . . . inform the mind of what is beneficial or harmful for the composite of which the mind is a part' (AT VII: 83; CSM II: 57, italics added). Our Nature is, as it were, the mechanism by means of which the body exercises its power to act on the soul in all forms of rational sense-perception. We might say that certain motions in sense-organs 'Naturally cause' or 'Naturally induce' certain thoughts in the soul (cf. AT IV: 603–4; CSMK III: 307).

Two things seem absolutely clear. First, a person's Nature is essentially something created by God (to secure the welfare of the substantial union). Second, our Nature is or essentially involves a one–one correlation between movements in the pineal gland and certain kinds of thoughts in the soul (both between movements in the gland normally caused by states of the sense-organs and thoughts which are instances of *sentire*, and between 'volitions' and movements of the gland which normally cause the limbs to move in a particular way). God is directly responsible for all of these correlations by building them into our Nature.

227 The Port-Royalists exemplify this point in their account of the perception of pain. They argue that it is possible for a mind separated from a body to be tormented by fire of hell or of purgatory because, 'even when [the mind was] in the body, the pain of burning was . . . nothing else but a thought [*conscience*] of suffering which is felt on *occasion* of what happened in the body to which God had united it. Why, therefore, may we not conceive that the justice of God may so dispose a certain portion of matter in regard to a mind, as that the movement of that matter may be an *occasion* to that mind of afflictive thoughts, which is all that can happen to our minds in corporeal pain?' (*PRL* I.ix).

This idea is mirrored in Arnauld's recurrent phrase 'the institution of the Author of Nature' (*Ideas, passim*).[228]

There is a clear sense, then, in which God is represented as the *sine qua non* of mind–body interaction. Far from being excluded by Descartes' use of causal idioms in this context ('cause', 'power', 'produce', 'act on', 'move'), this idea must be explicitly incorporated within it. In his view, certain movements in the eye, for instance, are '*ordained by Nature to make* the soul have the sensations' of seeing colours and light. This phrase is not to be read as a conjunction. His doctrine is not to be paraphrased 'certain movements in the eye bring about certain sensations in the soul *and* (incidentally) this causal relation is God's handiwork'. Rather, 'These movements are ordained-by-Nature-to-make-the-soul-have certain sensations (thoughts)' expresses a *primitive* (hence indecomposable) relation.[229] We might express this more compactly by employing the phrase 'Naturally cause'. In sense-perception, movements are the Natural causes of thoughts (sensations), while in voluntary action, thoughts (volitions) are the Natural causes of movements. It is essential to 'Natural causation' that it be contrasted with efficient causation. In particular, the Natural cause of a voluntary action cannot be a mechanical (or efficient) cause of the motion of matter. It is equally essential to a Natural cause that it must be instituted by God. On Descartes' view, 'our Nature' as the union of mind and body can be viewed as the totality of correlations 'ordained by Nature' between thoughts and bodily states, and this whole pattern of correspondence *must* be the work of God. By the definition of 'our Nature', God is absolutely *essential* to *Descartes*' doctrine of mind–body interaction. But there is a deeper truth here too: it is His activity alone which renders mind–body interaction at all intelligible. We will argue that removing God from this account would leave nothing that made sense to Descartes.

We might speculate that he made use of the alternative idiom of 'occasioning' in order to forestall a clear and present danger of being misunderstood. The use of causal terminology might be expected to produce the impression, even among his seventeenth-century contemporaries, that he was offering a naturalistic or scientific explanation which was to be *contrasted* with explanations in which God played an essential role.[230] Perhaps he thought that he could scotch this unintended interpretation by making prominent use of alternative formulations involving occasionalist locutions. How could any reputable paraphrase of his theory of

228 Wilson aptly christened this doctrine 'Natural Institution' (1978: 205). Loeb (1981: 131 n. 9) objects: 'In support of this, Wilson quotes a passage where Descartes states, "Of course the nature of man could have been so constituted by God that that same motion in the brain would exhibit something else to the mind" .... This is a thin textual basis for emphasizing God's role since on Descartes' view even the "eternal truths" ... are dependent on God's will'. Loeb fails to note that God is *directly* implicated in every one of the *numerous* passages that mention the Nature of man.

229 Or rather, a correlative pair of primitive *powers* (here, of the body to act on the soul and of the soul to be acted on by the body); see pp. 173–7.

230 They might perhaps be expected to treat the claim that God created 'our Nature' as a supplementary hypothesis which could be discarded by hard-headed 'scientific' thinkers.

vision omit mention of God when he had taken pains to express the view that a certain condition of the eyes '*gives occasion to the soul to form the idea of* light'?

In so far as Descartes' conception highlights the role of God in mind–body interaction, it has one essential attribute of occasionalism. (It also partakes of the spirit of Malebranche's occasionalism in calling attention to the utter dependence of humans on God in all the operations of the rational soul (*Recherche* II.ii.6).) But is it, strictly speaking, a form of 'occasionalism'? This depends on what further implications this label is taken to have.

One common implication that modern philosophers attach to it is the idea of particularity. Occasionalism requires God's intervention not just once for all (or even occasionally!), but constantly, from moment to moment and from case to case.[231] (On this view, there is, as it were, no such thing as God's acting at a distance.) For example, Russell took (Malebranche's version of) mind–body occasionalism to call for a specific individual intervention by God to account for each instance of someone's performing a voluntary action: 'When I will to move my arm . . . it is not my will that operates on my arm, but God, who, by His omnipotence, moves my arm whenever I want it moved' (Russell 1921: 35).[232] (This job-specification will ensure that God is kept busy!)[233] In this respect, Russell and James contrasted 'occasionalism' with other theocentric doctrines, in particular with a doctrine of 'pre-established harmony' (that both attributed to Leibniz).

It is a moot point where Descartes might be fitted on this spectrum. On the one hand, the phrases 'our Nature' and what is 'ordained by Nature' suggest the idea of a permanent endowment and an enduring set of regularities. On the other hand, he held the doctrine that God's continuous intervention is required to preserve His creation from moment to moment. 'So was Descartes *really* an occasionalist or an advocate of pre-established harmony?' There is little to be gained from further debating this question; the distinction postdates Descartes. (The debate might take

231 In Malebranche's version, God intervenes from moment to moment not just in mind–body interaction, but in every so-called 'causal' relation in the physical world too.

232 Garber offers a similar explanation. Occasionalism implied, to Descartes' contemporaries, that 'the changes that one body appears to cause in another upon impact, the changes that a body can cause in a mind in producing a sensation or a mind can cause in a body in producing voluntary action, are all due directly to God . . . [e.g.] it is God who is the actual cause of my arm's movement when I decide to raise it to wave; my volition is only an occasional cause' (Garber 1992: 299).

Compare this account: according to Malebranche's theory of 'Occasional Causes', 'when we appear to act on outward things, or outward things on us, there is here no true causality, but the *apparent cause* is simply the *occasion* of the Divine intervention. The intercourse between mind and body is thus kept up by the constant intervention of the Deity. When, for instance, I resolve to move my arm, the movement follows, and this is not due to my resolve, but simply to the action of the Deity on *occasion* of my resolve. My will is not, therefore, the true cause of any movement in my body, but simply the *occasional* cause – that is, the *occasion* – of the production of the movement by the Deity' (T. S. Baynes, note XXI to his edition of *PRL*, Edinburgh: Sutherland & Knox (2nd edn), 1851).

233 James wryly commented that Leibniz 'freed God from the duty of lending all this hourly assistance' (1911: 195).

on the slightly unreal character of debates about whether Mill was *really* an act-utilitarian or a rule-utilitarian.) But there is a strong case for saying that either of these is far closer to Descartes' own view than is 'Cartesian Interactionism'.[234]

Causing vs. occasioning

It is a commonsensical notion that causal explanations are sought in order to answer questions of the from '*Why* did this happen?'; equally, that ascertaining its cause makes a happening *intelligible*. Finding causes for events removes intellectual puzzlement and often confers powers to influence or control what happens. The relation cause–effect is conceptually bound up with the notion of making sequences of events intelligible.

This aspect of (efficient) causation is prominent in Malebranche's thinking and provides his rationale for distinguishing causing from occasioning. He defined causation as '*necessary* connection': 'A true cause as I understand it is one such that *the mind perceives* a necessary connection between it and its effect' (*Recherche* VI.ii.3, italics added). What is at issue here is a kind of intelligibility since he was concerned with what we *understand*. He argued that 'men are not the true causes of the movements they produce in their bodies' because *nobody knows how* to move his arm, i.e. what must be done to move his arm by means of animal spirits; only God knows how to do this (*Recherche* VI.ii.3, italics added). In contrasting occasioning with causing, he meant to exclude this conception of necessity from the connotation of the term 'occasion'. His statement that a movement in the eyes *occasions* the sensation of colour entails that there is *no intelligible connection* between the movement and the sensation. Equally, to affirm that my will to move my arm is the occasional cause of the movement of my arm is expressly to deny that there is a necessary connection between the two things. This is his own explanation of why '*x* occasions *y*' is inconsistent with '*x* causes *y*'. He exploited this implication of lack of intelligibility in arguing that one movement of matter cannot be the cause, but only the occasion, of another movement of matter.

On the other hand, Malebranche's use of the idiom of occasioning is meant to give some sort of explanation of why something happens. Wherever experience reveals to us perfect regularities without necessary connection, there we have paradigms of occasional causes, and God's direct intervention in the world is the general form of the explanation of these regularities. Malebranche's strategy, we might say, is to invoke divine intervention to make something (partially)

234 He was apparently understood by the Port-Royalists to advance a form of occasionalism in respect of sense-perception. 'It is false . . . that all our ideas come through sense. On the contrary, it may be affirmed, that no idea which we have in our minds has taken its rise from sense, except *on occasion* of those movements which are made in the brain through sense, the impulse from sense giving occasion to the mind to form different ideas [than it would have formed without it]' (*PRL* I.1). Arnauld too championed what he called Descartes' occasionalism in opposition to Malebranche's more complex theory of sense-perception.

intelligible that would otherwise be (completely) unintelligible. For example, my now having the sensation of colour would be completely unintelligible were it not the case that it is occasioned (Thanks be to God!) by certain movements now taking place in my eyes.[235] Although this relation of movement to thought is impenetrable to the human intellect, the activity of God makes it intelligible that it should be both exceptionless and unintelligible. This clearly must not be understood to mean that acts of God provide explanations that stand on the same level as natural laws or serve the same purposes as scientific explanations. On the contrary, Malebranche's assertion that one thing occasions another entails a negative claim about the *possibility* of constructing a causal explanation.[236]

This double standard of intelligibility is a second essential attribute of occasionalism. Making sense of a particular contrast between occasioning and causing requires appeal to the relevant standards of what is intelligible (and unintelligible). So too does the very idea of a particular way of making something, as it were, intelligibly unintelligible. As a direct consequence, variation from age to age (or from one philosopher to another) in the criteria of intelligibility produces different concepts of efficient causation and of occasioning. Applying inappropriate concepts in interpreting a specific doctrine is a source of misunderstanding and confusion. We will suggest that it is precisely one such unremarked modification in the concept of intelligibility that accounts for much of the difficulty that modern commentators have in making sense of Descartes' account of mind–body interaction. The rest can be ascribed to their failing to notice or to appreciate the fact that all of his causal idioms in this context are to be read as incorporating the qualification 'by Nature' or 'Naturally'.

To keep our bearings, let's start from a crude sketch of Descartes' conception of intelligibility. There are two forms of intelligible connections. One kind holds between certain modes of thinking: logical relations among thoughts (entailment, contrariety, mutual contradiction). The other kind holds between corporeal substances: mechanical relations of displacement by impact; or more generally, motions of matter linked by mechanisms (gear-trains, systems of wires, springs, and pulleys, etc.). Any connection not overtly having one of these basic forms is intelligible only in so far as it can be reduced or analysed into sequences of such transparent connections. This amounts to laying down particular, stringent criteria for judging whether or not explanations are successful, i.e. whether or not they make things intelligible. By Descartes' lights, there *can* be *only two* patterns for

235 The Port-Royalists gave precisely this argument. Although it would otherwise be completely unintelligible why I should suddenly have the thought 'I see light', God's intervention gives some account: 'no idea which we have in our minds has taken its rise from sense, except *on occasion* of those movements which are made in the brain through sense, the impulse from sense giving occasion to the mind *to form different ideas [than it would have formed without it]*' (*PRL* I.1, second italics added).

236 Hence his position *cannot* be described as invoking God's actions as explanatory hypotheses of last resort.

making connections intelligible. They are mutually exclusive[237] and jointly exhaustive.[238] We suggest that he characterized a successful explanation as one that revealed a 'resemblance', 'similarity', or 'affinity' between things. Consequently, to claim that two things 'resemble' each other is, in this sense of this term,[239] to assert that they are *intelligibly* connected.[240] (This is comparable to Malebranche's claiming that there is a 'necessary connection' between them.)

This conception of intelligibility is correlative to a conception of (absolute) unintelligibility. Anything which is definitely not a mechanical relation among corporeal things or a logical relation among thoughts *cannot* be explained; it *must* be opaque to reason. (These are logical impossibilities, not contingent lacunae in human knowledge.)[241] It follows immediately that correlations between thoughts and states of the body *must* be unintelligible. *A fortiori*, it is *impossible to explain* the correlation of sense-based thoughts with states of the sense-organs or to explain the correlation of bodily movements with volitional thoughts. There can be no such thing as a statement or theory that makes these soul–body correlations intelligible.[242] For this reason, there *can* be *no* 'resemblance', 'similarity', or 'affinity' between thoughts and movements in (or of) the body; this denial is unconditional or categorical.

Descartes shared this conception of intelligibility with many of his near-contemporaries. It informs several arguments in the Port-Royal *Logic*, and it is common ground between Arnauld and Malebranche. Although a staple of seventeenth-century speculation, it is doubly (and very deeply) alien to twentieth-century philosophical thinking. First, (efficient) causation has been divorced from the concept of mechanism, and it is now commonly equated with some form of

237 The reason is akin to the category-difference that Ryle emphasizes in trying to get rid of the 'bogey of determinism' (1954: 21–4). We cannot analyse arguments with causal concepts ('compel', 'determine', etc.) or describe sequences of events with logical concepts in terms of inference-licences, contrariety, etc.

238 Ironically, the Rationalists' notion of 'necessary connection' is commonly accused of having conflated these two distinct kinds of intelligibility!

239 There is probably a different use in speaking of the resemblance between an object and the image imprinted by it on the retina or in the brain (*Optics* V–VI, e.g., AT VI: 130; CSM I: 167).

240 It is this sense of 'resemble' that is relevant to understanding the so-called 'Causal Similarity Principle': namely an effect must resemble its (efficient) cause (AT V: 156; CSMK III: 539–40). This formulates in an obsolete jargon the requirement that ascertaining the cause must make the occurrence of an event *intelligible*.

241 Bedau (1986: 485ff.) argues that Descartes' view is not (as is sometimes held) that it is inconceivable *that* distinct kinds of substance interact, but rather that it is inconceivable *how* distinct kinds of substance interact. There is in our view something right about this, though Bedau's gloss – 'the means by which totally different substances interact . . . simply escapes us' (p. 486) – seems misguided.

242 This doctrine must be clearly distinguished from that with which it is now likely to be confused: namely that there is no intelligible connection between animal sentience (sense-perception, appetites, emotions, desires, memories, etc.) and states of the body (the sense-organs, the stomach, the brain, etc.). Descartes held that mechanical explanations could in principle be given for all aspects of (animal) sentience, so that physical science could make animal behaviour fully intelligible.

regularity.[243] Exhibiting something as an instance of a confirmed regularity makes it fully intelligible.[244] Only anomaly (or irregularity) is unintelligible. (The shift from mechanism to regularity eliminates the logical space for Descartes' occasionalism,[245] namely his invoking God as the author of 'our Nature' in order to make it intelligible that a well-documented *regularity* is in principle *unintelligible*.) Second, the very idea of absolute unintelligibility is now treated as deeply unintelligible. It is an axiom of modern science that *everything* can in principle be explained; nothing is, as it were, *ex officio* beyond the limits of possible scientific theories. Any anomaly can be identified only provisionally.[246] The further progress of science may exhibit it as an instance of a hitherto unrecognized regularity. And once subsumed under a well-confirmed generalization, it is made fully intelligible. (This change eliminates the degree of freedom essential to the occasionalist ambition to make something intelligibly unintelligible.)

Later evolution in the concept of efficient causation which are linked to a decisive change in the criteria for making sequences of events intelligible, distances twentieth-century discussions of causal interaction of mind and body from any doctrine that would have made sense to Descartes. (There has been a gradual and progressive transformation of intellectual frameworks, a conceptual analogue of continental drift. A whole ocean now separates us from him.) He held that a perfect regularity could be absolutely unintelligible, *a fortiori* not even a *possible* case of efficient causation. In the case of basic correlations of thoughts with bodily movements, he offered an essentially theological explanation based on the notion of Natural causation. It requires a sustained effort of imagination to regenerate his conception of Natural or occasional causes. For lack of it, today's philosophers are like savages listening to the speech of highly sophisticated men: they put the oddest interpretations on Descartes' words and draw the strangest conclusions from them. Making a better job of it has potential *philosophical* interest. (It might, for instance, expose an over-simplified or one-sided conception of causation widely shared among twentieth-century philosophers.)[247]

243 It is effectively reduced to 'constant conjunction' in Hume, but latterly takes more sophisticated forms.

244 It seems to be implied that *only* this makes something intelligible, i.e. that explanations in terms of mechanisms are accepted only because they are backed by observed regularities. Wittgenstein throws out a challenge to this philosophical prejudice, suggesting that pushes and pulls are a *primitive* form of causal explanation ('Cause' 387, 395–7).

245 Russell lodged a version of this objection against Malebranche's occasionalism: Leibniz's doctrine of pre-established harmony had 'the advantage' of being able to account for the perfect correspondence between the series of thoughts and the series of movements 'without the perpetual intervention of God' (B. Russell, *The Philosophy of Leibniz*, Cambridge: Cambridge University Press, 1900, p. 136).

246 This methodological principle negates a crucial presupposition of Descartes' advocacy of complete freedom for scientific enquiry from interference by the Church. He reasoned that fundamental Christian doctrines can be established by pure reason prior to, and independently of, any scientific enquiry; hence they fall in principle outside the scope of any possible experiments or scientific theories.

247 This is the avowed purpose of Wittgenstein's remarks in 'Cause'.

Efficient causes: intelligibility and resemblance

Having given a first sketch, we need to go back over the canvas and fill in some details. We start with the sixteenth/seventeenth-century conception of efficient causation.[248]

What is understood as the hallmark of causal interaction between corporeal substances is a kind of intelligibility. On this view, the prototype of the relation '*x* is the efficient cause of *y*' is a mechanism linking *x* to *y*. In the simplest cases, the question 'What made . . . happen?' is definitively answered by establishing that something was pulled by a string or pushed by a stick. In a slightly more complicated case, discovering a mechanism terminates the causal enquiry. For example, we may contrast *not understanding* how a clock works when we simply see the hands moving round the dial with *understanding* how it works once we have opened it up and traced through the gear-train. These seem to be everyday *paradigms* of explaining something or making it intelligible.[249] Descartes took them all at face value.

Underlying his notion that discovering a connecting mechanism makes corporeal interactions *intelligible* is the more basic idea that there is one relation between corporeal things that is *completely* intelligible, namely the displacement of one object by the impact of another moving object.[250] It is an axiom of Descartes' mechanics that one object can be set in motion only by the impact of another moving object, and the truth of this principle is seen *by the Natural light* (AT XI: 38–43, CSM I: 93–6; cf. *Principles* II.37, CSM I: 240–1). Consequently, observed instances of displacement by impact are transparent to reason just as they appear. A paradigm of intelligible interaction would be observing one billiard ball to be set in motion by the impact of another moving ball. Sequences of such transparent interactions are heir to the same intelligibility as in the interlinked movements of the cog-wheels in a gear-train. This is the basis for his principle that revealing a mechanism connecting two things makes a particular interaction between them fully intelligible.

Descartes built this concept of mechanism into his notion of efficient causation.[251] It is a criterion of adequacy for any causal explanation that something be exhibited, immediately or proximately, as being produced from displacements by

248 There is evidence that Descartes' conception of efficient causation was fairly widespread among his contemporaries, but this point is tangential to our concerns.

249 Indeed they are still paradigms among non-philosophers in the twentieth century. (This point is stressed by Wittgenstein in 'Cause'.)

250 This has the striking implication that any explanation having this form is final and complete. Hence there is no such thing as refining or improving it by incorporating some further hidden mechanism. (This is not even a possibility.)

251 More accurately, this is an essential component of the relation of efficient causation between finite substances. He held that God is the efficient and total cause of the existence and motion of all corporeal substances. We leave God's actions out of account for the purpose of the present exposition.

impact.[252] In some cases the observed movement of an object must be accounted for in terms of the impact of myriads of imperceptible particles; in other cases, changes in the observed properties of things must be explained by reference to changes in the local motions of their parts which are themselves produced by impact.

Descartes took pride in the intelligibility of his own mechanical explanations. In his view, the search for an efficient cause is terminated by the discovery of a *mechanism* which can be *seen* to produce the effect from the cause. Natural science aims to make the behaviour of corporeal things fully intelligible, and it achieves this end completely to the extent that it discovers the mechanisms underlying observed regularities. (Descartes took the revolutionary step of subsuming the whole of the behaviour of non-human animals within the scope of possible mechanical explanations.)[253] The peculiar intelligibility claimed for his physics is directly linked to success in the revelation of mechanisms.[254]

The crucial role of this particular conception of intelligibility is nowhere clearer than in Descartes' criticism of scholastic explanations which invoked 'real qualities':

> we *understand very well how* the different size, shape and motion of the particles of one body can produce various local motions in another body. But there is *no way of understanding how* these same attributes (size, shape and motion) can produce something else whose nature is quite different from their own – like the substantial forms and real qualities which many philosophers suppose to inhere in things; and we *cannot understand how* these qualities or forms could have the power subsequently to produce local motions in other bodies.
>
> (*Principles* IV.198, CSM I: 285, italics added; cf., e.g., AT II: 200, CSMK III: 107)[255]

Some of the details of his own position may be unclear. In some sense of the phrase 'what is sensed', he excluded the possibility that what is sensed could be

252 This is more of a demand than a discovery. It could be seen as the *stipulation* of criteria for determining what counts as a successful attempt at explanation; and equally for determining what calls for explanation (cf. AT XI: 42; CSM I: 95).

253 The *Treatise on Man* is principally devoted to sketching possible mechanisms that have enough complexity to account for *all* forms of animal sentience and locomotion but function on the simplest possible mechanical principles.

254 Malebranche stressed this aspect of Descartes' physics. He conceded ironically that 'Descartes was not given to us by God to teach us everything that can possibly be known, as Averroes says of Aristotle'. But he added: 'if you want to be basically instructed in physics . . . you would not know how to do anything unless you followed his method, that is, unless you reasoned as he does on the basis of clear ideas, always beginning with the simplest ones' (*Recherche* VI.ii.4).

255 As Bedau (1986: 489f.) points out, Descartes' otherwise puzzling analogy, frequently repeated (e.g., AT III: 667–8; CSMK III: 219), between mind–body interaction and the alleged action of 'real qualities' like heaviness on bodies is a dialectical strategy: his opponents already admit that the action of real accidents is unintelligible to reason, so they have before them a (misapplied) model of mind–body interaction.

anything other than a purely mechanical mode of extension of a corporeal substance, since it must bring about changes in the local motions within the sense-organs. At the same time, he admitted the possibility of sensations *of* colour, light, taste, pain, etc., and he described possible mechanisms to explain all these forms of sense perception. What is required to make sense of his position is a clarification of the sense in which colours, light, tastes, etc. can be *identified* with mechanical states of matter (see above, pp. 129–34). Evidently he understood the doctrine of 'real qualities' to be incompatible with any such identification. And he took his own explanation of the various forms of sense-perception to be the antithesis of explanations by 'real qualities' precisely because we *can understand* how 'the size, shape and motion of the particles of one body can produce local motions in another body'![256]

His thought is now hard to grasp because the relevant notion of intelligibility has largely disappeared from the post-Humean philosophical conception of causation. What Descartes took to be the paradigm of an intelligible mechanical interaction, that is, a single instance of one billiard ball's being set in motion by the impact of another moving ball, Hume treated as the paradigm of an unintelligible ('brute') fact. On Descartes' view, the observation of some matter's being displaced by other moving matter gives us the material for drawing the distinction *post hoc/propter hoc* in a *single instance*,[257] whereas Hume denied that a single observation could justify any statement stronger than 'First one thing moved, then the other'. The very same particular interactions of corporeal substances which Descartes claimed to be transparent to reason Hume proclaimed to be opaque to reason.[258] Descartes thought that exhibiting a mechanism connecting two movements (e.g., a taut string) is a complete, full-dress causal explanation of a particular event (e.g., a person's falling off a dock when a ship moves away from a wharf). Hume denied precisely this point, arguing that no possible description of a single sequence of events can license distinguishing a causal connection from a mere coincidence; this distinction necessarily requires reference to *other* sequences of events in order to justify the claim that the original sequence of events instantiates a 'constant conjunction'. On Hume's view, discovery of a mechanism can't abrogate this logical requirement (though it might alter our perceptions of which regularities were relevant to explaining a single sequence of events).

How should we view this confrontation? Did Hume discover the true *nature* of causal explanation? Did he refute Descartes' concept of intelligibility? We might

256 Garber argues that Descartes failed in this ambition because he had to invoke God as the cause of motion, thereby using God to accomplish what had been done by the substantial forms of the schoolmen (Garber 1992: 305).

257 We might make this point by saying that an observation of impact (or of shoving with a stick or pulling with a string) is a *criterion* for stating that one thing happens *because* another has; not a *symptom* of the truth of a statement of constant conjunction (cf. Wittgenstein, 'Cause' 410).

258 Of course, discrepancies about what is transparent to reason or about what is known by pure reason must witness to differences in what is to be understood by the term 'reason'.

think it better to say that Hume's 'improvement' on Descartes amounted to the substitution of one *concept* of intelligibility for another, since it demonstrably alters what it *makes sense* to say. Hume dissociated causal claims from any commitment as to the existence of actual mechanisms.[259] This amounts to the stipulation of new criteria for making something intelligible. Equivalently, it is the substitution of one concept of causation in place of another one. This is clear from the fact that what counts as giving a causal explanation is decisively altered. On Hume's view, establishing uniform correlations of sensations with local movements in sense-organs is revealing a *causal* connection between body and mind, whereas on Descartes' view this causal claim is demonstrably false.[260] Our Nature as the union of body and soul consists of correlations of movements and thoughts that are perfectly regular, since they are ordained by God; but they are not causal, since they *cannot* be mechanical. Hume abolished Descartes' doctrine of occasionalist interactionism by conceptual fiat.[261]

To sum up: a certain conception of intelligibility is built into Descartes' conception of efficient causation, at least as it is applied to the behaviour of corporeal things. (This, we might say, is an important aspect of his *rationalism.*)

Natural causes: unintelligibility and non-resemblance

It is crucial to make this point clear in order to grasp his antithetical conception of the interaction between mind and body. He had the conviction that these correlations must be absolutely or in principle *unintelligible* or *opaque to reason*. They *cannot* be *explained* or *understood*. It seems clear that there could be nothing parallel to a mechanism to clarify the power of the mind to move the body or the power of the mind to be influenced by states of the body. There can be no *mechanism* whose input is moving matter and whose output is *thoughts*.[262] Equally, there can be no *reasoning* whose premises are thoughts and whose conclusions are *movements*.[263] If we follow the misleading practice of making use

259 He seems committed, however, to the *possibility* of introducing a mechanism between any two links in a causal chain. On his view, there is no bedrock in causal explanation.

260 In fact, their positions are not quite so directly comparable, since what Hume meant by an 'impression' is *not* what Descartes understood by a 'sensation'. We ignore this complication.

261 This was not an arbitrary (i.e., unmotivated) change. On the contrary, Hume refashioned the concept for two purposes. First, it opens up the possibility of framing causal laws governing the mind; especially the possibility of exhibiting the laws of the association of ideas as the counterpart of universal gravitation in his 'Newtonian mechanics of the mind'. Second, it makes intelligible the idea that acts of the will are the causes of voluntary actions, and the stimulation of sense-organs the causes of impressions; hence it opens up the possibility of a unified science of mind and matter. Nothing less than a *conceptual* revolution could have made the impossible possible!

262 'Body, as far as we can conceive, being able only to strike and affect body, and motion, according to the utmost reach of our ideas, being able to produce nothing but motion; so that when we allow it to produce pleasure or pain, or the idea of a colour or sound, we are fain to quit our reason, go beyond our ideas, and attribute it wholly to the good pleasure of our Maker' (Locke, *Essay* IV.iii.6).

263 *Pace* Aristotle, who notoriously described practical reasoning in just these terms (*De Motu Animalium* 701^{a}6–25).

of *unqualified* causal idioms in paraphrasing his doctrines, we must be clear that *lack of intelligibility* characterizes so-called 'causal interaction' between corporeal and incorporeal substances. It must in principle be *impossible* to explain *how* any such interaction occurs on the model of giving mechanical explanations of movements. Alternatively, if we stick closely to his idiom, for instance, that certain movements in the eye are *ordained-by-Nature-to-make-the-soul-have* certain sensations, then we should bear in mind that this relation differs from efficient causation in respect of not making it *intelligible* why someone has these sensations when his eyes are stimulated in the appropriate way. The concepts of Natural causes and of efficient causes are essentially different in precisely this respect.

It is clear that Descartes used the phrases 'taught to us by Nature' and 'ordained by Nature' to express this view. They are used *in contrast to* 'intelligibly connected'. He meant these expressions to convey the thought that the (divinely instituted) correlations between things are intrinsically or necessarily 'unintelligible':

> Why should that curious tugging sensation in the stomach which I call hunger tell me that I should eat, or a dryness of the throat tell me to drink, and so on? I was not able to give any explanation of all this, except that nature taught me so. For there is absolutely no connection [*affinitas*] (at least that I can understand [i.e. no *intelligible* connection]) between the tugging sensation and the decision to take food, or between the sensation of something causing pain and the mental apprehension of distress that arises from that sensation.
>
> (AT VII: 76; CSM II: 53)[264]

In this passage, what is unintelligible are certain regular, non-logical correlations between distinct thoughts. But precisely the same point holds in respect of the correlation of thoughts (sensations or volitions) with bodily movements. To say that the 'Natural correlations' between mental and corporeal properties are 'unintelligible' is to say that they are absolutely 'inexplicable'. There is nothing comparable to the 'story' about the internal workings of the clock which enables us to understand *why* the sensation of pain is annexed to the violent local motion of particles in the foot which is caused by a sword blow. Such mind–body correlations are *not* 'beyond the present capacities of his philosophy to explain', but rather '(logically) impossible to explain'.[265]

It is ironic that one common criticism of Descartes' Dualism points to the *a*

264 Very crudely, the picture is that if there is a genuine connection between things, then either it is intelligible (in which case I can learn it for myself) or it is not (in which case I must have been taught it by Nature).

265 We might liken Descartes' position here with Victor Cousin's thesis that we cannot perceive things as they are in themselves. '*Je ne dis pas que le problème est insoluble*, je dis qu'il est absurde et enferme une contradiction. *Nous* ne savons pas ce que ces causes sont en elles-mêmes, *et la raison nous défend de chercher à le connaître . . .* ' (*Cours d'Histoire de la Philosophie au 18me siècle, 8me leçon*; quoted by Mill, *Logic*, I.3.7).

priori impossibility of his *explaining* mind–body interaction. That is precisely his *doctrine*, not a *problem* for it.[266] It is part of what he meant to be understood, not something that he would have preferred to pass unnoticed. He expressed it in the claim that the interaction of body and soul is a *primitive* notion (AT III: 665–6; CSMK III: 218). In his view, this is consistent with treating it as something 'ordained by Nature', since this description, by invoking the action of God, expressly puts the matter beyond the reach of metaphysical or scientific explanation.

It is even more ironic to accuse Descartes of a fallacy in localizing a logically impossible mechanism of mind–body interaction in the pineal gland, or invoking the animal spirits as the medium of mind–body interaction. He couldn't have been trying to explain the mechanism of this two-way interaction since he held it to be in principle inexplicable. In his system, the pineal gland had a totally different role. It explains the unification of sensory inputs and the amplification of mechanical forces, and both matters are still thought to require explanation in modern physiology even if the preferred mechanism is different (e.g., we no longer talk about animal spirits). The pineal gland has a pivotal function in the working of the body-machine, and it plays the very same roles in Descartes' mechanical explanations of *animal* sentience (where there is no question of any interaction between the body and the soul!).

To repeat: The conception of souls and bodies as distinct kinds of substances is understood to entail that any connection between them is absolutely inexplicable or in principle opaque to reason. The idioms of 'gives occasion' and 'ordained by Nature to make' are intended to make this point explicit, and it has to be understood as implicit in all Descartes' uses of causal idioms in discussions of mind–body interaction.

He had other ways of expressing the notion of this inexplicability. In some cases, this point seems obvious. For example, he frequently invoked the metaphor of movements in the brain 'presenting signals' to the mind or soul. An injury to the foot, say, produces a motion in the pineal gland which in turn 'gives the mind its signal for having . . . the sensation of a pain as occurring in the foot' (AT VII: 88; CSM II: 60). The point of the metaphor is to capitalize on the familiar idea that symbols are *arbitrarily* associated with what they signify.[267] This is made explicit elsewhere:

> Now if words, which signify nothing except by human convention, suffice to make us think of things to which they bear no resemblance, then why could *Nature* not also have established some *sign* which would make us

266 *Prima facie*, this is an odd objection to raise within the framework of the post-Humean conception of causal connection as observed regularity (cf. Bedau 1986). Is it a component of this conception that the assertion of a causal connection, though independent of any *actual* mechanism, implies the logical *possibility* of inserting a mechanism between *any* two events in a causal chain?

267 In another sense, these mind–body correlations are far from arbitrary, since they were ordained by God for the specific purpose of subserving our welfare: see pp. 183ff.

> have the sensation of light, even if the sign contained nothing in itself which is similar to this sensation?
>
> (AT XI: 4; CSM I: 81, italics added)

> There is no reason to be surprised that certain motions of the heart should be Naturally connected . . . with certain thoughts, which they in no way resemble . . . . In the same way when we learn a language, we connect the letters or the pronunciation of certain words, which are material things, with their meanings, which are thoughts.
>
> (AT IV: 603–4; CSMK III: 307)

Just as there is no 'intelligible connection' between a sign and what it signifies, so there is no 'intelligible connection' between the movement in the brain and the thought in the mind.

In other instances, his expressions of the incomprehensibility of mind–body interactions are not so readily intelligible, at least to modern readers.[268] The principal exhibit under this heading is his denial that two things 'resemble' each other.[269] For example, in describing love as involving motions of the heart which make the soul imagine lovable qualities in the object loved, he noted 'that certain motions of the heart [are] *Naturally connected* in this way with certain thoughts, which they *in no way resemble*' (AT IV: 603–4; CSMK III: 307, italics added). It seems impossible to make sense of this remark by taking 'resemble' naively (in any available everyday sense);[270] it is at best a gratuitous parenthesis, at worst sheer nonsense. But the remark itself, by suggesting that Nature can take lack of resemblance in its stride, further implies that this feature is precisely the unintelligibility that Descartes regularly invoked Nature to make *intelligibly* unintelligible. The very same point is suggested in the rhetorical question 'why could *Nature* not . . . have established some sign which would make us have the sensation of light, even if the sign contained *nothing* in itself which is *similar to* the sensation?' (AT XI: 4, CSM I: 81, italics added; cf. AT VI: 112, CSM I: 165).

According to our interpretation, correlations 'ordained by Nature' are essential ingredients in every case of mind–body interaction, and Descartes drew attention to this doctrine both by making use of occasionalist idioms and by drawing attention to absence of 'resemblance' between thoughts and bodily movements. Lack of resemblance between thoughts and movements amounts to a denial of

268 Compare Malebranche's statement: 'There is *no relation* . . . between instances of motion and sensations' (*Recherche* I.12, italics added): Yet in sense-perception, the one is the natural cause of the other.

269 Cf. Locke: it is 'no more impossible that God should annex such ideas [of the blue colour and sweet scent of that flower] to such motions, with which they have no similitude, than that he should annex the idea of pain to the motion of a piece of steel dividing our flesh, with which that idea hath no resemblance' (*Essay* II.viii.13).

270 The same point holds in respect of the so-called 'Causal Similarity Principle' (AT V: 156, CSMK III: 337–8; cf. AT VII: 188, CSM II: 132) and of the Aristotelian doctrine that knowledge requires 'resemblance' with its object (what is known) or that the knower must resemble what he knows (cf. *De Anima* 404^b16–18, 427^b4).

efficient causation. The correlation between them is a matter of *Natural* causation. Many earlier interpreters have achieved some degree of understanding of his conception without being side-tracked by his use of causal idioms. There is surely something perverse about the presupposition of modern commentators that Descartes' use of expressions like 'cause' must conform to the logical geography of the expression 'cause' in twentieth-century English (or worse yet, in twentieth-century *philosophers'* English).

Natural causes and the 'paramechanical hypothesis'

Some philosophers (e.g., Russell) have given an indirect argument for occasionalism in Descartes' account of voluntary action on the grounds that the very idea that the mind might 'produce' the motion of matter seems to be inconsistent with his axiom that matter can be set in motion *only* by the impact of other moving matter; his 'whole theory of the material world . . . was rigidly deterministic' (Russell 1946: 590). Our own argument has taken a very different route. But does the doctrine of Natural causes solve this notorious conundrum? There is a tremendous temptation to suppose that an 'occasional cause' must still be something like a 'paramechanical cause',[271] even if bolstered up by God. My volition to move my arm, on this view, constitutes a (non-mechanical) *intervention* in the mechanical flow of things. This doctrine might be preferable to the apparently nonsensical idea that the mind intervenes *mechanically*, and adding God to psychokinesis might undercut some of the more obvious objections.[272] Yet it still seems that Natural causes flatly contradict the axiom that matter moves *only* by the impact of other moving matter.

From the very beginning, this has been a crux in interpreting Descartes. Various strategies have been explored. Some commentators (Garber 1992: 303) have argued that he did not intend the axiom to hold with full generality (cf. *Principles* II.40; CSM I: 242): *his* axiom is rather that *matter* only moves other matter by impact, but this expressly leaves open the possibility that mind can also move matter (although not by impact). Others have argued that Descartes' axiom concerning the conservation of motion relates only to speed, not to direction; here the picture is that the soul, like a fountain-keeper, uses the pineal gland to divert the flow of animal spirits and thus brings about physical changes.[273] These are ways of trying to reconcile paramechanical causes with the axioms of mechanics.

The issues raised here are extraordinarily complex and widely ramifying. On the one hand, there is the contention that Descartes' system of mechanics is 'rigidly

271 Perhaps something like 'psychokinesis' (cf. Williams 1978: 288ff.).

272 For instance, it might provide a straightforward explanation of why I can will my arm to move but not will my hair (or for that matter, my pineal gland!) to move: God has deemed it beneficial to my welfare to make the one a 'basic action' but not the other (see p. 177).

273 Leibniz put forward a version of this suggestion, which has been adopted and adapted by a number of commentators: Russell 1946: 583, 590; Rée 1974: 101–2; Williams 1978: 281; and Gaukroger 1995: 369–70.

deterministic' (Russell 1946: 590). But it is not clear what the content of this doctrine is.[274] In particular, it is arguable that any form of Laplacean determinism was inconceivable before Leibniz developed the principle of the conservation of momentum and combined it with the supposition of perfectly elastic impact (Russell 1900: 81). On the other hand, it is clear that Descartes envisaged a strictly mechanical explanation of the whole gamut of animal behaviour. Yet it is not clear that his conception of the operation of *bêtes-machines* committed him to any view that full knowledge of any one momentary state of the natural world would entail full knowledge of its state at every later time. On the contrary, he might have held the view that animal behaviour is predictable only locally (within a single 'behaviour-cycle'),[275] but not globally. This would be a plausible analogue of his conception of the functioning of hydraulic automata.

We cannot debate these complex issues here. But we want to put forward the possibility of a quite different way of seeing 'occasional causes'. On this view, he really did leave no logical space for any 'paramechanical' operations of the mind; the soul *cannot* interfere, mechanically or paramechanically, in the corporeal world. One might find evidence for this view in the following passage:

> The soul cannot produce any movement in the body without the appropriate disposition of the bodily organs which are required for making the movement. On the contrary, when all the bodily organs are appropriately disposed for some movement, the body has no need of the soul in order to produce that movement, and, as a result, all the movements which we in no way experience as depending on our thought must be attributed not to the soul, but simply to the disposition of the organs. Even the movements which we call 'voluntary' occur principally as a result of this disposition of the organs, since, although it is the soul that determines the movements, they cannot be produced without the requisite disposition of the organs, no matter how much we may will this to happen.
>
> (AT XI: 225; CSM I: 315)

If the bodily organs are appropriately disposed, then a mechanical explanation of the movement is in principle available; i.e. no ghostly pushing or shoving is needed to explain the movement. Indeed this would happen whether or not the soul wills it. How then can thought (volition) be part of the efficient and total cause of the movement? Even when the act is 'voluntary', the occurrence of the movement *requires* the appropriate disposition of the organs, and this disposition is *sufficient*

274 On one interpretation, Descartes had a 'hydrostatic model [of mechanics], where it is not motions but instantaneous tendencies to motion, not speeds but atemporal displacements, that matter'. This has often been thought to have the paradoxical consequence 'that different instants in the universe will be causally insulated from one another, so that no earlier state of affairs can have any effect on a later one' (Gaukroger 1995: 368). Even if this implication were denied, however, 'the notion of instantaneous tendencies to motion actually prevents Descartes from dealing with the continuous motions required by kinematics' (p. 376). We can't here pursue these difficult issues further.

275 Compare Russell (1921: ch. 3).

to produce the movement! Therefore, in Descartes' view, human freedom cannot be visible in contra-mechanical interventions in natural history; there can be no such thing. Volitions are idle wheels in the *mechanism* of all physical human behaviour.

Is this doctrine *obviously* crazy? Modern philosophers might be inclined to react by saying that if volitions are idle wheels, surely we should apply Occam's razor to them! But this reaction presupposes a particular view of what Descartes is doing, namely offering a causal explanation of human *behaviour*, of human *bodily movements*. In fact, Descartes offered separate 'causal' explanations of animal and rational voluntary *action*, with different senses of both 'cause' and 'action'. He warned us against confusing the 'two principles of motion': 'the principle depending solely on the animal spirits and organs exists in the brutes just as it does in us', but we must not 'jump to the conclusion . . . that the other principle, which consists in mind or thought, also exists in them' (AT VII: 230–1; CSM II: 162). The 'principle of movement' which governs brute actions has a role in efficient causation; the principle of movement which governs rational actions has a role in Natural causation. There is no movement whatever which cannot be perfectly 'imitated', i.e. performed, by an animal or even by a machine or automaton (AT VI: 58; CSM I: 140–1); any *movement* can be given a complete mechanical explanation. But it is *only* humans who can act in the rational or 'restricted' sense; it is only human acts that can express thoughts or exhibit intelligence, virtue, and vice. The 'principle of motion' of a rational voluntary action is a volition, the result of practical deliberation, and consequently is crucial in the *moral* evaluation of human action. The proposal to 'prune away' the volition with Occam's razor amounts to the proposal to prune away moral agency! But the idea that human beings are morally responsible for their voluntary actions is not an explanatory hypothesis (see pp. 202–4). The soul *cannot* interfere in the corporeal world, it is not part of the mechanical 'order'; but it can make a difference in the *moral* world, it is part of the 'moral order'.

Occasionalist interactionism

If we were forced to choose between 'occasionalism' and 'interactionism' as labels for Descartes' account of human sense-perception and voluntary action, we would prefer the first to the second. It has the great advantage of stressing the pivotal role of God in the account of the substantial union. Precisely this point is completely absent from standard expositions of Cartesian Dualism, and the result is a caricature of Descartes' thinking. The term 'occasionalism' has the further virtue of respecting his metaphysical principle that there can be no such thing as efficient causation between thoughts and movements.

The immediate danger is that 'occasionalism' is taken to be logically incompatible with any use of causal idioms or any talk of mind–body interaction. This implication generates all manner of anxiety and confusion in reading Descartes' texts, and it fosters the mistaken idea that his advocacy of occasionalism was the result of the primitive state of physiology and psychology in his day. Any version of occasionalism is now liable to ridicule as a relic of the Stone Age of philosophical thinking.

In our view, the usual debate about how to interpret his doctrine of the relation of body and soul rests on three failures. Two we have explored here: the failure to understand his conception of efficient causation, and the failure to notice or explore his conception of Nature and the associated notion of Natural causation. Once we have clarified these matters sufficiently, we will see that we face no dilemma in expounding his doctrine. On the contrary, it becomes clear that he used the different idioms of (Naturally) causing and occasioning to develop a single, consistent conception of a God-ordained one–one correlation between basic thoughts and certain states of the body. The trouble faced by most later interpreters has been that subsequent changes in the concept of causation have eliminated the possibility of making sense of his doctrine of Natural or occasional causes. It is difficult to find any space between constant conjunction and efficient causation. We have tried to work our way upstream, as it were, in order to recapture his vision.

A third difficulty that stands in the way of seeing his doctrine aright is blindness, once again, to the systematic ambiguity of S-predicates (explored on pp. 179–84): one fallacy of equivocation underpins another. It is commonly held that Descartes advocated both a causal theory of action and a causal theory of sense-perception. (Although these are both now viewed by some, though not all, as respectable philosophical doctrines, his dualistic interactionist version of them is universally seen as a muddle.) The truth is that he elaborated a *mechanical* causal account of *animal* action and *animal* sense-perception and a *Natural* causal account of *rational* action and *rational* sense-perception. It cannot but foster confusion to talk nonchalantly about 'causal theories of action and perception', without making these crucial distinctions.

Dissolving the apparent dilemma in interpreting Descartes' texts has been our primary concern. But in the protracted debates about his interactionism/occasionalism, two further things are taken for granted that are wholly unwarranted and that have implications of the greatest importance.

First, attention is directed wholly at the nature of the *relation* between mind and body, not at the nature of the *relata*.[276] It is taken for granted that we clearly understand what the *sensations* are that are somehow correlated with local motions in the sense-organs, and that we clearly understand what the *volitions* are that are somehow correlated with movements of the body; the only question is how to describe Descartes' conception of *how* these things are correlated with each other. The very idea that it makes sense to think of these relations as being causal seems

276 And, of course, the word 'relation' itself needs careful handling! We have already stressed that there are no relational judgements in the framework which Descartes inherited; below (p. 175) we argue that the idiom of 'powers' (e.g., the power of the soul to move the body) is a result of that framework.

to presuppose that these sensations and volitions be conceived as some sort of amorphous or inarticulate experiences.[277] In sense-perception, they must be visual, auditory, etc. impressions, and pains, pangs of hunger, feelings of anger, etc.: these occurrences (what passes before our minds) are the data given to us through the senses. In voluntary action, the volitions must be conceived as acts of will, i.e. as 'non-physical episodes which constitute the shadow-drama on the ghostly boards of the mental stage' (Ryle 1949: 64). In both cases, the mental counterparts of bodily movements are conceived as being inarticulate and non-propositional. They are 'objects' that may intelligibly stand as terms in the relation '*x* causes *y*'. This is the shared presupposition of both parties to the debate about occasionalism and interactionism.

Evidently, however, our Nature consists in the correlation of *thoughts* with bodily movements, and by 'thoughts' Descartes here meant articulate judgements (or at least the articulate contents of judgements). What he called 'sensations' and 'volitions' must have propositional content;[278] they can certainly be affirmed, and their affirmations can be assessed as true or false. The whole idea that movements in sense-organs are efficient causes of sense-based judgements would be at loggerheads with his principle that making judgements is an exercise of freedom. Conversely, his evident concern to differentiate rational from causal explanations of human behaviour would conflict with the spirit of the notion that volitions with articulate thought-content are the efficient causes of bodily movements. In any case, the debate over occasionalism/interactionism seems to lose much of its intuitive appeal if we pay attention to his conception of the nature of thoughts. Conversely, participating in this debate is apt to perpetuate the misconception that Descartes divorced the concept of a thought from the notion of having articulate thought-content.

Second, in the most basic cases, both '*x* causes *y*' and '*x* occasions *y*' are thought to express *external* relations between the terms *x* and *y*.[279] Paradigmatic causal statements are held to be contingent and empirical, and it is a requirement that each of the two terms can be identified independently of the other (on the model of fire and smoke). In so far as '*x* occasions *y*' is normally held to be an even weaker relation, the same requirement must be applicable to statements of this form. Interpreters do not offer occasionalism as an *antithesis* to the thesis that mind–

277 This distinction between sensation and judgement is crucial for making sense of Malebranche's conception of hallucination: 'There have been those who believed they had horns on their head and others who imagined they were made of butter or glass .... They were mad .... [But] it should be noted that these madmen really see themselves as they think they are – error is not strictly in the sensation they have but in the judgement they form .... They err solely in the fact that they believe that their body is like the one they sense' (*Eclaircissement* VI).

278 Here again we must note the ambiguity of S-predicates.

279 For simplicity, we exclude any consideration of causal statements one term of which has the form 'the cause of ...' or 'the effect of ...', or one term of which can be so defined. The 'internal' relations generated in this way are clearly logical relations between *expressions*; the supposition that *all* internal relations are relations between expressions is akin to the idea that all necessity is logical necessity, and would have been wholly alien to Descartes (see pp.183ff.).

body correlations are external. On the contrary, Descartes is invariably taken to have developed some form of the doctrine that any relation between a thought and a movement must be contingent. (This might be seen as a straightforward consequence of his dualism provided that both thoughts and movements were seen as mental and physical *things* or *objects*. It may seem tautological to state that there are no necessary connections between any two distinct things.[280] This principle might be the heir of the Aristotelian metaphysical axiom that any two substances must be capable of existing independently of each other.)

The notion that Cartesian mind–body connections must be external is the essential basis for the Wittgenstein-inspired refutation of Cartesian Dualism. The conclusion of this argument is that the doctrine of causal interaction fails to meet the general epistemological requirement for making intelligible causal statements, namely that the terms of causal relations must be identifiable independently of each other. Now it might seem that basic sense-impressions and acts of will are items in the stream of consciousness (what passes before the mind) of which each person is immediately aware, and this seems to guarantee the possibility of one's identifying these items independently of knowing anything about the movements in or of one's own body. But the Private Language Argument is taken to have demonstrated that this plausible claim is untenable. Wittgenstein has purportedly shown that, independently of outward behaviour, there are no criteria for individuating inner states. In this way he is claimed to have fired a broadside into the Cartesian conception of the mind and sunk it once for all.

This 'refutation' seriously misrepresents its target. Unlike '*x* causes *y*', the expression '*x* occasions *y*' in Descartes' usage describes a relation that is not merely external. (Is it ever suggested that defending an *occasionalist* interpretation might rescue Descartes from this conceptual shipwreck?) Every instance of one thing's occasioning another is ordained by God, and whatever God wills is, in some sense, necessary (see below, pp. 183–8). This general principle holds for the system of correlations that constitute 'our Nature' as the union of mind and body. Any Natural correlation of a thought with a movement (as in rational sense-perception) or of a movement with a thought (as in rational desire) *could not be other than it is*; the actual correlation is the sole one among all 'conceivable' correlations which best secures our welfare by the most efficient uniform means.

280 Could this not be the burden of Wittgenstein's challenge to the grammatical remark 'A pain is *something*' (*PI* §304)? We may be strongly inclined to epitomize the claim that 'pain' and 'pain-behaviour' are not synonymous expressions in the formula 'Pain is one thing, pain-behaviour is another thing'. But then we are liable to infer that the concept of pain and the concept of pain-behaviour are independent of each other, i.e. that each of them can be explained without reference to the other. That conflicts with our acknowledging that we treat pain-behaviour as a *criterion* of being in pain, and that we do explain what 'pain' means in terms of what we call 'expressions of pain'. One way to eliminate such confusion is to resist the temptation to describe what a word means in terms of its standing for a quite particular 'object', since that form of representation of grammar is what surrounds the workings of our language with a fog (cf. *PI* §§1–3).

In some sense, all these relations are *internal*. A particular movement of the pineal gland would not be the movement it is if it were not tied to the particular thought which it in fact occasions the soul to have, and a particular volition (of the sort which terminates in an action of the body) would not be the volition it is if it were not tied to the particular movement of the pineal gland which is in fact occasioned by it. We might need to explore whether Descartes' conception of these necessary connections succeeded in meeting the demand that inner states be *conceptually* linked to bodily behaviour, but we have no right to assume that it is irrelevant. We can be certain, however, that Cartesian Dualism misrepresents a crucial aspect of Descartes' Dualism, namely the non-contingency of the fundamental mind–body correlations that constitute our Nature (see pp. 183–8).

This point has an important corollary. Despite the lack of relevant textual evidence, he is regularly held to have analysed voluntary action as a 'portmanteau' concept. For example, my stealing an apple must be a conjunction of two distinct things: one is the movement of detaching the apple from the tree and placing it in my pocket, the other is the performing of certain mental acts (say deciding to remove the apple with the intention of depriving its owner of any benefit from having grown it).[281] What is explicitly built into this conception is the independence of the two components that jointly make up the concept of a particular voluntary action. But, if the Natural correlations of volitions and movements are severally necessary, then any items paired together by Nature are *internally* related.[282] In respect of these rational voluntary actions, the analysis as 'portmanteau' concepts definitely misrepresents Descartes' position. In each case, neither component of the 'conjunction' would be what it is if it were not correlated by Nature with the other one.[283]

Different 'theories' of mind–body interaction are as different in content as the kinds of reason that are offered in their support. Failure to heed this principle of textual interpretation has led twentieth-century Anglo-American philosophers to attribute to Descartes an account of causal interaction that he definitely did *not* hold. His complex and subtle doctrine of Natural interaction lies beyond the range of the artillery lined up against Cartesian Dualism.

281 Cf. Mill: 'Now what is an action? Not one thing, but a series of two things; the state of mind called a volition, followed by an effect. The volition or intention to produce the effect, is one thing; the effect produced in consequence of the intention, is another thing; the two together constitute the action' (*Logic* I.iii.5).

282 The matter is further complicated by the distinction between movements of the pineal gland and the observable movements of the body that are their mechanical consequences. The latter give rise to the concept of 'necessarily normally connected'; see p. 187.

283 That volition and movement are not separable embodies an important insight: '"Willing, if it is not to be a sort of wishing, must be the action itself. It cannot be allowed to stop anywhere short of the action"' (Wittgenstein *PI* §615). This has a moral implication: what I take pride in or feel shame about, or what merits praise or blame, is not merely the intention which I had in doing something, but 'the whole history of the incident' (*PI* §§643–4).

The substantial union of mind and body

The analysis of Descartes' conception of the two-way interaction between the soul and the body is a crucial part of the stage-setting for his account of the substantial union of these two substances in each individual person. It doesn't by itself, however, clarify this extremely puzzling (and even apparently paradoxical) aspect of his conception of the person.[284]

It is worth noting straight away that Descartes took knowledge that a person is a union of mind and body to be something *unproblematic*, something of which everyone is *conscius* (AT V: 222; CSMK III: 357). 'People who never philosophize and use only their senses' conceive the union between soul and body without difficulty; 'it is the ordinary course of life and conversation' which teaches us how to do this (AT III: 692; CSMK III: 227). By contrast, the idea that a person is a pair of substances, an immortal soul and a body-machine, is apparent only to somebody who has won through to this insight by dint of sustained metaphysical reflection and 'withdrawal of the mind from the senses'. (Even intelligent and reflective people are easily led astray into conceiving of the soul as the form of the body, or even into the nonsensical doctrine that the soul is a substantial form.) As a consequence of the many temptations to fall into error and heresy, Descartes put great emphasis on arguments to prove the 'real distinction' between soul and body, while his remarks on the 'substantial union' are comparatively infrequent and low-key:

> many more people make the mistake of thinking that the soul is not really distinct from the body than make the mistake of admitting their distinction and denying their substantial union, and in order to refute those who believe souls to be mortal it is more important to teach the distinctness of parts in a human being than to teach their union.
>
> (AT III: 508; CSMK III: 209)

None the less, his view of the union is perfectly visible to the attentive reader.

The following six points are clearly essential parts of his doctrine and will have to serve as our navigational aids.[285]

1 Each person, though in some sense constituted by two substances (a soul and a body) that are capable of existing independently of each other, is also in some sense a single thing:

284 Our account of the substantial union is in marked disagreement with those of Wilson (1978: ch. VI) and Cottingham (1986: ch. V). Nevertheless both of them have done something extremely important in focusing attention on this neglected aspect of Descartes' concept of a person.

285 These 'navigational aids' come from chronologically diverse sources; we feel reluctant to invoke Voss' 'Leibnizian hermeneutic' unless forced to – 'Time for Leibniz is God's way of allowing contradictory propositions to be true . . . the appearance of conflict among Descartes' statements can often be alleviated by supposing that he sometimes changed his mind' (1994: 274). Voss argues that there is a radical shift between Descartes' view in the *Meditations*, where he held that 'there exists an entity composed of soul and body', and his view post-*Principles*, where he is committed to the view that 'there is no such thing as man' (p. 274). This case turns on what is meant by 'entity'.

> Everyone feels that he is a *single person* with both a body and a soul so related by nature that the soul can move the body and feel the things which happen to it.
>
> (AT III: 694; CSMK III: 228*, italics added)

It is enough of an entity in its own right to have a welfare, and equally to have a history, life, or career. A person is not a logical fiction, but must be in some sense substance-like: this is what is marked by the phrase '*substantial* union' ('*unio substantialis*' or '*unio essentialis*': AT III: 508). He even went as far as suggesting that it is 'possible' to call the union of mind and body a 'complete substance' by characterizing the soul and the body of a person as 'incomplete substances'. This apparently self-contradictory expression he explained by claiming that a substance can be called 'incomplete'

> insofar as it is referred to some other substance in conjunction with which it forms something which is a unity in its own right . . . [In this way] the mind and the body are incomplete substances when they are referred to a human being which together they make up.
>
> (AT VII: 222; CSM II: 157)[286]

He connected this notion in turn with the claim that the union of mind and body is an '*ens per se*' (literally: 'an entity in itself' or 'an essential entity'), by contrast with an '*ens per accidens*' (literally: 'accidental entity'):

> the body and the soul, in relation to the whole human being, are incomplete substances; and it follows from their being incomplete that what they constitute is an *ens per se*.
>
> (AT III: 460, CSMK III: 200; cf. AT III: 492–3, CSMK III: 206)

The difficulty here can be brought into sharp focus by noting that the phrases '*per se*' and '*per accidens*' are standard scholastic terminology for contrasting *essential* attributes with *accidental* properties. Calling a person an '*ens per se*' is equivalent to affirming that the union of mind and body is essential ('*essentialis*') and to denying that it is accidental ('*accidentaria*') (AT III: 508; CSMK III: 209). Hence what must be done is to clarify how there can be a *necessary* connection or *internal* relation between two distinct *substances*, each of which must be capable of existing independently of any other substance!

2 Descartes drew a contrast between the mind's being 'lodged (or present) in' the body and the two substances being 'intimately intermingled and conjoined':

> I am not merely present in my body as a sailor is present in a ship, but . . .

286 Peter Markie ('Descartes' Concepts of Substance', in Cottingham 1994) apparently misreads this passage when he concludes that Descartes held that the union of mind and body was a *substance* of which the mind and body (also substances in the same sense) were parts (65–6). Voss makes a parallel criticism (1994: 290 n. 27).

> am very closely joined and, as it were, intermingled with it, so that I and the body form a unit.
>
> (AT VII: 81; CSM II: 56)

The simile of the sailor and his ship is meant to present a model of two substances that are merely glued together or externally conjoined.[287] The *unit* designated 'sailor plus ship' (or 'angel plus body', cf. AT III: 493; CSMK III: 206) seems to be a paradigm of what in scholastic jargon is called an '*ens per accidens*'.[288]

3 Sense-perception and Imagination are described as 'faculties' that are not essential to the mind (cf. AT VII: 78, CSM II: 54; AT VII: 73, CSM II: 51); they are 'species of thoughts' and hence 'belong to the soul', but nevertheless 'belong to the soul only insofar as it is joined to the body' (AT III: 479; CSMK III: 203). Alternatively,

> we experience within ourselves . . . all the sensations such as those of pain, pleasure, light, colours, sounds, smells, tastes, heat, hardness [etc.]; . . . [these] must not be referred either to the mind alone or to the body alone, [but] . . . arise from the close and intimate union of our mind with the body.
>
> (*Principles* I.48; CSM I: 209*)[289]

This has implications for the disembodied soul: 'the human mind separated from the body does not have sense-perception [and Imagination] strictly so called' (AT V: 402; CSMK III: 380).[290]

4 He held that the union of mind and body is a 'primitive notion', and that with this notion are linked the further 'primitive notions' of two powers which 'belong to the union of the soul with the body', namely the power of the soul to move the body and the power of the body to act on the soul (AT III: 665; CSMK III: 218). The former is apparently involved in the capacity for voluntary action and the

287 We might say that the mind 'lodged in' the body has no *right* to use the word 'I' (or '*my* body') to refer to the body in which it is lodged; cf. 'the body which by some special right I called "mine"' (AT VII: 76; CSM II: 52). Here 'no right' means 'no God-given right'. But this metaphor is only as clear as the notion of the substantial union.

288 It is evident that the phrase 'very closely joined and, as it were, intermingled' is equivalent to 'substantially united' (AT VII: 228; CSM II: 160). One implication might be a reductive logical analysis of any statement whose grammatical subject was 'the sailor and his ship'. At the first stage, this would be treated as a conjunction of a pair of independent judgements, one predicating a property of the sailor, the other predicating something of his ship. (Cf. p. 162, n.281)

289 Note: 'must not be referred either to the mind alone or to the body alone' may sound like 'must be referred to (i.e. predicated of) the union of mind and body'; but this would make nonsense of his logico-metaphysical principle that only substances can be the logical subjects of judgements. 'The mind alone' must mean 'the mind on its own, i.e. not united to the body'; likewise, *mutatis mutandis*, for 'the body alone'.

290 'Separation' normally contrasts with 'union', but is compatible with distinctness. (Indeed distinctness and union are both descriptive of living human beings.) But there are some anomalous usages, such as 'it is not clear by natural reason alone whether angels are created in the form of minds distinct from bodies, or in the form of minds united to bodies' (AT V: 402; CSMK III: 380*).

power of the passions to produce bodily movement, the latter in sense-perception (hence in sensations and passions) and probably also Imagination. Consequently, the substantial union seems to be, as it were, the substrate for a large part of his account of what might be called 'Human Nature'.[291]

5 What Descartes referred to as 'confused thoughts' – especially the confused thoughts connected with the internal senses – are repeatedly said to 'arise from' the union of mind and body. For example, the 'emotions or passions of the soul' are presented 'as *confused thoughts*, which the mind does not derive from itself alone but experiences as a result of something happening to the body with which it is closely conjoined' (*Principles* IV.190; CSM I: 281, italics added). Emphasis on confused thoughts is explicit in contrasting the substantial union with the sailor in his ship: for if I were lodged in my body as a sailor is lodged in his ship,

> when the body needed food or drink, I should have an explicit understanding of the fact, instead of having *confused* sensations of hunger and thirst. For these sensations of hunger, thirst, pain and so on are nothing but *confused* modes of thinking which arise from the union and, as it were, intermingling of the mind with the body.
>
> (AT VII: 81; CSM II: 56, italics added)

These first five points seem to present an obvious difficulty for the interpreter. How can we make sense of 'powers' and 'faculties' that can be referred neither to the body alone nor to the mind alone? Mustn't these be 'emergent' properties which count neither as modes of thinking nor as modes of extension? (Couldn't this be what the adjective 'confused' gestures at?) How else can we describe what it is that the 'sailor in his ship' or the mind 'merely lodged' in the body lacks? Yet, if they are genuinely 'new' or 'emergent' properties, then don't they require a third kind of substance in which to inhere, namely the union itself,[292] and a third sense of 'I' to refer to this substance? But this idea comes into flagrant collision with his ('official') metaphysical dualism.[293] How can we steer a course between the Scylla of making a person an *ens per accidens* and the Charybdis of undermining Descartes' expressed dualism?

The real difficulty, we think, about Descartes' conception of the person is not to discover a hidden solution to the enigma of how he conceived of the 'substantial

291 The term 'human nature' now strikes philosophers as vague and rather suspect. In Descartes' texts, 'human nature' ('our Nature as union of mind and body') is both precise and central to making sense of his concept of a person (see pp.168ff.).

292 Note that for Descartes the idea of a third type of property of human beings that counted neither as thought nor as extension would, given his logical framework, *require* a third type of substance; *pace* Cottingham (1986: 131), there is no room for a view that embraced exactly two kinds of substance but allowed three kinds of properties.

293 This, arguably, is what motivates Cottingham's claim that the *union* of mind and body bears a special new kind of property: 'phenomenological' properties or 'subjective' qualities, a 'what it is like' (cf. 1986: 126). But Cottingham himself holds that these 'phenomenological properties' do not fit happily into Descartes' 'official dualistic schema' (p. 127).

union'. Rather, it is to recognize that the explanation that he repeatedly gave really amounts to a clear and complete answer to the question. His own explanation crucially involves the concept of Nature, but this concept is seldom noticed and even more rarely analysed. Here then is the sixth buoy for navigating between Scylla and Charybdis.

6 The notion of the substantial union of mind and body is identified with 'our Nature', in one sense of this multiply ambiguous phrase. In its widest sense, 'By my own Nature . . . I understand nothing other than the totality of things bestowed on me by God' (AT VII: 80; CSM II: 56*). In a more restricted sense, 'my Nature' is to be understood as 'what God has bestowed on me as a combination of mind and body' (AT VII: 82; CSM II: 57). This is what is crucial for grasping the doctrine of the substantial union: the phrase '*our Nature as* union of mind and body' is a slogan that recurs in his discussions of the topic (especially in *Meditation* VI). It points clearly to God's role. Descartes' use of the term 'Nature' is intended to signal to the attentive reader the vital fact that *God* is responsible for the substantial union of mind and body.

The strategy we will follow begins with a preliminary clarification of 'our Nature (as union of mind and body)': this is to be explained as a distinctive pattern of strict correlations between thoughts and movements in the brain. This generates, as a (divinely intended) by-product, a further pattern of normal (non-strict) correlations between thoughts and movements or conditions of the body (see pp. 168–72). The (strict) Natural correlations in a certain sense just *are* the 'primitive notions' of the power of the soul to move the body and the power of the body to act on the soul; these two powers play a role, respectively, in what might be called 'basic actions' and 'basic sense-perceptions'. What might be called 'non-basic' actions and sense-perceptions are in some sense grounded in these (see pp. 123–7). These Natural correlations and connections are (directly or derivatively) *ordained by God*, and this has two vital implications. First, they must serve human *welfare* (pp. 178–80). This point is crucial for making sense of the idea that the 'basic sensations', particularly those tied to the internal senses, are 'confused thoughts' (pp. 180–3). Second, Natural correlations have a kind of *necessity* (pp. 183–8).[294] (It follows from this that the power of the soul to move the body and the power of the body to act on the soul in a sense belong to the *nature* (essence) of the soul and the body respectively, when they are united.) It is precisely this necessity which justifies the description of the substantial union as an *ens per se* rather than an *ens per accidens*; it alone makes sense of the notion of a necessary connection between two distinct substances. It is this, finally, that enables us to make sense of one of Descartes' most puzzling remarks (see pp. 188–91):

294 Herein lies one major point of disagreement with Wilson's version of the 'Natural Institution' doctrine.

> It does not seem to me that the human mind is capable of forming a very distinct conception of both the distinction between the soul and the body and their union; for to do this it is necessary to conceive them as a single thing and at the same time to conceive them as two things; and this is absurd.
> (AT III: 693; CSMK III: 227)

The account we give here is complex and multi-stranded, and it is crucial not to lose sight of the main point, namely that Descartes had a distinctively *theocentric* conception of the substantial union of mind and body. This gives a crucial role to the notion of the *welfare*, in particular the *moral* welfare, of a person. And it gives rise to a kind of *internal* relation between mind and body, notwithstanding the fact that mind and body are 'really distinct'.

'Our Nature'

Clarification of Descartes' conception of the substantial union must begin from considering our Nature, namely what God has bestowed on each of us as a combination of mind and body. There seem to be at least four distinct but closely related uses of the term 'Nature' that need to be understood here.

First, there is the expression 'ordained *by Nature*'; this can be read as synonymous with 'instituted *by God*'. *What* God (or Nature) has ordained is a set of mind–body correlations. Normal adult human life manifests a vast array of systematic (normal although not absolutely invariable) correlations of thoughts and bodily movements (both movements within the body and movements of parts of the body). Many of these (especially expressing thoughts in speech and understanding the speech of others) involve learned habits and human conventions, but all of these correlations ultimately rest on a system of (absolutely invariable) correlations between thoughts in the soul and movements in the pineal gland. In addition, various distinct and logically independent thoughts are correlated with each other, for example, the sensation of thirst and the desire to drink (AT VII: 76; CSM II: 53). (This sketch will be further elaborated below.)

Second, this pattern or system of correlations 'ordained by Nature' is itself what Descartes called '*our Nature* as the union of mind and body'.[295] This point is made clear in many texts, though it is generally masked in modern English translations where 'by Nature' in this sense ('*naturâ*' or '*naturellement*') comes out in English as 'naturally': 'There is no reason to be surprised that certain motions of the heart should be naturally connected in this way with certain thoughts, which they in no way resemble' (AT IV: 603–4; CSMK III: 307). This is too easy to read either simply as meaning 'of course' (like '*natürlich*' in German) or as a reference to the 'natural relation' of causation,[296] but this is contrary to Descartes' intentions.

295 In this use (unlike the previous one), the noun '*natura*' is combined with other applicatives such as 'this' ('*haec*') and 'that' ('*ista*').

296 For example, Loeb (1981: 137) reads this adverb as 'Descartes' own foreshadowing of a Humean, constant conjunction, or regularity analysis of causation'.

It is to forestall such misunderstandings that we capitalize such occurrences of 'Naturally', as well as 'Nature'. Obviously the word 'natural' has the same difficulties; for instance, modern English readers are unlikely to be struck by its vital occurrence here, and they may even mistakenly accuse Descartes of a *non sequitur*: 'This deception of the senses is *natural*, *because* a given motion in the brain must always produce the same sensation in the mind' (AT VII: 88; CSM II: 61, italics added).

Third, by virtue of these God-instituted correlations between thoughts and gland-movements, the soul (and arguably also, *mutatis mutandis*, the body) has a 'nature' that it would not have had were it not united to the body.[297]

> There are two facts about the human soul on which depend all the knowledge we can have of its nature. The first is that it thinks, the second is that, being united to the body, it can act and be acted upon along with it.
>
> (AT III: 664–5; CSMK III: 217–18)

This is clearly the key to the two 'primitive notions' of the power of the soul to move the body and the power of the body to act on the soul. These two powers are said respectively to belong to the *nature* of the soul (when united to the body) and of the body (when united to the soul): 'Everyone feels that he is a single person with both a body and a soul so related *by nature* that [*un corps & une pensée, lesquels sont de telle nature que*] the soul can move the body and feel the things which happen to it' (AT III: 694; CSMK III: 228*, italics added).

Finally, Descartes claimed that '*(my) Nature* teaches me' various things. In particular, it teaches me 'that I have a body which has something wrong with it when I have the sensation of pain, which needs food and drink when I have the sensation of hunger or thirst, and so on' (AT VII: 80; CSM II: 56*). Likewise, my Nature teaches me to decide to take food when I have the sensation of hunger, and to take a drink when I have the sensation of dryness in the throat (AT VII: 76; CSM II: 53). More generally, (my) Nature teaches me 'by these sensations of pain, hunger, thirst, etc. . . . that I am very closely joined and, as it were, intermingled with' my body (AT VII: 81; CSM II: 56). In all these passages the phrase 'my Nature teaches me' seems to be offered as an explanation for my making a non-logical inference of one judgement from another.[298] Although these inferences may sometimes yield false conclusions, as in the case of phantom pains or dropsy, they are implanted in us by God; given his benevolence, there must be 'some truth' in these Natural patterns of thinking. Thanks be to God, what I am

297 Bedau (1986: 496–7) argues on these grounds that Descartes' account of the 'natures' of mind and body as thought and extension respectively must be incomplete. This may underplay the *prima facie* difficulty (see pp. 188–91).

298 In this respect, 'what Nature teaches me' is radically different from what I know 'by the Natural light' ('*lumen naturale*'), namely 'common notions'.

taught *by Nature* is generally true, and this is conducive to my welfare, but it may occasionally be mistaken (AT VII: 85; CSM II: 59).[299]

The first two uses of 'Nature' are intimately connected. 'Our Nature', or the pattern of correlations ordained by Nature, is described as 'what God has bestowed on us' (AT VII: 82; CSM II: 57). There can be no intelligible relation between a mode of thinking and a mode of extension, and he expressed this point by claiming that they 'bear no resemblance' to each other (see pp. 152–6). None the less there is no reason that *Nature* could not have established some movement in the eyes which would, like a sign, make us have the sensation of light even though the sign in itself contained *nothing* which is *similar* to the sensation (cf. AT XI: 4; CSM I: 81). The action of God is the only way of making regularities between thoughts and movements at all intelligible (and equally non-logical connections between distinct judgements); they remain absolutely inscrutable, but it is at least intelligible *that* they should exist and be unintelligible (to human reason). Any discernible patterns of correlation between a person's thoughts and movements *must* be God's handiwork precisely because both logical and causal connections are out of the question. As previously noted, Descartes' use of occasionalist idioms manifests his intention to stress this feature of mind–body interaction: without God, the substantial union would be dissolved.

The fact that God is directly responsible for the design and creation of our Nature has two crucial corollaries which show how the other two uses of 'Nature' link in. One is the conceptual connection between our Nature and human welfare: my Nature 'teaches me things' which are in general conducive to my welfare (see pp. 178–80). The other is the notion that some kind of *necessity* attaches to whatever God has ordained. The power of the soul to move the body and the power of the body to act on the soul are directly underpinned by the correlation in which our Nature consists (see pp. 173–7); to say that these powers constitute the *nature* of my soul (when united to the body) and of my body (when united to the soul) is to refer to the necessity of what God has explicitly ordained (see pp. 183–91).

But first we need to arrive at a more refined understanding of Descartes' conception of our Nature. We know that God has endowed us with a set of strict correlations between movements in the pineal gland and (S-predicate-involving) thoughts in the soul. These correlations are invariable or, as it were, 'hard-wired'. There is no such thing as a breakdown in this Super-Machine.[300] But we also know that movements in the pineal gland are related *mechanically* (i.e. by the mechanism of nerve-tuggings and the flow-patterns of the animal spirits) to other states of the body. In particular, when the body-machine functions properly, they are caused by changes in local movement within the sense-organs, and they bring about movements of muscles and locomotion. These mechanisms, however, may

299 Again, 'there is a big difference here' between 'what Nature teaches me to think' and 'what is revealed to me by the Natural light' (AT VII: 38; CSM II: 26–7).

300 This principle is *morally* (not logically) certain, and it captures one aspect of the idea that Natural correlations are *necessary* (see pp. 183ff.).

be absent altogether (e.g., in the congenitally blind or deaf), they are subject to wear and tear, and they are liable to breakdowns, either transient or long-term (e.g., in the nerve-tuggings that originate in the stump of an amputated limb). Nevertheless, since the body-machine normally (usually) functions normally (properly), the strict correlations of thoughts with movements of the pineal gland becomes an integral part of a more widely ramifying pattern of correlations between thoughts and states of matter.

First, 'our Nature' induces (non-strict) correlations between thoughts and conditions within the rest of our bodies apart from the pineal gland.[301] This results from the fact that the movements of the pineal gland are *normally* correlated with conditions in the rest of the body, especially in (animal) sense-perception and (animal) locomotion. In this way, God has indirectly instituted a correlation of the thought 'I see_1 light' with increased local movement in my eyes and the thought 'I feel_1 pain in my foot' with violent local movement in my foot (cf. AT VII: 85–9; CSM II: 59–61). Equally, He has indirectly correlated the thought 'I (shall) move_1 my foot out of the fire' with the movement of withdrawing my foot from the fire. And so on. We might say that somebody's exhibiting these correlations is a criterion for his body's being in good working order. But it makes sense to deny that these correlations hold. For example, my making the judgement 'I feel_1 pain in my foot' does not *entail* that there are violent local motions in my foot; hence it does not entail that I feel_1 pain in my foot. And my making the judgement 'I (shall) move_1 my foot' does not entail that I move_1 my foot; for various reasons I may lack the power to do so.

Second, 'our Nature' induces non-strict correlations between some thoughts and states of corporeal things external to our bodies (the 'proper objects' of the external senses). This results from the fact that the senses function mechanically. It is part of the concept of seeing_1 something that the object seen_1 bring about an alteration in local motions within the seer_1's eyes by originating or modifying a stream of corpuscles that strike the eyes. Every one of the five external senses works in a similar way. When they function *normally*, there is a regular correlation between certain local motions in the sense-organs and certain mechanical conditions in what is sense-perceived. Otherwise, they are deemed to function abnormally or not at all. As a consequence of holding this conception of sense-

301 Commentators (e.g., Williams 1978: 289; Dicker 1993: 218) sometimes claim to discern a conflict between the thesis that 'the soul is united to all the parts of the body conjointly' (*Passions* I.30; CSM I: 339) and the thesis that 'There is a little gland in the brain where the soul exercises its functions more particularly than in the other parts of the body' (*Passions* I.31; CSM I: 340); the tension that Wilson discerns between the 'Natural Institution' view and the 'Co-extension' view (1978: 206ff.) in effect comes down to this. Since these two remarks occur in consecutive paragraphs, this *cannot* be right. Arguably the second refers to the *strict* Natural correlations between mind and body, the first to certain of the *non-strict* (but nevertheless God-ordained) Natural correlations. The first is sometimes expressed as the claim that the mind is 'coextensive with the body' (AT VII: 442; CSM II: 298). He explained (e.g. AT V: 270, CSMK III: 361; cf. AT V: 342, CSMK III: 372–3) that what was at issue was not an 'extension of substance' but an 'extension of power'. (On the powers of the union, see below pp. 173–7.)

perception, Descartes was committed to the doctrine that 'our Nature' indirectly correlates the thought 'I see$_1$ light' with the existence of something with a certain property outside me (in the direction I am looking), say, the sun. We might say that 'our Nature' induces a correlation between ('basic': see p. 176) sense-based thoughts and what makes them true (cf. *Passions* I.23; CSM I: 337). But these correlations hold only on the supposition that my sense-organs are functioning properly. Hence the occurrence in me of sense-based thoughts like 'I see$_1$ light' does not *entail* that there are any corporeal substances that exist outside me. This argument is developed at some length in the first half of *Meditation* III.

Third, connections between different *thoughts* are themselves induced by the set of thought–movement correlations which constitute our Nature. There is a kind of shadow cast on thinking by certain mechanical connections in the normal functioning of the body. The result is an inclination to fail to distinguish thoughts – an inclination to 'confusion' that is, in some sense, 'taught to me by Nature':

> Why should that curious sensation of pain give rise to a particular distress of mind; or why should a certain kind of delight follow on a sensation of tickling [*ex sensu titillationis*]? Again, why should that curious tugging in the stomach which I call hunger [*illa nescio quae vellicatio ventriculi, quam famen voco*] tell me that I should eat, or a dryness of the throat tell me to drink, and so on? I was not able to give any explanation of all this, except that *Nature taught me* so. For there is absolutely no connection [*affinitas*] (at least that I can understand) between the tugging sensation and the decision to take food, or between the sensation of something causing pain and the thought of distress [*cogitationem tristitiae*] that arises from that sensation.
>
> (AT VII: 76; CSM II: 52–3*, italics added)

In fact, the claim that Nature connects together sensations arising from the internal senses with perceptions of bodily needs or desires to act suggests that my making these connections must promote my welfare. Various thoughts *are* grouped together in our minds although their connection (being non-logical) is absolutely opaque to reason and can be explained only as ordained by God (for our welfare). We do not in general distinguish them because it is evidently beneficial to the union of body and soul that, in general, we do not do so. This is the key to Descartes' conception of Naturally confused thoughts. (For details, see pp. 180ff.)

To summarize: our Nature consists in a strict correlation between thoughts and movements of the pineal gland. But additionally, given the way the body-machine works, our Nature induces a *normal* correlation between sense-based thoughts and local movements in the sense-organs or between rational and animal voluntary actions; and less immediately, between thoughts and the perceptible properties of perceived things. Finally, mechanical connections between welfare-related conditions of the body get mirrored back into 'Naturally confused thoughts'.

The powers of the union

To talk of the strict Natural correlations constituting our Nature just *is* to talk of the power of the body to act on the soul and the power of the soul to move the body.[302] (It follows from this and our discussion (on pp. 145ff.) that these two powers *cannot* be understood as '(efficient) causal powers': there is no question of the body transferring motion to the mind or of the mind interfering contra-causally in the bodily mechanism.) The first of these powers plays a crucial role in sense-perception, the second both in the natural expressions of passions and in voluntary actions; arguably in all of these cases via certain of the *non-strict* Natural correlations.

Descartes outlined his general conception of sense-perception in the final sections of *Principles* IV.

> 189. *What sensation* [*sensus*] *is and how it operates* . . . . Sensation comes about by means of nerves, which stretch like threads from the brain to all the limbs . . . . [Movement in several of the nerve ends] is then transmitted to the other ends of the nerves which are all grouped together in the brain around the seat of the soul [the pineal gland] . . . . The result of these movements being set up in the brain by the nerves is that the soul or mind that is closely joined to the brain is affected in various ways, corresponding to the various different sorts of movements. And the various different states of mind, or thoughts [*mentis affectiones, sive cogitationes*], which are the immediate result of these movements are called sensory perceptions [*sensuum perceptiones*], or in ordinary speech, sensations.
>
> (*Principles* IV.189 (AT VIIIA: 315–16, CSM I: 280*))

The topic here is sensory perception *in human beings*, i.e. exercises of the faculty of sense-perception (*sentire*). Now, a faculty is a power, and the Aristotelian tradition in which Descartes worked relied on a distinction between 'active' and 'passive' powers. These powers came in internally linked pairs, for example, 'fire has a[n active] power to melt gold . . . gold has a [passive] power to be melted [by fire]', etc. (Locke, *Essay* II.xxi.1). Plausibly, 'the *faculty* of sensory perception' (together with 'the faculty of Imagination') is simply the 'passive power' which is internally correlative to the 'active power' of the body to act on the soul. (It could also therefore be called 'the power of the soul to be acted on by the body'.) To talk of powers within this tradition is, in effect, to talk of patterns of correlation between sets of properties (e.g., between fire's burning and gold's melting); this pattern can be viewed from either one side or the other, and powers are assigned to one or the other substance accordingly. Indeed it *must* be so viewed, since there are no relational judgements within the Aristotelian framework (see pp. 62–3): powers are, as it were, what you get when you try to pack correlations

302 It is the fact that our Nature is in a certain sense necessary that warrants the description of these two powers as part of the nature (essence) of the soul and body respectively when these two substances are united to each other (see pp. 188–91).

into one of the *correlata* so as to obtain a subject-predicate judgement. To a first approximation at least, we suggest that the faculty of sensory perception (the power of the soul to be acted on by the body) is the relevant pattern of strict Natural correlations viewed from the 'mind' side. The active power of the body to act on the soul is then the relevant strict Natural mind–body correlations viewed from the 'body' side. Since to have a Nature is to be a substantial union of mind and body, it follows that only a soul united to a body can possess the faculty of sensory perception, and only a body substantially united to a soul can possess the power of the body to act on the soul.

This suggestion links the faculty of sensory perception and the power of the body to act on the soul with the strict Natural correlations between soul and body. A fuller account of human sensory perception (one that allows us to distinguish between dreaming and more normal exercises of the faculty of sensory perception)[303] might build on the non-strict Natural correlations between mind and body; i.e. it might make reference to the Naturally normal causes of the gland-movements which constitute exercises of the power of the soul to move the body, perhaps both the normal bodily causes ('movement in several of the nerve ends') and the normal external causes of those movements (e.g., light). It is unclear (and pointless to speculate about) what the details of such an account would be, or how, precisely, one might wish to link up 'human sensory perception' with animal and rational sensory perception (as discussed on pp. 72ff.), although they surely are linked.[304]

We suggested that the active power of the body to act on the soul is essentially correlative to the passive faculty of sensory perception. Descartes went so far as to claim that 'although an agent and patient are often quite different, an action and passion [sc. an exercise of an active power and of a passive power] must always be a single thing which has these two names on account of the two different subjects to which it may be related' (*Passions* I.1; CSM I: 328). It may seem

303 Given that the so-called Dreaming Argument (in *Meditation* I) forms part of his polemic against empiricism, i.e. the view that what is acquired from and through *the senses* is 'most true', he must have conceived dreaming to involve the exercise of the faculty of sense-perception.

304 It *may* be that human sense-perception entails both animal and rational sense-perception. Neither animal nor rational sense-perception entails human sense-perception, since the first is possessed by animals, the second, logically possibly, by disembodied souls. (This logical possibility underlay Descartes' rationale for having introduced the restricted senses of S-predicates. That manoeuvre was meant to isolate the truth of the judgement 'I see_2 light' from falsification by such circumstances as being asleep or even having no body. Of course, philosophers today of the 'world-involvingness' persuasion would object to the idea that there could so much as *be* a thought with this type of reference-failure. Descartes would rule out the actualization of such a logical possibility on other grounds: for God to place such thoughts in a disembodied mind would be for Him to deceive, and 'it is self-contradictory that men should be deceived by God' (AT VII: 428; CSM II: 289). In *Meditation* II, before he had proved God's existence and deduced His non-deceptiveness, he could not demonstrate that this logical possibility was none the less an impossibility in another sense; see p. 183ff. Cf. Arnauld: 'The sensations of pain, hunger, and thirst can, if you want, prove nothing concerning the existence of my body, taken alone; but when we consider God along with these, they prove it demonstratively'; and 'the same holds for other sensations' (*Ideas* ch. 28).

strange that an exercise of a power of fire and an exercise of a power of gold could be 'a single thing', and stranger still that an exercise of a power of the soul and an exercise of a power of the body could be 'a single thing'. (That sounds dangerously close to saying that a mode of thinking is identical with a mode of extension!) But his claim is simply that the exercises of correlative active and passive powers are internally related: that is, the judgement that the agent has exercised one power necessarily has the same truth-value as the (distinct) judgement that the patient has exercised the other power, just as the judgement that the fire has the property of having melted the gold is necessarily interchangeable with the (distinct) judgement that the gold has the property of having been melted by the fire. (We might today prefer to say that here a single *fact*, i.e some *one* thing, corresponds to a *single* relational judgement when it is true; this is precisely what Descartes *could not* say, given that there was no such thing as a relational judgement within the framework of Aristotelian logic. He was forced to express the same insight in the somewhat awkward idiom that action and passion are 'a single thing'.) This has a striking consequence: though we might be inclined to worry about having to choose between saying that human sensory perception is an exercise of the power of the body to act on the soul and saying that it is an exercise of the power of the soul to be acted on by the body, from Descartes' point of view this choice *doesn't matter*. Human sense-perception is, as it were, 'a single thing' that can be described in these two different ways.

What about the converse power, the power of the soul to move the body?[305] That power is involved both in the Natural expression of passions (e.g., the blushes that accompany shame, the laughter that accompanies joy: AT V: 65; CSMK III: 237) and in human voluntary action. In conformity with our overall policy, we neglect the first and focus on the second. Exercises of this power, in so far as it relates to human voluntary action (cf. *Passions* I.41; CSM I: 343), can be identified with those volitions 'which terminate in our body' in contrast with those 'which terminate in the soul itself, as when we will to love God' (*Passions* I.18; CSM I: 335). We know that *in human beings* 'each volition is Naturally joined to some movement of the gland' (*Passions* I.44; CSM I: 344). Plausibly, the power of the soul to move the body is the relevant pattern of strict Natural correlations, viewed from the 'mind' side (*Passions* I.41; CSM I: 343: 'And the activity of the soul consists entirely in the fact that simply by willing something it brings it about that the little gland to which it is closely joined moves in the manner required to produce the effect corresponding to this volition'). Evidently only a soul united to a body can possess such a power. There must be a correlative passive power of the body to be moved by the soul, which can be identified with the relevant pattern of strict Natural correlations viewed from the 'body' side.

This suggestion links the power of the soul to move the body, and the correlative

305 Descartes suggested that 'If "corporeal" is taken to mean anything which can in any way affect a body, then the mind too must be called corporeal in this sense' (AT III: 424, CSMK III: 190; cf. AT III: 694, CSMK III: 228; AT V: 223, CSMK III: 358).

passive power, to the strict Natural correlations between operations of the soul and movements of the pineal gland. A full Cartesian account of human voluntary action, one which allows us to distinguish between volitions performed when the body is, say, temporarily paralysed, and cases 'when our merely willing to walk has the consequence that our legs move and we walk' (*Passions* I.18; CSM I: 335), would have to extend consideration to the non-strict Natural correlations between volitions and movements in the remoter parts of the body. Again, there is no point in speculating here about the details of how to link up human voluntary action with what we earlier called animal and rational action.[306]

Note also that (because of the essential equivalence between the judgements that the soul exercised its power to move the body and that the body exercised its power to be moved by the soul) in a certain sense it does not matter whether we say that human voluntary action is an exercise of the one power or of the other. To view it as an exercise of the power of the soul to move the body is to view it as an object of *conscientia* (cf. p. 113), and the *conscientia*-judgement that the soul exercised its power to move the body is necessarily interchangeable with the judgement that the body exercised its power to be moved by the soul. (This might seem self-contradictory unless we bear in mind that *conscientia* is not infallible.)

It will no doubt have struck you that the cases we have been dealing with all along are of a very limited and simple variety. We have been talking about seeing light, not about seeing trees, much less about seeing Rembrandts. And we have been talking about walking, not about writing a poem or stabbing an enemy. These are, of course, just the examples that Descartes himself used repeatedly. The reason for this, surely, is that it is at this 'basic' level that he conceived Nature to operate. The pattern of correlations set up by God is between movements of the pineal gland and what might be called 'basic sense-perceptions' and 'basic actions'. It would have been at best a wild extravagance, even an impediment to our welfare, for God to have annexed a different motion of the pineal gland corresponding to every possible (*sentire*- or *agere*-) thought-content.[307]

The precise demarcation of this 'basic' level is unclear, and so too is the form of analysis that he envisaged carrying out. It would be pointless to try to improvise them. ('Seeing light' is a basic sense-perception; but what about 'seeing variations in light and dark'? 'Seeing colour'? 'Seeing red?' 'Seeing *eau-de-nil*?'[308] 'Walking' is a basic action; but 'walking swiftly'? 'Dancing'? 'Executing a *pas-de-deux*'? etc.) For Descartes' purposes, the details don't matter at all; it is only

306 Plausibly, what should be said here would parallel what should be said about human sensory perception (see n.304 above).

307 Arguably it would be a nonsensical supposition. Might not the logical multiplicity of sensory judgements exceed the logical multiplicity of movements of the gland?

308 Also, of course, we would need to ask about 'seeing shape', 'seeing size', etc. We noted (p. 75, n.41) that his use of the term 'sensation' was apparently restricted to the 'proper objects' of the senses; for example, in the case of sight, 'light and colour' are 'the only qualities belonging properly to the sense of sight' (AT VI: 130; CSM I: 167). Thus the suggestion here sees a parallelism between the proper objects of the senses, on the one hand, and so-called basic actions, on the other. The issues here are interesting but go well beyond the scope of this work.

the possibility of an 'analysis' of sense-perceptions and actions that is metaphysically significant.

None the less, it is important to clarify what Descartes took this basic level to *exclude*. On the one hand, certain higher-level perceptions and actions are excluded (seeing trees, seeing Rembrandts, writing poems, stabbing enemies). It seems intuitively plausible that these higher-level perceptions and actions in some way or other involve or depend on basic ones. Surely one cannot see a Rembrandt unless one sees light and colour, nor stab an enemy unless one moves one's arm![309] On the other hand, the basic level of perception (or action) excludes all reference to the finer-grained bodily mechanisms that occur between the sense-organs (or muscles) and the pineal gland. God did not annex to a particular movement of the pineal gland such thoughts as 'I see my retina being bombarded by particles', 'I see the animal spirits racing up the optic nerve', 'I move my pineal gland', or 'I flex my left quadriceps'.

Descartes elaborated on this last point in respect of sense-perception (*sentire*) by the internal senses. The sensation of pain in the foot, he argued, is correlated with a particular motion of the pineal gland:

> God could have made the Nature of man such that this particular motion in the brain indicated something else to the mind [rather than giving it 'the sensation of pain as occurring in the foot']; it might, for example, have made the mind aware of the actual motion occurring in the brain, or in the foot, or in any of the intermediate regions .... But there is nothing else which would have been so conducive to the continued well-being of the body.
>
> (AT VII: 88; CSM II: 60–1)

According to God's design, this particular motion of the gland is normally caused by my foot's being painful, and this is normally connected with damage to my body and the need to withdraw my foot from the source of the pain (see pp. 181ff.). What *good* would it do us if this gland-movement gave rise to the thought that the gland-movement occurred? 'The most useful thing for us to know about the whole business' is that our foot hurts and hence that we need to respond appropriately. Descartes might offer a parallel argument to show why walking rather than moving my pineal gland or moving my left quadriceps was made by God into a basic action. If I am being attacked by a lion, I need to run, and the most useful thing for me to be able to do is 'just to do it'.[310] This reasoning brings out the first crucial implication of the fact that God is responsible for the creation of our Nature, viz. the conceptual link between our Nature and our *welfare*.

309 Cf. also *Passions* I.44 (CSM I: 344): 'each volition is naturally joined to some movement of the gland, but through effort or habit we may join it to others'. Some of these further connections might accurately be described as acquiring a 'second nature'.

310 This was a point that Malebranche misunderstood or deliberately distorted. He argued that we do not know how to move our arm because we are ignorant of the workings of the body-machine, and he concluded that even the simplest voluntary actions are not within our power.

Welfare

The pattern of basic thought–movement correlations instituted by God is claimed to be expressly designed to promote our welfare as the union of mind and body. For this reason, one must be able to demonstrate that some of its apparently puzzling details can be vindicated as manifestations of God's benevolence (e.g., the bodily mechanism that gives rise to the phenomenon of 'phantom pains' in missing limbs). The concept of welfare is an essential component in the explanation of Descartes' conception of the substantial union.[311]

Considerations of welfare are especially prominent in the discussion of 'confused thoughts' (see below, pp. 180–3). On the one hand, there are the 'confused thoughts of pain, hunger and thirst'. These (and some closely related thoughts) are planted in us by Nature for our preservation. On the other hand, there are 'confused sensations of colour, light, taste, etc.' Through bad habits of thinking, we commonly confuse these with obscure judgements about the nature of what we perceive by the senses (*Principles* I.46; CSM I: 208).[312] It might seem to be a deficiency in God's design that we have these sensations correlated by Nature with local movements in the sense-organs, since God could have correlated any thought He pleased with a particular movement in the eye or ear (AT VII: 88; CSM II: 60). But the blame lies with us, not with God. We use these sensations for the wrong purpose when we draw conclusions from them about the *nature* of corporeal substances.[313] God gave them to us for a different purpose, namely to make us vividly aware of things that are beneficial or harmful to us, and for this purpose they are 'clear and distinct' enough (AT VII: 83; CSM II: 57). For this reason, 'there is absolutely nothing to be found in [the sensations which Nature has given us] that does not bear witness to the power and goodness of God' (AT VII: 87; CSM II: 60).

We must bear in mind, however, that 'sensory perceptions are related *exclusively* to this combination of the human body and mind' (*Principles* II.3; CSM I: 224,

311 Here, more perhaps than in any other part of the book, our self-denying ordinance of refraining from discussing the passions (proper) pinches. Amélie Rorty ('Cartesian Passions and the Union of Mind and Body', in A. Rorty 1986) has a useful discussion of some of these issues; though we have points of disagreement, we cannot explore them here.

312 It is crucial to distinguish here between Natural confusion (non-logical connections between thoughts which are 'taught to me by Nature' (cf. pp. 169ff.), confusion between which is generally conducive to our welfare) and confusion due to 'a habit of making ill-considered judgements' (AT VII: 82; CSM II: 56). The former is further discussed below (pp. 180ff.). These two sorts of confusion are themselves commonly confused – by ordinary human beings, according to Descartes; but also by some commentators (e.g., Grene 1985: 36). Descartes was not in a position until *Meditation* VI to make the distinction.

313 Colour, taste, etc. are claimed to be no part of the *nature* of matter (*Principles* II.4, CSM I: 224; cf. AT XI: 26, CSM I: 89). This is liable to be misunderstood. They are not unreal; on the contrary, they are genuine 'modes of extension' (see above, pp. 129–34). But Descartes held that corporeal things have such properties only *per accidens*. The *nature* of matter is limited to what is *essential* to being a corporeal substance, namely the attributes necessarily involved in being an extended thing. Sense-perceptions are evidently not given to us by God for discovering this since, in Descartes' view, reason alone is competent to settle this question and to investigate the essential properties of corporeal substances (in arithmetic and geometry).

italics added). They are signals to the soul of what is beneficial or harmful to the Union. If an angel were lodged in a human body, the *composite* would have no welfare; hence, were God to correlate certain local movements of the body's eyes with the angel's having the sensation of colour, He would be defenceless against the charge of being a deceiver. For this reason, Descartes held that the angel must have the thought that there is a certain local motion in the surface of a coloured object rather than the sensation of colour (AT III: 493; CSMK III: 206). Without consideration of welfare, this reasoning would be utterly opaque.

But we need to clarify Descartes' conception of welfare. Welfare is a moral concept: it is closely analogous to Aristotle's notion of happiness (*eudaimonia*) as the supreme good of man. Welfare depends on knowledge of basic principles of metaphysics and physics (*Principles*, Preface (AT IXB: 14; CSM I: 186)), and its achievement also depends on the right use of reason (AT IV: 267; CSMK III: 258). It belongs with freedom and responsibility as characteristics of moral agents; indeed, freedom is a major component of welfare (AT V: 82–3; CSMK III: 324–5). Welfare is tied to the notion of a life or career; even if it may increase or decrease with the passage of time, at any period in someone's life it is constituted as much by his past actions and past thoughts as by present ones (AT IV: 305; CSMK III: 268). (It is not conceived as a present state of mind that is externally related to a moral agent's past.)[314] For all these reasons, the concept of human welfare ('our welfare') is tied to the notion of the *union* of mind and body. *Our* welfare is the welfare of the Union.

But in what sense can it be true to say that a *union* of mind and body has a welfare? In fact, it would be better to say that *only* the union of mind and body has a welfare. The body has its own health, the mind has its. Knowledge stands to the soul as health to the body; it is even called the soul's 'health' (AT V: 327; CSMK III: 370).[315] Each form of 'health' has a crucial role in promoting the other. Knowledge of metaphysics and physics underpins sound medicine which in turn can be used to improve physical health,[316] while bodily health – apart from Naturally giving us joy (AT IV: 605; CSMK III: 307) – is a precondition for achieving the intellectual freedom and detachment from the senses which is necessary for rigorous reasoning and the accumulation of knowledge, since ill health leaves the sick person immersed in his body and in his senses, hence in a certain sense less free (AT III: 424, CSMK III: 190; AT IV: 282,

314 On the model of Mill's conception of conscience as a feeling of discomfort that accompanies present recollection of past wrongdoings.

315 Welfare crops up in unexpected places in Descartes' reasoning. The very possibility of knowledge about the nature of things depends on the uniformity and rational transparency of the principles embodied in God's creation. Thus the simplicity of the operations of God, and clarity and distinctness, are welfare-related concepts. Seen in this light, familiar principles of rationality take on a new aspect. So, Occam's razor is not a heuristic maxim, but part of the moral order of the world. Further exploration of these ideas must be left for another occasion.

316 Descartes wondered 'whether it is possible to discover a system of medicine which is founded on infallible demonstrations' (AT I: 105; CSMK III: 17); 'the preservation of health has always been the principal end of my studies' (AT IV: 329; CSMK III: 275).

CSMK III: 262–3). Both bodily health and knowledge are essential to the welfare of the Union, but neither constitutes the *welfare* of one component. There is a certain sense in which neither component *has* a welfare. The body no more has a welfare than any other machine does; health in an animal or in an 'inanimate' body is comparable to the smooth, efficient functioning of a mechanism. Likewise, the disembodied soul which survives the death of the body seems to lack a welfare in virtue of its ceasing to be a moral agent for lack of the power to act.[317] It is tautological to say that our welfare is the welfare of the substantial union.

Since our Nature is the pattern of correlations of thoughts and movements which God has ordained for our welfare, it inherits a moral dimension from the essentially moral character of the concept of welfare. The person is the moral agent, and the doctrine of the substantial union is clearly meant to elucidate not merely mind–body interaction as conceived in 'philosophy of mind', but also the nature of moral agency. (This concept finds no place whatever in expositions of Cartesian Dualism.)

Confused thoughts

Considerations about the power of the body to act on the soul to produce 'basic sense-perceptions' (cf. p. 176) and about welfare (cf. pp. 178–80) are essential prerequisites for clarifying Descartes' conception of '(Naturally) confused thoughts'. We noted earlier that this is a key to understanding the doctrine of the substantial union. For in his view, if I were merely lodged in the body like a sailor in a ship,

> when the body needed food or drink, I should have an explicit understanding of the fact, instead of having *confused* sensations of hunger and thirst. For these sensations of hunger, thirst, pain and so on are nothing but *confused* modes of thinking which arise from the union and, as it were, intermingling of the mind with the body.
>
> (AT VII: 81; CSM II: 56, italics added)

This suggests that there are certain thoughts which are somehow *intrinsically* confused. How can we make sense of this idea? By Descartes' own explanation (*Principles* I.46; CSM I: 208), 'confusion' is the opposite of 'distinctness'; it is also something remediable: by dint of effort and attention, we have the power to perceive clear things distinctly. Someone's thought is confused if, when required to do so, he fails to distinguish it from various other thoughts that are in fact distinct (or different) from it.[318] What we need to do is to explain how

317 The question to what extent a disembodied soul is a full moral agent was one debated in medieval theology. (Cf. G. R. Evans, *Philosophy and Theology in the Middle Ages*, London: Routledge, 1993, p. 92.)

318 For a fuller treatment of Descartes' conception of confusion, see K. Morris 1995. Lilli Alanen ('Sensory Ideas, Objective Reality, and Material Falsity', in Cottingham 1994) presents a conception of 'material falsity' which bears some resemblance to the conception offered here of 'confusion': 'a confused idea, in order to be materially false, involves, in addition, implicit unnoticed false judgements about what it contains or presents, confusedly, to the mind' (p. 246).

anybody can be led *by Nature* to confuse thoughts that are in fact distinct. Although the upshot would be a kind of 'intrinsic' confusion, this would not contradict his general explanation of 'confusion' provided it is within one's power to avoid even this form of confusion when this is necessary for sound understanding (or, exceptionally, for one's own welfare).

This form of 'Natural confusion' is particularly conspicuous in respect of sensations arising from the first internal sense. For example, 'I feel$_1$ thirst' expresses both the thought 'My throat feels$_1$ dry' and the thought 'I want$_1$ (or need$_1$) to drink' (cf. AT VII: 80–1; CSM II: 56). (A case like dropsy demonstrates that the two are distinct, since the dropsical man judges correctly that his throat is dry, but judges falsely that his body needs drink.) Again, 'I feel$_1$ pain in the foot' expresses both the thought that I feel$_1$ something wrong with my foot and the 'thought of distress' (*cogitatio tristitiae*)[319] – likewise, presumably, 'the decision to withdraw the foot from what is causing pain', which parallels the 'decision to take food' that accompanies the sensation of hunger (AT VII: 76; CSM II: 53).[320]

These non-logical connections are the counterparts in thought of mechanical connections that are part of God's design of sentient machines. In an animal, or in a person who acts instinctively and without thinking, the feeling of thirst (i.e. feeling$_1$ thirst) gives rise to the desire to drink (i.e. desiring$_1$ to drink) and to seeking drink (i.e. trying$_1$ to find something to drink). Similar connections hold in the cases of hunger, pain, sexual appetites, and fear. The body-machine groups together certain animal feelings with animal desire (Imagination) and movement. A feeling triggers off other states of sentience and an appropriate behaviour cycle.

On Descartes' view, it seems, 'Natural confusion' takes the form of failing, in the ordinary course of life, to make any distinction between the thoughts corresponding to these animal-states which are grouped together by Nature. It inclines me, for example, to conflate the thought reported by 'I feel$_1$ hunger' with the (rational) desire for food ('I want$_1$ food') and the intention (volition) to find something to eat ('I will go food-seeking'). Similarly, I confuse the thought reported by 'I feel$_1$ thirst' with the perception 'My body needs drink' and with the (rational) desire to drink, or the thought 'I feel$_1$ pain in my foot' with the desire to move my foot. These Natural confusions are evidently conducive to my welfare, just as the groupings of the corresponding mechanical states are generally conducive to the preservation and efficient functioning of animals. A confusion ordained by Nature obviates the need for me to make an inference; my Nature takes care of me automatically by inducing me to identify these distinct

319 *Pace* the common complaint that Descartes didn't, indeed couldn't, give any explanation of why the sensation of pain is something disagreeable (e.g., Williams 1978: 286).

320 What gets bundled together in particular cases may be no more – and no less – definite and uniform than what are treated as criteria for applying a particular 'psychological predicate'. We tentatively suggest that Descartes ascribed to Nature the correlations among judgements that Wittgenstein assigns to grammar.

thoughts,[321] and this is beneficial except in extraordinary circumstances (e.g., if I suffer from dropsy).

The notion of thoughts that are Naturally confused seems to be peculiarly appropriate for sensations arising from the *internal* senses since they have a very close and immediate connection with bodily health. It is readily extended from pain, hunger, and thirst to some of the more primitive passions such as anger and fear. Just as the desire to drink is not normally distinguished from the feeling of thirst, so the desire to shun the feared object is not normally distinguished from the emotion of fear (cf. *Principles* IV.190; CSM I: 281). We can perhaps extend this notion of Naturally confused thoughts to some sensations arising from the external senses, at least in cases where welfare is conspicuously involved. I may not make any distinction between seeing that a tree is about to fall on me, a feeling of fear, and the desire to get out of the way; or between feeling the ground giving way under my feet and the desire to get away from the edge of a cliff; and so on. Again, 'a man's Nature urges him to go for' 'what is responsible for the pleasant taste': i.e. we Naturally fail to distinguish between the thought that the food tastes pleasant and the thought that the food is good for us (AT VII: 83–4; CSM II: 58).[322]

We might even say in such cases that it is *part of* having certain sense-perceptions that one has certain passions and desires. If this idiom is understood to describe *logical* relations between distinct thoughts, it is inappropriate; the thoughts are logically independent of each other. What in fact is reported are quasi-logical relations[323] (or even 'experienced identities') between modes of thinking that reflect connections in the body-machine between modes of extension.

Thus to say that 'I feel thirst' expresses a 'confused thought' is to say that it expresses a whole set of distinct (i.e. distinguish*able*) thoughts which the thinker (commonly) does *not distinguish* from each other (i.e. none of which he distinctly perceives). Indeed it is generally in his interest for him *not* to separate out the different elements in each thought-package. 'Confused thoughts' are what 'emerge' from the union of mind and body. The absolutely inexplicable *links* between distinct thoughts are what characterize 'confused thoughts' as the thoughts of a mind united with a body. These Natural confusions are a very certain sign that the soul is united to the body: a mind not united to a body *could not*, in a certain sense (pp. 183ff.), have certain 'confused bundles' of thoughts. The reasoning here depends on the axiom that God is benevolent. An angel lodged in

321 Keeping them distinct is, as it were, a luxury that I can't afford. This is roughly parallel to Hume's account of how experience produces (causally) the sentiment of belief without any need for a person's engaging in any form of reasoning: Nature deemed learning from experience too important to leave to the vagaries of reason.

322 Descartes, however, denied that there is a 'Natural error' (comparable to that which occurs in dropsy) 'when someone is tricked by the pleasant taste of some food into eating the poison concealed inside it': 'the only inference that can be drawn from this is that his Nature is not omniscient'. Presumably the thought here is that 'what is responsible for the pleasant taste' *is* good for us in this case, but the poison, which also happens to be in the food (unbeknownst to our limited Nature!), is not.

323 Mimicking the phrase 'Natural causation', we might here speak of 'Natural implication'.

a body would not have the sensations of pain, thirst, light, colour, taste, fear, etc.; more particularly, God would not have arranged things so that the angel was designed not to distinguish distinct thoughts. Since there is no question of welfare in the absence of a substantial union (see pp. 179–80), any form of *Natural* (i.e. God-given) confusion in an angel's thinking would be a design-*fault*. Thus the fact that I have 'confused sensations of hunger, thirst and pain' makes it *morally* certain (see p. 185, n.331) that my mind is intermingled with my body.

'Natural necessity'

The system of connections between thoughts and movements which constitutes 'our Nature' *must* have been ordained by God because there is no 'resemblance' whatever between any thought and any movement. As we argued (pp. 152–6), this means that any such connection is absolutely unintelligible or opaque to reason.

It seems natural to conclude that any Natural connection is wholly accidental or contingent. Nothing except the arbitrary fiat of God underpins it. Its being as it is rests merely on the whim of the Creator.[324] Surely, in respect of God's will, 'Anything goes!' But this line of reasoning utterly distorts Descartes' conception of 'our Nature'. In his view, the order instituted by God is, in a certain sense, *essential* or *necessary*. There are powerful *a priori* reasons for concluding that our Nature could not have been different from what it actually is. No other arrangement of things (though others are 'possible' in the abstract) could be so conducive to human welfare (and equally simple, uniform, and efficient). So all of these abstract 'possibilities' are really *impossible*.[325]

Consider, for example, the correlation of the sensation of pain in the foot with the motion in the brain which is generally produced by physical injury or damage to the foot. This is what God has actually ordained, manifestly for our welfare. We might imagine that He could, for instance, have correlated no thought with this state of the body, or perhaps some *other* thought, say, the thought of the motion of the pineal gland. But

> The sensation of pain as occurring in the foot . . . stimulates the mind to do its best to get rid of the cause of the pain, which it takes to be harmful to the foot. . . . [T]here is *nothing else* which *would have been so conducive* to the continued well-being of the body.
>
> (AT VII: 88; CSM II: 60–1, italics added)

Admittedly, the motion in the brain which gives occasion to the mind to have the

324 This deflationary or derogatory attitude is conspicuous in treatments of the idea that the truths of arithmetic and geometry are created or legislated by God. Some take this doctrine to undermine the claim that these truths are truly necessary; like *everything* else, they rest on nothing more than God's will. But why not argue, instead, that they rest on *nothing less* than God's *explicit* fiat? What else could make them 'truly necessary'? (Or more different from accidental general truths?)

325 This pattern of argument is clearly exhibited in Locke's discussion of personal identity (*Essay*, II.xxvii.13 and 27).

sensation of a pain in the foot may sometimes occur otherwise than as the mechanical effect of injury to the foot, for example, in the case of an amputee who mistakenly judges 'My foot hurts'. Even here the actual arrangement of things best secures our welfare: however God had created 'our Nature', it would be bound to mislead a person from time to time, and the actual arrangement demonstrably maximizes the benefit and minimizes the risk of error (AT VII: 88–9; CSM II: 61).

Similarly, the correlation by Nature of the sensation of thirst with dryness in the throat is the best possible means of securing human welfare 'because the most useful thing for us to know about the whole business is that we need drink in order to stay healthy' (AT VII: 88; CSM II: 61). In the case of an individual afflicted with dropsy, this arrangement gives rise to a Natural deception by the senses. 'Yet it is much better that [dryness in the throat] should mislead on this occasion than that it should always mislead when the body is in good health' (AT VII: 89; CSM II: 61). In this way, careful reflection demonstrates that, in a certain sense, what God ordained *could not* have been otherwise than it is.

What these arguments introduce is a distinctive kind or grade of *necessity*.[326] Descartes' strategy is to vindicate God's benevolence in designing the detailed structure of our Nature. He rebutted counter-arguments by showing that Natural correlations which appear to be less than perfect because they are injurious to some individuals are in fact the best of all the abstract possibilities that were open to God in creating the world given His general determination to foster human welfare. Given the axiom that God is benevolent, no alternative scheme of correlations of thoughts with movements is even possible; what is ordained by Nature must be *the best of all possible* arrangements.[327] Therefore, in a certain sense, everything explicitly ordained by Nature or instituted by God must be *necessary*.[328] This whole pattern of correlating thoughts with movements (and the derivative Natural correlations among thoughts and actions) is necessary in the same sense in which it is *necessary* that God must have arranged His Creation to maximize human welfare by the simplest and most uniform means.[329]

This pattern of reasoning tends in the direction of Leibniz's notorious 'Principle

326 Until fairly recently, analytic philosophers have been antagonistic to this idea. It has been a Leitmotiv in twentieth-century analytic philosophy that there is only one kind of necessity. This was sounded in Wittgenstein's *Tractatus*: 'The only necessity is *logical* necessity'. It continued to echo and re-echo in the principles 'All necessary truths are analytic', 'Necessary truths are true by linguistic convention', and 'Essence is the shadow of grammar'.

327 Cottingham (1986: 140) suggests that 'natural selection can play the beneficent role in this system which Descartes assigns to God' (see *infra* for a discussion of some further complications). But (post-Darwinian) 'nature' is *not* 'beneficent', hence this suggestion misses precisely the dimension of necessity under discussion here.

328 In effect, this inverts Loeb's deflationary argument (1981: 131 n. 9). He argues that the fact that God ordained the union between mind and body is of minimal importance, since after all God ordained *everything* (even the eternal truths). We argue that the fact that God ordained the union between mind and body is of maximal importance, since what He explicitly ordains (e.g., the eternal truths, but also the union between mind and body) has a kind of *necessity*.

329 'God made our body like a machine, and he wanted it to function like a universal instrument . . . . If the body did not induce this misleading state [dropsy], it would not be behaving uniformly . . . and then there would be a defect in God's constancy' (AT V: 163–4; CSMK III: 346).

of Sufficient Reason', later parodied by Voltaire in the form 'Everything is for the best in the best of all possible worlds'. The underlying idea is the principle that God must always act for good reasons – indeed for the best of reasons. (Only a confusion between reasons and causes would lead one to infer, from the fact that God is not subject to constraint, that He does not act with reason.) This is understood to hold quite strictly: not in the form that God could not act if there were overriding reasons for His doing something different, but rather in the form that God could not act if the reasons for two different actions were equally good.[330] This has the consequence that any alternative course of action must be definitely less eligible than anything that God has actually chosen to do. So whatever is true is *necessarily* true. (We might coin the phrase 'morally necessary' to express this conception.)[331]

The difference between Descartes and Leibniz does not concern so much the pattern of reasoning as what it is applied to. Leibniz took his principle of sufficient reason to be all-embracing: it applies to each and every individual substance and property, hence (derivatively) to each and every individual human action or historical event. In his view, there is a sense in which any property that something has must be a property that it *necessarily* has: nothing whatever is contingent. Descartes didn't hold this radical and seemingly paradoxical view. He applied his reasoning to *generalizations*, not to singular propositions. In his view, we think, necessity characterizes what we might call 'the Natural *Order*' (or 'the ordered system of created things established by God' (AT VII: 80; CSM II: 56)). Indeed it belongs to 'Nature' in all its forms. My Nature, 'the totality of things bestowed on me by God', 'includes many things that belong to the mind alone . . . much that relates to the body alone . . . and what God has bestowed on me as a combination of mind and body' (AT VII: 82; CSM II: 57), and there is a kind of necessity linked with each of these three aspects of my Nature (although we have here focused on the last). There is a 'Natural necessity' that belongs to the principles of logic that govern the relations between the modes of thinking which inhere in a rational soul; logical relations among thoughts are transparent to reason (perceived by 'the Natural light'). There is equally a 'Natural necessity' that pertains to the principles of mechanics (the 'Natural laws') which govern the interactions of corporeal substances (and their modes) in God's Creation; it is in this sense, as Malebranche later argued, that efficient causation is a 'necessary

330 In a human being this would be called 'indifference', but 'the indifference which belongs to human freedom is very different from that which belongs to divine freedom' (AT VII: 433; CSM II: 292). 'The supreme indifference to be found in God is the supreme indication of his omnipotence. But as for man, since he finds that the nature of all goodness and truth is already determined by God . . . he will embrace what is good and true all the more willingly, and hence more freely, in proportion as he sees it more clearly' (AT VII: 432; CSM II: 292). We cannot pursue these issues here.

331 Descartes used the expression 'morally certain', commonly glossed as 'certain for all practical purposes'. This is in our view likely to have seriously misleading connotations today, unless 'practical' is linked with 'moral' and 'moral' is linked with God's goodness. What is 'morally certain' is 'morally *necessary*', and what is morally necessary really is *necessary*.

connection'. And finally there is a *Natural* necessity that belongs to the uniform pattern of connections that God has ordained in each human being between modes of thinking of the soul and modes of motion of the body: no other pattern is compatible with God's benevolence and omnipotence, since the actual ordering maximizes welfare while achieving the greatest conceivable simplicity of apparatus and uniformity of its functioning.

At all these levels, Descartes held that certain kinds of generalizations about the connections between things have various kinds of necessity that stem from their being the framework of God's Creation. But Descartes didn't exclude the possibility that there are contingently true singular judgements or even that there may be contingently true generalizations about kinds of things and their interrelations. At the same time, he didn't think that *all* connections between thoughts and movements are *external* or *contingent*. (As previously noted, the Legend misguidedly ascribes that doctrine to him in virtue of describing 'Cartesian Interaction' as *causal*.)

What goes for 'necessity' goes for 'possibility' too; there are different 'grades' of possibility. It is (in some sense) 'conceivable' or 'possible' that God could have correlated any thought whatever with physical injury to the foot. At the same time, it is 'evident' that nothing other than correlating the sensation of pain in the foot (i.e. the thought 'I have a pain in my foot') with injury to the foot could have been ordained by God. So (in some sense) it must be 'inconceivable' or 'impossible' that this component of 'our Nature' could be different from what it actually is, hence 'necessary' that it is as it is (AT VII: 88–9; CSM II: 60–1).[332] In one sense, it is possible for something to have a property if the nature or essence of this thing doesn't exclude its having this property. In another sense, it is possible for something to have a property if God has not ruled this out in ordering His Creation. 'Possible' in the first sense is compatible with 'impossible' in the second sense.[333] It is in the *second* of these two senses that the correlations of thoughts and movements ordained by Nature are held by Descartes to be *necessary*.

We should note that, in his view, this is a substantial principle, not a stale truism. It doesn't amount to the general thesis that whatever ordering of thoughts and movements God has established is just the ordering of thoughts and movements that it has pleased God to establish. Rather, Descartes held that each one of the particular basic (or primitive) correlations of a thought with a movement has *evidently* been ordained by God and can thereby be *seen* to be necessary. In setting up a one–one correlation of movements with thoughts,

332 There is a precise parallel for this double use of the term 'conceivable' in Malebranche's argument about the nature of 'pure mind' at the beginning of *Recherches* III.i.1. On the one hand, 'a mind without volition is conceivable' ('*il est possible de concevoir . . .* '); on the other hand, 'the power of volition, though not essential to it, is inseparable from mind . . . so a mind incapable of willing . . . is inconceivable' ('*il n'est pas possible de concevoir . . .* '). The argument for the second position turns on the idea that 'an intelligent being could not conceivably have willed to produce the mind in this state [sc. without volition]'.

> the best system that could be devised is that [the movement of the pineal gland] should produce the one sensation which, of all possible sensations, is most especially and most frequently conducive to the preservation of the healthy man. And experience shows that the sensations which Nature has given us are all of this kind . . .
>
> (AT VII: 87; CSM II: 60)

So these Natural correlations *could not have been otherwise* given 'the immense goodness of God'.

The question of how to understand the precise scope of the necessity involved in the notion of the substantial union is a delicate one, in at least two respects. First, it applies directly only to the *strict* Natural correlations between thoughts and gland-movements; it cannot (by definition) apply directly to the non-strict correlations between sensations and the conditions of the sense-organs or between volitions and the movements of the limbs, etc. On the other hand, it is only these non-strict correlations that 'justify' the strict ones: God's reason for correlating *this* sensation (say, the sensation of pain in the foot) with *this* movement of the pineal gland is that this movement of the pineal gland is *normally* caused by a painful foot. If this correlation did not *normally* hold, then (*per impossible*) God's design would be faulty. What we might therefore say is that the non-strict Natural correlations *Naturally necessarily normally* hold.

Second, it might be thought to be easier to make out a case for the necessity of the connections between conditions of the body and specific *internal*-sense-based judgements than for that same necessity with respect to specific *external*-sense-based judgements, for the simple reason that the links between bodily health and the proper objects of the internal senses (pain, thirst, etc.) are tighter and more direct than those between health and the proper objects of the external senses (light, colour, sounds, etc.). Hence we might be able to see why God instituted a Natural correlation between the sensation of pain in the foot with the motion in the brain which is generally produced by physical injury or damage to the foot, without seeing a parallel case for the sensation of red. But it is easy to misunderstand what the question is here; we are likely to think that what is being suggested is the possibility, apparently consistent with God's benevolence, of 'qualia inversion'.[334] If we see that 'the sensation of red' is a *thought* with propositional content, not a subjective 'quale' of an experience, this suggestion is transformed into the idea that God might have correlated the thought that the rose is red with the rose's being (say) green, which is manifestly inconsistent with God's non-deceptiveness! The real question here parallels the one Descartes raised

333 Williams (1978: 107) arguably conflates different senses of 'possible' when he argues that the fact that (according to Descartes) God can separate mind and body doesn't amount to much, since after all God can do *anything* (even alter the eternal truths! i.e. do what is logically impossible).

334 'I can imagine a being for whom the wavelength of light coming from a rose was "flagged" in a way that, from the subjective point of view, was quite different from the way in which it is "flagged" for me' (Cottingham 1986: 141).

about the sensations of pain and thirst: why did not God correlate the thought *that my pineal gland is moving in such and such a way* with my pineal gland's moving in such and such a way, and instead correlated *the sensation of red* with that gland-movement (a movement normally caused by the presence of something red)? The answer is obvious: it is much more useful for me to know about the colours of objects than to know about my own gland-movements. Even if redness (unlike pain) does not signal any *specific* threat or benefit to my bodily health, none the less 'the proper purpose of the sensory perceptions given me by Nature is . . . to inform the mind of what is beneficial and harmful' (AT VII: 83; CSM II: 57), and that it can do only if sensations of colour or sound, as opposed to thoughts of gland-movements, are correlated with the gland-movements.[335]

The doctrine that 'our Nature' is in some sense '*necessary*' is precisely what is encapsulated in his insistence that a human being, a substantial union of mind and body, is an *ens per se* rather than an *ens per accidens*.[336] Indeed Descartes connected the phrase '*ens per se*' with the phrase '*essential* union' ('*unio essentialis*') and contrasted this with the phrase 'accidental union' ('*unio accidentaria*') (AT III: 508; CSMK III: 209). It is also implicit in his claim that the whole pattern of Natural correlations of thoughts and movements must be *innate*; they cannot be derived from sense-experience, but rather they are presupposed by the possibility of learning anything through the senses (AT VIIIB: 359; CSM I: 304). Being *a priori*, they must also be necessary. Thus the statements of the general correlations of thoughts and movements that constitute 'our Nature' are, in some sense, 'necessary or essential truths'.[337] In Descartes' theocentric system, there are really no other possibilities.

A person: both one thing and two things?

Acknowledgement of the ambiguity of the terms 'necessary' and 'possible' is necessary for making sense of an aspect of Descartes' Dualism which is commonly

335 Moreover, of course, we skew the case by focusing on distance senses like sight and hearing. How do matters stand with taste or smell? The sensation of putridity or the sensation of sweetness have more direct connections with bodily health than sensations of red or green. For example, 'our Nature' teaches us to seek out what tastes pleasant, surely because what tastes pleasant is normally good for us.

336 It is a presupposition of this account that the principle 'one mind, one body' is itself *necessary* – not *logically*, but 'morally' necessary. This is an *axiom* in Descartes' Dualism. It is not a proposition that demands, or even admits of, confirmation. Within 'the ordered system of created things established by God', there is no such thing as a body's being substantially united with two or more souls, and no such thing as a mind's being substantially united with more than one body. (Reflect on the implications of these 'possibilities' for the notion of *moral responsibility* for thoughts and actions!) These are not real possibilities, but merely cases of the imagination's running wild. Even to raise doubts about the truth of the principle 'one mind, one body' requires jumping outside the very framework in which Descartes' conception of a person makes sense. (Nor could the soul be united to anything other than a human body: as Leibniz remarked 'Nature does not permit these fictions', *Essais* 242.)

337 Arguably the real difficulty here is with the term 'truth' rather than 'necessary'. The solution may be recognizing that axioms or common notions are not (strictly speaking) *judgements*. Consequently, they cannot be 'truths' in the same sense that genuine judgements are. (We can't pursue these 'proto-Tractarian' ideas here.)

seen to be problematic or paradoxical. It seems that he ran a serious risk of contradicting himself about the *nature* of the rational soul.

On the one hand, the whole essence of the soul is to be a thinking thing. The attribute of thinking is inseparable from the soul; indeed, every soul must always be thinking. But particular kinds of thinking are not part of its essence. Specifically, all those modes of thinking which arise from its union with the body are not essential to its existence; namely, sense-perception, Imagination, and volitions which terminate in bodily action.

> I find in myself faculties for certain special modes of thinking, namely Imagination and sense-perception. Now I can clearly and distinctly understand myself as a whole without these faculties; but I cannot, conversely, understand these faculties without me, that is, without an intellectual substance to inhere in.
>
> (AT VII: 78; CSM II: 54)

This line of argument seems to yield the conclusion that what is essential to the soul is what 'regards the soul on its own': 'only the notion of thought, which includes the perceptions of the intellect and the inclinations of the will' (AT III: 665; CSMK III: 218). Thus the soul is 'really distinct' from the body and can be separated from it. As two substances, each can exist independently of the other.

On the other hand, it is an essential property of the soul that it has the powers to move the body and to be acted on by the body. These powers are explicitly asserted to be as much a part of the *nature* of the soul as thinking is even though these powers 'belong to the soul only in so far as it is joined to the body' (AT III: 479; CSMK III: 203).

> There are two facts about the human soul on which depend all the knowledge we can have of its *nature*. The first is that it thinks, the second is that, being united to the body, it can act and be acted upon along with it.
>
> (AT III: 664–5; CSMK III: 217–18, italics added)

This line of argument seems to yield the conclusion that a soul is *essentially* (indeed, 'by its nature'!) united with a body.

These two conceptions of the nature or essence of the soul seem to collide with each other. And they give rise to apparently conflicting conceptions of a human being: the first conception of the nature of the soul seems to imply that the human being is an *ens per accidens*, whereas the second seems to imply that it is an *ens per se*. Both points of view are expressed, side by side in the same documents:

> a human being is an *ens per accidens* . . . in relation to its parts, the soul and the body . . . . But if a human being is considered in himself as a whole, we say of course that he is a single *ens per se*, and not *per accidens*.
>
> (AT III: 508; CSMK III: 209)

A person is both *essentially* two things and *essentially* one thing. There is indeed a great difficulty in

> forming a very distinct conception of both the distinction between the soul and the body and their union; for to do this it is necessary to conceive them as *a single thing* and at the same time to conceive them as *two things* . . .
> (AT III: 693; CSMK III: 227, italics added)

Most commentators see Descartes as 'in a philosophical mess' here.[338]

Perhaps it would be better to see him as struggling to put across a difficult point. Descartes explained that there are two points of view about the nature of a person. From one, a person is a combination of *two substances* each of which can exist independently of the other. From the other, a person is a *single thing* characterized by its own 'primitive notions'. (A person is two things, and a person is one thing, but a person is not *both* two things and one thing!) Our difficulty is to make sense of the idea that these two aspects can both belong to the *essence* of a person. We can do so if we acknowledge the ambiguity of the term 'necessary', and hence the ambiguity of the related terms 'essence' or 'nature' and 'attribute'. Before I have established the existence and benevolence of God, I find it 'conceivable' that I am no more than a thinking thing. (By the same token I find it 'conceivable' that a disembodied soul could have *sentire*- and *agere*-thoughts.) But later, having ascertained these metaphysical truths, I find this no longer 'conceivable'; I could not be a soul not *united* with a body given that I am *conscius* of my freedom (or capacity for voluntary action) and of having sensations and Imagination. (A mind merely 'conjoined' but not '*united*' to a body *could not* have these faculties.)[339] At the same time, it is now 'conceivable' that I can survive death as a disembodied soul. But in this state, it seems, I would no longer have the properties that depend on my being substantially united with a body: I would cease to be an active moral agent, and I would lose the capacity for sense-perception and Imagination: 'The human mind separated from the body does not have sense-perception [and Imagination] in the restricted sense' (AT V: 402; CSMK III: 380*).[340]

What we might say today is that in a human being, mind and body are internally related. There are obstacles to Descartes' putting the point like this, but these arise from a wholly unexpected source. They have nothing to do with his dualism: the problem is *not* that distinct substances cannot be internally related, since there *is* no problem here once we recognize that there are different 'grades' of necessity. Rather, the difficulty is that there were no relational judgements within the

338 'It is hard to see how to avoid interpreting this statement as on overt admission on Descartes's part that his position on the mind-body relation is self-contradictory' (Wilson 1978: 207).

339 For this reason Descartes refused to answer the question 'Do angels have sense-perceptions in the restricted sense?', since he thought that 'it is not clear by natural reason alone whether angels are created in the form of [*instar*] minds distinct from matter, or in the form of minds united to matter [*instar [mentium] corpori unitarum*]' (AT V: 402; CSMK III: 380*).

340 *Pace* Hilary Putnam, 'The Meaning of "Meaning"' (in his *Mind, Language and Reality*, Cambridge: Cambridge University Press, 1975, p. 220) on 'the assumption of methodological solipsism'. The Legend typically contradicts what it would understand by this remark. Thus Geach (1957: 116–17) and Kenny (1966: 353) claim that on Aquinas' view it made no sense to talk about disembodied beings who could see, feel pain, etc., and they *contrast* this with Descartes' view.

framework of Aristotelian logic, and hence no internal-relational judgements. Talk of 'powers' is what does duty for talk of relations within the Aristotelian framework (cf. above, pp. 173–4); instead of the relational judgement 'Fire melts gold', we get the twin judgements 'Fire has the active power to melt gold' and 'Gold has the passive power to be melted by fire'. Correspondingly, what does duty for talk of *internal* relations within the Aristotelian framework is talk of '*essential* powers' or 'powers belonging to the *nature* of . . .' This is precisely how Descartes characterized the power of the soul to move the body and (apparently) also the power of the body to act on the soul.

His description of the human being as 'a single thing' from one point of view and as 'two things' from another sounds paradoxical. But even today, similar paradoxicality characterizes *any* attempt to talk about 'internal' relations. Think here of Wittgenstein on pain and pain-behaviour:

> 'But you will surely admit that there is a difference between pain-behaviour accompanied by pain and pain-behaviour without any pain?' – Admit it? What greater difference could there be? – 'And yet you again and again reach the conclusion that the sensation itself is a *nothing*.' – Not at all. It is not a *something*, but not a *nothing* either!
>
> (*PI* §304)[341]

We have tried to reconstruct a multi-faceted conception of essence that makes possible the apparent impossibility that the human being is both a single thing and at the same time two things. If this task of interpretation is truly impossible, there seems no hope of salvaging Descartes' doctrine that a person is an *ens per se*. Unless we keep in mind the notion of there being different kinds of *necessity*, we are bound to lose sight of at least one aspect of his account of the substantial union.

SUMMARY

In this chapter we have tried to elaborate on the four principles we picked out at the beginning. This was a lengthy examination of a very intricate and complex philosophical position which combines within it a range of ideas that are relatively unfamiliar to modern readers. We tried to draw out the implications of these ideas and the interrelations among them in order to expose an intelligible pattern in Descartes' thinking about the nature of a person as a substantial union of mind and body. But the account may itself be so complex that it threatens to defeat its own purpose. We here summarize the main elements of this account.

341 Wittgenstein, we might say, felt that his contemporaries were inclined to over-emphasize the 'real distinction' between mind and body; his attempts to combat this temptation made him look to some like a behaviourist, who saw the two things as one. Descartes felt that ordinary people (as well as philosophers) were inclined to over-emphasize the union of mind and body; in attempting to combat this temptation he managed to give some people the impression that he saw mind and body as merely contingently or accidentally conjoined.

1 There are two and only two kinds of (finite) substances: corporeal things and thinking things (minds or rational souls). The properties of minds are all modes of thinking; the properties of bodies are all modes of extension. The distinction between substances and modes is absolute. In particular, neither a thought nor a geometrical shape is a *thing* (a substance). Since only a thing (a substance) can be the logical subject of a judgement, there are (apart from God) two and only two kinds of *logical* subjects of predication: *res extensae* and rational souls. Hence there are no 'mental particulars' other than minds. The Two-Worlds View, from Descartes' perspective, exemplifies the fundamental confusion of treating modes as substances.

2 The essence of the mind is thought, the essence of the body is extension. The boundary between the mind and the body is grounded in the distinction between the intelligent (the rational, the intellectual, hence the moral) and the mechanical (the instinctive, the automatic, the causally determined). Metabolism, sentience, and locomotion in animals can be explained by the principles of mechanics; hence 'sapience' and 'sentience' fall on opposite sides of the mind–body boundary. Animals, and likewise the human body not united to a rational soul, are living, self-moving, and sentient machines which lack free will, hence cannot make judgements and cannot be moral agents. The distinction between mind and body (thus between mental properties and bodily properties) is, however, masked by ordinary language which uses many predicates ('sees light', 'feels pain', 'remembers being burnt', 'walks', etc.) which are *systematically ambiguous* between expressing mental and bodily properties. In one sense such predicates are applicable to animals (which lack rational souls) and to human bodies; in another sense they express modes of thinking which can be exhibited only by rational souls. It is a fundamental form of confused thinking to fail to distinguish the ideas in each of these pairs. That is, effectively, to fail to distinguish two things which are 'really distinct', namely minds and corporeal things. The twentieth-century conception of 'consciousness' (enshrined in the Cartesian Legend's description of Descartes' boundary between mind and body as that between consciousness and clockwork) exemplifies just this form of confused thinking.

3 Human bodies and their properties are objects of sense-perception. Minds and their properties cannot be objects of sense-perception. There is a first-/third-person asymmetry in the epistemology of singular judgements about bodies: each person has (fallible) sense-perception of his own body and certain of its states through the two internal as well as the five external senses, of another's body only through the external senses. There is a different first-/third-person asymmetry in the epistemology of singular judgements about minds: one cannot have *conscientia* (the capacity to apprehend and reflect on one's own thinking) of another's thinking. Being *conscius* of its own modes is an essential property of the rational soul, but it is a potentiality, not a (cognitive) performance; it is, moreover, susceptible to inability to recall and even to self-deception (especially in respect

of moral character and the passions of the soul). But every mode of thinking has a propositional content, and this can be fully expressed in articulate speech; hence there is no such thing as essentially private (incommunicable) thoughts. Thus both the internal senses and *conscientia* exhibit forms of epistemological asymmetry, but neither carries the implication that first-person knowledge-claims about 'states of consciousness' are incommunicable or incorrigible. 'Cartesian Introspection' and 'Cartesian Privacy' would make no sense to Descartes.

The Legend does not recognize the internal senses, and there is a case for saying that it simply confuses these with *conscientia.* (This would be an instance of the fundamental confusion between mind and body). Moreover, the Legend misses out crucial aspects both of *conscientia* and the internal senses. On the one hand, *conscientia* maintains its links with *conscience*; hence human beings have *conscientia* of their voluntary actions and their moral character. These are 'operations of the soul', but not included anywhere in the Legend's characterization of the Cartesian mind. On the other hand, the objects of the internal senses include pain, hunger, anger, and fear. These are therefore properties of the body, but are normally counted by the Legend as 'states of consciousness' and hence as *mental.*

4 The interaction between mind and body is 'rationally unintelligible'; in a human being, a mind and a body are 'substantially united'. It is part of the doctrine (hence not a *problem* for the doctrine) that the interaction between mind and body cannot be made rationally intelligible; only logical or mechanical 'interactions' are intelligible, and these are neither. The regular correlation of modes of thinking and modes of extension (in sense-perception or Imagination and in voluntary action) is to be characterized solely in terms of the operation of 'Natural' or 'occasional' causes. These qualifications are absolutely vital; apart from indicating rational unintelligibility, they signal the central involvement of God in mind–body union. Our Nature as the substantial union of mind and body underlies both the faculty of sense-perception and the capacity for voluntary action. It was instituted by God for the preservation of human welfare, and as a consequence has a certain kind of necessity. It is this that Descartes tried to bring out in his description of the union of mind and body as an *ens per se*, by contrast with an *ens per accidens* like the sailor in his ship. For all of these reasons, Descartes' doctrine is fundamentally at odds with 'Cartesian Interactionism'.

Here, then, is a summary sketch of the conception that we call '*Descartes*' Dualism' to distinguish it from so-called 'Cartesian Dualism'. (Etymologically it has a claim to the title 'Cartesian Dualism'. But since that title has been firmly usurped by an interloper, we have refrained from trying to claim it back.) We have tried to show that this picture has at least as strong a textual grounding as Cartesian Dualism. We have also tried to argue that Descartes' Dualism is less confused and internally contradictory than Cartesian Dualism. It seems to us that our interpretation plainly meets the general criteria for being a *good* interpretation of the corpus of his texts.

5

REVISIONS

DESCARTES' DUALISM: NEGLECTED ASPECTS

We summarized the main elements of our interpretation at the end of the last chapter. We want now to offer a different form of recapitulation, to organize our findings horizontally rather than vertically, so to speak. Our overarching theme is the desirability of placing Descartes' thinking in its intellectual context. (This ought to go without saying.) We have advocated looking at the concepts and doctrines he inherited and at how (and why), in some cases, he modified them. We have urged the importance of relating ideas across frameworks that *he* took to be interconnected and of resisting the inclination to fall in with modern compartmentalization of issues. And we have stressed the need to investigate *his* philosophical targets and *his* methods of addressing them.

One of our themes is the persistence of traditional concepts and doctrines in Descartes' philosophical system. These have implications and interconnections that are unlikely to strike us today. (There is a clear need for painstaking and sensitive clarification of these concepts; we have done little more than scratch the surface here.)

For example, his notion of *conscientia* inherits much of its content from the scholastic tradition, and this rules out treating it as identical with the late twentieth-century conception of introspection. First, *conscientia* retained its internal relations with the notion of *moral* conscience. Central to Descartes' whole pattern of thinking is the idea that moral virtues and vices are *paradigms* of 'states of mind', of which I can be *conscius* (even though I may exhibit *mauvaise foi* in evaluating my moral character). Second, *conscientia* is a form of knowledge. Hence anything of which I am *conscius* is something that can be put into words and communicated to others. *Conscientia* is articulate self-knowledge, not prelinguistic 'experience'; there is nothing 'essentially private' about its subject-matter. Finally, Descartes narrowed the range of functions which are to be counted as operations of the rational soul, and he thereby modified the traditional scope of *conscientia*; but this very modification presupposed his retention of the scholastic doctrine that the logical subject of any *conscientia*-judgement is the rational soul.

Various other traditional concepts have played important roles in our interpretation. Prominent among them are the notions of the internal senses, correlative active and passive powers, essence, and substances.

We have also emphasized the pivotal role of deeply entrenched scholastic doctrines in shaping his thought. Much of Descartes' Dualism makes good sense only when his ideas are integrated into the background of Aristotelian logic and Aristotelian metaphysics. This framework includes the axioms that all judgements must be subject-predicate in logical form, that all inferences must be syllogistic, that the only genuine entities are substances and modes of substances, that every mode must inhere in a substance, etc. Careful account must be taken of the implications of his axiom that rational souls are the only non-corporeal *substances*. When combined with the Aristotelian doctrine that only substances can be the *logical subjects* of singular judgements, this has dramatic consequences. It shows that '*cogito*' (i.e. '*I* think') is the minimal move in the language-game of reporting one's own thoughts; it demands that, in a certain sense, the soul itself, as well as modes of thinking, must fall within the scope of self-knowledge (*conscientia*); and it precludes the intelligibility of framing questions about the 'ownership' of particular thoughts (the problem of the 'unity of consciousness') or the 'numerical identity' of the thoughts of different thinkers.

Other traditional doctrines have been highlighted in our interpretation. Among them are scholastic psychology (especially the categorization of the soul's faculties and the doctrine of the sensitive soul) and Christian ethics (especially the treatment of *conscientia* as the essential complement to moral responsibility for the free operations of the soul).

Another of our concerns is integrating the various elements of his wide-ranging system, sometimes in unfamiliar ways. We have argued that metaphysics and logic are inseparable in his thinking, and have worked out some of the implications of this proposition. Similarly, we have shown that his conception of the substantial union is essentially connected with fundamental principles of physics and theology. We have suggested that he conceived the rational soul as the seat of moral agency and the bearer of moral responsibility, and we have pointed towards an essentially moral motivation for his search for unshakable foundations of knowledge. We can look at these patterns of integration either from the bottom up or from the top down.

In many of his specific doctrines, apparently disparate elements are intermingled and intimately conjoined. His analysis of human sense-perception affords a paradigm. Consider the case of human vision, for example, someone's making the basic judgement 'I see light'. Here logic, metaphysics, mechanics, physiology, and theology are all directly involved. It is a matter of logic to settle what is the logical form of the thought expressed by this utterance and how this form compares with the logical form of the judgement 'It seems to me that I see light'. It is an issue in metaphysics to distinguish between two kinds of modes: namely, duration, order, and number, on the one hand, and sensations, emotions, and appetites, on the other. This is important for understanding why the sensation of light is classed together with the sensations of pain, pleasure, colours, sounds, tastes, etc. Since sense-perception essentially requires the production of a mechanical change in the appropriate sense-organ, it is an issue in mechanics to determine what can intelligibly be said to be visible to a sentient creature, i.e. to work out what, in one sense, light must *be*. Physiology is crucial to explaining the unification of the visual input from the two eyes and the amplification of the effect of light on the eyes as manifested in overt bodily response (e.g., in my taking flight); for this purpose Descartes gave a pivotal role to the pineal gland. Finally, theology is involved:[1] in a human being, the thought of seeing light must be correlated by Nature with the physical conditions of the eye (or the pineal gland). It is through the intervention of God that a change in the eye 'gives occasion to the soul' to have the sensation of light, i.e. to judge 'I see light'. To leave out any one of these diverse considerations would be to misrepresent Descartes' analysis of human vision. It lies, as it were, at the intersection of several different conceptual frameworks.

Conversely, what we might think of as a relatively isolable body of doctrine tends to ramify in many unexpected directions. His theology is a good example. It includes a whole range of traditional considerations about the nature and powers of God, the relation of reason to faith, the immortality of the soul, the relation of human freedom and moral responsibility to God's providence and omniscience, and the maximum simplicity and intelligibility in the workings of God's creation. But these ideas have implications that may now be unanticipated. For example, it is certainty about God's nature that underpinned the fundamental principles of the 'new physics'. These include the general claims that the laws of mechanics are mathematical in nature and fully intelligible or transparent to reason, and that all mechanical explanation is based on the 'geometrical' properties of matter, as well as the more specific claims that no two bits of matter can occupy the same position at the same time, that matter acts on other matter only by impact, and that the total quantity of motion is always conserved. We are entitled to certainty that God's creation is simple, uniform, and elegant, or that it is constructed on rational principles. Theology informs Descartes' building a particular conception of *intelligibility* into the concept of efficient causation. Hence theology extends into his account of the substantial union of mind and body. The regular concomitance of sense-based judgements with states of the sense-organs and of actions with volitions can be explained only as something instituted by God for the sake of human welfare. This makes up our God-given Nature. Moreover, since these correlations are expressly instituted by God, they must have a kind of necessity. In a certain sense, God's essential attributes guarantee that our Nature could not be other than it is. To eliminate God from Descartes' story of mind–body interaction leaves nothing that makes sense at all. The same point holds in respect of his conception that we must have infallible *conscientia* of making judgements

1 Although not what he called 'theology in the strict sense', whose concern is with 'anything dependent on revelation'. Rather he appealed to 'natural theology', concerned with 'metaphysical' questions 'to be examined by human reason' (AT I: 144; CSMK III: 22).

and of withholding assent from thoughts. His position is underpinned by the moral certainty that God could not hold us responsible for any action that is in principle beyond the scope of self-knowledge. In these and other conspicuous ways, elements of Descartes' theology crop up in other departments of his thinking.

Finally, we drew attention to the importance of looking at Descartes' targets and methods. In particular, we have stressed his opposition to empiricism and to the doctrines of real qualities and of sensitive souls; and we have stressed his use of the technique of disambiguation to rout the target doctrines with the accusation 'the Fallacy of Equivocation'.

We haven't explored these doctrines in detail; but even a superficial understanding of what it was that he attacked helps in keeping one's bearings. It is noteworthy that, in several central respects, 'Cartesian Dualism' is barely distinguishable from the positions that Descartes went to enormous lengths to undermine! The Legend sees little fundamental difference between him and the (British) empiricists; he supposedly tried to build objective knowledge on the foundation of subjective experience or sense-data.[2] He is treated as if he *subscribed* to the doctrine (perhaps in a purified version) that what I have acquired 'either from the senses or through the senses' is 'most true' (AT VII: 18; CSM II: 12). It is equally noteworthy that these sense-data themselves, and all the other mental particulars which allegedly populate the Cartesian inner world, have all the earmarks of 'real qualities': they are not called 'substances', but they are meant to be the logical subjects of judgements,[3] in particular the *relata* in judgements expressing mind–body causal interactions. Most wonderful of all, Descartes' 'rational soul' is in effect retransformed by the Legend back into a sensitive soul; it performs all the functions (sense-perception, sensation, Imagination, even the conferral of life and the power of self-movement) that the traditional sensitive soul

2 Santayana made the perceptive observation that the conception of experience among the British empiricists is itself distinctive. 'Experience, as practical people understand it, is not every sort of consciousness or memory, but . . . the intellectual fruit of a material intercourse. It . . . means so much knowledge and readiness as is fetched from contact with events by a teachable and intelligent creature; it is a fund of wisdom gathered by living in familiar intercourse with things' (George Santayana, *Soliloquies in England and Later Soliloquies*, New York: Scribner, 1922, pp. 198–9). It is arguably this commonsense conception of experience that was championed by Bacon and Hobbes, when they urged the importance of putting theories or political principles to the test of experience. But it underwent a metamorphosis at the hands of Locke, Berkeley, and Hume. 'Here was an odd transformation. The self-educated merchants and indignant reformers who, thumping their desks dogmatically, had appealed so roundly to the evidence of their senses, little expected that their philosophy was directed to turning them in the end into inarticulate sensualists, rapt in omphalic contemplation of their states of mind' (p. 192). The magnitude of this change is apparent in the temptation to treat adjectives such as 'subjective' or 'private' as pleonastic when attached to the term 'experience'. Empiricism, it might be claimed, has reshaped the concept of experience, thereby turning its back on the everyday notion. 'The disadvantage of radical empiricism is that it shuts out experience' (p. 201).

3 Like Malebranche's ideas, they are 'real [spiritual] beings, since they have real properties [and] they are [numerically] different from one another' (*Recherche* III.ii.3). Compare Locke's notion that simple ideas are 'positive beings' or 'things' (*Essay* II.xxv.6), that they are terms in causal relations (II.xxvi.2), and that they exhibit numerical diversity (II.xxvii.3).

did.[4] Allegedly only a careless confusion between consciousness and self-consciousness stood in the way of his ascribing minds or rational souls to animals! He once complained ironically to his correspondent Chanut: 'A certain Father Bourdin thought he had good reason to accuse me of being a sceptic, because I refuted the sceptics; and a certain minister tried to argue that I was an atheist, without giving any reason other than the fact that I tried to prove the existence of God' (AT IV: 536; CSMK III: 299). Might he not suspect a family resemblance between these and the Legend's reconstruction of his thinking?

One conspicuous method he used for attacking the doctrines he opposed is disambiguation. We put special stress on the systematic ambiguity of what we call S-predicates. These are a very wide category. To a first approximation, they include all forms of sense-perception (*sentire*) by the internal as well as the external senses; all forms of Imagination (*imaginari*) including goal-seeking and learning from experience; and all forms of bodily movement (*agere*). A moth which flutters against the outside of a window at night is a creature to which the predicate 'sees light' is correctly applicable. So is an adult human who looks towards a lighthouse at night and makes the report 'I see light'. But, on Descartes' view, the predicate 'sees light' has a different sense in these two cases. Similar reasoning supports the doctrine of the systematic ambiguity of all S-predicates. This doctrine, in our view, is one of the fundamental elements of Descartes' Dualism. It is effectively screened from view by the Legend.

In his view, confusion or failure to distinguish the distinct meanings of S-predicates was a principal source of empiricism and the doctrine of sensitive souls. These doctrines ultimately rest on fallacies of equivocation. Empiricism rests on confusing, say, $seeing_1$ light with $seeing_2$ light (and thence ascribing the certainty which attaches to the second to the first). This movement of thought can lead directly to the doctrine of sensitive souls: since animals see_1 light and $seeing_2$ light requires a soul, if you confuse $seeing_1$ with $seeing_2$, you end up supposing that $seeing_1$ requires a soul – thus to fall in with the 'almost universal' opinion that 'animals see just as we do . . . when we think that we see [*dum sentimus nos videre*]' (AT I: 413; CSMK III: 61–2*). Empiricism itself leads us to confuse the two meanings of the expression 'principles of movement' (and thus to suppose that if the behaviour of two organisms is indistinguishable to sensory observation, then the 'principle of movement' must be the same in both cases);[5] this in turn encourages the doctrine of sensitive souls. The disappearance of the 'ambiguity thesis' not only distorts the understanding of Descartes' conception of the person, it eliminates one of his major therapeutic methods. Making sense of his dualism presupposes a sound understanding of *what* he was attacking and *how* he did so.

4 The doctrine of 'the unity of sensitive and intellective souls' is claimed to be something 'forged by Descartes' (Anthony Levi, *French Moralists*, Oxford: Clarendon, 1964, p. 25).

5 'Most of the actions of animals resemble ours, and throughout our lives this has given us many occasions to judge that they act by an interior principle like the one within ourselves, that is to say, by means of a soul which has feelings and passions like ours' (AT II: 39; CSMK III: 99).

ASSESSMENTS OF DESCARTES' DUALISM

Suppose we were right about what Descartes' conception of the person is; what is to be said about this conception itself? In some sense at least, Descartes' Dualism is clearly a 'better' position than Cartesian Dualism, in so far as it is the less confused and more consistent of the two. It is also clear that many of the criticisms commonly levelled against particular elements of Cartesian Dualism, in so far as they are *not* elements of Descartes' Dualism, will have no force against the latter. For example, although Cartesian Privacy is a prominent and much-reviled strand in Cartesian Dualism, it is no part of Descartes' Dualism, and hence the standard criticisms of Cartesian Privacy (the Private Language Argument and the impossibility of 'building objective knowledge on subjective foundations') leave Descartes' Dualism untouched. Again, the doctrine of Cartesian Introspection may have appeared to be an internally inconsistent relic of obsolete, pre-Freudian psychology; but *conscientia* does not purport to be a performance or to be infallible except about one operation of the mind, namely judgements made in the specious present. Similar remarks apply to the Legend's interpretation of the *Bête-Machine* Doctrine, which takes Descartes to have denied that animals feel pain, hunger, or anger and supposes this to be virtually a *reductio ad absurdum* ('impossible to defend without appearing downright ludicrous').[6] Finally, many standard criticisms of Cartesian Dualism presuppose the Two-Worlds View, but since Descartes, far from being committed to this doctrine, saw it as an exemplary instance of a fundamental kind of confused thinking, these criticisms too have no force against him.

But don't these negative points pale into insignificance when you consider Descartes' Dualism in its own right? Even if it is immune to some standard criticisms of Cartesian Dualism, others hold with at least equal force. For example, it too offends against Strawson's principle that 'the concept of a person is primitive'. It also opens a Pandora's box of insuperable new problems. Most of its distinctive doctrines will be judged to be either manifestly false (disproved by everyday experiences which must have escaped his notice) or wildly implausible (hypotheses that are highly unlikely to survive in the Darwinian jungle of contemporary theory-building); some might be branded 'Nonsense'. These criticisms apply both to the general logical, metaphysical, and scientific framework of his system and to the specific elements of Descartes' Dualism.[7] The Aristotelian doctrine that all judgements are subject-predicate in form might seem to stem from an 'observational' shortcoming, namely failing to note the existence of relational judgements in everyday discourse (e.g., 'Plato taught Aristotle').[8] The

6 Patricia Churchland, quoted in Leiber (1988: 309).

7 Exhibiting the untrustworthiness of self-evidence, 'the systems of such great metaphysicians as Descartes and Spinoza consist in large measure of false judgments which their originators nevertheless held to be the most certain of all truths' (Schlick 1974: 148–9).

8 On Russell's view, only *experience* will show whether a complete inventory of logical forms must include 13-term relations! Other critics argue that *no* judgement has subject-predicate structure in its pure Aristotelian form: the notion of a term, as conceived in Aristotelian logic, 'has no application whatsoever' (P. Geach, *Reference and Generality*, Ithaca: Cornell University Press, 1963, p. 34).

logico-metaphysical doctrine that only substances can be the logical subjects of judgements is refuted by the obvious fact that I can judge that *the thought* I just had is brilliant or that *the pain* in my foot is agonizing. Cartesian physics (whose principles are that matter acts on other matter only by impact, a vacuum is impossible, etc.) has long since been supplanted by Newtonian and post-Newtonian mechanics (which acknowledges action at a distance, the possibility of empty space, etc.). The idea that the soul is always thinking is immediately refuted by the fact that we sometimes sleep (or at least the fact that we sleep without dreaming). The thesis that animals cannot think or display intelligence has been disproved by modern psychology: recent experiments with bonobo chimpanzees put it beyond reasonable doubt that some animals can engage in quite complicated thinking, and it is debatable whether they don't also demonstrate some capacity in animals to use and understand language. Modern computer technology has already disproved Descartes' contention that a machine cannot use language, and it might be on the verge of producing a thinking machine (one capable of passing the Turing test). Normal human beings plainly have visual experiences; 'Those who [like Descartes, on our reading] doubt the existence of visual experiences . . . might want to ask themselves what it is that we have and ['blind-sighted'] patients lack'.[9] The doctrine of *conscientia* falls foul of recent research which shows that we may be mistaken even about having just made a sense-based judgement: you may think that you judged that you saw no eye-glasses on the woman who dashed by, when in fact you judged that she was bespectacled but (seconds later) misremembered what you judged.[10] Any theory of mind–body interaction that makes God the intermediary is clearly desperate: 'Today, both Occasionalism and Preestablished Harmony are regarded as historical curiosities – theories too fantastic to warrant serious consideration' (Dicker 1993: 222). (Presumably because the 'theory' that God exists is too implausible?) In any case these same doctrines are plainly contradicted by the facts of daily life, e.g., the fact that I can invite someone to dinner and he may come (Russell 1921: 35–6). (Being a Cambridge empiricist, Russell is content to state something trite provided it is true. By contrast, being both French and a rationalist, Descartes was just the sort to lose sight of the most salient data of everyday experience in the swirling mists of his fevered metaphysical speculations.) In modern philosophy of mind, Cartesian Dualism is generally presented as the worst of all available theories, but, if our version of his dualism were put into circulation, there is little doubt that it would seem worse than the worst!

This verdict may well cast doubt either on our motives or our sanity. Aren't we really in the nasty business of 'spitting on Descartes' grave', trying to demonstrate that he was even more confused, stupid, and outdated than had hitherto been thought? Our 'defence' of his dualism has the character of making the droplets of

9 John R. Searle, *Intentionality*, Cambridge: Cambridge University Press, 1983, p. 47. James would add that it is equally indubitable that we have kinaesthetic sensations (James 1890: I.488–9).

10 Cf. Dennett (1993: 117ff.); Dennett wants to argue that there may be no fact of the matter.

latent nonsense into a sea of patent nonsense. The accused might prefer to dispense with the assistance of his self-styled *amici curiae* and stand alone to face the lesser charges of Cartesian Dualism! Alternatively, it might seem that we are advocating a particularly quixotic form of philosophical fundamentalism. ('Back to Descartes! Important insights have been lost, the framework of sound thinking has degenerated over the past three centuries, and things have gone from bad to worse. Down with the predicate calculus: modern logic is a curse. Animals really are machines. All mechanical interaction is by impact. Bring back God to solve the mind–body problem!') In either case it will be asked: what could the *philosophical* interest of our enterprise possibly be?

METAPHYSICS AND CONCEPT FORMATION

As a first step towards answering this question, we want to propose two interpretative principles that are violated not just by the standard critiques of Cartesian Dualism, but also by the schematic critiques of Descartes' Dualism just adumbrated. The first principle is to attend scrupulously to the modal qualifications that are conspicuous features of Descartes' statements. The second is to reflect sensitively on what *he* meant by *all* the terms that occur in his seemingly bizarre doctrines in order to work out the content of *his* thoughts.

Metaphysics, as traditionally conceived, is the science of *necessary* or *essential* truths. These were deemed to have an altogether different status from the *contingent* generalizations of the natural sciences. Descartes thought that essential truths can be established by pure reason. This does not imply that the same kind or pattern of reasoning must be employed in every case, but it does imply that the conclusions are known independently of sense-experience, even if they are truths *about* corporeal things (as he conceived arithmetic and geometry to be). He also thought that essential truths have a role in reasoning different from that of contingent judgements. They establish the limits of natural science and fix the framework for determining the correctness of observation-reports and the admissibility of explanatory hypotheses. For example, the principle that there *cannot* be a vacuum has the consequence that there *must* be imperceptible matter in any space where no matter is sense-perceived, and the principle that matter *can* be moved *only* by the impact of moving matter implies that the moon *must* stay in orbit around the earth because it is constantly bombarded by particles from the far side. Essential truths have a distinctive status in Descartes' thinking.

Given this general conception, any attempt to refute or disconfirm metaphysical truths by counter-examples and counter-evidence is manifestly question-begging. Although many doctrines of Descartes' Dualism will be dismissed brusquely because they are held to be refuted by everyday experience (or to be likely to be disconfirmed by future scientific research), he didn't simply 'fail to notice' the relevant facts; 'the facts' are generally not in dispute. What is at issue is the intelligibility of the *descriptions* of the recalcitrant 'data'; any empirical 'refutation' begs the question. *Of course* we say both 'I weigh 11 stone' and 'I think that

11 is a prime number'. Does it follow that one and the same *particular* (a person) is the *logical subject* of both judgements? In Descartes' view to suppose so is to let oneself be misled by ordinary language into confused thinking (into supposing that both modes of thinking and modes of extension may properly be predicated of the *same* logical subject). Likewise, I can *of course* make the statement 'Plato taught Aristotle', and others can understand what I have said. (That people say such things could hardly have escaped his notice!) The question, however, is how to describe the *logical form* of this utterance, i.e. whether I have formulated a single judgement with two logical subjects, two different subject-predicate judgements, or no determinate judgement at all; and noting the variety of *grammatical* structures in ordinary language is irrelevant to that debate. (The Port-Royalists showed some sophistication in dealing with this form of objection.) *Of course* people sometimes report, on awaking from sleep, that they have had no thoughts (that their sleep has been dreamless). In reply to this objection, Descartes argued that sleepers *must* have had thoughts of which they were *conscius* at the time, and that it is their inability subsequently to recollect these thoughts which is mistakenly taken to show that they had none.[11] *Of course* I can write an invitation to come to dinner, and of course the invitee may respond by turning up to dinner. Very probably Descartes himself did both these things at some time in his life. The question is whether either of these actions can correctly be described as *causal* interactions between mind and matter, and telling anecdotes is irrelevant to this debate.

Other criticisms seem to presuppose a close analogy between Descartes' Dualism and complex scientific theories. But this disregards his contention that his metaphysical claims are not open to confirmation and disconfirmation in the way that empirical generalizations are. It is now widely agreed that philosophy of mind treats the issue of building and testing *theories*. On this view, *all* discourse about states of mind, whether everyday and unstudied or scholarly and scientific, is concerned exclusively with the explanation and prediction of human behaviour in all its complexity. Consequently, it is treated as an open question whether the most powerful and economical explanation need involve the 'postulation' of a mind in any form. And even under the supposition that some concept of a mind is required, there would be supplementary questions as to whether the mind is to be treated as a *substance* or whether Descartes' version of dualism provides the best (or even any!) explanation of behaviour.

From his point of view, none of his doctrines are hypotheses, and it makes no sense to subject them to any form of empirical confirmation or disconfirmation, however indirect.[12] We can make this absolutely clear by a consideration of

11 It would be more reasonable to suppose that the soul ceased to exist when it ceased to think than that it could exist without its essential attribute (thinking): you might as well suggest that a corporeal substance could exist without being extended (AT III: 478; CSMK III: 203)!

12 The idea that he viewed the existence of the rational soul (the bearer of moral responsibility and what is subject to redemption at the Last Judgement) as an explanatory *hypothesis* seems perverse. (Or even the idea that 'the Cartesian ego is the substratum of those states of mind about which doubt is impossible' (Kenny 1989: 89)). Can you seriously imagine that *he* would listen to (say) Dennett's trenchant critique of Cartesian Dualism and conclude: '*Je n'ai plus besoin de cette hypothèse*'?

experiments which are now supposed to prove that animals can think. Montaigne had cited many instances of 'intelligence' or 'reasoning' in animals, for example, the way that swallows choose nesting sites located on the warm side of a building and sheltered from the prevailing wind. Correspondents raised other examples from the behaviour of pets and domestic animals. If the question were whether animals *do as a matter of fact* think, then these reports, if properly corroborated and experimentally confirmed, *might* settle the question in the affirmative.[13] But Descartes refused to treat the issue in this way. The question is what 'think' *means*, for he claimed that animals *cannot in principle* think. His conception is one very generally accepted among his contemporaries: only if animals have *rational souls* is it *possible* for them to have *thoughts*. Whether they do have rational souls is not a question that can be settled by gathering evidence about complicated patterns of behaviour that individual organisms exhibit. Whatever routines animals perform can be explained mechanically provided they are sufficiently intricate or sophisticated mechanisms, and since God is the Creator of all finite substances, it is certain that there is no rational limit to the possible complexity of the living mechanisms that are called 'animals'. The question whether animals have rational souls *cannot* be settled by any observational or experimental evidence about the degree of *complexity* of behaviour exhibited by individual animals. Indeed this is absurd given the axiom that possession of a rational soul would make an animal a *moral agent*. Could anybody seriously think that moral agency is an *observational* property of any organism?

In fact, complexity of behaviour is equally irrelevant in respect of human beings. It is part of the *essence* of a person to have a rational soul. Descartes surely didn't *postulate* that human beings are free and responsible moral agents whose characters include moral virtues and vices.[14] Hence the common charge that the mind, as *Descartes* conceived it, can be discarded as an idle wheel in the mechanism of an explanatory theory of human behaviour surely misses its target. He was supposedly struck with the apparently limitless complexity of human behaviour and concluded that it couldn't be given a purely mechanical explanation. To account for the intricate individual and social behaviour of civilized and educated people he allegedly held it to be necessary to hypothesize that human beings have beliefs, desires, intentions, emotions, etc., hence that they have minds.[15] (If human bodies are machines, then they *must* be inhabited by ghosts!)

13 Or they might *not*. This would depend on what we chose as the criteria for thinking, and there is surely much latitude here. For example, we might take the acid test to be the ability to participate in a *conversation*. (Cf. Leiber 1988: 340: having spent a great deal of time 'in intimate contact' with chimpanzees, 'I felt love, awe, affection, and cheer'; but 'I know now that I am never going to have a conversation with a chimpanzee'.) The concept of 'conversation' manifestly has a moral as well as a purely intellectual aspect.

14 It would even be absurd to describe him as 'being of the *opinion*' that humans have rational souls; rather it is part of rational human life that, *ceteris paribus*, we *treat* each other as moral agents.

15 'That there are minds or souls attached to some bodies is simply a hypothesis, introduced to account for certain observed facts' (A. M. MacIver, 'Is There Mind–Body Interaction?', in Vesey 1964: 308).

This line of argument is open to empirical disconfirmation by experiments with computers or animals, but only on the presupposition that he held the view that it is the *degree of complexity* of human behaviour that eliminates the possibility of giving a purely mechanical explanation of human *actions*. That would surely have struck him as absurd, morally perverse, and even blasphemous. There could be no sequence of movements of the human body that *could not* be produced as the output of a *God-built* mechanism. ('The difficult He can accomplish instantly, the impossible may take a little time.') Descartes affirmed explicitly that *any* bodily movement performed by a human being could be performed by a machine or an animal if it were given an appropriate disposition of its organs. What a machine cannot do is 'act in all the contingencies of life in the way in which our *reason* makes us act' (AT VI: 57; CSM I: 140, italics added). In his view, all bodily movements whose principle of motion is volition or thought are voluntary acts of *moral agents*. Consequently, he connected the possession of a rational soul with the *intelligibility* of characterizing human actions as voluntary, intelligent, morally responsible, virtuous and sinful. What could this have to do with what cognitive scientists now call 'the degree of complexity of behaviour'?[16]

It is part of the framework of modern science that there is nothing that in principle lies outside the scope of scientific explanation. (Any lacunae in explanations *must* be provisional; ephemeral challenges to scientific ingenuity, not permanent barriers to human thought.)[17] Descartes disagreed: there are many matters that can be demonstrated by pure reason, some of them independent of empirical science (the existence and benevolence of God, the real distinction between the soul and the body, the perfect freedom and responsibility of the soul for assenting to ideas), others of them the *a priori* or metaphysical preconditions for (rational) science (the impossibility of a vacuum, the necessity of impact for mechanical interaction, the conservation of the quantity of motion). To dispute these 'axioms' isn't to correct Descartes' 'prejudices' and 'blindnesses', but to replace his concepts with our own *different* ones.[18]

16 Suppose somebody told you, with all apparent seriousness, that you *must* appraise the behaviour of bonobos in terms of virtues and vices if you once concede that they have demonstrated any real capacity to use and understand linguistic symbols? Or that a computer that passed the Turing test would *thereby* prove itself to be a potential *sinner*?

17 Compare Dennett's discussion of the 'wild-eyed inventor engaged in a debate with a tough-minded philosopher'. The inventor wished to construct a device that would automatically 'record' and then 'replay' an orchestra and chorus performing Beethoven's Ninth; the philosopher insisted that this was impossible. Dennett concludes that the philosopher 'mistook his failure of imagination for an insight into necessity' (1993: 48), and clearly wants us to draw the conclusion that all alleged 'metaphysical truths' and 'metaphysical impossibilities' are in the same boat.

18 Dennett (1993: 38) reprints a famous Sidney Harris cartoon which depicts two scientists. One of them has written a complex mathematical formula on the board, in the middle of which he has written 'Then a miracle occurs'. The second is pointing to these words and saying 'I think you should be more explicit here in step two'. (It is meant as an informal *reductio ad absurdum* of Descartes' conception of mind–body interaction.) Dennett and Descartes would disagree only in their assessment of which of the two scientists was confused. (We look forward to seeing a certain respected national newspaper publish a photograph of Descartes with the caption '"Dennett was wrong", says Descartes'.)

Descartes himself made sharp distinctions between essential and accidental truths. One may wish to reject this distinction (and many post-Quinean philosophers will insist upon doing so); what is absolutely certain is that without heeding it, there is little hope of arriving at *Descartes'* conception of the *nature* or *essence* of a person.

Inattention to the distinction between essential and accidental truths in his writings is, we think, linked with a failure to consider carefully enough *Descartes'* own conceptions of concepts which play a central role in his doctrines. Consider again the claim that animals cannot think. For most modern philosophers, the issue is one about the behavioural capacities of individual organisms; it can in principle be settled, for example, by a repeatable experiment with a single chimpanzee, for nothing is relevant apart from this organism's satisfying the appropriate behavioural criteria on particular occasions. But this is definitely *not* Descartes' understanding of the issue. His question is 'Do (any (non-human)) animals have *rational souls*?' (This is definitely *not* the question addressed in twentieth-century philosophy of mind, experimental psychology, or cognitive science.) What then are the criteria for possessing a soul? It is clear that he did *not* consider this to turn on observations of the behaviour of single organisms. Correspondents raised with him the objection that he could not coherently deny that some individual animals can think while affirming that human infants, idiots, and senile adults can think. These critics based their reasoning on the observation that many a cat is much more self-sufficient and capable of looking after its welfare than a new-born baby, or that a well-trained dog may be able to carry out a complex routine beyond the capacity of a human being who has a severe mental handicap. In other words, his critics presupposed that the attribute 'thinking' is to be ascribed to or withheld from an individual organism on the basis of *its* observed behaviour patterns. Descartes took a different view of the matter. It is of the *essence* of a human being to have a rational soul; and rationality is an *essential* difference (*differentia*) between two 'species', that is, men and brutes (cf. AT V: 278; CSMK III: 366). Hence a new-born baby or an idiot *must* have the capacity to think;[19] indeed *any* human being must always be thinking, however inept his behaviour may be. Having or lacking a rational soul must be an attribute of an entire species (or natural kind). From his point of view, then, it is doubly absurd to draw any conclusions about whether any *species* of non-human animal has as part of its *essence* the possession of a rational soul by starting from observations about how individual members of that species compare in respect of life skills with infants or idiots. His own understanding of the doctrine that animals cannot think can be ascertained from the way he actually met criticisms, and it is very different from what is challenged by modern critics of Cartesian Dualism.

No doubt post-Quinean worries will also affect reactions to our talk about sameness and difference of concepts (e.g., to our distinguishing Descartes'

19 'I should not judge that infants were endowed with minds unless I saw that they were *of the same nature as* adults' (AT V: 345; CSMK III: 374, italics added).

concept of *conscientia* from the modern philosophers' concepts of consciousness and introspection). We can't here engage in a thorough discussion of this issue; but a response might proceed by noting that there are different paradigms to follow in philosophy. Quine stands at one extreme, in seeing no principled distinction between the conceptual framework and the content of a theory and, accordingly, emphasizing the continuity between empirical science and philosophy. In advocating this way of seeing things, he makes use of the concept of 'being open to revision in the light of experience', and this is well-chosen to make everything look homogeneous. At the opposite extreme stands Wittgenstein, who took himself to be stressing the distinction between concept-formation (explanation) and concept-application (use) as well as emphasizing the difference between philosophy (describing the grammar of our language) and empirical science (explaining phenomena).[20] In making propaganda for his way of seeing things, he made use of the contrast between discovery and stipulation (invention) or between measuring the length of a rod against a metre stick and using a rod to introduce a new unit of length; these analogies were carefully chosen to highlight the contrast between treating a generalization as answerable to observational data and making a free decision to replace one convention for using words by another different one (even if the decision were prompted by experience). Although we can juxtapose these two paradigms of philosophical investigation, nothing would count as proving one or other of them to be 'correct'. We leave Quine's conception to one side, and follow Wittgenstein's example, at least for the purpose of making a case for the philosophical interest of Descartes' Dualism.

Definitions or explanations of terms have generally been taken to be *necessary* truths or statements of the *essences* of things (or concepts). One might invert this truism: any necessary truth in part determines or defines its constituent concepts.[21] Many of the seemingly bizarre doctrines which are integral to Descartes' Dualism are best viewed from this perspective. According to his understanding, they are essential truths (appropriately framed with the modal terms 'must' and 'cannot'), and they therefore hold the key to grasping *his conception* of 'thinking', 'the rational soul', 'machines', '*conscientia*', 'sense-perception' ('*sentire*'), 'feeling pain', 'cause', etc. Many of these 'essential truths' may strike us as strange today, for instance, the claim that animals can't think, or that the human body is a sentient machine, or that we perceive (and may misperceive) pain or thirst with our internal senses. But instead of discarding these (under the rubric 'nonsense'), instead of taking him to make blunders in describing concepts familiar to us now, we should treat him as describing *different concepts* that may be more or less alien to twentieth-century philosophers.

20 It does not follow from his distinction that some contrast between framework and content is not applicable to the enterprise of characterizing the frameworks of particular sciences or even 'the grammar of our language'.

21 As this line of argument is commonly associated with Wittgenstein, we might be said to be practising 'Wittgensteinian hermeneutics' in interpreting Descartes' texts. (It is not to be confused with the abrasive (or even abusive) method of treating other philosophers which is commonly associated with the adjective 'Wittgensteinian'.)

By focusing sharply on what he advanced as essential truths, we have tried to elucidate his conception of the person as a substantial union of mind and body. We think his system of thought can be made intelligible, but only if we respect the necessary truths that he formulated as determining the concepts with which he worked. Modern critics have themselves to blame for making his concept of a person literally inaccessible.

CONCEPTUAL CHANGES

Different philosophers may have different concepts, and important concepts may vary over time. There are several levels at which such changes can occur, not all of which may be immediately obvious. Carefully plotting conceptual changes has enormous consequences for our understanding of Descartes.

Let's start with the simplest kind of case. We have argued that many of his concepts differ in fundamental ways from the modern concepts with which they are usually identified. In fact, some of these concepts have gone through a whole series of intermediate changes. We have sketched some evidence for this in respect of '*conscientia*' or 'consciousness', and we have alluded to sequential shifts in understanding of some other concepts, such as 'sensation', 'perception', 'state of mind', and 'necessary'. Many of these generate serious problems in interpreting previous philosophers' interpretations of Descartes.

For example, what he called 'the mind' ('*mens*', '*esprit*') is strictly rational and deliberative; it has nothing to do with animal sentience. Moreover, being identical with the Christian rational soul, it has an essential moral aspect. As a result, he took moral character traits (virtues and vices) to be paradigms of modes of thinking (or 'states of mind'). In all these respects what modern philosophers call 'the mind' and 'state of mind' are enormously different from his conceptions. Correlatively, what modern philosophers build into the concept of the human body is entirely different from what Descartes built into it. He saw the body as a sentient machine. Modern philosophers find the phrase 'sentient machine' paradoxical. Correspondingly, they treat '*unconscious* machine' as a pleonasm. Moreover, they dismiss as seriously confused the idea that the *body* is sentient (e.g., that *it* can feel pain or hunger).[22] Descartes also saw us as having a kind of corrigible but asymmetrical access to certain states of our own bodies through the internal senses, whereas many philosophers now take 'first-/third-person asymmetry' to be diagnostic of the mental. What follows from all this, we suggest, is not that Descartes was egregiously confused, but rather that his *concepts* of mind and body must be very different from the ones now current among philosophers.

Analogous remarks apply to his conception of cause. In his view, causal interaction between corporeal substances is characterized by a kind of intelligibility, exemplified in the sort of understanding we achieve when we observe one

22 Some quote Wittgenstein with approval: 'isn't it absurd to say of a *body* that it has pain?' (*PI* §286). They ought to note that this is a question, not an assertion.

billiard ball set in motion by the impact of another moving ball. More generally, revealing a mechanism connecting two things makes their interaction intelligible. Descartes built this idea of mechanism into his concept of efficient causation. But, post-Hume, both the relevant notion of intelligibility and the (related) relevant notion of efficient causation have altered beyond recognition. What Descartes took to be the paradigm of intelligible mechanical interaction, that is, one billiard ball's being set in motion by the impact of another moving ball, Hume treated as the paradigm of an unintelligible fact. He argued that mechanisms make nothing intelligible; they merely postpone our ignorance. This amounts to the substitution of one *concept* of intelligibility for another and the concomitant substitution of one *concept* of causation for another. Failure to appreciate this shift generates serious misunderstanding of Descartes' conception of mind–body interaction. In *his* language, it is *nonsensical* to speak of *causal* interaction between thoughts and movements. His doctrine can be phrased in *post-Humean* jargon as two-way causal interaction, but this is liable to generate fresh confusion by eclipsing his supplementary doctrine that *God* alone is capable of instituting the regular correlation of thoughts and movements which constitutes our Nature.

In these and many other cases ('pain', 'sensation of pain', 'conscious', 'sense-perception', 'imagination', 'sentient', 'machine', 'nature', 'subject' and 'predicate', 'inference', 'substance', 'property', 'relation', etc.), the change in the conceptual landscape between Descartes and (say) Dennett, Searle, Nagel, and Davidson seems colossal. It is comparable to the stylistic gulf separating Giotto from Picasso or Purcell from Prokofiev. Anyone unaware of it faces an acute danger of radically misinterpreting Descartes and of thinking at cross-purposes with him even when trying to analyse or criticize his thought.

Changes in *concepts* have a very distinctive kind of importance: they shift the boundary between sense and nonsense. This is comparable to altering the rules of a game: for instance, to changing the regulation size and shape of a tennis court or to introducing the castling rule into pre-modern chess. If the rule-change is conspicuous and widely accepted or enforced, the pre-reformation game ceases to be played and the post-reformation one usurps its place. Something previously excluded may now be allowed, or something previously legitimate may now be banned. Such differences are, in a clear sense, fundamental. The same holds of shifts in concepts. In Cartesian mechanics, for example, there is no such thing as action at a distance; matter *can* act on other matter *only* by *impact*. This determines whether some movement of matter needs to be explained or not, what form the explanation must take, and whether or not a proffered explanation is correct or complete. Hence this principle fixes the *concept* of 'mechanical explanation'. As a consequence, by incorporating the notion of action *at a distance*, Newtonian mechanics altered the *conceptual* landscape. It didn't simply replace one theory of mechanics by an improved theory, but rather advocated as a form of 'mechanical explanation' something that Cartesian physics had expressly disqualified for the title 'mechanical *explanation*' in virtue of its form. This was a (successful) attempt to move the goal-posts.

In philosophy, concept-shifts alter the 'geometry' of reflections in a similarly decisive way. In particular, they involve changes in what kinds of questions are deemed admissible. Whether a question arises is often relative to accepting or rejecting a conceptual framework. 'Refutations' of Descartes typically proceed by raising impossible questions (i.e. questions that *cannot* be raised within *his* framework) and then pointing out (often with malicious glee) that he provided no answers whatever to them. For example, he has long been accused of providing no answer to the question why any particular thought must belong to a thinker. How could he vindicate his claim that '*Cogito*' (a report of the occurrence of a particular thought) entails '*Sum res cogitans*' ('I am a thinking *substance*')? He might be excused this omission by the patronizing observation that he *assumed*, having been educated in Aristotelian metaphysics, that every mode must inhere in a substance.[23] But that doesn't excuse him from having failed to address the question why a particular thought inheres in only one soul or why a person's successive thoughts inhere in a single persisting mental substance. He stands accused of having no answer to the question 'What property must a thought have in order to be *my* thought?' But, within his logico-metaphysical framework, this question is comparable to the question 'What property must the colour blue have in order to belong to *this* chair?', though most of his critics would agree that this latter question 'does not arise'. Similar considerations hold in respect of his alleged inability to answer the question, 'How can one ever be certain that two people have numerically the same thought?' Rigorous attention to his ontology and the metaphysical distinction between substances and modes removes the logical space needed for framing these questions; they are, as it were, 'geometrically excluded'.

Many of the most common and allegedly most damning criticisms of Descartes involve raising questions that similarly transgress the bounds of sense which are the correlates of his conceptual framework. The question '*How* do mind and body causally interact?' is supposed to checkmate his account of the union of mind and body. But if we understand what he would countenance as the only possible form of answer (viz. making such an interaction rationally intelligible by describing a *mechanism*), we understand that this question cannot intelligibly be framed. Likewise, his only conceivable strategy for answering the question 'What does "see light" *mean* (in the "strict sense")?' is supposed to be an appeal to private ostensive definition, and that is to play into checkmate by the Private Language Argument. But if we realize that the rational senses of S-predicates involve attributions of articulate thoughts to the rational soul, we should see clearly enough that each of these concepts can be systematically explained in terms of the corresponding animal sense of the S-predicate (which itself is linked to responsive behaviour). And so on.

23 For example, Russell (1946: 589): '"I think" is his ultimate premise . . . . When he goes on to say "I am a *thing* which thinks", he is already using uncritically the apparatus of categories handed down by scholasticism.' Cf. Dicker on 'the substance theory' (1993: 50ff.).

We could express this point more trenchantly. The standard objections to Descartes' concept of a person are all appropriate questions to marshall against Cartesian Dualism. The fact that most, if not all, of them cannot be raised within the complex logical, metaphysical, moral, and theological framework of his thinking has a dramatic implication. It shows that Cartesian Dualism is worse than an 'unnatural' interpretation of his philosophy; it is not even a *possible* one. It is 'geometrically excluded' by prominent features of the system of ideas that it purports to reconstruct.

SWAPPING NEW FOR OLD

A second aspect of concept-change has similar importance: concepts can be gained or lost over time. (This might seem to pose a threat to mutual intelligibility.) We have called attention to a number of examples that are of crucial importance for interpreting Descartes' Dualism. Loss of some of his concepts is correlated with modern blindness to certain aspects of his philosophy, while the later introduction of some other concepts conjures up urgent questions that he *could not* have considered.

Here is one clear example: Descartes' concept of the internal senses has disappeared entirely from the mainstream of modern Anglo-American thinking; it has no counterpart in philosophy of mind. This loss (a casualty of Progress?) is related to the fact that the objects of both his internal senses (pain, hunger, thirst, anger, fear, joy, etc.) have been 'extruded' from the body and reallocated to the mind. (We can't here explore the reasons or motives for this shift.) One consequence of this loss is a tendency to treat one's own body itself as if it were simply one *external* object among others.[24] Another is divorcing the concepts of pain, anger, and so on, from the concept of welfare. (This changes the 'geometry' of all these concepts. So it eliminates much of the scope for speaking of *erroneous* judgements about pain and thirst. By removing the possibility of 'deception by the internal senses', this revisionist account of the grammar of 'feels pain' or 'feels hunger' draws the conclusion that these phrases cannot signify forms of *perception*.) This (allegedly Cartesian!) severing of the conceptual connection between pain and welfare is indispensable for making the picture of pain as a 'private inner object' so attractive (or dangerously seductive) to modern philosophers. This *grand mal* has, in turn, called forth a *grand remède* in the form of 'the Private Language Argument'. The demise of the internal senses has had a string of effects.

We have drawn attention to some other clear cases of concepts which played important roles in Descartes' thinking but which must now be listed among Missing Persons:

1 *Conscientia*. This is self-knowledge which embraces mental acts with proposi-

24 Once upon a time, the 'external world' was what lay outside one's own skin. Was this a primitive superstition?

tional content (entertaining thoughts, making judgements, framing volitions and desires, etc.), voluntary actions, states of intellect and character, and the moral evaluation of past and present thoughts, actions, and character. There is no close modern analogue: the very idea of moral *knowledge* has all but disappeared from twentieth-century thought (having been replaced, at best, with 'pain attendant upon the violation of duty'), while 'consciousness' takes in forms of sentience that lack propositional content.

2 The rational soul. Having a soul is an *essential* attribute of human beings, and it embraces capacities both for judging and reasoning and for operating as a free and responsible *moral agent*. 'The mind' plays an altogether different role in twentieth-century thought.

3 *Moral* necessity. This is a kind of necessity which depends on arguments excluding possibilities on the grounds of being inconsistent with the benevolence, omnipotence, and uniformity of God's creative and sustaining activities. It gives rise to a distinctive kind of internal relation (especially correlations ordained by Nature between movements and thoughts) for which there is no modern counterpart.

4 Subject and predicate in Aristotelian logic. These correlative concepts are tied to the doctrines that every judgement *must* be subject-predicate in form and that there *can* be *no* genuine relations.[25] In Descartes' system, *only* substances *can* be the logical subjects of singular judgements. All of these concepts are incommensurable with the conceptual apparatus of the predicate calculus.[26]

5 Nature. To talk of 'Nature', whether in the form of 'our Nature as union of mind and body', 'the laws of Nature', or 'the Natural light', is virtually always, directly or indirectly, to talk of God.

We should note that subtracting one concept from a system of concepts necessarily alters the interconnections between all of the ones that are left. Nothing remains completely unchanged. For example, dropping the internal senses has all sorts of repercussions for Descartes' thinking. It compels us to redraw the boundaries between the faculties of sense-perception, Imagination, and intellect or else to drop the axiom that these three faculties give an exhaustive schema for classifying the operations of the soul. It abrogates the immediate inference from the fact that animals are sentient to the conclusion that they feel pains, bodily appetites, and emotions. It generates a lacuna in allocating self-knowledge between *conscientia* and sense-perception, and it thereby motivates extending the scope of *conscientia* to include what had been the objects of the internal senses. The knock-on effects parallel those of simplifying a game by removing one of its rules. For example, to repeal the rule of castling in chess would, in an obvious sense, amount to a reduction in the power of the rooks relative to the other pieces.

25 Russell called it an 'untenable *metaphysical hypothesis*' that all judgements have subject-predicate form (1956: 109)!

26 It is less the case that modern logicians have discovered the true logical form of the judgement 'Socrates taught Plato' than that they have introduced a new *concept* of logical form.

Concepts get added as well as subtracted, and this has similarly fundamental repercussions. In particular, it licenses raising questions that were previously 'geometrically' excluded. A simple model might be the extension of the set of natural numbers by the addition of negative integers. In the pre-reformation system, it makes sense to subtract 2 from 4, but not 4 from 2, whereas in the post-reformation system, the question 'What is $x-y$?' makes sense for *any* pair of numbers. This amounts to a change in the concept of a number and in the definition of the operation of subtraction.[27]

We have called attention to various concepts that have been added to the system of concepts with which Descartes worked, and we have argued that failure to appreciate these changes distorts modern evaluations of his work.

1 Particulars. These are the logical subjects of singular judgements. They include a vast range of things that Descartes excluded for the reason that they are not substances. They generate the logical space that is filled by the items of the so-called 'Cartesian inner world'.
2 Relations. Relations are logical constituents of judgements distinct from objects and properties. To acknowledge their existence is not to discover *the* logic of multiple generality but to jettison Aristotelian logic and to adopt a different form of representation for the logical structures of judgements and inferences.
3 Humean impressions and acts of will. These are non-propositional items in the stream of consciousness, things which pass before our minds and of which we are aware by the power of reflection or inner sense. They provide the raw materials for concept-formation by abstraction, and they are the terms of causal relations in mind–body interaction. They are paradigms of objects in the inner world or subjective experiences. Descartes' system of thought leaves no room for any concept that fills any of these conditions, let alone all of them.
4 Inner sense. This is conceived as providing the experiential basis of ideas of reflection. Without this notion, empiricists might have difficulty in defending the claim that everything in the intellect originates in the *senses*.
5 Phenomenological properties. These are what is predicated of inner objects in descriptions of immediate experience. (They are, for instance, the attributes of Humean impressions.) They may be considered to be more or less ineffable, especially when presented under the labels 'raw feels' and 'the what's-it-like'. Descartes *could* not have entertained this concept.

These conceptual innovations give rise to two powerful temptations. One is to read modern ideas into Descartes' account. For example, we may suppose that he *must* have argued that the difference between a mind 'lodged' in the body like a pilot in a ship and a mind 'united' with a body is to be drawn in terms of the

27 The system of signed integers (positive and negative integers) is '*a new form of expression*; and there is nothing so absurd as to try and describe this new schema, this new kind of scaffolding, by means of the old expressions' (Ludwig Wittgenstein, *Remarks on the Foundations of Mathematics*, 3rd edn, Oxford: Blackwell, 1978, p.138).

absence or presence of the 'phenomenology' of embodiment. The other is to suppose that he missed out something vital. For example, were we to acknowledge what his conception of modes of thinking is, we might then upbraid him with the rhetorical question 'Where's the what's-it-like?' Both forms of anachronism are equally out of place.

DIVISION OF LABOUR

A third level at which concepts can alter dramatically over time has to do with changes in principles of relevance. What is counted as relevant or irrelevant to whether a concept is correctly used or not? Such changes can be exemplified by the now-familiar and widespread policy of banishing questions from discussions of logic by branding them as 'metaphysical' or 'psychological'.

This dyslogistic use of 'metaphysical' is notorious among the Logical Empiricists. But it has precedents, for example, in Mill's *Logic*, and it persists to the present day.[28] The term 'metaphysical' probably carries the connotation 'non-logical' for most readers of this book.

'Anti-psychologism' is an equally strong theme in much modern philosophical logic. Syllogistic logic was expounded in terms of 'concepts', 'judgements', and 'inferences'; hence every inference was held to be the transition from a pair of judgements to a third judgement.[29] As early as Mill, this formulation was thought to hold the danger of contaminating logical issues with psychological ones. He distinguished between the *act* of judging (allegedly something psychological) and the *object* of judgement (apparently an abstract entity). Frege built this distinction into his exposition of the predicate calculus. He announced as one of his fundamental principles 'always to separate sharply the psychological from the logical, the subjective from the objective'.[30] He used the term 'psychological' to exclude matters from consideration in his logic; much modern philosophy of logic continues to stress the distinction between logic and psychology (e.g., by distinguishing 'arguments' from 'inferences' or 'propositions' from 'thoughts'). Consequently, the term 'psychological', just as much as the term 'metaphysical', is apt now to carry the implication 'non-logical'. (Similar points could be made for the term 'epistemological' as now excluding 'theological' and 'moral', etc.)[31]

28 For example, one influential commentator characterizes Frege's doctrine that the True and the False are two objects as a 'merely metaphysical' idea precisely in order to exclude it from his own reconstruction of Frege's philosophy of logic.

29 Descartes framed at least one logico-metaphysical principle in a 'psychologistic' idiom: namely only substances and modes of substances have any 'existence outside the mind' (see pp. 133–4).

30 *FA* p. x.

31 The material of *Meditation* IV is seldom mentioned in the ubiquitous discussions of doubt and certainty that take rise from *Meditations* I–II. A recent commentary on the *Meditations* which reprints most of the text omits the whole of *Meditation* IV on the grounds that it introduces into Descartes' reasoning about epistemology two 'extraneous' topics, error and free will!

Peter Schouls, in 'Human Nature, Reason, and Will' (in Cottingham 1994) aims to correct the impression that the *Meditations* is simply a validation of reason as opposed to a 'validation' of the will; this reading is congenial to our plea for reading Descartes' epistemology as having a moral dimension.

These are particular cases of the emergence of a modern consensus about principles of relevance. This development incorporates many changes that separate modern readers from Descartes. These are of decisive importance for understanding and appreciating his philosophy. For better or worse, he clearly did *not* share twentieth-century notions about the division of philosophical labour. Putting his individual doctrines in their wider settings changes the appearance of the whole intellectual landscape. This is a large part of what we have tried to do in this work, in connecting his conception of the logical forms of judgements directly with his system of metaphysics, his principles of mechanics with his analysis of sense-perception, his concept of the rational soul to his theology and ethics, and so on. In weaving together all of this material, we have done something that would be excluded, almost *ex vi terminorum*, by anybody who set out to clarify 'Descartes' Philosophy of Mind'. He held the concept of the rational soul, the concept of sense-perception, the concept of a bodily sensation or appetite, and the concept of an occasional cause each to be *essentially* multi-faceted. His system of thinking is organic, and its very life is destroyed when it is dissected according to the approved modern procedures. 'Divide and conquer!' seems a recipe for disaster in trying to analyse a system of ideas as tightly interwoven as his is.

For example, we have stressed the moral and theological aspects of his concept of the rational soul. What is crucial here are the ideas of freedom, intelligence, responsibility, virtue and vice. On his view, it is solely in virtue of having a rational soul that a person *can* have these attributes. In his notorious doctrine that animals lack minds, it is *this* concept of the mind (or rational soul) that Descartes denied applied to animals. Consequently, most of the modern 'refutations' of his doctrine plainly miss their target. It is not enough *for this purpose* to show that Köhler's apes engaged in problem-solving, that a sheep can distinguish a wolf from a goat, that a dog wags its tail when its master gets up from his armchair to take it for its habitual evening walk, that a computer can carry out a complex mathematical calculation, or even that bonobos have very considerable abilities to make differentiated responses to variable verbal instructions. In Descartes' view, none of this would settle the question whether any behaviour of any animal manifests either intelligence or moral values, nor whether any animal should be regarded as free, morally responsible, and subject to redemption by Christ. Making clear the 'multidimensional' nature of the rational soul makes clear too that the question whether animals have rational souls hangs out of reach of any conceivable scientific enquiry. The answer doesn't have the character of an opinion or hypothesis to be confirmed or disconfirmed by observations of animal behaviour, but rather the character of a way of living and acting towards animals which is an integral part of a wider system of human values. Modern chatter about 'postulating the mind' is worlds away from Descartes' conception that human beings are unique among animals in having rational souls. Like a matador, the twentieth-century cognitive scientist confronts only an enfeebled remnant of his allegedly mighty adversary before administering the *coup de grâce*.

Unless we are sensitive to the possibility of such changes, then the task of hearing Descartes with our twentieth-century ears really is a hopeless one.

PHILOSOPHICAL IMAGINATION

The question 'What is the *philosophical* interest of our enterprise?' might seem now to be even more pressing than it was originally. If our reasoning above (pp. 206–7) carries any force, then his position might no longer be dismissed out of hand as being internally inconsistent and riddled with factual errors. We proposed, instead, that his metaphysical truths be seen as determining or defining concepts which are very different from our modern ones in some fundamental respects. He didn't write a lot of nonsense about *the* (invariant) concept of a person, but rather a lot of sense about something different, namely *his* concept. This defence seems sure to provoke a further negative reaction: what of *philosophical* value or interest is to be gained from studying Descartes' system of thought? It may seem that there is literally *nothing* to learn from him, no nuggets of gold to mine from his texts, and nothing capable of being transported into twentieth-century philosophy and exploited now for our own benefit.

Many twentieth-century philosophical exponents of the Legend take Descartes to be mapping out the logical geography or the grammar of our discourse about persons, the mind, the body, mental states and processes, etc. In this way they show a kind of respect: they treat him as someone seriously engaged in the proper business of philosophy. They take him to being offering logical analyses of the very same concepts that are still the focus of philosophical debate and investigation. (Others, with a different conception of the proper business of philosophy, see him as offering a proto-scientific explanation of human behaviour, complete with unobservable hypothetical entities like the rational soul.) At the same time, they take him to be seriously or fundamentally confused about this shared subject-matter. His findings are *mis*descriptions and *mis*representations of a whole system of invariant (or at least, unchanged) concepts. (And his primitive psychology is hopelessly out of step with modern cognitive science.)

If our sketch of Descartes' Dualism carries any conviction, then it has an obvious implication for this strategy of treating his thinking. We have demonstrated that many of his most central concepts are essentially different in various ways from the modern concepts with which the Legend identifies them; also that subsequent additions and deletions of concepts have effected substantial changes in the interrelations among apparently enduring concepts. Roughly speaking, the whole conceptual landscape has undergone radical transformation. As a consequence, the Legend's critical investigation begins from *projecting* a modern conception of the mind on to Descartes. It then castigates him for giving a mistaken analysis of something that he couldn't have known anything about! The Legend's damning evaluation of his philosophy is pre-ordained by its notion of how to treat his work with *respect*.

There might be a different conception of how to show respect to Great Dead

Philosophers, one which caters for the possibility of significant changes in systems of concepts.[32] We have tried to attend as carefully as possible to what Descartes wrote, to cultivate some sensitivity to the significant nuances of his statements, and especially to work out, on the basis of what he formulated as essential truths, how he understood (and would have explained) the constituent concepts. We want to distance ourselves from the prejudice that he *must* have been exploring the very same concepts that are deployed by twentieth-century analytic philosophers. If you keep this *possibility* clearly in view, you should have little difficulty in finding telling evidence for fundamental differences between these two systems of concepts. You should then see too that most of the strident modern criticism of Descartes is irrelevant to what he thought and wrote.

By disregarding conceptual change, Anglo-American analytic philosophy constructs a picture of gradual but significant progress. Thanks to the labours of such giants as Kant, Frege, and Wittgenstein, we are now far better equipped to map out the logical geography of 'mental conduct concepts' than were Descartes, Locke, Hume, or even Russell. We want to urge a different picture of the history of philosophy. We should see philosophers themselves not solely as spectators, but also as agents of conceptual change, and we should look at the evolution of a particular philosophical tradition less as the accumulation of knowledge about unchanging concepts, more as a series of *motivated* conceptual changes. This picture contrasts, on the one hand, with a picture according to which philosophy is the discovery of truths of some kind (about logical forms, the grammar of our language, the neurophysiology of perception, etc.), and on the other hand, with a picture according to which such concepts simply undergo a kind of random continental drift (as it were, Brownian movement on a geological time-scale).

Looking at things in this way might help to alleviate the uneasy sense that many readers might feel, that if talk of 'discovering philosophical truths' is replaced by talk about 'changing concepts', then philosophers can say what they like: 'anything goes'. This in turn might help to clarify what the philosophical interest of an enterprise like ours might be.

Let's take the concept of pain as an example. Many analytic philosophers are inclined to think that its 'grammar' has now been definitively mapped out. Students are taught to rehearse a whole litany of 'grammatical truths' about 'our use of the word "pain"': that pain is a mental state, that it makes no sense to talk about being mistaken about being in pain or failing to notice a pain, that 'to feel a headache' is synonymous with 'to have a headache', that pains have various 'phenomenological' and 'hedonic' qualities (ranging from being awful or unbearable to being stabbing or burning), etc. Such philosophers may fail to notice that Descartes had a very different conception of pain, and in so far as they attend to its details, they naturally take them to be nonsensical. We have shown his picture

32 Also for the possibility of synchronic diversity, for instance, between Ryle and Merleau-Ponty. We ignore this point here, even though it has some secondary importance in respect of the diversity of interpretations of Descartes' thought.

to contain several elements: painfulness (which is a property of the body related to illness and injury), an 'internal sense' (which has a sense-organ that is mechanically affected by what is sense-perceived), animal sense-perception (which causes health-preserving animal responses), and the sensation of pain (which is a confused thought which is occasioned by a movement in the body, normally by some violent local motion in the injured or diseased part of the body, for the welfare of the person). Built into this picture are some striking ideas: pain is no *thing*, hence nothing of which one can say that it has the *property* of being unbearable, intermittent, sickening, throbbing, etc.; an amputee's judging that he feels a pain in his missing foot is a paradigm case of *deception* by the *senses*; one may *fail to notice* that one's foot is painful; etc. These ideas all conflict with entrenched features of the received philosophical analysis of the concept of pain.

What could we conceivably learn from making this conflict visible? Descartes did not see himself to be in the business of delineating *the* ordinary use (*sic*) of the *word* 'pain' (or even the grammar of '*mal*' or '*douleur*' in early seventeenth-century French). But this doesn't mean that his attempts to penetrate the *nature* of feeling pain have no interest for analytic philosophers. They might consider whether his conception of pain can't be used to illuminate some aspects of the modern concept of pain (perhaps to be equated with the everyday use of 'pain') that are cast into shadow by the 'received' conception.[33] They might even use his conception to bring to consciousness some of the preconceptions or prejudices that underlie the consensus about how correctly to analyse the concept of pain.

Let's review a few of the details of Descartes' account and consider what of value they might indicate. First, he argued that the sensation of pain is internally related to threats to or loss of welfare. Emphasizing this facet of the concept would undermine part of the motivation for philosophers' insisting on distinguishing pain from injury, and it would eliminate the possibility of treating pain as the paradigm of an 'immediate private experience'. Second, Descartes took it to be an essential feature of any pain that it be located somewhere in the sufferer's body;[34] or more accurately, he held that the minimal (complete) move in the language-game of expressing a sensation of pain specifies a pain-location (e.g., 'I feel a pain *in my foot*'). This explains why he took an amputee's report of a phantom pain to be an unequivocally mistaken judgement. Adopting this point of view would undermine the case for the modern philosophical dogma that 'feel' cannot be a perceptual verb in the phrase 'feel pain' (on the grounds that misperception is grammatically excluded), and it would demand a reconsideration of why analytic philosophers make such very heavy weather of the analysis of pain-location. Third, Descartes definitely excluded treating pain as a *thing* or as something *mental* (a mode of *thinking*), *a fortiori* as a paradigmatic 'mental entity'. This point of view already

33 See Katherine J. Morris, 'Pain, Injury and First-/Third-Person Asymmetry', forthcoming in *Philosophy and Phenomenological Research*.

34 Contrast: 'It is a rule of grammar that a person's pain is where he indicates, avows, etc., not a truth of metaphysics that pains are *in* bodies' (Hacker 1990: 50).

incorporates two allegedly 'Wittgensteinian insights', and it would remove the logical space in which debates about phenomenological properties and 'the what's-it-like' are now conducted. In general, Descartes' conception of pain belongs to a different framework: he had different ways of delineating the logical forms of expressions of pain, different notions of what is central and what is peripheral, different accounts of which forms of words are in order as they are, and different ways of conceiving of concept-identity and concept-difference.

The point of these reflections is not at all to say that Descartes' way of seeing pain was 'right', and that our modern conception is 'wrong'; or even that his conception is clearly preferable to ours. (His conception might cast into shadow some aspects of our use of 'pain'.) Our point is rather to illustrate the way in which very different conceptions can be justified or motivated: his conception is not arbitrary. Making sense of it, or clarifying its rationale and implications, could prove to be philosophically interesting.

First, it might lead us to see aspects of concepts to which we have been blind. Descartes discerned certain patterns among concepts, patterns no less apparent to the attentive mind than the different ones now stressed. Some forms of aspect-blindness may impose intellectual costs on us now; they might explain why we have become entangled in certain philosophical problems or antinomies. We have just illustrated this point with the concept of pain. Earlier we have explored other concepts and made similar suggestions in respect of knowledge of states of one's own body, the problem of the 'unity of consciousness', the concept of sense-perception, knowledge of one's own voluntary actions, and 'the mind–body problem'. Becoming sensible of neglected aspects of various concepts might hold out the best possibility of *dissolving* some of our present puzzles, problems, and antinomies. Many of the concepts that are central to contemporary philosophizing are difficult to survey. It would be astonishing if we had nothing to learn from serious attempts of other highly intelligent people to map out complex conceptual landscapes.

Grasping neglected aspects might take a less specific form with more wide-reaching repercussions. We have drawn attention to the integratedness of Descartes' philosophy by contrasting it with the modern pattern of the division of philosophical labour. In particular we stressed the modern divorce of epistemology and philosophy of mind from ethics and *moral* psychology. This has many dramatic consequences. Without excluding all consideration of moral agency, the question of 'animal intelligence' could scarcely be raised. Modern discussions of personal identity focus on memory rather than responsibility, while discussions of self-deception focus on present beliefs and desires rather than character or past actions. Moral deliberation has ceased to be a paradigm of reasoning, and the active powers of the rational soul have been whittled down to mysterious and redundant 'acts of will'. Virtues and vices are not considered to belong to the subject-matter of philosophy of mind. These transformations are of the utmost importance for the conduct of philosophical investigations. They seem to be exempted from any serious philosophical scrutiny, yet they predetermine much of the content of modern conceptual analysis.

Second, making a sustained effort to grasp Descartes' vision of things might lead to greater *self*-awareness. We today are too ready to accuse others (especially long-dead others) of inability to see important patterns in things that are perfectly familiar and plainly visible. Of course, we note, these others are labouring under various misconceptions. They are the victims of obsolete doctrines, the prejudices of their times or places, deficiencies in factual knowledge, etc. Are we today immune to all such intellectual diseases? Isn't there the slightest possibility that we ourselves might be tainted by prejudice or blind to something? If we could acknowledge the real possibility of aspect-blindness in ourselves, we might see the merit of a different procedure for showing respect to Descartes. We might read his texts with more humility, making a serious attempt to weigh his words in order to work out the content of his thoughts. We might be able to keep alive the hope of learning something important from a great thinker rather than assuming that we already are in firm possession of privileged access to the truth.

What needs to be envisaged is the possibility of recognizing a conflict of frameworks and responding to it intelligently. There is a clash of two different 'forms of representation'. Our up-to-date principles have essentially the same status as Descartes' discarded ones: both articulate forms of representation (not, as it were, the unvarnished truth about the nature of things). You might conclude that we are arguing that all principles are *mere* forms of representation, or that they are *nothing more than* ways of seeing things. We would prefer to say that all such principles (new or old) are *nothing less than* ways of seeing things or norms of describing them. The word 'mere' is altogether out of place: forms of representation have *enormous* importance and power precisely because they mould our concepts, shape our speech, and determine what questions arise and what count as answers to them.

The old-fashioned ways of seeing things deserve no less *respect* than their modern equivalents (even if they don't have the same attraction for us now): none is uniquely privileged (not even the doctrine of the forms of judgement and inference which underlies quantification theory). If we saw this aright, we might be led to the radical view that sympathy and imagination can be seen as internally connected,[35] and that, so seen, they are intellectual virtues of the greatest importance to philosophers.

35 The kind of 'technological' imagination the need for which Dennett stresses so strongly (1993: e.g., 16ff.) is, precisely, one that sees no such internal connection.

BIBLIOGRAPHY

Anscombe, Elizabeth and Peter Thomas Geach, (trs and eds) (1954), *Descartes: Philosophical Writings*, Edinburgh: Thomas Nelson & Sons Ltd.

Armstrong, D. M. (1984), see Malcolm and Armstrong (1984).

Baker, Gordon and Katherine J. Morris (1993), 'Descartes UnLocked', *British Journal of the History of Philosophy* I.

Bedau, Mark (1986), 'Cartesian Interaction', in Peter A. French, Theodore Uehling, Jr. and Howard K. Wettstein (eds), *Midwest Studies in Philosophy*, vol. X, Minneapolis: University of Minnesota Press.

Churchland, Paul (1984), *Matter and Consciousness*, Cambridge Mass.: MIT Press.

Cottingham, John (1978a), '"A Brute to the Brutes?": Descartes' Treatment of Animals,' *Philosophy* 53.

—— (1978b), 'Descartes on "Thought"', *Philosophical Quarterly* 28.

—— (1986), *Descartes*, Oxford: Blackwell.

—— (1993), *A Descartes Dictionary*, Oxford: Blackwell.

—— (ed.) (1994), *Reason, Will and Sensation*, Oxford: Clarendon.

Curley, E. M. (1979), *Descartes Against the Sceptics*, Oxford: Blackwell.

Dalmiya, Vrinda, 'Introspection', in Dancy and Sosa (1992).

Dancy, Jonathan and Ernest Sosa (eds) (1992), *A Companion to Epistemology*, Oxford: Blackwell.

Davidson, Donald (1980), *Essays on Actions and Events*, Oxford: Oxford University Press.

Dennett, Daniel (1993), *Consciousness Explained*, Harmondsworth: Penguin.

Dicker, Georges (1993), *Descartes: An Analytical and Historical Introduction*, Oxford: Oxford University Press.

Garber, Daniel (1992), *Descartes' Metaphysical Physics*, Chicago: University of Chicago Press.

Gaukroger, Stephen (1995), *Descartes: An Intellectual Biography*, Oxford: Oxford University Press.

Geach, P. T. (1957), *Mental Acts*, London: Routledge.

Grene, Marjorie (1985), *Descartes*, Brighton: Harvester.

Gunderson, Keith (1964), 'Descartes, La Mettrie, Language, and Machines', *Philosophy* 39.

Hacker, Peter (1986), *Insight and Illusion*, revised edn, Oxford: Clarendon.

—— (1987), *Appearance and Reality*, Oxford: Blackwell.

—— (1990), *Wittgenstein: Meaning and Mind*, Oxford: Blackwell.

Harré, Rom (1964), *Matter and Method*, London: Macmillan.

Haugeland, John (1985), *Artificial Intelligence*, Cambridge Mass.: MIT Press.

James, William (1890), *The Principles of Psychology*, New York: Henry Holt & Co.

—— (1911), *Some Problems of Philosophy*, London: Longman & Green.

Keeling, S. V. (1968), *Descartes*, 2nd edn, Oxford: Oxford University Press.
Kenny, Anthony (1966), 'Cartesian Privacy', in George Pitcher (ed.), *Wittgenstein: The Philosophical Investigations*, New York: Anchor.
—— (1968), *Descartes: A Study of his Philosophy*, New York: Random House.
—— (1975), *Will, Freedom and Power*, Oxford: Blackwell.
—— (1985), *The Legacy of Wittgenstein*, Oxford: Blackwell.
—— (1989), *The Metaphysics of Mind*, Oxford: Clarendon.
—— (1993), *Aquinas on Mind*, London: Routledge.
Leiber, Justin (1988), '"Cartesian" Linguistics?', *Philosophia* 18.
Loeb, Louis (1981), *From Descartes to Hume*, Ithaca: Cornell University Press.
Lott, Tommy L. (1986), 'Descartes on Phantom Limbs', *Mind and Language* 1.
McDowell, John (1994), *Mind and World*, Cambridge: Harvard University Press.
Malcolm, Norman (1977), *Thought and Knowledge*, Ithaca: Cornell University Press.
—— and D. M. Armstrong (1984), *Consciousness and Causality*, Oxford: Blackwell.
Merleau-Ponty, Maurice (1962), *The Phenomenology of Perception*, tr. Colin Smith, London: Routledge.
Morris, John M. (1980), 'What the Skeptic Cannot Doubt', *Philosophical Forum* 11.
Morris, Katherine J. (1995), 'Intermingling and Confusion', *International Journal of Philosophical Studies* 3.
Rée, Jonathan (1974), *Descartes*, London: Allen Lane, 1974.
Rorty, Amélie Oksenberg (ed.) (1986), *Essays on Descartes' Meditations*, Berkeley and Los Angeles: University of California Press.
Rorty, Richard (1980), *Philosophy and the Mirror of Nature*, Oxford: Blackwell.
Russell, Bertrand (1900). *A Critical Exposition of the Philosophy of Leibniz*, Cambridge: Cambridge University Press.
—— (1912), *The Problems of Philosophy*, London: Williams & Norgate.
—— (1921), *Analysis of Mind*, London: Allen & Unwin.
—— (1946), *History of Western Philosophy*, London: Allen & Unwin.
—— (1956), *Logic and Knowledge*, ed. R. C. Marsh, London: Allen & Unwin.
Ryle, Gilbert (1949), *The Concept of Mind*, London: Hutchinson.
—— (1954), *Dilemmas*, Cambridge: Cambridge University Press.
Schlick, Moritz (1974), *General Theory of Knowledge*, tr. A. E. Blumberg, New York and Vienna: Springer.
Stout, G. F. (1964), 'Mind and Matter', reprinted in Vesey (1964).
Strawson, P. F. (1959), *Individuals*, London: Methuen.
Vesey, G. N. A. (ed.) (1964), *Body and Mind*, London: Allen & Unwin.
Voss, Stephen (ed.) (1993), *Essays on the Philosophy and Science of René Descartes*, Oxford: Oxford University Press.
—— (1994), 'Descartes: The End of Anthropology', in Cottingham (1994).
Williams, Bernard (1967), 'Descartes', in Paul Edwards (ed.), *The Encyclopedia of Philosophy*, vol. II, London and New York.
—— (1978), *Descartes: The Project of Pure Enquiry*, Harmondsworth: Penguin.
Wilson, Margaret Dauler (1978), *Descartes*, London: Routledge.
—— (1994), 'Descartes on Sense and "Resemblance"', in Cottingham (1994).

INDEX OF CITATIONS FROM DESCARTES

AT VOLUME

XI

NAME INDEX

SUBJECT INDEX

Page numbers in **bold** denote major section devoted to the subject.